Rwenzori

Histories and Cultures
of an African Mountain

Editors

Cecilia Pennacini
Hermann Wittenberg

FOUNTAIN PUBLISHERS

Kampala

Fountain Publishers
P.O. Box 488
Kampala
E-mail:fountain@starcom.co.ug
Website:www.fountainpublishers.co.ug

© Cecilia Pennacini and Hermann Wittenberg 2008
First published 2008

All rights reserved. No part of this publication may be reprinted or reproduced or utilised in any form or by any means, electronic, mechanical or other means now known or hereafter invented, including copying and recording, or in any information storage or retrieval system, without permission in writing from the publishers.

This book has been published thanks to a contribution of the University of Turin, Department of Anthropological, Archeological and Historical-Territorial Sciences, the National Museum of the Mountain "Duke of Abruzzi" (Turin), and the Piedmonte Region.

Cover picture: Vittorio Sella, "Native (milk porter) met on the road bordered by *papyri*", Rwenzori, 1906 ©2007 Fondazione Sella-Biella

Layout: Robert Asaph Sempagala-Mpagi

ISBN 978-9970-02-755-2

Cataloguing-in-Publication Data

Rwenzori: Histories and Cultures of an African Mountain. – Kampala: Fountain Publishers, 2008
__ p; __ cm.

Includes tables and figures

ISBN 978-9970-02-755-2

1. Rwenzori I. Histories II. Cultures III. African History

Contents

iv

Foreword

It is a rare privilege to be involved in the celebrations marking such an important centenary as the first ascent of the Rwenzori by Luigi Amedeo of Savoy, better known as the Duke of Abruzzi. The Rwenzori Mountain, more than any other African massif, has in the past attracted speculation and interest related to the mystery surrounding the sources of the River Nile. Already in 150 AD, Claudius Ptolemy wrote about the Mountains of the Moon as the source of the Nile, but it was only in 1906 that the range was finally mapped by the Duke of Abruzzi, together with his ten companions and scientists. Previously, the American explorer Stanley had called the massif Rwenzori, from the local place-name "rwenzururu", which means the "place of the snow". Recognition must also go to Vittorio Sella, the photographer of the expedition. Thanks to his photographs, the world got a tangible look at world of perennial ice at the equator.

The Italian Embassy in Kampala coordinated the preparatory phases and the celebrations that culminated in a reception at the Uganda Wildlife Authority on 23 June 2006. It honoured the alpinists who scaled the massif by following the "Footsteps of the Duke" route. The Ministries of Tourism, of Internal Affairs and the Ministry of Defence of Uganda, the Ugandan National Museum, the Ugandan Mountain Club, the Uganda Tourism Board, the University of Makerere and Kyambogo, and the Uganda Society also participated. Many Italian institutions were also involved, among them the Region Valle d'Aosta, the Italian Alpine Corps, the National Museum of the Mountain in Turin, the Universities of Turin and Brescia, and the CNR. Both the Italian and Ugandan press reported on the celebrations and gave it broader public visibility.

The range of contributions in this publication bears concrete testimony to the anthropological, scientific and geographic realities of this beautiful and unique massif. It is hoped that this book will be a catalyst for further studies and research projects, particularly in the area of climate change, as evidenced by the melting of the glaciers.

A special word of thanks goes to the Piemonte Region and to the Museum of the Mountain in Turin, who, together with the University of Turin, have played an important role in these celebrations. I also thank the firm Ferrino of Turin who sponsored expedition tents, as well as the climbers who re-enacted the historical ascent by following the footsteps of the Duke. The last word of thanks goes to all those who have given support to these celebrations.

Umberto Plaja
Italian Ambassador in Uganda

Preface

I am very happy about this academic Uganda-Italy cooperation, as realized between the Institute of Languages here at Makerere University and the Department of Anthropological, Archaeological and Territorial-Historical Sciences at the University of Turin. We recently renewed our Agreement on cooperation, lasting until 2012. One of the outcomes of this valuable cooperation is the present volume, upon the publication of which I heartily salute the organizers of the scientific conference that preceded it, the authors of the articles and the editors. Indeed, I want to thank the University of Turin, His Excellency the Ambassador and the staff of the Embassy of Italy in Kampala, the Italian Ministry of Foreign Affairs, and our own Ministry of Foreign Affairs, for their part in establishing and strengthening this relationship.

The Mountains of the Moon on the Uganda-Congo border and the surrounding areas are certainly a very important, fascinating feature of our cultural, economic and political geography and history. They are likely to remain a major object of scientific, geographical-geological, and tourist curiosity. It is, therefore, important to illuminate the region from a variety of perspectives. The authors of this book have tried to do this, from the vantage points of history and politics; ethnography and anthropology; linguistics and literature; and nature, culture and religion. We, in Uganda, in fact do need to look at the Rwenzoris, as indeed at any mountain or other feature of our country's geography, as a gift of God and a resource, as something we need to look after wisely. Whether we follow in the footsteps of the Duke of Abruzzi in 1906 and conquer the highest peak, Mt. Margherita; or whether we intimately participate in the forging and development of a culture – as Bakonjo-Banande, Babwisi or

Bamba – or simply seek to understand such a culture in order to deepen and broaden our understanding of the world and of life, no matter who we are or where we are from on the globe: the Mountains of the Moon should make us pause and humbly ponder the majesty of creation. I trust that the essays in this book, inspired as they all are by this great mountain, will enhance the reader's appreciation of the silent power of the Rwenzoris, and indeed of nature in general.

I look forward to more results out of this cooperation between Makerere and Turin. The study of the cultures and histories not only of the Rwenzoris but also of the broader Great Lakes Region will, I hope, result in a documentation centre/archive, or, even better, a museum here at Makerere, plus the protection of the most important sites of our cultural heritage. Our educational, cultural and tourist industries will greatly benefit from this, and I shall be happy to act as a kind of catalyst in the development. Pro futuro aedificamus: We build for the future! For God and My Country.

Prof. Livingstone S. Luboobi
Vice Chancellor
Makerere University

The Rwenzori Centenary Celebrations (1906-2006)

One hundred years ago, the Duke of Abruzzi ascended the Rwenzori Mountains with ten other Italians. This ascent made news worldwide, since the climbers had for the first time reached its highest peak that was later named Margherita after the Italian queen mother. The motivation to climb the Rwenzori arose out of a curiosity to "discover" one of the sources of the Nile, the mythical Mountains of the Moon already cited by Claudius Ptolemy in his treatise "Geography" in the year 150 AD.

One hundred years after that historic expedition, Italy and Uganda have jointly commemorated the first scientific exploration of the Rwenzori through a number of cultural and sporting activities.

As president of the organizing committee for the celebrations, I have had the privilege to work directly with every person participating in the various events. I confess having already been involved in the celebrations of the 90th anniversary of the climb, and since then I have always felt sympathy for those climbers who departed from Naples by boat in 1906, who went through the newly constructed Suez Canal, and docked at Mombasa. From there they entered the heart of Africa by railway and reached Lake Victoria in just two days. Speke, Burton and Grant, the early explorers of the sources of the Nile, had struggled for years to reach the area. Just fifty years later, Lake Victoria was not only reachable via a spectacularly beautiful train journey, but people and goods from the coast could also be transported everywhere across the lake by a regular service of steam boats. The climbers arrived at Entebbe, then the capital city of the Protectorate of Uganda. But the journey was not over, for to reach the Rwenzori, the Duke Luigi Amedeo of Savoy and his guides and scientists had to walk another 300 kilometres. This safari took them through hills, swamps and forests before at last viewing the peaks of the Rwenzori.

One of the purposes of the present celebration was to commemorate the efforts of those climbers who participated in the 1906 adventure, unveiling the last secrets of the Mountains of the Moon and its people. Luigi Amedeo, the Duke of Abruzzi, was a mountaineer, an expert explorer, a Prince of the House of Savoy and a military man. Some people say that he was also a poet. After verifying the route that the Duke chose for climbing the mountain and assessing the difficulties represented by the swamps, the cold and then the ice of the peaks, I can assert without doubts that the Duke was a man who loved to explore, and that he was not deterred by fatigue and adversities. Today, we would define him as a "real man", someone who would not accept half measures.

The Duke was also a down-to-earth person who interacted with ordinary people. In 1920 he established an innovative farming community in Somalia, at a time when warfare, colonialism and imperialism were the order of the day. He was a man who stood aloof from money and personal glory; and from my point of view, this makes him a great man. I am therefore proud to have contributed to the commemoration of a small part of his life.

The commemorative climb in June 2006 was spearheaded by the Italian Alpine Corps, lead by Gen. Antonio Vizzi and Capt. Felicetti. A descendant of the Duke's head guide, Mr. Giuseppe Petigax from the Courmayeur School of Climbing, also participated. Many other people joined the climb: Ugandan authorities like Gen. Ivan Koreta, deputy commander of the UPDF, Mr. Moses Mapesa, head of the UWA, as well as several researchers and journalists. During the commemorative climb, the University of Brescia and the Ev-K2-CNR installed instruments for climate monitoring. Lastly, a plaque was unveiled at Margherita Peak (5109 metres) in remembrance of the event.

An important role in these celebrations was played by the Museum of the Mountain in Turin that, together with the Department of Anthropology of the University of Turin and in collaboration with the Sella Foundation, organized an exhibition with a catalogue entitled "The People of the Moon". The exhibition was held both in Turin and at the National Museum of Kampala. Pictures by Vittorio Sella, who accompanied the Duke in 1906, and by Craig Richards, taken a hundred years later, gave viewers the opportunity to understand the geography and the life of the people of the Moon. Other events, like a seminar organized by the University of Turin, the University of Makerere and Kyambogo in Kampala, attracted academics and researchers. Other parties involved were the Ugandan Ministry of Tourism, the Uganda Wildlife Authority, the Nommo Gallery that hosted a painting competition, the Bakonzo people, the Kingdom of Tororo, and Kampala Club which hosted an Open Tennis Tournament. Special thanks go to Dr. Pietro Tombaccini, Deputy Head of the Italian Mission in Kampala, for his contribution to the celebrations and the organization of the marathon in Fort Portal.

Uganda is a growing country; unfortunately some people still identify this nation with the period of Amin Dada's rule, but I do wish that the government's new emphasis on tourism, together with the Rwenzori Centenary Celebrations, will see more interest in a country that can boast of preserving half of the last 600 mountain gorillas, a country that has the largest reserve of wild animals and fresh water on a plateau of 1,200 metres. Uganda is truly the Green Pearl of Africa.

In conclusion, let me thank the Duke and his expedition, for it is their historic efforts getting us together in these 2006 commemorative events. Finally, I would like to express my gratitude to all those who have made this publication possible, especially Prof. Cecilia Pennacini and the other members of the Italian Ethnological Mission in Equatorial Africa supported by the Italian Ministry of Foreign Affairs.

Pietro Averono
Cultural Officer
Embassy of Italy, Kampala

The Exhibition "The People of the Moon: Rwenzori 1906–2006"

In June 1906, Luigi Amedeo of Savoy, the Duke of Abruzzi, successfully concluded a mountaineering and exploring expedition, an important step in the history of the geographical discoveries concerning the sources of the Nile. He was the first person to reach the highest peaks of the Rwenzori, known as Ptolemy's "Mountains of the Moon", the vast mountainous massif that stretches between Uganda and the present-day Democratic Republic of Congo, in the region of the Great African Lakes.

In Europe, the sources of the Nile were still, in the second half of the nineteenth century, one of the great unsolved geographical enigmas handed down from ancient times. As early as the fifth century BC, Herodotus tackled the problem of the sources of the Nile in the second book of his Histories, personally travelling to the town of Elephantine on the border between Egypt and Nubia, the farthest point of his search. Aristotle described a river to the south of Libya that shared a common source with the Nile, rising from a mountain of silver located near the great lakes. The Romans even coined the term "fontes Nili quaerere" to indicate something that was impossible. In the second century AD, in his Geography, the geographer Claudius Ptolemy wrote that the Nile sprang from two circular lakes fed by rivers flowing from a mountainous chain covered by perennial snow: the Lunae Montes, or Mountains of the Moon. No mountains covered by perennial snow were found in the latitude indicated by Ptolemy however, and the mystery remained unsolved for almost seventeen centuries, despite much conjecture on the part of geographers and scholars.

It was only during the mid nineteenth century that the fever for exploration spread into the equatorial African regions. In 1857, the Royal Geographical Society entrusted John Speke and Richard Burton with an expedition to look for the sources of the great river. Departing from Bagamoyo, they came upon an enormous expanse of water after eight months' march: Lake Tanganyika. Speke, alone, succeeded in pushing on northwards and on 3 August 1858 he discovered a veritable inner sea: Lake Nyanza, later renamed Lake Victoria in honour of the British queen. On his return, he claimed to have discovered the sources of the Nile. In his turn, during 1857, the explorer Henry Morton Stanley completed the first circumnavigation of Lake Victoria and far-ranging reconnaissance of the swampy lands up to the mouth of the Kagera, which he called the Alexandra Nile and considered the farthest spring area of the great river. On 24 May 1888, while travelling along the south-west coastal plane of Lake Albert, he glimpsed "a peculiar shaped cloud [...] which assumed the proportions and appearance of a vast mountain covered with snow" and knew he had found Ptolemy's legendary Lunae Montes, the Rwenzori massif.

When the Duke of Abruzzi turned his attention to equatorial Africa, the white blanks on the maps of the continent were thus much reduced compared to the past, and the mystery of the sources of the Nile had been resolved. However, the Mountains of the Moon were themselves still very much unknown: the banks of cloud permanently enveloping the mountain chain prevented any idea about the precise orography of the region, while the adverse weather conditions and state of the terrain made every attempt to approach the peaks extremely difficult. Between summer 1899 and spring 1906 a good seventeen expeditions went to the Rwenzori, all ending with scant success. The list of attempts made to ascend the mountains is long and varied and includes military personnel, explorers, scientists and colonial residents: the best organized team was sent by the British Museum, departing from London in November 1905.

On 7 May 1906, twenty-one days after leaving Naples, the expedition led by the Duke of Abruzzi reached Entebbe, the political and administrative capital of the British Protectorate of Uganda. From this point, mountaineers, guides and bearers progressed on foot: three hundred people loaded with provisions, climbing equipment and instruments trekked the 290 kilometres of paths to Fort Portal, the last British outpost before the mountains. On 28 May, the Rwenzori finally appeared on the horizon, beyond the hills to the north of Kaibo. On 1 June, the expedition began to wind up the slopes of the massif, snaking into the valley of the Mobuku stream. The fairy-tale surroundings of the rain forest were a surprise: however, what delighted the eye soon revealed itself to be treacherous to forward progression. Mud and boggy ground increased in consistency; and the caravan sank into thick, black, sticky slime. After hours of incessant rain, every movement meant a super-human effort. Progressing upwards, the forest gave way to more open slopes covered with groundsel and lobelia and stretches of flat terraces, the home to fearful swamps. On 7 June, at Bujungolo, at a height of 3,798 metres, a base camp was set up under an enormous overhanging roof of rock dropping sheer to the valley below. The place was dark, damp and wild, but offered shelter against the rain. Two days later, the expedition started to explore the head of the valley, struggling against constant downpours, fog and clouds that prevented clear vision and orientation. Finally, on 18 June, the duke, Joseph Brochererel, Joseph Petigax and César Ollier climbed the Alessandra and Margherita peaks, the highest in the range. Between 10 June and 16 July the seventeen main peaks, distributed among the six mountain groups of the Rwenzori chain, were scaled, and a good twenty-eight ascents were completed. At the same time the geographical, geological, botanical and zoological characteristics of the massif were studied. *The expedition made contact with societies and cultures that lived on the slopes and at the foot of the mountainous massif, but the lack of a professional anthropologist prevented in-depth scientific study of the variations in the languages, cultures, economies and social organizations of the groups encountered.*

The outstanding success of the Duke of Abruzzi's arduous mountaineering expedition was due in large part to an impeccable, almost military-style organization, in which every detail was meticulously prepared and carried out following tried and tested methods proven on his previous expeditions outside Europe. It must also not be forgotten that the presence of a prince of a reigning house also guaranteed full collaboration from the 'establishment' of the British colony as well as much respect from the local populations.

In 1996 the Museo Nazionale della Montagna "Duca degli Abruzzi" of Turin and the Piemonte Region initiated an international collaboration to promote this moment in Italian mountain exploration, organizing the exhibition "Rwenzori Discovery", held in Turin and in the Uganda Museum in Kampala. This traced the main stages of the 1906 expedition through the historic photographs taken by Vittorio Sella.

Ten years later, on the occasion of the centenary of the 1906 expedition, the Turin National Mountain Museum and the Piemonte Region, together with the University of Turin and the Italian Embassy in Kampala, with the collaboration of the Sella Foundation, created and organized an historical and anthropological exhibition titled "The People of the Moon. Rwenzori 1906–2006". The expedition focused on the populations that the duke of the Abruzzi had met during his expedition and which still live on the slopes of the Rwenzori massif.

This exhibition opened as different versions in both Italy and Uganda, and examined various moments in the past and present history of the region from an anthropological-visual stance. The

xvi

exhibition traced developments over time, starting with the photographs taken in 1906 by Vittorio Sella, moving on to those amassed a year later by Jan Czekanowski, the first professional anthropologist who travelled in the Rwenzori region in 1907. These images have had been complemented by photographs taken in the same places one hundred years later by the contemporary photographer Craig Richards. The images of these three photographers (each with their very individual eye) showed, over a stretch of a hundred years, a world in transition between the antique and the modern, revealing a human universe rich in history and culture. Vittorio Sella immortalized a valuable heritage with the eye of a man of his times, struck above all by the diversity and exoticism of a world so far away and diverse. Jan Czekanowski was a sensitive and enlightened man who gives us a historical and social description of the territories he travelled in. His diaries reveal a surprisingly modern stance, though his photographs show the influence of ethnographic conventions of the positivist period, in which the human subjects are represented according to the canons of anthropometric photography and scientific documentation. Craig Richards travelled to the Rwenzori region in 2005, as part of the preparatory research for the exhibition. Thus, a century later, he followed in the steps of the Duke of Abruzzi with a profoundly different eye and sensitivity than that of Sella and Czekanowski. In the first place, Richards searched for a "contact" with the people – something that in the past was almost always missing – establishing relationships of curiosity and reciprocal liking with the people photographed. This allowed him to shoot images full of significance, of almost "pictorial" quality – thanks to a masterly use of black and white – capable of abstracting themselves from the environmental and temporal context.

Finally, the centenary of the first ascent of the Rwenzori by the Duke of Abruzzi was also the occasion to give voice to the Bakonzo, the true "sherpas" of the Rwenzori, highly valued guides and bearers of the 1906 expedition and of all those that have followed to this day. *The history of great explorations and ascents has generally been written by the men who organized or carried them out; the story of the men who have in part made them possible, thanks to their familiarity and knowledge of the terrain, has almost never been told. In this light, a number of by now very elderly guides were tracked down and interviewed with the aim of finding out if the Italian expedition has remained in the collective memory, even a hundred years later. To our surprise, we discovered that the memory of the duke and of his great expedition is still very much alive today among the people of the Mobuku valley and that the Duke of Abruzzi still holds the record for being the most generous "tourist".*

What do Ptolemy's Mountains of the Moon signify for the Bakonzo, men of the mountain? What is their relationship with the peaks, with the snow and ice? These and other issues led to the definition of a picture in which two contrasting worlds find themselves climbing the same mountain, sometimes alongside each other, but with widely differing visions and objectives.

Cristina Natta-Soleri
National Museum of the Mountain
Turin

Introduction

Cecilia Pennacini and Hermann Wittenberg

The research papers and essays collected in this volume bear testimony to the fact that no mountain region in Africa has attracted as much scholarly and general interest as the Rwenzori massif on the border of Uganda and the Democratic Republic of Congo. For more than a 100 years, the geography and the people of the Rwenzori region have been the subject of an extraordinary range of academic and popular writing, a heritage to which the authors of these papers both contribute and reflect on.

Written on the occasion of the Abruzzi Centenary celebrations in 2006, these papers were presented at two interdisciplinary conferences, held in Turin (at the National Museum of the Mountain) and Kampala (at the Uganda Museum) respectively. The conferences were organized under the auspices of a Cooperation Agreement established between the Department of Anthropological, Archeological and Historical-Territorial Sciences of the University of Turin, and the Institute of Languages of Makerere University. Active since 2004, the agreement has facilitated an exchange of scholars and students between Italy and Uganda. The exchange has provided researchers and students with exciting opportunities to share research, and to reflect together on the anthropology, languages and history of an important Ugandan region, using a multidisciplinary approach in the field of social sciences. The conferences and the proceedings we are now publishing are the first tangible outcomes of this joint effort. One of the strengths of this book is thus the fact that it represents a collaborative intellectual project that has brought together Western and African scholars, united in their endeavour to interrogate the history of an African mountain, and explore the complexities of the diverse cultures that are associated with the region. This book cannot adequately reflect the many discussions and exchanges of ideas

1

that took place before, during and after the conferences, but several of the papers nevertheless give a sense of the intellectual bridges that have been formed, demonstrating the fact that meaningful knowledge is always dialogic. To use the phrase of one of the contributors (Stanley Baluku), the Rwenzori has become a "bridge of cultures", not only for diverse local communities, but also for researchers from different parts of the world.

Looking at the titles of the chapters in this book, readers will notice that the Rwenzori has been studied from a wide range of perspectives and academic interests. This interdisciplinary approach is reflected in contributions from the disciplines of anthropology, linguistics, political science, history, literary studies, musicology, religion and lexicography; and in many papers these approaches have been integrated. A great variety is also shown in the different subjects examined by the contributors. Since the book presents the proceedings of the conferences, a degree of heterogeneity is inevitable[1]. In certain cases, authors embrace divergent positions; and it is clear that the differences in culture and methodology inevitably preclude a single, unified point of view or position. This pluralistic representation of the region is however a value in itself, since it enables the reader to appreciate the complexity of situations and points of view involved in this study.

The articles deal with a wide variety of topics, but most of them explore the relationship between the specific characteristics of this mountain territory on the one hand, and the dynamics of culture and identity formation on the other. A central concern is thus the unique relationship between geography and culture in the Rwenzori region. In some papers, a long historical record going back several centuries is examined, but the majority of contributions deal more specifically with the last century, mainly considering the period from the time of the Duke of Abruzzi expedition to the present. This period has seen some profound changes among the different societies living in the region, at a political, economic and cultural levels. Several authors (Stacey,

Muhindo, Pennacini) try to clarify these processes, among them the most striking and interesting: the centralization of Bakonzo society. This process, with all its contradictions and difficulties, is still evolving as we write, not having been completed yet. We are thus in the fortunate position to observe processes of fundamental political and social change that involve an entire society. Bound up with this process, as we know, are the forces of violence and conflict, which have marked the history of the entire nation so deeply. Violence and conflict have become – for reasons that some of the articles try to explain (Muhindo, Jourdan) – crucial in this frontier region and more generally in the Semliki Valley, already since the sixteenth century, becoming more pronounced in the present day. Through the various analyses found in this book, we hope that the complex history of the populations living on and around the massif, and particularly the history of the Bakonzo mountain farmers, can now be understood more clearly.

Other major subjects connected with the cultural and historical life of the region are developed in the book: aspects of traditional cultures and their dynamics of change, for example the funerary Banande rituals (Remotti) and Bakonzo circumcision customs (Zavaroni); artistic and musical expression (Facci-Nannyonga, Crupi); history and analysis of different local languages (Ndolelire, Mutaka); traditional and "universalistic" religions (Gusman, Muranga); the increasingly difficult existence of pygmy groups throughout the region, subject to marginalization processes caused by old cultural attitudes, as well as the recent establishment of natural parks that forbid them to continue their traditional hunter and gatherer economy (Forno); and lastly, the ways in which European travellers, writers and scholars have seen and depicted the region and their inhabitants (Czekanowska, Wittenberg). As one can see, the broad choice of subjects and approaches, although not pretending in any way to be a complete or exhaustive analysis of the region, forms a vivid mosaic of scenes of past and present human life on this mountain.

But most importantly, as Anna Czekanowska has pointed out in her precious reconstruction of her father's adventurous travel through the Great Lakes region in 1908 (Jan Czekanowski was the first professional anthropologist to come to this area, whose extraordinary essays in Polish and German remain insufficiently known), the most promising idea springing from this book is "the recognition of traditional culture by contemporary African scholars and their vital interest in the history and culture". Even though the colony, as a political entity, died almost fifty years ago, Western colonization of African culture and consciousness has continued, and this has become an irreversible process. In religion, as in all the most important aspects of cultural life, the exchange between Europe and Africa has been intense, but almost exclusively uni-directional. Another consequence of this state of affairs, connected with the spread of the Western school system with its associated values, is a sort of detachment of the most educated members of Ugandan society (who of course correspond to its elite) from their own original culture. And moreover, this trend has affected research and teaching in African universities, were African anthropology and more generally African Studies have not fully developed. This book and the conferences on the Rwenzori are possibly signs of a different emerging trend, improving the study and the systematic reconstruction of the African past, and presenting cultures, languages and religions through an equal, reciprocal and fertile exchange of ideas.

Among the many individuals and institutions that have contributed to the conference and to the publication of this book we would like to mention the Italian Ethnological Mission in Equatorial Africa, founded by Francesco Remotti in the 1970s to support ethnological research among the Banande of the Congo, and now directed by Cecilia Pennacini. All the Italian contributors to the book are members of the Mission, which has had ongoing financial support from the Italian Ministry of Foreign Affairs. The Italian Ambassador, Umberto Plaja, and all the staff of the Italian Embassy in Kampala have always been highly supportive of this project, as have the many Ugandan institutions involved in it. We wish to thank the colleagues and students of the Makerere Institute of Languages and its director, Manuel Muranga, together with the Vice Chancellor of Makerere University, Livingstone Luboobi and the other Makerere researchers involved in the project. We are also much in debt to the Uganda Museum, who hosted the conference and the exhibition "The People of the Moon. Rwenzori 1906-2006", to its director Ephraim Kamuhangire, to the curator Rose Mwanja and to all the staff; to the Uganda Society and especially to John Twesigye; to the people and the institutions that helped us during fieldwork in Kasese district: the Kasese District administration, the Uganda Wild Life Authority, the Rwenzori Mountaineering Service; to Fountain Publishers and especially to Alex Bangirana.

A special word of thanks goes to the National Museum of the Mountain in Turin and to its director, Aldo Audisio; to the Piemonte Region and to the Councillor for Culture and Youth Politics, Gianni Oliva; to the Sella Foundation in Biella and especially to Angelica and Ludovico Sella; to the Faculty of Letters and Philosophy of the University of Turin and to its Dean, Renzo Massobrio; to the Department of Anthropological, Archeological and Historical-Territorial Sciences, and its director, Paola Sereno and to all its staff; and finally to the Rector of the University of Turin, Ezio Pelizzetti, who has constantly morally and materially supported our African research and our Cooperation Agreement, making the conference and the publication of the proceedings possible.

Figure 1   **Stacey T., *Tribe: The Hidden History of the Mountains of the Moon*, London, Stacey International, p. 24.**

Note

1. This heterogeneity is also present in the transcription of local words, in the end notes and in the bibliographic apparatus. We in fact decided to leave authors free to adopt the solutions used in the tradition they belong to.

The Snows of Rwenzururu
and the Kingdom

Tom Stacey

Consider these mountains. Consider this phenomenon of creation, this massif on the equatorial girdle of the world, some 70 miles in length overall, and 40 wide, with its clusters of mighty peaks of which, until recently, five were glaciered and the entire upper canopy under permanent snow.

Do you know this sacred place: this place of awesomeness and beauty almost beyond description? Who reminded us that "Goodness, truth and beauty" were "a three-strand cord, not easily broken"? Why, another Italian, if probably by adoption: the philosopher Plotinus?

Do you know there is no such place in the world that compares with Rwenzori? Its glaciered plateaux lie at 16,000 feet; its peaks rise to nearly 17,000 feet, over 5,000 metres, higher than the greatest mountains of Europe. The vegetation and wildlife of Rwenzori reach almost to the snouts of its glaciers, and of course overlap the outer fall of its snows.

It is a world of its own. Its abundant rainfall usually contributes as much as half of the waters that feed, via the Semliki, the central African reaches of the White Nile. That rainfall, and the infra-red and ultra-violet light reaching its territory above, say, 11,000 feet, induce the famous surreality of gigantic species among its prevailing vegetation of senecios, lobelias, heathers and helichrysums, which occur nowhere else on the globe except on a far lesser scale on other East African heights: Kilimanjaro, Kenya, and Elgon.

To our Rwenzori we ascribe an unprecedented array of unique species for so compact a piece of territory, a mountain-island, as it were – all the species derived from its combination of altitude and climate: its 15 species of mammals, some of them formidable and famous like the Rwenzori black leopard, the Rwenzori colobus, and the hyrax; its 25 species of reptiles; its 18 unique birds, including the brilliant turaco and its daringly designed sunbirds; its score upon score of strictly Rwenzori insects, mosses, fungi.

Do you know this place? Its hidden gulches? Its high, steep-sided, silent lakes, its literally impenetrable forest-swathes of helichrysums (impenetratable to man), the ferocious descent of its temperatures nightly within the space of a single hour from the heat of a European summer's afternoon to below zero; its comparable caprice of meteorological changeability in a matter of minutes, from clear heavenward infinity to an assault of hail, snow, and fog?

Do you know that place, whose first comprehensive European intruders we are here to honour: them and their intrusion? Have you lived it? Of course you have been hearing of it in these lectures, and learning from the accompanying display of photographs. Some of you non-Rwenzururians will have climbed into those mountains, perhaps as botanists and zoologists. Of us Basungu, none will have known it with quite the persistent devotion of the late Guy Yeoman, to whom I wish to give honour at this centenary, and none with the same length of experience and loyalty as Henry Osmaston, cartographer and forester, nine years my senior, whose greetings I bring to this conference and whose new Guide to Inner and Upper Rwenzori I have brought to Kampala the first copies.

There is also myself: whose acquaintance with and commitment to these mountains, and supremely to their people, goes back 52 years. My territorial, geographic acquaintance was dramatically refreshed as recently as 2001, when, at the age of 71, I re-ascended the mountains to that great glacier world of Mount Stanley at 16,000 feet, with my friends Syayipuma Augustine and Mudenge, respectively of Ibanda and Nyakalingija, only to be halted at that height by the sudden descent of fog – at the hand of the dispenser of Rwenzori weather.

Yet there is a people – one kind of people – who can be said to "live" Rwenzori and its central snows, whether they have seen or approached the snow-citadel in the reality or know it as symbol-in-the-mind. Let me call them the Banyarwenzuru. This ethnic collective – whose habitat is the mountain massif, Rwenzururu, and its immediate environs – are prevailingly comprised, of course, by the Bakonzo, whose home or ancestral home is or was the mountains, and their immediate neighbours and spiritual associates of the Rift at the north-west of the range, the Bamba. What essentially distinguishes the approximately 900,000 Bakonzo from the four million or more of their fellows of blood and language in the lowlands of Congo-side, the Banande, is the Bakonzo's presence on Rwenzori or in the mountains' immediate vicinity.

The Lukonzo word for their place, Rwenzururu, first misheard and mis-transcribed by H.M. Stanley in 1889, means the Place of Snow; and whether it is the reality or the symbol, Nzururu, *snow*, is and remains the presiding deity. These people of this language, with its regional mountain lilt and dialect, varying even between the north and southern reaches of the mountains, and its mountain vocabulary, these people of this physique and physiognomy, this fortitude and highland culture, and the snow- and peak-dominated cosmology, this history and this mythology, *live* their Rwenzururu.

Rwenzururu provides their pantheon, as Mount Olympus provided the pantheon of the Greeks, whose civilization, in combination with that of the Hebrews, have fed the only civilization we Basungu can honour as ours. The Bakonzo's is a snow and mountain cosmology. It cannot but infuse the self-view of the Bakonzo and inform their *embitha*, that unspoken sense of unity and uniqueness whose influence within the Bakonzo people socially and politically is in direct ratio to its privacy. For a century the ethnic resilience of the Bakonzo in relation to their territory has been repeatedly misjudged – unperceived, underestimated or misread – by the powers beyond, whether colonial or Ugandan. Bakonzo historians and chroniclers have all observed and described this phenomenon.

Are we still to upraise the significance of this cosmology? Do not our Christian churches presume that a Christian Trinitarian cosmology has overlaid the inherited deities of a pagan past? Let us pick our words here with care. I will not seek to oppose the God of Love with the mythologies of geography and climate such as bear daily upon the lives of mountain-dwelling people. Terminologically, the Christian "God" in Konzo liturgy, *Nyamuhanga*, is drawn from the traditional Konzo pantheon: the creative force, from which all materiality is ultimately descended, whose very name combines the reproductive *nya* with *hangi*, the roaming, ranging, ubiquitously flowing spirit, to which the *mu* brings enduring personal life. By the same requirement the territorial deity Nzururu, deification of semen, makes for fixity in the flux: drifting, swirling snow (yet clothing *rock*); spilling water, hail, yet solid, iconic water; dangerous, glittering, unendurable water; corniced, cloud-piercing exquisite snow, shrouding its vast metropolis of rock. This is a cosmology of workable symbols for the people of the mountains to which a God of Love may bring not nullity but His light.

Begot of Nzururu is Nyabirika, the Preserver of Snow, who in turn has begat that snow-dwelling deity of a name known to every Mukonzo, man, woman, and child, and respected by Christian and secularist alike – a name which we who have also climbed to the snows do not dare to breathe in his own snowy heartland, a name which means in translation "the great one, spirit-lord who does not climb" yet a name we may speak (with apt reverence) here in this archival precinct of the nation: Kitasamba.

Kirsten Alnaes, that distinguished Norwegian anthropologist of the Bakonzo, is owed a special debt for her tabulation of Konzo deities. She has described Kitasamba thus, in her doctoral thesis on the spirit-singing of the Bakonzo: a "giant force that controls the environment and the livelihood and so the lives of all Konzo: in short he personifies the totality of all life ... the dominant male force, distant, snow-dwelling and unrelenting but protective and life-giving".

Kitasamba is moreover the spirit of music. His prime instrument is the collective *endara*, of ever-flowing inventiveness. Yet he is the over-arching musician of all instruments, and so also of beauty. His colour is red, as of blood and life; but most especially is his presence betrayed by the crepuscular pink on a bank of snow in the region of his dwelling. That is the region of his sanctuary. One climbs up there in awe. Men climbing to the snow-girt peaks of the mountains are to have no sexual intercourse before setting out, on pain of death from Kitasamba.

There, confronting the climber from the highest hut, Elena, immediately across from where you are, the twin peaks soar cloudwards a further 1,000 feet, virtually unscaleable pinnacles, 400 yards apart, each exactly 15,944 feet high: Kitasamba and his sister, Nyabibuya, the female and healing principle. This is all the inviolate and inviolable heart of Bakonzo territory.

Luigi Amedeo di Savoia, Duke of Abruzzi, possessed formidable qualities. Yet he was, I venture, awfully grand. His two scientific volumes giving the account and findings of his expedition were, as we know, ghosted for him by a Dottore who was not actually a member of the expedition at all, and who refers to the prince throughout at SAR: Sua Altezza Reale. His Royal Highness really hadn't the time, he explained in his preface, to write books.

These works give a few lines to the Bakonzo he recruited, without whom (I venture) he could not possibly have achieved what he did. Local Bakonzo had been engaged as guides and porters from the time of the expedition of C.S. Moore and Sir Harry Johnston in 1900, and each of the five intervening expeditions aimed at conquering and mapping the high peaks: all those predecessors were British, and all – one way or another – may be said to have been frustrated by Kitasamba.

The prince and his ghost-writer speak of 80 Bakonzo, all presumably hunters from the Mubuku valley, whom he recruited for the first three legs of the ascent, to the rock shelter of

Bujongolo, above the bamboos, the expedition's base camp. Of these, fifteen were selected for higher porterage, but none went into the snow. None of their names was recorded, and there is not a moment's speculation as to why a Mukonzo might be unwilling to breach the snows of their Olympus. They were commended for cleverness with their sticks on the climb, but remain uncredited for knowing all the tracks and intricacies of covert routes and tunnels which any ascent entails.

It does not seem to have been of significance to the prince that the Bakonzo already had names for each stream, gully, crag, overhang, waterfall, for every (or virtually every) species of creature or plant the expedition encountered. That he was entering territory sacred to the Bakonzo did not occur to him, least of all that it might belong to what in Christian terms we might call the "ground of the Soul", and to that Spirit which had no further to climb.

The Mukonzo political economist here in our midst, and well known to you all, Arthur Syahuka-Muhindo, is also the leading indigenous chronicler of the Rwenzururu movement. He has been a voice, in his writings, urging the recognition of the relationship between cosmology and political motive and action. There I stand with him, in my own experience of this place and these people, and have given sufficient expression of it in what I too have written. In this short address today I have said enough in summary of the extent to which the cosmology of the Bakonzo is shaped by the astonishing terrain they inhabit and the unique inviolability of the heartland, which their own habitation encircles and of which every Mukonzo is implicitly a guardian.

The inner heights are ever present to a mountain-dwelling Mukonzo. When (in 1954) I first traversed the length of the range along the upper contour of habitation, from what was then Bwamba; across the northern spine of the range to Burahya, and southwards into Bunyangabo and then Busongora, finishing in what under the Rwenzururu breakaway administration was known as Kambasa and Kyatenga, on Congo side, not a day or a night passed without my and my Konzo companions' awareness of the great inner heights of snows and glaciers, the cradle of thunder and lightning. In every turn in the weather, there was the arm of Kitasamba.

There in the highest village of the Tako valley, and the first human habitation man or spirit would encounter descending southwards from the snow peak (then) of Luigi di Savoia, my prime, beloved, companion and guide Isaya Mukirane and I were to decide upon the creation of the Bakonzo Life History Research Society (BLHRS). That was the intimately cultural Bakonzo-Bamba Rwenzururu-wide network which our journey had helped to make possible, and which was to lead to the political movement for self-determination (in acceptable UN-speak, at least of that time) and a declaration of an independent mountain-wide Rwenzururu, under the then presidency of Isaya Mukirane himself. Independent, I would say, that August of 1962, of the kingdom of Toro, and thus of Uganda and indeed of Britain itself, whose writ as the colonial power still had a couple of months to run. Isaya made his declaration from his new *kahindangoma* – his drum headquarters – in that self-same Buswagha territory of highland southern Busongora where he had first mooted the BLHRS.

Isaya's and his Bamba comrades' Rwenzururu movement and its fledgling army always sensed they were, in the final analysis – "when push came to shove" – undefeatable. In the first place they enjoyed, with varying degrees of passion and reluctance (yet more the former than the latter), the support of virtually the entire Bakonzo-Bamba community. Second, they had their inner territory: knowledge of its ways, familiarity with its climate and its weather, and virtually inexhaustible provisions therefrom – territory instantly hostile and dangerous to any stranger-force, yet into which they themselves could ever melt and seemingly vanish. Third, and of course relatedly, they had the spirits: the mighty spirits of the snows Nzururu, Nyabirika, Kitasamba: He Who Can Climb No Higher, and his cohorts. I have described this all at length in what I have written in book form. Let me bring you one or two fragments of this history.

When I visited (at Obote's request) Isaya at his rebel hideaway for a month or two the following year, 1963, after Rwenzururu's secession, he commanding his gossamer nation, I found myself echoing St. Paul: "In our frailty is our strength." The presumption, the defiance, was almost absurd. Yet it was, astonishingly, effective. It was cosmology as political, and now military, action … with bows for agitating monkeys out of trees and spears for sticking wild pig. Isaya's vision and his people's *always* had the inner and the upper, centred upon the inviolable snows, to call upon or to withdraw to. Kitasamba would do the rest.

The white disc in the centre of our new Rwenzururu flag was Nzururu's central snows. When, during my presence there at that time, Congo-side, Isaya was writing to the prime minister (as he still was), Milton Obote, and to the secretary-general of the UN – and various others in between – one typed and officially stamped missive ended:

> By this copy, Rwenzururians are advised to stand firmly in their homes – the God, King of Rwenzururu is sending down the Rwenzururu heavenly spirits with sharp swords which will slash down those who are disturbing and invading the innocent country Rwenzururu.

One knew whom he meant, though I doubt if U. Thant, in New York's UN headquarters, quite picked up the reference. Anyone who has endured, unprepared and unprotected, a Rwenzori hailstorm at 8,000 feet, with accompany lightning and heavenly rumbling, would know what was being warned of.

When Isaya wished, despite by own earnest initiative, to break off negotiating with Obote and his interior minister, Felix Onama, he withdrew with his entourage inward and upward to what he called his, or Rwenzururu's, 'furthest Private Cave'. There was very little I or anyone else could do about that. Nzururu's heights were the true, permanent, prevailing reality and sanctum.

Soon enough, Isaya, married as he was to the granddaughter of the outstanding northern Konzo chieftain of the first quarter of the century, Rhuandika, was no longer president but king, ceremonially enstooled or installed as Omusinga Kibanzanga, He Who Is Not To Be Moved, by a gathering of representative elders and seers; and his court and followers sang their kingdom (as the Konzo sing all that is important to them):

> *Sitwendihula!*
> *We cannot give up the struggle!*
> *We can never give up the struggle!*
> *We shall never give up the struggle*
> *Until we have won our goal!*

Thus they sang, and thus – in a modern context – they still sing.

Fearful privations and assaults were visited in those early years of the Kingdom of Rwenzururu. Yet miraculously it survived. There are those among us here who grew up in the midst of it, those of that self-same kingly family. It survived a ruthless assault in late 1964 by Uganda's military, recently shed of its British officers, sweeping the highland ridges, burning, looting, and shooting anyone in flight. It survived the death of Rwenzururu's first king, Isaya Mukirane, on 28 August 1966. It survived a devastating assault in September 1967 by Ugandan troops, which ravaged the seat of government, its palace and parliament building, and put the community to flight.

Yet, first under the regency, and an effective premiership, and at the end of the decade after the formal installation of Isaya Kibanzanga's 18-year-old eldest son Charles Wesley as Omusinga, King of Rwenzururu, the little highland state had reasserted its presence and taken shape. The ministerial line-up was expanded to include Defence (a portfolio taken by Charles Wesley himself), Finance, Internal Affairs, Regions, Justice, Education, Churches, Works, Labour and never-to-be-quite-overlooked Foreign Affairs. Four further senior roles were at the centre of affairs: the Speaker of the National Assembly, the Chief Justice, the Deputy Minister of Defence, and the Deputy Minister of Finance. There was a uniformed army, with its own training college, uniformed police, a treasury, courts, schools at primary level, churches, and an ubiquitous and occasionally somewhat pitiless poll-tax collection.

There was drawn up and promulgated a formal Treatise of Aims, *Ebilhubirirwa,* unmistakably the work of civilized men – imbued with generosity, and premised on lasting ideals of mankind with an insistent urgency: freedom, peace, unity, tolerance, the collective weal, the sanctity of culture and heritage, and the essential rightness and benison of God's creation. The disabled and elderly were given due protection, the role of women was to be advanced, and – note this – tribalism in any negative sense was to be "stamped out". Charles, as king, led morally, culturally, and politically, with dignity and with as full a personal responsibility as was reasonably possible. There were inevitable fallings-away from the ideal.

The ending of the Kingdom's administrative and political separation from Uganda (and likewise from Congo, in that there was anything coherent from which to have seceded from) was a planned, rational and orderly affair, carefully negotiated with government in Kampala. It took place on 15 August 1972, precisely 20 years to the day after Rwenzururu's declaration of its independence, at a massed rally and formal ceremony at Kasese. That was during Milton Obote's second term of office.

The Bakonzo now had their own administrative district, Kasese, far from comprehensive in terms of tribally occupied territory, yet comprising the whole of their southern heartlands. The Bamba had Bundibugyo, with a 60 per cent or greater complement of Bakonzo therein. There were very soon to be two Konzo-oriented dioceses, Protestant and Roman Catholic, and a third regionally based Seventh Day Adventists (SDA) province. The medium of education in Konzo area schools was Lukonzo, and administrative documentation accordingly. They had their own ethnically Konzo members of parliament. Charles Wesley's own paramountcy among his ethnically and linguistically identifiable Banyarwenzururu fellow citizens was implicitly acknowledged, albeit in a Uganda which had not yet returned, under the maturer presidency of Obote's ultimate successor, Yoweri Museveni, to expressed recognition of the role of ethnicity in Uganda's regions and the recognition of inherited paramountcy on a "cultural" basis, in the politically correct terms of our times.

As Uganda – and this audience – knows well, that claim to the formalization by Kampala of Obusinga bwa Rwenzururu, with Charles Wesley and his line as heir to Omusingaship, carries ineradicable support in the heart of the Bakonzo and indeed most Bamba too. I note with interest the renewed backing for Obusinga by the Mwamba patriot, Peter Mupalya, one of the original triumvirate of separatist leaders, headed by Isaya Mukirane, which launched the original independent entity.

What is overwhelmingly evident is that the issue of Banyarwenzururu assertion of their cultural – and I daresay territorial – identity on their own snow-citadel mountain territory by the symbolism and mystical authority of *obusinga*, is not going to be eradicated. Time will strengthen it, not diminish it. It has become rooted above all in the mythology which rightly or wrongly surrounds the defiance and effectiveness and relative nobility of that 20-year *montagnard* kingdom of more than a third of a century ago, throughout which the people's mountain cosmology took centre stage. That extraordinary piece of equatorial Africa's history could belong to no other piece of geography but that centred upon the Rwenzori massif, which hides, protects, fortifies and revivifies, by its ferocity and its bounty, its darkness and dazzling beauty, none but its own … by courtesy of its gods.

Migrations and Social Formation in the Rwenzori Region

Arthur Syahuka-Muhindo

Introduction: Social formation in the Semliki Valley

Social formation in the Rwenzori region began with immigration to the Semliki from the seventh century onwards, from all directions – west, north-west, north, north-west, south-west and south. The earliest migrations constituted the Batembuzi society, which, as it differentiated, gave rise to the Bacwezi who, in turn, formed the first political associations in Kitara. Spatial population distribution in early Kitara came to follow particular regions, and the emergence of the state redefined the context of population movements within the region, thereby redefining the context of settlements and political relations among groups.

The Semliki Valley was the melting pot in which many different groups of immigrants to the region coalesced into clans before moving east into the heartland of Bunyoro-Kitara where they mingled with immigrants from the north, north-east and south to form the Bakitara people[1]. The Semliki Valley received in reverse emigration groups of Bakitara, or Bacwezi, from the heartland Bunyoro-Kitara, fleeing the violence associated with state formation. Beginning with the rise of the Bacwezi dynasty, the population began to drift westward. Cattle keepers and agriculturalists fleeing the economic coercion imposed by, first, the emerging Bacwezi ruling group and then the Babito group, moved westward until they reached the eastern slopes of the Rwenzori Mountains. Pastoralist groups occupying the savannah grassland plains of Busongora increasingly extended their grazing activities to the Semliki Valley where the Abasonga people already practised cattle-keeping.

18

Westward population movement, resulting from state formation processes in the Bunyoro-Kitara heartland, notably the rising power of the Babito, increased from the seventeenth to the nineteenth century. Warfare and political centralization in the Bunyoro, Nkore, Mpororo and Toro kingdoms tended to push groups of people to the peripheral areas of these emerging polities. From the Bunyoro-Kitara heartland, populations moved westward and southward. When the Toro kingdom formed, population moved further west into Busongora, the Semliki Valley and subsequently into the Rwenzori Mountains.

In Busongora, the Semliki Valley, and the Rwenzori Mountains, the different groups of immigrants coalesced into the Bakonzo and Bamba who, in the 1960s, violently challenged the authority of the rulers of the Toro Kingdom in the form of the Rwenzururu movement. The Rwenzururu movement created a state known as the Rwenzururu Kingdom. The historical significance of the Rwenzururu Movement, arising on the eve of the departure of British colonialism, was not only its attempt to create a state, but also what this effort revealed about local and regional dynamics in the pre-colonial and colonial periods. The Bamba and Bakonzo tribes were formed on the periphery of the Kitara Empire. They thus included remnants of the earliest immigrants as well as a variety of different groups of people – agriculturalists and pastoralists alike – who came to Busongora and the Semliki Valley fleeing political and military pressures, or the warfare violence associated with state formation in the kingdom areas to the east of the Rwenzori Mountains, along with those later fleeing the turmoil caused in the nineteenth century by the Kilongalonga slave raiders and traders. The turmoil of the nineteenth century pushed these groups into physical and cultural isolation – the Bakonzo in the Rwenzori Mountains and the Bamba in the inaccessible Bwamba plains – thus sealing their fate as marginal tribes in Toro Kingdom. These people not only preserved historical traditions elsewhere obscured by the creation of the colonial Toro Kingdom and the British colonial state, but retained linguistic forms – Lukonzo and Kwamba – that sharply distinguished them. Thus, although originally part of the Kitara people, the Bamba and Bakonzo became different in relation to other peoples in the region and so became discriminated against on the basis of tribe of culture. In reaction, they aspired to be recognized as nationalities, leading to their violent struggle to establish the Rwenzururu state[2].

The history of the peoples of the Semliki Valley illustrates the wide range of variables in the process of state formation and especially the role of violence involved. Not only was the Semliki Valley the melting pot in which different groups of immigrants to the region coalesced into the Bakonzo and Bamba tribes, but also the valley formed the periphery of Toro Kingdom. The history of social formation in the Semliki Valley demonstrates that whereas different elements combined in the process of state formation, the violence of the late nineteenth and early twentieth century was the major means by which different peoples were brought under the control of a single state. Until then, violence had been minimal in the evolution of the state in the Semliki Valley. Archie Mafeje made this point regarding the rise of Bahima and Batutsi controlled states elsewhere[3]. What he fell short of clarifying was the exact socio-political dynamic that brought forth the state in the new forms he identified. History of state formation – the shedding and reconstitution of roles by different social groups and their impact on the character of the emergent (new) states – if properly researched, has the beneficial potential of redirecting our understanding of the problematic of the state in the interlacustrine region. It may also be the avenue through which we may better understand the current crisis of the state not only in Uganda, but the entire Great Lakes region.

The history of the Semliki Valley peoples also dispels the myth of the disappearance of the Bacwezi and demonstrates that what has been misinterpreted as their disappearance was in fact the political transformation of their conditions of existence. This arose from the decline of the Bacwezi rule and the "new"

Babito's ascendance to power in a process that divided the Kitara Empire into new and centralising kingdom states[4]. People belonging to one polity were forcefully drawn into another, and this process continued into the colonial period. The Bakonzo and the Bamba tribes, having been forcefully drawn into colonial Toro, would in the 1960s violently challenge the authority of the rulers of that kingdom, seeking to secede and establish a separate state, the Rwenzururu state. Thus Bakonzo and Bamba tribal nationalism arose on the basis of colonial contradictions in the Toro Kingdom, which gave contemporary significance to grievances of the long past.

There has been a tendency to characterize those who established the Babito dynasty as an alien group in the history of state formation in Bunyoro-Kitara. It is commonly believed that the Babito were of Luo origin and came from the north. My contention is that the Luo peoples, wherever they may have come from, did not arrive in Bunyoro-Kitara as Babito. Instead, the Babito was the new clan formed from existing clans that defined itself as a political clan – as the successor to the Bacwezi rulers. Thus, in the Rukidi tradition, the Babito became the ruling clan comprising both agricultural and pastoral groups. Originating from the king's court, the Babito clan quickly expanded and extended to most parts of the empire since it was associated with power[5]. The Babito clan became one of the largest clan groups, numbering 156 sub-clans[6]. Buchanan argues that between the sixteenth century and the nineteenth century this rapid growth of the royal clan eventually contributed to the political instability of the state[7]. The Babito of the ruling lineage adopted the pastoral culture in which cattle were not only the measure of wealth and power but also a symbol of status. The forceful acquisition of cattle created friction between the Bacwezi pastoralists and the new Babito chiefs. The Bacwezi pastoralists responded by migrating south-west to Busongora, and further south of the Katonga River into contemporary Ankole. In this way, Bahima pastoralism became predominant in Busongora and the Semliki

Valley following the formation of the Babito-dominated Kingdom of Bunyoro-Kitara.

Centre-Periphery Migration in Bunyoro-Kitara

In all, there were eight major distinctive waves of migration from the Bunyoro-Kitara heartland to Busongora. The Abagabu represent the first wave of migration to reach Busongora. They were predominantly Bari-Sudanic speakers, and had been associated with the Isaza tradition. They fled south-west to Busongora at the collapse of the Isaza ruling system. They were an agricultural-pastoral group when they occupied central and northern Burahya[8]. The second wave of migration in the westward direction was made up of Baranzi, trekking back to Busongora following the overthrow and killing of their leader Bukuku by Ndahura (of Babito)[9]. In other words, tribal fighting that characterized the rise of the Babito to power in Bunyoro caused this Bahima group to relocate in Busongora. The third wave was that of the Basingo (Omurarra Cow Totem group) as Bahima, who came to Busongora during the Bacwezi period[10], followed by the Bafunjo and Balisa from Rwanda, also with Sanga cattle during the Bukuku period[11]. The fifth wave of migration into Busongora was that of the Bazira and Bahati clans. The sixth was the Baisanza and Basambo[12]. The seventh was that of the Baitira, Bacwamba, Bane, and Bairuntu clans. These were originally one clan recognizing a common totem: the elephant (*njovu* in Luganda, *njojo* in Runyoro-Rutoro). They moved from Buganda and Busoga, where the elephant clan is associated with the Kintu group of migrants that are believed to have arrived in the area from Mt. Elgon by the thirteenth century. They reached the Semliki Valley in the seventeenth century. In the Semliki Valley this led to the formation of the Bakira clan of the Bakonzo. The places they "colonized" or occupied during their westward movement are known as Kitswamba, west of the Rwimi River in Busongora, Kicwamba in Burahya and

Bunyaruguru. On adopting cattle culture they formed the Embazi Cow Totem group, and later, as a Bakonzo clan, the buffalo (*mbogho, mbogo*). The last major migration wave involving Bahima people was the Basana, a subdivision of the Basengya. The Basana went to Busongora, becoming the most numerous Bahima clan in the Busongora area, while the Bangere travelled to Buganda, where they were assimilated as the Namunjjona (crow) clan[13].

Kitara traditions indicate that clan formation was a continuous process; a clan was formed from different peoples. Clans changed, reflecting changes in their socio-economic conditions or when their members acquired new skills. For example, the Basehe formed as a clan in the Semliki Valley, but they relocated in "Buyaga", part of Kitara, as the "Bayaga", following their adoption of a cattle-keeping culture and their acquisition of a special skill to interpret the winds in order to determine the weather conditions over the lake. They used this skill to cross Lake Anekbonyo (Albert) "safely", taking their possessions, including cattle, with them[14]. Likewise, when agricultural people acquired cattle and adopted a pastoral culture, they changed totems or formed new clans to reflect their new socio-economic situation. When the Bakira had cattle, their totem was the Embazi cow, but they changed it to a buffalo once they lost their pastoral culture and became cultivators on the east bank of the Semliki Valley, at Bukira, near Burangwa.

The Peopling of Semliki Valley Region and the Rwenzori Mountains

From the seventh century to the immediate pre-colonial period there were several migrations, largely along the western flank of the Great Rift Valley, from the Equatorial Province of the Sudan (from the southern Sudanese mountains) southward to the Rwenzori Mountains. There were also migrations from the west and southwest of the Rwenzori Mountains. The earliest immigrant groups mingled in the Semliki Valley and the Busongora plains where they coalesced into the different clans that subsequently migrated eastward into heartland (Bunyoro) Kitara. In heartland Kitara, clans from the Semliki Valley encountered groups, also organized as clans, that came from the north-west and north-east. These coalescent groups, taken together, were the Batembuzi – the forerunners of the Bakitara people.

At this point Kitara society was not organized beyond clan level. For the immigrants from the west, as for the immigrants to Kitara arriving from elsewhere, the clan was the vehicle by which their existing traditions were preserved. Buchanan observes that these clan traditions testified to a steady stream of immigrants entering the Kitara complex from the west. All were Bantu speakers who travelled from the Semliki Valley beyond the Rwenzori Mountains around and across the southern end of Lake Anekbonyo (Albert)[15]. The Bantu-speaking clans represented the primary ingredient in the tribal makeup of Kitara, an importance that is attributable to their number and their cultural influence. Their political institutions, for example, involved a more hierarchically structured clan organization than other intrusive groups of the pre-dynastic period, including the pattern of two titles for their leaders used in alternative traditions[16]. Not only was their influence great in terms of political organization, but they are also reputed to have introduced cattle and the mixed agricultural-pastoral economy that afterwards characterized the "Kitara Complex". This economy originated in the Semliki Valley. As it expanded to the other parts of the Kitara complex and was modified, the "Semliki economy" continued to be the basis on which Kitara society evolved and social reproduction organized.

Clan traditions of the Semliki group that moved into the Rwenzori Mountains (and some to the Mitumba hills), following social strife of one kind or another in the Semliki Valley, as well as traditions elsewhere in Kitara, are distinctive and show that new clans formed following the fragmentation of the old ones as they absorbed new members, so that a single migration was not exclusively composed of genealogically related lineages. These traditions also show that there was a tendency for pastoral groups to move continuously, thus spreading throughout the Kitara complex, although originally their concentration was in heartland Bunyoro – the counties of Buyaga, Bugangaizi, Buhekura (Buwekula) and Mubende.

The Semliki Valley population migrated to other parts of Kitara as the Barungu and Abasonga clans. These clans first formed in the Rwenzori Mountains and the Semliki Valley. The earliest Barungu settlement was in Burangwa, the hill territory straddling the Lume, a tributary of the Semliki River, and Muroho River, a tributary of River Tako. Kiraro in Burangwa territory was the main centre of Barungu clan coalescence. Buchanan hypothesizes that Kiraro was not a place name[17]. However, there is a Kiraro located in Burangwa territory[18] where a church, a primary school, and a market place today exist in the village, each bearing the Kiraro name.

Konzo tradition suggests that the Barungu (otherwise, Bahira – guinea fowl – a wild bird totem) hived off the Abasonga (grasshopper) clan as the Semliki Valley economy differentiated. Ecological conditions in the Semliki Valley played a role in the formation of the Abasonga. The Abasonga emerged as a cattle-keeping clan in the rich pastureland in the Semliki Valley and first "colonized" the Busongora plains from where they dispersed[19]. They introduced the small horned and humped (*engolomojwa*) cow to the Kitara heartland. The Abasonga and Barungu terminated their migration in Buganda, where they dropped their Kitara names but retained their totems, the grasshopper and guinea fowl, as clans according to Buganda custom[20]. In Buganda, the Grasshopper clan is generally regarded as being earlier than "Kintu", who is the earliest cultural hero of Buganda and Busoga traditions[21]. This seems to confirm their early arrival in Buganda.

The Bagahi/Babwijwa, the Bayanja[22], the Baranzi/Baami[23] also originated from the Semliki Valley[24]. Together with the Barungu/Abasonga and the Bayaga[25], this western stream of immigrants formed the larger and more influential component of Bakitara in the pre-Babito period. Moreover, Kitara as a whole adopted the cattle and mixed agricultural-pastoral economy that originated from the Semliki Valley. Constantly modified, the "Semliki economy" formed the basis of social reproduction in the Batembuzi, Bacwezi and Babito eras. Thus, the migrations of the western stream had an extensive impact on the region.

Peopling of the Rwenzori Mountains and the Creation of Bakonzo and Bamba Tribes

The peopling of the Rwenzori Mountains is related to two simultaneous processes: the arrival of new streams of immigrants in the Semliki Valley and the hindering of their eastward movement by the rising kingdom of Bunyoro-Kitara. The earliest immigrants in the Semliki Valley were able to subsequently disperse east to the shores of Lake Victoria and beyond. This was not the case with later migrants whose eastward expansion was checked by the rising Bunyoro-Kitara Kingdom under Babito rule. The stream that could not make it to heartland Bunyoro-Kitara from the Semliki Valley originated specifically from the Ndu people of the West Nile region of contemporary Uganda. The movement of peoples caused their southward migration to the Semliki Valley from southern Sudan into West Nile.

Ndu (Kebu) people were the original inhabitants of the West Nile region of contemporary Uganda[26]. The Ndu people moved southward into the Semliki Valley, arriving there at a very early date[27]. It is not known why these people moved from their original land in West Nile. Buchanan, relying on Kitara traditions, suggests that the initial movements had been precipitated by some cataclysmic event such as famine[28]. However, later waves of Ndu migration to the Semliki Valley were linked to their contact with outsiders from the north – the Lugbara who immigrated to West Nile from Sudan[29].

The Lugbara came in three distinct waves[30]. The earliest Lugbara group to arrive in West Nile was the Moru-Madi division (or simply the Madi division), who claim to have come directly from Moru in Sudan. They came to the West Nile via Mount Midigo, which is situated in the extreme north of the present day Aringa County in Arua District. Their territory lay between the Nile River to the east and the Liru, Wati and Luku mountains to the west. The next group of settlers to arrive in Lugbaraland was that group which belongs to the Jaki division of the Lugbara. This group broke away from the Bari in the Sudan. After many years of wandering, they finally settled near Mount Liru, from where they spread to other areas. From them come such Lugbara clans as Taraa, Oleba, and Rubu, who occupied what is modern day Maraca county[31]. The third wave comprised the Banale division, which, according to Lugbara tradition, was the last to arrive in Lugbaraland. From Moru in the Sudan they first migrated to western Acholi (presently Gulu District) via the Nile valley. From Gulu they migrated to the west side of the Nile (Miri), crossing near Gimara and eventually settling on Mount Wati[32]. By the end of the first quarter of the nineteenth century, the whole of Lugbaraland (Arua District) was occupied by Lugbara 'chieflets'. It is possible that each wave of Lugbara migration into West Nile caused a corresponding migration of Ndu further south.

Effects of the Lugbara people on the Ndu people seem to have been a continuous southward and westward movement of the Ndu into the Semliki Valley. Ndu migrations in the nineteenth century were halted by Belgian colonialism from the west and British colonialism from the south and east. Earlier, the Ndu had moved southward until they reached the Rwenzori Mountains, where they became known as the Babundu. The eighteenth century Babundu were either exterminated by disease or integrated into the local population[33].

It is difficult to draw definite conclusions about the role of disease as a stimulus for migration. It has been argued that references to sleeping sickness north of Lake Edward may represent the incorporation of the more recent experiences with the devastating sleeping sickness epidemic of the Semliki Valley at the beginning of the twentieth century and its subsequent evacuation into traditions that refer to earlier events. On the other hand, Webster indicates that sleeping sickness spread into Busongora from Bunyoro during the major droughts of the late sixteenth and beginning of the eighteenth centuries[34]. John Ford has suggested that sleeping sickness may have been endemic in the Semliki Valley before the outbreak of the 1905 epidemic. He notes that a tradition told to Van Hoof by the Belgian territorial administrator M. Hackaers in 1926 indicated that a succession of peoples settled in the Semliki Valley only to be driven out by outbreaks of sleeping sickness. Ford wrote:

> The Mabundu, for example, who live in the Nepoka, were settled over 200 years ago in the Semliki Valley; they abandoned that part of the Ruwenzori, so they say, to escape the ravages of sleeping sickness ... Similarly, the Bakumu or Babira, whose vanguard coming from the east, passed around the south of Ruwenzori and then spread northwards and westwards, to the district of (B)Uvumu and Mombasa, only remained for a short time in the Semliki Valley where the dreadful diseases killed more of their people than the wars they had had to wage in order to force their way across the high plateau dominating the fatal valley[35].

The in-and-out movements of the Babundu and Babira suggest that the Bamba groups formed in the area long after the Babundu had arrived, perhaps during the later part of the eighteenth century. Suffice to conclude therefore that the Bamba tribal formation began during that time.

Ndu or Babundu migration southward occurred mainly into the Semliki Valley, and was largely confined to the western shores of Lake Albert (through the Mahagi territory) and along the banks of the Semliki River, which connects this lake to Lake Edward south of the Rwenzori Mountains. After staying in the Semliki valley for some time, the Ndu peoples began to move eastwards, following a course similar to that of their predecessors into southern Bunyangabu and southern Burahya. They terminated their eastward movement in Burahya when they encountered streams of westward population movement caused by the emergence of Babito rule in Bunyoro. Thus, the process by which the Bakonzo tribe was formed and confined to the Rwenzori Mountains began in the seventeenth century. It began when the population in the savannah pastureland from the Semliki River to the Muzizi River was forced to take refuge in the mountains following various forms of social strife arising from disease and drought in the sixteenth and seventeenth centuries, and later the violence associated with warfare and slave raiding during the second half of the nineteenth century. The intersection of the agricultural Banyoro moving west with the Ndu migrants on one hand, and the initial effect on them by Babito rule on the other, is represented in the Bakonzo tradition of Kibiniro.

Bakonzo tradition in Burahya has it that a man known as Kibiniro from Isale arrived in Burahya with a large party of followers more than four hundred years ago. In Burahya, Kibiniro and his party encountered a people who were moving westward. Fighting his way, Kibiniro led his party to the eastern slopes of the Rwenzori Mountains where they remained and multiplied. Kibiniro was of the Bashu clan, and this is how the Bashu (the dominant Semliki Valley clan) first spread in the south-eastern parts of the Rwenzori Mountains.

My interpretation is that, rather than being the name of a person, Kibiniro represents a particular historical period when groups of migrants from the Semliki Valley, and groups moving westward from Bunyoro, met each other in Burahya. These groups mingled, subsequently coalescing into the Bakonzo tribe[36]. The Bakonzo tribe formed in the southern and south-eastern parts of the mountains, although the different groups comprising the tribe were not collectively known as Bakonzo until another tribe – the Batoro – emerged and formed itself into a polity as the Toro Kingdom, in the belt between the Rwenzori Mountains and the Bunyoro-Kitara Kingdom. The distinct difference between Batoro and Bakonzo was not only geographical. The Bakonzo comprised coalescent groups from many of the previous migrations in the Kitara Empire, who became secluded in the mountains where they preserved old customs and traditions of the Batembuzi, Bacwezi and even the Babito periods. The different groups of people that settled in the mountains evolved a common language that combined the elements of Bantu and Nilo-Saharan languages. It was the Luyira that combined with Lukobi to form the Lukonzo language. Luyira and Lukobi were spoken in the south-eastern and south-western slopes of the Rwenzori Mountains respectively. Luyira was the hill peoples' variant of Ruhyana, while Lukobi was the more archaic language of the Semliki Valley, preserved in the western highlands of the Rwenzori Mountains – Burangwa.

The massive Rwenzori Mountains and the Ntoroko plains shielded migrants in the lower Semliki valley from the political influence of Bunyoro-Kitara Kingdom. The rulers of the Bunyoro-Kitara Kingdom had no interest in territory beyond the area containing the salt deposits of Lake Katwe[37]. This was also the context in which the Bamba tribe formed in the lower Semliki Valley and the Bwamba plains.

In the Rwenzori area the Ndu, who had long integrated with the local population, differentiated into two broad categories – cattle-keepers and blacksmiths. Traditionally, the Ndu were blacksmiths[38]. Farming and cattle-keeping were the two most important aspects of the Lugbara economy[39]. During their peaceful coexistence with the Lugbara immigrants, the Ndu supplied metal goods (hoes, arrowpoints, spearheads, bracelets, bangles and rings) to the Lugbara in exchange for cattle[40]. As the Lugbara population increased and the Ndu were forced to migrate farther south, it became difficult for the former to obtain iron ore and goods. Some Lugbara communities attempted to solve this problem by absorbing Ndu groups into their own chieflets. The Aya in Terego and the Nyangilia in Kakwa adopted this method and succeeded in transforming their own areas into "manufacturing centres"[41]. Compared to the "manufacturing centres" farther south, these two centres were limited and managed to serve only local, or at most, regional needs[42]. For the rest of Lugbaraland, iron goods could only be obtained through long distance trade with the Ndu in the south[43]. There emerged traders among the Ndu who, in addition to metal tools, also traded Katwe salt in markets established along the axis from Lake Katwe to Lugbaraland. This group subsequently withdrew from other economic activities to concentrate on cattle-keeping and the salt trade. They became known as Basongora because of their practice of using sharp implements for hunting and specialized sharpened sticks (mambo) for spreading animal skins to dry. When new herdsmen later arrived in the region, they too were called Basongora; otherwise they were called Bahima[44]. The Ndu-Basongora lived in the areas of the northwest shores of Lake Edward in the Kyavinyonge, Kasindi and Muramba areas[45]. This part of the Semliki Valley, a savannah grassland area, was suitable for rearing cattle; the reason it attracted Bahima immigrants from other places.

The other group of Ndu immigrants to the Rwenzori region remained blacksmiths. By far the smallest number, they tended to live in the mountains where they excavated the ore which they smelted to fabricate spears, arrows, and hoes. While it has been argued in the past that metal hoes were introduced to the Rwenzori area by Banyoro immigrants and traders, more recent research has adduced new evidence that metal hoes, even if of inferior artistic quality, already existed in the western parts of the Rwenzori Mountains and had spread to the Isale hills by the time Bunyoro hoes were introduced by later immigrants. The rudimentary technology of the Babundu was long used in salt mining at the Katwe and Kasenyi salt lakes before Bunyoro implements were known there.

Oral tradition on either side of the Rwenzori Mountains clearly indicates that immigrants from the "Sudan", a reference to the Babundu, first developed the hoe in the Semliki valley. This is partly supported by Heinzelin's excavation at Ishango (or Isango) at the mouth of the Semliki River. Heinzelin suggests that a hunting and fishing population with late Mesolithic industries preceded Bashu settlement in the area and had contact with Bantu occupants[46]. From this, I make two critical observations. First, the original Nande groups were Sudanic peoples (i.e. non-Bantu groups), and the Bantu occupants they came in contact with were the immigrants from the south-west and the Bacwezi tribes moving westward into the Semliki Valley. The admixture resulted in the formation of the principal proto-Cwezi Bakonzo/Banande clans – the Babinga[47], Bakira[48], Bahira[49], Baswagha[50], Batangi[51], Bahambo, and Bashu among others. Second, the study of the social and environmental history of the Semliki Valley demolishes the myth of Cwezi disappearance. The chronology of immigration into the Semliki Valley region indicates that the earliest immigrants to arrive in the region were Sudanic peoples (non-Bantu speakers), followed by Bacwezi groups (Bantu speakers), and finally Babito. In this regard, the so-called disappearance of Bacwezi may simply mean that either they dispersed to new areas away from the centre of the Bacwezi empire and mingled with other peoples, the process, for example, by which previous Bacwezi groups became designated as clans of the Banande and Bakonzo; or that their supposed disappearance may simply be a result of the present limitations of the study of early African civilizations. Randall Packard makes the crucial point that:

> ...the literature on African political systems in fact is filled with references that attest to the role of cosmology in general in shaping patterns of political action. Yet as numerous as these sources are, the historical relationship between cosmology and action has yet to

be explored in a comprehensive fashion. This is because studies of political process and history have failed to examine in sufficient detail indigenous political ideas and the relationship of these ideas to the wider world view of the peoples being studied. In most cases, the discussion of the cosmological dimension of sovereignty has been limited to observations concerning the general relationship between authority and the problem of maintaining the fertility of the land, and has not paid adequate attention to either the complexity or pervasiveness of this linkage between politics and cosmology[52].

"Failing to explore the depth and breadth of indigenous political perceptions, has", Packard argues, "encouraged a fragmented view of the impact of these perceptions on political action."

While indigenous ideas about the nature of sovereignty are shown to come into play on specific occasions – the most important of which involve periods of ecological crisis – at other times, cosmology appears to have little significance for politics, and both motivations and actions are ascribed either implicitly or explicitly to universal categories of thought and behaviour as defined, for example by Bailey[53], Sahlins[54] and Swartz *et al*[55]. Political actors thus appear to take on and divest themselves of cosmological notions as the situation dictates, operating at one moment by universal rules of political behaviour, and at others in a culturally defined mode[56]. Packard elaborates this point with a suggestion by Evans-Pritchard regarding his study of Zande witchcraft, how individual perceptions of the world cannot be laid aside, but come into play on certain occasions if not on others. Instead, these perceptions serve as a permanent (albeit changing) lens through which experience is interpreted and actions are given form[57]. This is the elaboration of the rectitude of "tribe".

Konzo oral tradition maintains that metal hoes were produced locally by blacksmiths before Bunyoro hoes were introduced[58]. This tradition maintains that the original local Bakonzo hoes were fabricated from melted rock, but acknowledges that these were found to be inferior to the Bunyoro hoes, which were fabricated from *"obuthale"*, presumably iron ore. However, *"obuthale"* seems to have referred to any material used for making metal tools[59].

Following the arrival of Banyoro immigrants during the eighteenth century, iron ore was obtained from Bugangaizi markets in the heartland of Bunyoro. Since Banyoro immigrants of the eighteenth century were mainly agricultural people, and trade between Busongora and the heartland of Bunyoro expanded during that century, local production of hoes was undermined as tools of better quality could be obtained through trade[60]. However, when warfare and violence intensified in Toro and resulted in the cessation of trade between Busongora and Bunyoro, cultural recession followed, resulting in cultivators in the mountains resorting to using wooden implements as hoes[61]. The situation was not helped by British colonialism outlawing local manufacturing, following the Abayora rebellion that highland Bakonzo organized in response to British colonialism in the area during the later part of the 1910s.

Oral tradition in the Bwamba part of the Semliki Valley region suggests that the population began to move into the mountains following an outbreak of sleeping sickness, roughly two hundred years ago. The Bwamba plains became depopulated until they were re-colonized or re-occupied by the Bamba, who migrated eastward from Bubira[62]. In the southern and south-eastern parts, population had repeatedly sought refugee in the hills so that the thick tropical forest that covered the slopes of the Rwenzori Mountains was pushed back to 7,000 feet above sea level as the area became settled[63].

While population dwindled in the Bwamba plains, the middle Semliki Valley west of the Rwenzori Mountains teemed with fresh waves of immigrants. The plains were covered with a savannah-type grassland, suitable for cattle-keeping. Bahima from Busongora increasingly drove their herds into the Semliki Valley. In time, ethnic integration occurred between the various groups of herdsmen – the "Ndu-Basongora" and "Hima-Basongora", later to disintegrate in the turmoil of the nineteenth century, specifically, the violence associated with state formation, slave raiding, and Belgian and British colonialism, coupled with the ensuing outbreak of epidemic disease.

Through intermarriage with local tribes, the Ndu had long adopted the Bantu languages of the local people among whom they lived. Espousing the theory of language change in historical contexts in eastern and southern Africa, Christopher Ehret makes the following observations. First, when two (or more) language groups settle among one another and establish regular and frequent patterns of interaction, one (or more) of these groups usually changes its primary language. Second, in such a situation it normally takes at least one generation for bilingualism to become widespread. Third, it takes at least another two generations for a complete shift in language affiliation to occur[64]. This theory applies to the development of dialects near the Rwenzori Mountains, and is borne out by the nature and character of language forms of the various Lukonzo/Kinande dialects spoken in this area[65].

However, Ehret does not indicate possible intervening factors which can enhance or inhibit the speed at which language change occurs. In the pre-colonial period, when intermarriage was one of these factors, language change through this process may have occurred slowly. The more speedy forms of language change occurred against a background of social strife, including warfare among political states. Warfare and epidemic diseases, which caused flight, invigorated the process of inter-group contact while undermining traditional tendencies through social disorganization and reorganization. This was true of immigrants into the Rwenzori Mountains, especially in the period after 1850, when the surrounding lowland region witnessed incessant warfare compounded by slave raiding.

In the Semliki Valley epidemic diseases affecting both cattle and humans aggravated the social situation. Epidemic disease produced traumatic effects similar to those of warfare, acting as a social brake with consequences for community and culture. At the same time, processes of adaptation that followed had renewal effects, one of these being language development and acquisition. Survivors of either war or epidemic disease tended to seek greater interdependence, thereby enhancing inter-group contact through collaboration, intermarriage and exchange of vital services such as healing and spirituality. Development of mutually intelligible languages was therefore vital for both interaction and "inter-ethnic" communication leading to a cohesive tribal formation or grouping such as Bakonzo or Bamba.

The period from the mid-nineteenth century onward witnessed frequent wars in the Rift Valley region in general and the Semliki Valley in particular. Warfare destroyed networks of production and inter-group association in very important ways. Groups of people lost control of their main economic and social activities. The necessity to survive social strife caused by warfare or disease drew members of different tribal groups closer. Groups that were more settled and more numerous gained advantages over those who were fewer in number, or socially disorganized. This happened to the Ndu-Basongora and other small immigrant groups[66]. In time, the Ndu groups attached themselves to, or were absorbed into, the largest of the Bakonzo clans, the Bashu. This pattern was also followed by the Abahambya from Bunyoro who lived in the Kiyanja area on the north-western shores of Lake Edward in the upper Semliki Valley, and subsequently withdrew to the Rwenzori Mountains during the 1890s fleeing the Kilongalonga slave raiders from southwest and the Abarusura (Bunyoro) army from the east[67]. The Abahambya, who were descendants of Babito, also found it feasible to attach themselves to the Bashu clan who already claimed historical links with the Babito of Bunyoro[68]. Because of its high rate of absorption of immigrant groups, the mainstream Bashu clan differentiated into the Bashu-Bandu and Bashu-Banyalubango[69]. This categorization brings together the

Banisanza (or Banyisanza) and Babito into a single clan formation, both of whom trace their origin in the Bunyoro-Kitara Kingdom.

However, because of their peculiar group occupation, the Ndu cattle-keepers were not fully absorbed into the Bashu clan. Known as Basongora, whose totem is the grasshopper, they remained a distinct sub-clan of the Bashu. In the 1880s they formed the Basongora chiefdom, which by 1918 extended to River Kanyampara in the east and River Semliki in the west. Other Bashu sub-clans belong to the bushbuck and sparrow totems, suggesting Babito predominance in these clans. The agricultural group among the Ndu formed a sub-clan of Basyangwa, which has since completely dissolved into the mainstream Bashu clan in the Rwenzori Mountains[70]. This is an example of the way in which warfare and environment, including environmental adversity, has influenced societal forms in the Semliki Valley and the Rwenzori Mountains.

I have emphasized that the creation of the Babito-controlled state in Bunyoro-Kitara provided the impetus for the westward migration of the subjugated Kitara tribes into the Semliki Valley. Evidently, therefore, population movements occurred in every direction – west to east and vice versa, north to south and vice versa. Population moved westward in one part of the Rift Valley, while in another part movement was eastward. Interposed between these were numerous alternating north-south population movements. These became more dramatic, mainly in the nineteenth century, due to a combination of population pressure, warfare, slave raiding and trade, and colonial conquest.

While migration, population increase and reinvigorated economic activities call attention to the influence of the natural environment as migration occurred in search of new opportunities, such as agricultural grazing and hunting areas, it was warfare that provided the catalyst for rapid population movements across different ecological zones, causing problems of adaptation, and generating new tribal formations. Colonial conquest warfare initially reinvigorated tribal and ethnic population movements, but these soon halted once colonial governments were established. Colonial warfare generally covered wider territorial areas than previous African conflicts. It was also more rapacious, owing to superior European organization and more technologically advanced weaponry, and generally led to greater population movements than previous conflicts[71]. In almost every case, wars of colonial conquest were followed by devastating epidemics[72]. These, too, affected the character of social formations in the Semliki Valley and the Rwenzori highlands.

Warfare, Environmental Adversity and State Formation in the Semliki Valley, 1850-1900

Endemic warfare does not seem to have been a feature of the Semliki Valley until the 1850s. No doubt contact between groups of immigrants generated tensions, but this does not seem to have resulted in extreme forms of violence. The period 1850 to 1900 was the period during which warfare and generalized violence seems to have become a regular feature of society, entailing at one time or another the Maniema slave raiders and ivory traders, the armies of Bunyoro and Toro, Rwanda irregulars, and African agents of European colonial rule. Thus, violence in the Semliki Valley during this period was an extension of warfare occurring in the kingdom states to the east of the Semliki Valley, arising from the process of the founding of Toro Kingdom and the Bunyoro conquest (or reunification wars), slave raiding and European colonialism.

Banande/Bakonzo traditions emphatically point out that their people moved from the lowlands generally, and the Semliki Valley in particular, to the western slopes of the Rwenzori Mountains owing to a combination of drought, disease and war violence during the 1880s and 1890s. Disease and drought had no doubt occurred in the Semliki Valley before, and these had caused earlier migrations to the highlands. Recent work on the climatological history of the lakes region of East Africa suggests that the migration periods cited in Banande/Bakonzo tradition(s) – the middle of the sixteenth century to the middle of the seventeenth century and the end of the seventeenth century – were marked by extended dry weather which led to drought conditions and famine[73]. Those conditions evidently caused people throughout the region to look for wetter lands near lakes, rivers, forests and mountains and may well have contributed to the movement of Nande cultivators out of the Semliki Valley[74].

There was no hint of the state in the Semliki Valley and the surrounding hills until the sixteenth and seventeenth century droughts. These droughts caused competition between the herdsmen and cultivators over deteriorating water and land resources. Packard suggests that cultivators, who preferred to resist domination by herdsmen, and to maintain their agricultural existence, may have chosen to move away from the centres of Bahima control[75]. Under conditions of drought, farmers reduced to desperate straits by famine might well have accepted service among pastoral neighbours who had valuable and mobile resources such as cattle[76]. This view is supported by the Bahima-Babito chiefs' consideration of their political authority over Busongora to the east of the Semliki River[77]. Based on this evidence, the establishment of the Bahima-controlled chiefdoms did not necessarily entail the use of physical violence. Rather, it was mothered by the occurrence of long-lasting environmental adversity. At least in this instance, the conquest myth attributed to the Bahima does not seem to hold. With respect to Busongora and the Semliki Valley, there is little evidence of armed confrontation between the herdsmen and cultivators in the initial establishment of political control by the Bahima over the Banande/Bakonzo cultivators.

Political transformation in Busongora and the Semliki Valley evidently occurred in a complex of ecological change in the valley and violence in the kingdoms of heartland Bunyoro-Kitara.

Periods of drought, accompanied perhaps by outbreaks of sleeping sickness, altered the ecological and political balance between herdsmen and farmers in the region. In response, Banande/Bakonzo cultivators moved their settlements to the slopes of the mountains and northward into the forest[78]. At the same time, other cultivators became the clients of herdsmen, whose economy came to dominate the valley. These changes culminated in the consolidation of the Bahima-Babito authority over Busongora and the establishment of the Babito kingdom of Kisaka at the beginning of the eighteenth century[79].

Pastoral domination of the valley was accelerated by the arrival of new groups of herdsmen fleeing the political turmoil disrupting western Ugandan states during this period. The violence that occurred in the neighbouring kingdoms accelerated migration of herdsmen from kingdoms to the Semliki Valley. Instances of such violence include the Bunyoro invasion of Nkore during the reign of Ntare IV (1713-40), the Nkore invasion of Buhweju during the same period, the succession wars in Nkore that followed the death of Ntare IV, and the civil wars following the break-up of Mpororo at the end of the eighteenth century. All contributed to western Uganda's political instability and stimulated the migration of pastoralists into the upper Semliki Valley[80].

The arrival of new immigrants contributed to the social and economic transformation of Busongora and the Semliki Valley, and furthered the dominance of herdsmen over Banande/Bakonzo cultivators. During the later years of the eighteenth century, and the beginning of the nineteenth, this shift in political balance between the valley's two major economic groups was completed by the consolidation of the herdsmen's political control over the west bank of the Semliki Valley, under the Babito princes of Busongora, and their Bamoli allies. Both of these ruling groups subsequently extended their political influence into the Mitumba mountains[81]. Thus the state that was first formed in the Semliki Valley region was organized by Bahima and Babito, both later arrivals.

The Effects of External Violence on Society and State in the Semliki Valley: Formation of Kisaka, Bugaya, and Kiyanja chiefdoms

Three embryonic states emerged in the Semliki Valley and Busongora: the kingdoms of Kisaka, Bugaya, and Kiyanja. The first was the Kingdom of Kisaka, that subsequently influenced the formation of the Bugaya and Kiyanja kingdoms.

The Kingdom of Kisaka, situated in Busongora, extended westward to the east bank of the Semliki River. However, military force does not seem to have been instrumental either in the formation of the Kisaka chiefdom nor in its expansion. Perhaps, instead, some form of economic coercion was involved.

Initially, the expansion of Babito authority and the establishment of the Babito kingdom of Bugaya began during the reign of Mairanga, who ruled Kisaka at the beginning of the nineteenth century. Additional Babito expansion occurred during the reign of Mairanga's successor, Kioma (or Kighoma), in response to military incursions into Busongora by the Toro armies in the 1850s and 1870s. Military violence affected the inhabitants of Kisaka, resulting in the formation of armed regiments for the defence of people and property. Such regiments, led by clan leaders, were deployed against the invading Toro forces.

The main reason for the Toro military incursion into Busongora was the determination of King Kaboyo of Toro to wrest the control of the salt lake and cattle resources of Busongora from the ruler of Kisaka[82]. Kaboyo's raids into the region throughout his reign caused many Babito-Bahima to seek refuge to the west of the Semliki, thus furthering the expansion of Babito authority over this region, while Bakonzo cultivators sought the safety of the mountains.

The second state was formed as a result of Babito expansion. This was the Kiyanja chiefdom started by the Bamoli. Some Bamoli already lived on the southern half of the Semliki's west bank as clients of the Babito rulers of Kisaka. Expansion of the Bamoli settlements to the west of the Semliki River and the foundation of Kiyanja began with the arrival of a new group of migrants from the south end of Lake Edward during the mid-eighteenth century. These people, known locally as Bakingwe, engaged in lake-side commerce and had a similar culture to the Banande/Bakonzo peoples who formerly occupied the Semliki Valley. The Bakingwe settled around Katwe under the Barenge clan, who traced their origins to Rwanda and Ndorwa[83].

Among the Bakingwe were immigrants from Buganda of Bukunja ancestry. The Bakunja, with a maritime tradition, were reputed to have introduced canoe transport on Lake Edward, invigorating salt trade around the lakes region, and were subsequently responsible for the rise of the Kiyanja chiefdom.

Unlike the Kisaka and Bugaya states set up by the Bahima-Babito, the Kiyanja chiefdom was set up by the Bamoli and the Bakingwe, that is, by agriculturalists and traders. The Bakingwe generally took an active interest in the transport of salt and soon expanded its trade using the fast, lightweight canoes which they supposedly introduced to convey salt to lakeshore markets. These became centres for the exchange and distribution of salt throughout the hinterland. Such markets were also the basis of inter-state rivalry involving Bunyoro, Nkore and Buganda. Later, with the advent of European colonialism, they would also become part of imperial rivalry between Britain and Belgium.

The success of the Bakingwe in the salt trade brought them wealth and prestige which they used to extend their political influence over the Katwe region. While they evidently accepted the overlordship of the Babito, they acquired direct control over the islands and lakeshore around Katwe, and became chiefs over the region[84]. They might well have founded a Bakingwe state had Kabalega and British colonialism not intervened. The Bamoli retained substantial influence in the region because of their role as mediums for Wamara, but they were officially subordinate to the Bakingwe. Their subordination apparently encouraged the Bamoli to expand their settlements to the west of the Semliki River, where they established the chiefdom of Kiyanja at the beginning of the nineteenth century[85].

By the early nineteenth century the Babito and Bamoli had established their authority over most of the upper Semliki Valley. More chiefdoms formed along the western slopes of the Rwenzori in the nineteenth century. A junior group of the Babito, known locally as Banisanza (or Bashu Banyisanza) subsequently crossed the Semliki Valley and settled around Mount Lisasa, north of Isale, after unsuccessful attempts to establish themselves in the plains just south of the equatorial forest. Two other groups, claiming Babito connections, expanded their settlements into the mountains from the plains, during the early nineteenth century. The first, led by Mukumbwa, settled south of Isale near Luvere. The second, and more important, represented in Bashu traditions by Kavango (or Kabango), settled at Kivika (or Kibika) on the slopes of Mount Mughulungu in Isale. Kavango's descendants eventually expanded their political authority into most of the present Bashu region[86].

Violence in Busongora and the Semliki Valley at the Close of the Nineteenth Century

In preceding sections I discussed how population migrations and ecological conditions influenced the character of social and political formations in Busongora and the Semliki Valley in the pre-1850 period. I now turn to the effects of violence on society and the environment.

Population displacement caused by violence associated with the westward expansion of the Toro Kingdom was exacerbated during Bunyoro's expansionist wars in Toro and Busongora. By the time Bunyoro forces overran Toro in 1889, people and markets remained only at Lake Katwe in Busongora. Bunyoro assaults on this area displaced people and destroyed the existing salt trade that had hitherto provided a means of livelihood. Some residents of Lake Katwe fled to the hills of Kyangwe (or Kyango) and Isale across Lake Edward, while others fled to the mountain slopes of Bukonzo north of the lake. This was not the first time people from Busongora had moved into those areas. The first movement had taken place centuries before during the southward migration of the Bahima[87]. However, this earlier movement was not caused by military violence; rather the agricultural community shifted to the mountain slopes as a result of land pressure created by the demands of the traditional grazing system.

Bunyoro's assault on Toro and Busongora complicated an already volatile situation. The Toro Kingdom had experienced persistent social and political strife as a result of the numerous succession wars following the death of Omukama Kaboyo (ca. 1870), the founder of the Toro Kingdom. Fighting erupted in one region after another and warfare repeatedly disrupted production and displaced populations. Ingham describes how Toro Kingdom was destroyed by internal and external violence[88].

Between 1876 and 1893, the population endured no less than six expeditions at the hands of the Abarusura. Each involved horrific loss of life, and social and economic disruption. Kabalega's initial expeditions were successfully repulsed, and he had to retreat and reorganize his forces before he could attack again – a process that took nearly ten years. From 1885 to 1891, the history of Toro is one of complete disorder and total confusion. Whole sections of the Toro population were compelled to move from their homeland and to take up residence in parts of Bunyoro. Apparently, Banyoro from the north were made to settle in their place[89]. By this time, Kabalega had acquired firearms with which his army, the Abarusura, subdued Toro. In 1889, Kabalega's forces completely eliminated the last vestiges of the Toro state, and put the young future Toro king, Kasagama, to flight. The conquest of Toro resulted in the annexation of Toro and Busongora as administrative regions of the Bunyoro Kingdom.

A population decline followed the Bunyoro military campaigns, undermining production and exchange, and disrupting social and political institutions. Whereas Kaboyo's conquest (1850-1878) caused tribal disharmony, the Kabalega wars of conquest produced the opposite result. The Abarusura military activities ironically stimulated a great deal of tribal integration among survivors. Through population displacement, relocation and adaptation by survivors, new communities formed via de-ethnicization and social reconstitution. The violent disruption of society in the Semliki Valley relegated the Bakonzo, fleeing to the safety of the mountain, to a stateless status. By 1900 a state remained only in the Isale highlands and the upper Semliki Valley in the form of the Bashu chiefdom of Isale.

Because of the Kabalega wars and the effects of the Sudanese, whom Captain F. Lugard introduced in the area in 1891, the people of eastern Toro fled into central and southern Bunyangabu as well as south central Burahya. Having lost their herds to both the Abarusura and Sudanese soldiers, many turned to agriculture and were thus "de-classed". In most of Toro Kingdom this process led to the blurring and eventual disappearance of the social distance between the Bahima (pastoralists) and the agricultural Batoro[90]. The Bahima in Busongora, however, remained a distinctively pastoral people.

In Busongora, the flight of the Kisaka rulers to the west of the Semliki River marked the demise of the local state, which was replaced by agents of the Bunyoro state. The region was later redrawn into the Kingdom of Toro under British colonial rule, with the Semliki Valley becoming part of Belgian Congo following the Congo-Uganda boundary settlement in 1918[91]. By the end of the nineteenth century the effects of a long period of warfare resulted in epidemic disease. Throughout the first two or three decades of the twentieth century disease had a significant impact, with disruptive effects on society and its political institutions. Much of the disruption occurred in the war-torn areas of lowland Busongora and the Semliki Valley. On both sides of the Rift Valley and within it there had been widespread and profound political disorder that brought misery to the ordinary peasantry. Survivors of violence and disease responded by fleeing to the mountains. Emphasizing the generality of violence and its effects on populations on both sides of the Semliki Valley, John Ford wrote:

> The British portion of the Western Rift Valley was devastated by the colonial wars but its people's miseries were trivial compared with the horrors that were endured by the inhabitants of the Eastern Congo. The confrontation of the Europeans and the Arab slave traders set in motion the most appalling outbreak of inter-tribal strife on top of genuine attempts by the inhabitants to preserve themselves from one or other invaders ... Large-scale destruction of human communities can only take place after relatively long intervals in which they had time to grow and establish themselves. It is evident that the stresses to which the indigenous peoples were subjected between 1885 and 1895 had a profound effect upon the epidemiology and epizootiology and trypanosmiasis in the Rift. The first cases of sleeping sickness were identified in 1905[92].

In other words, the violence of the later period of the nineteenth century in the Rift Valley reproduced the environmental adversity of previous centuries. However, with or without human activity, the environment is always in a state of flux. Howe defines the environment as:

> ...the matrix of physical, biological and social circumstances surrounding man and affecting his well being. It is the milieu in which he has lived during the many hundred thousand years of his biological evolution. It is the sum total of his habitat, economy and society and, as such, embraces not only his life support system of air, water, food and shelter, but also the multiplicity of provocative forces bearing down on him and affecting his health. It is, in effect, a reservoir of physical, chemical and biological forces which

support or threaten, and which have, among other powers, mutagenic properties over the genotype of living things. The environmental complex is in a continuous state of flux; it is ever changing[93].

Several factors affect the health of human beings, including the physical environment influenced by the weather and climate, the availability and quality of water, and the biological environment – the domain of disease and disease organisms. Environmental diseases, which derive from the state of the biological environment, tend to assume epidemic proportions, these being cholera, smallpox, tuberculosis, leprosy, influenza, dysentery, and meningitis. Other environmental diseases include malaria and typhoid fever. Howe points out that disease in any given locality is the result of a combination of geographical circumstances which bring together disease agent, vector, intermediate host, reservoir, and man at the most auspicious time[94]. Violence did not only disrupt the habitat, it also disrupted the socio-cultural environment through forced, often unplanned relocations of populations, subjecting people to the disturbing prospect of resource depletion and unfamiliar environmental hazards. Not only does war as armed conflict lead to violent massive death, but it also disorients, undermines and disrupts the familiar routine of productive (not necessarily creative) activities in the economy, leading to forced scarcity.

Depopulation caused by war and war-related processes breeds important and unforeseen consequences. Whether the population is killed during fighting or flees from a given region that experiences fighting, the removal of a population has historically been followed by ecological transformation. Where cultivation and grazing occurred, these kept the bush at bay and the tsetse fly, carrier of sleeping sickness, was confined to wild areas, forming frontiers between nations. However, the removal of the population caused the land to revert to thorn trees and bush, creating a favourable habitat for tsetse fly and other disease vectors. This ushered in epidemic diseases which killed people as well as animals[95]. The situation in Busongora and the Semliki Valley, following the turmoil that occurred at the close of the nineteenth century, exemplifies to this. Violence and diseases, towards the close of the nineteenth century, altered the context of the state in the region; it re-emerged in the form of a colonial state.

Conclusion

In this paper I have attempted to reconstruct the history of the Semliki Valley, which was not only a corridor for both population movements and the spread of epidemic disease, but also a melting pot in which new societies were formed. I have illustrated the common origins of the people living in and around the Rwenzori region and shown how different tribes emerged. I have demonstrated that tribes formed when people's existence became confined to specific ecological areas so that tribe represented the social expression in a bounded or defined territory. Tribe thus embodied the collective expression of community that transcended clans and which both defined and was defined by the tribe's constituted system of social reproduction, language and customs. By tracing the historical links between the Semliki Valley and Bunyoro-Kitara, this paper illustrates the interaction of local and regional dynamics, and demonstrates how the histories of small, peripheral communities can enrich our knowledge of larger, regional, and national processes[96].

Cultural isolation among the Bakonzo has often been misrepresented as a matter of choice. The majority of Rwenzori Mountain inhabitants did belong to an ancient race, but this had little to do with cultural isolation. What is true is that warfare, regional violence and disease pushed the Bakonzo into seclusion in the mountains, and tribal relations with the Batoro, in turn, pushed the Bakonzo and Bamba into cultural isolation.

Some have seen this cultural isolation as natural[97]. Synge argues that the Bakonzo were an ancient "race", since they had been little affected by migrations from the north and northeast. They, in this view, merely retreated to the mountains, where they preserved their language and powerful, heavy "Negroid stature" and appearance[98]. This viewpoint sees the history of African peoples living in peripheral or remote areas as essentially static. I have shown in this paper that the Bakonzo belonged to the same social mosaic as the rest of the Kitara people, before they were forced into seclusion in the Rwenzori (and Mitumba) Mountains. My view is that the sustained cultural isolation was based on two crucial factors: the rise of an ethnic Toro state to the east of the mountains, and the decimation of the population in the Busongora plains and the Semliki Valley by violence and epidemic disease. Deprived of interaction with the population in the lowlands, the Bakonzo thus came to lead a secluded life. Cultural isolation and stagnation occurred among the mountain people in a particular historical and environmental context. The most spectacular consequence of colonial violence, especially towards the close of the nineteenth and early twentieth century, was the termination of the pre-colonial process of forming the indigenous state; instead ushering in the process of colonial state formation.

The view that the Bakonzo had not come into contact with other peoples is not valid. Synge and others see the Rwenzori mountain peoples as static and timeless. This was the folly of many colonial anthropologists. Ironically, the area through which Synge passed had seen much tribal integration that was interrupted only two decades before he arrived. However, it was not only colonial observers who misrepresent the history of the Rwenzori Mountains people. Even more recent writing by such prominent Ugandan writers as Mamdani[99] and Dani Wadada Nabudere[100], repeat the same fallacies because of the problem of uncritical reliance on colonial anthropology as written history. Perhaps this is too strong a criticism given the Bakonzo self-view and mythology. For the Bakonzo, their mythology stems from their mountains – "Rwenzururu" or "Rwenzura". It is no wonder, then, that their existence in the mountains should appear natural, both to themselves and their external observers, among them explorers, colonial anthropologists, and latter-day political scientists.

Notes

1. See Buchanan, C.A. 1973. 'The Kitara Complex: The Historical Tradition of Western Uganda to the 16th Century', PhD dissertation, Indiana University.

2. This insight derives from memoranda by Rwenzururu Movement leaders, among them Yeremiya S. Kawamara and Peter Kamba Mupalya, 'Bamba/Bakonjo Memorandum Testimonial Evidence', 16 September 1962. This was a memorandum to the Central Government Commission, chaired by F.C. Sembeguya, instituted to investigate the causes of the Rwenzururu Movement, known as 'The Commission of Inquiry into the Recent Disturbances amongst the Bamba and Bakonjo People of Toro'. Another Rwenzururu document was the 'Bakonzo/Bamba Petition' to the Central Government demanding separation from Toro Government before 9 October 1962, dated at Kasulenge 15 August 1962. It was written by Isaya M. Mukirane, Y.S. Kawamara and Peter K. Mupalya and witnessed by thirteen Bakonzo/Bamba leaders. (Rwenzururu documents in author's collections.)

3. See Mafeje, A. 1998. *Kingdoms of the Great Lakes Region: Ethnography of African Social Formations.* Kampala: Fountain Publishers.

4. See Mafeje, 1998; John Nyakatura, *Anatomy of an African Kingdom; A History of Bunyoro-Kitara,* NOK Publishers, New York, 1973.

5. Buchanan, (1973) chapters 7 and 8.

6. Bikunya, P. 1927. *Ky'Abakama ba Bunyoro,* Sheldon Press, London, 59-61.

7. Buchanan, (1973) 222.

8. Buchanan, (1973) 128.

9. Buchanan, (1973) 140-143.

10. Buchanan, 1973, 149-150.

11. Buchanan, (1973) 153.

12. Buchanan, (1973) 154-156.

13. Buchanan, (1973) 158.

14. Buchanan, (1973) 73-74.

15. Buchanan, (1973) 69.

16. Buchanan, (1973) 69-70.

17. Buchanan, (1973) 78.

18. This territory has been known by different names at different historical times – Burungu, Bukunja, Bukonjo, Buleha, and Bakonzo's legendary Bukobi. In 1891, Lugard identified its central position as Bukunja. Originally emerging as Burungu, Burangwa territory contracted with the passage of time until now only its mountainous portion remains known as Burangwa.

19. Abasonga tradition according to Eriya Kambere (former sub-county chief). Personal communication, 30 July, 2003.

20. Buchanan, (1973) 80.

21. Buchanan, (1973) 80-81.

22. The *mutima*, 'heart' clan in Buganda

23. Civet cat (totem) clan.

24. Buchanan, (1973) 82-86.

25. Original totem was *ente engaju* – a reddish-brown cow, later changing to a reddish bird known as *akafunzi* in the Runyoro language, *kanyamunkongi* in Rutoro, *kasanke* in Luganda, and *kisu* in Lukonzo.

26. See Shiroya, O.J.E. 1984. "The Lugbara states in the eighteenth and nineteenth centuries". In Salim, A.I. 1984 ed., *State Formation in Eastern Africa*. Nairobi:, Heinemann Educational Books. Nairobi, 200.

27. Shiroya, (1984) 198-203.

28. Buchanan, (1973) 71.

29. The Lugbara are a Sudanic-speaking people and are classed as members of the Moru-Madi sub-group of the Eastern Sudanic group. The Lugbara live on the Nile-Congo watershed where this forms the international boundary between the republics of Uganda and the Congo. The heart of Lugbaraland is the plateau, between 4,000 and 5,000 feet above sea level, consisting of open, almost treeless rolling plains, bounded by the watershed and the circle of mountains, Liru, Wati and Luku. The country is fertile and has many permanent streams and rivers, and a well-distributed rainfall. See Shiroya, 1984, 195.

30. Shiroya, (1984) 195-196.

31. Shiroya, (1984) 196.

32. Shiroya, (1984) 196.

33. Bakonzo tradition has it that at least one wave of Babundu arriving in the Butawu part of the Semliki valley in the nineteenth century perished in a series of military confrontations with the local forces from the Kiyanja

Kingdom. This information is available in Mr. Constantine Mbiwa's collections, which the author possesses.

34. Webster, J.B. 1979. "Noi! Noi!, Famines and Aids to Interlacustrine Chronology". In Webster, J.B. ed., *Chronology, Migrations and Drought in Interlacustrine Africa*, African Publishing, New York.

35. Ford, J. 1971. *The Role of Trypanosomiases in African Ecology*, Clarendon Press, Oxford, 177.

36. *Kibiniro* is a Lukobi (ancient Konzo) term for arena. In this regard the "Kibiniro-arena" represented the interaction of various migration groups encountering each other and mingling into a single identical "tribe". The name Burahya given to the territory in which the Kibiniro myth developed, defined the process and character of "'inter-tribal'" composition in that area in the seventeenth century. This is what Burahya literally means – it is a concept of archaic meaning.

37. Only with the emergence of the ivory trade did the area become of interest to the Babito, as became the case during the reign of Omukama Kabalega (1870-1899). Bunyoro-Kitara's conquest of Bulega country across the Semliki River in the 1880s was the first major external military engagement in the Semliki valley. Kabalega's rule affected the people of the lower Semliki Valley as it affected those south of the Rwenzori Mountains or Busongora – it caused flight to the mountains. In the Bulega and Mahagi areas, further flight was caused by the ravages of Emin Pasha's troops before they were recruited into Lugard's force in Uganda. See Lugard, F. 1893. *The Rise of Our East African Empire: Early Efforts in Nyasaland and Uganda*, William Blackwood and Sons, Edinburgh and London; Jameson, J.S. 1890. *The Story of the Rear Column of the Emin Pasha Expedition*, R.H. Porter, London; Werner, R.J. 1889. *A Visit to Stanley's Rear-guard at Major Bartleto's Camp on the Aruhwimi, with an Account of River Life on the Congo*, W. Blackwood, London.

38. Shiroya, (1984) 200.

39. Shiroya, (1984) 200.

40. There has been a tendency to suggest that cattle reached Uganda only from the north-eastern direction. This is because the introduction of cattle in Uganda has been associated with the movement of Hima groups. But a critical re-examination of the history of the Semliki Valley region points to new evidence that short-horned cows were first introduced there by Sudanic peoples as far back as the seventh century. Perhaps the main reason that the history of cattle-keeping in Uganda has been traced from the Hima is the fact that the cattle complex became established in the interlacustrine region to the extent that even when the Bacwezi disappeared, the Luo immigrants who established the Babito dynasty in

Bunyoro, and the Bahima who established the Bahinda dynasties in the kingdoms of Ankole, maintained the tradition of cattle-keeping. This may provide another explanation, namely that colonial historiography did not endeavour to research African history in a manner that it would bring out evidence of destroyed past civilizations. The point is that the Ndu-Basongora's civilization, having been decimated through wars and diseases in the Rift Valley region, seems to have lost their own history, and the tendency was to associate themselves with the Hima-Basongora.

41. Shiroya, (1984) 200.

42. Aluma of Ajibu-Anyavu, quoted in Shiroya, (1984) 201.

43. Shiroya, (1984) 201.

44. See Syahuka-Muhindo, A. 1994. "The Rwenzururu Movement and the Democratic Struggle". In Mahmood Mamdani and Joe Oloka-Onyango, eds, *Uganda: Studies in Living Conditions, Popular Movements and Constitutionalism*, JEP and Centre for Basic Research, Kampala. Pre-Bahima cattle-keeping in the Semliki Valley confirms that the Abasonga, the original Basongora, were the first pastoralists in area. However, influxes of Bahima pastoralists from heartland Bunyoro-Kitara with larger herds of Sanga (long-horned) cattle transformed the pastoral culture as the "indigenous Basongora" adopted Bahima cattle-keeping practices, while remaining culturally distinct from them. The Ndu-Basongora occupied a middle position between the Bahima and the local agricultural communities, largely Banande/Bakonzo. Disease – rinderpest, sleeping sickness, smallpox, etc. collapsed the distinction between the Bahima and the local agricultural community, Banande or Bakonzo. Epidemic rinderpest not only diminished animal stock but also in combination with other diseases affected the population, thereby causing a cultural recession in distinctive groups. However, warfare and epidemics that characterized Busongora and the Semliki Valley at the close of the nineteenth century, accelerated the process of cultural integration in the Rwenzori highlands, leading to a unified Bakonzo culture. The Kihyana culture that had thrived in the lowlands for several centuries collapsed; with it, the Bahima economic dominance in Busongora and the Semliki Valley.

45. The vegetation cover in this area suggests that indeed the area was previously used for herding cattle. This is the same area that the Basonga clan in the Kitara tradition formed.

46. Jean de Heinzelin, 1957. "Les Fouilles d'Ishango", Institut des Parcs Nationaux du Congo Belge, Brussels, 76, cited in Packard, R.M. 1981. *Chiefship and Cosmology: An Historical Study of Competition*, Indiana University Press, Bloomington, 59.

47. Composed of elements of Bito (a branch of Cwaa clans) and Bayaga, Bahunga, Abenyonyintono (small reddish bird – Buganda and Busoga).

48. Composed of elements traceable from Mount Elgon via Busoga and Buganda: Baitira, Banyasere, Bairuntu, Bacwamba and Bane.

49. Composed of elements of Basambo, Banyiginya, and Jo-Kisambo and Barungu.

50. Like the Bakira, also traceable from Mount Elgon, they are composed of elements of Basita, Baraha, Bajwaga, Abendiga (sheep, Buganda) and Byabasita (Kibale).

51. Composed of elements of Basingo, Pa-Bango, Abakimbire (Nkore, Rwanda, Kigezi).

52. Packard, (1981) 8.

53. Bailey, F.G. 1969. *Strategems and Spoils*, Schocken Books, New York.

54. Sahlins, M. 1963. "Poor Man, Rich Man, Big Man, Chief: Political Types in Melanesia and Polynesia". In *Comparative Studies in Society and History*, Vol. 5 No. 3, 285-303.

55. Swartz, M.J., Turner, V.W. & Tuden, A. (Eds.) 1966. *Political Anthropology*, Aldine, Chicago.

56. Packard, (1981) 8.

57. Packard, (1981) 8.

58. In earlier research, I pointed out that the technology used in the production/mining of salt at Lake Katwe came from the Congolese highlands of Isale, west of Lake Edward, and the Bukonzo mountains in present-day Uganda. See Syahuka-Muhindo, A. 1989. "The Rwenzururu Question". I have since discovered that Lendu immigrants who settled in the Semliki Valley actually introduced the fabrication of metal implements long before the region felt the influence of developments in the heartland of Bunyoro-Kitara. Most blacksmiths in the Rwenzori Mountains are indeed descendants of Lendu immigrants.

59. Artisans obtained *obuthale* (ore) from Buthale (place) in the mountain hills of Mahango in Kasese District.

60. On trade between Busongora and Bunyoro, see Kamuhangire, E.R. 1975. "The Pre-colonial Economic and Social History of East Africa with Special Reference to South-Western Uganda Salt Lakes Region". In Ogot, B. A. ed. *Hadith*, Vol. 5, East African Publishing House, Nairobi; and his "The States of Southwestern Uganda Salt Lakes Region During the Nineteenth Century", Seminar Paper, Department of History, Makerere University, Kampala. Also see Uzoigwe, G.N. 1972. "Pre-colonial Markets in Bunyoro-Kitara", in *Comparative Studies in Society and History*, Vol. 14.

61. Interview with Adonia Kanekerya Masereka, Ibanda (Kasese), October 1986.

62. A section of the Bamba, the Babulele, are related to a forest people known as Babira, who lived across the Semliki River.

63. See Winter, E.H. 1955. Bwamba Economy: *The Development of a Primitive Subsistence Economy in Uganda*, East African Institute of Social Research, Kampala; Parsons, J.D. 1960. "The Systems of Agriculture Practiced in Uganda. Memoirs of the Research Division". Agricultural Department, Uganda Protectorate, Kampala Research Station.

64. Ehret, C. 1971. "Southern Nilotic History : Linguistic Approaches to the Study of the Past".

65. There are three distinct but very closely linked dialects in the Lukonzo language: Kinande, spoken in Kivu Province of eastern Democratic Republic of Congo; Lukonzo in the highland parts of southern Rwenzori; and Lughendera in Bunyangabu, Burahya and Bundibugyo. Kinande exhibits marks of other eastern Congolese languages such as Kihunde, Kimbuba and Kibira. Lhughendera exhibits marks of Runyoro-Rutoro languages. Highland Lukonzo (also known as Luyira, meaning olden language), remains more indigenous. In addition Kinande has acquired Lingala and French words, while the Ugandan Lukonzo varieties have acquired English words. A similar situation exists in the Kwamba language, which also has two distinct dialects - Lubwisi and Bulebule. Bulebule is akin to Kibira languages, while Lubwisi is a combination of many languages: Lukonzo, Rutoro and Kwamba.

66. There were numerous small groups of immigrants who fled to the mountains as refugees. Some of the villages such refugees occupied were named after their original nationalities -- for example Bughungu (Bugungu) in Kitholu sub-county and Buhambya in Ihandiro sub-county. Bughungu in Kitholu sub-county became home to immigrants of Bugungu origin, while Buhambya in Ihandiro became home to the Abahambya, both groups being "refugees" from Bunyoro. The Abahambya men were remnants of the Abarusura, who fled to the Rwenzori mountains when Lugard's forces defeated them in 1891. Some Basongora (of Hima origin) who fled to the mountains completely lost the cattle-keeping culture, turning instead to agricultural life and thus becoming fully Konzoised.

67. Interview with Paulo Muhindo and Yofesi Mulisya, Kampala, July 2002. (Notes about Abahambya).

68. Regarding this claim, see Packard (1981), 55-71. Because people of Babito descent were the first to form chiefdoms in the Semliki Valley region, there was a tendency among many latter immigrants from Bunyoro to

belong to the Bashu clan. There could be other reasons as well, namely that since such people came from state societies, there was a tendency for them to belong to a group which was in the process of evolving a state system.

69. These are the Bashu of the royal lineage, descendants of Lubango, who was credited with the formation of a type of centralized state dominated by members of his lineage, who were of Bahambya origin.

70. Oral tradition in the hills of Bukonzo, west of Kanyampara.

71. See J.A. de Moor & Wesseling, H.L. 1989. *Imperialism and War: Essays on Colonial Wars in Asia and Africa*, E.J. Brill/Universitaire Pers Leiden, Leiden, 1989; and Headrick, D.R. 1981. *Tools of Empire; Technology and European Imperialism in the Nineteenth Century*, Oxford University Press, Oxford, 1981.

72. There is a wealth of literature on this subject, mainly by public health historians, e.g. Turshen, M. 1984. *The Political Ecology of Disease in Tanzania*, Rutgers University Press, New Brunswick; Lyons, M. 1992. *The Colonial Disease: a Social History of Sleeping Sickness in the Social History of Northern Zaire, 1900-1940*, Cambridge University Press, Cambridge; also see among others Caldwell, J.C. 1981. "The Mechanisms of Demographic Change in Historical Perspective", in *Population Studies,* 35(1), 5-27; Chipindulla, D.C. 1968. "The Maji Maji Rising in Kilosa Town", *Maji Maji Research Project Collected Papers*, University College, Dar es Salaam, Research Project No. 2/68/1/1; Crosby, A.W. 1972. *The Colombian Exchange: Biological and Cultural Consequences of 1492*, Greenwood Pub. Co., Westport, 1972; Ferguson, D.E. 1980. "The Political Economy of Health and Medicine in Colonial Tanganyika", in M.H.Y. Kaniki, ed., *Tanzania under Colonial Rule*, Longman, London, 1980; Gwassa, G.C.K. 1969. "The German Intervention and African Resistance in Tanzania", in Kimambo, I.N. ed., *A History of Tanzania*, East African Publishing House, Nairobi; Iliffe, J. 1967. "The Effects of the Maji Maji Rebellion of 1905-1912 on German Occupation Policy in East Africa", in Gifford, P. and Louis, R. eds, *Britain and Germany in Africa: Imperial Rivalry and Colonial Rule*, Yale University Press, New Haven, 1967.

73. See Cohen, D.W. 1974. "A Preliminary Survey of Climatic Trends in the Lake Region of East Africa", ASA Conference, Chicago; Riehl, H. & Meitin, J. 1979. "Discharge of the Nile River: A Barometer of Short Term Climatic Variation", in *Science*, Vol. 206, 1178-80; Herring, R.S. 1979. "Hydrology and Chronology: The Rodah Nilometer as an Aid to Interlacustrine Chronology", in Webster, J.B. 1979 ed., *Chronology,*

Migration and Drought in Interlacustrine Africa, Africana Publishing, New York.

74. Packard, (1981) 60.

75. Packard (1981) 61. "Bahima" were not a tribe. "Bahima" referred to people who were occupationally cattle-keepers.

76. Steinhart, E. 1979. "The Kingdoms on the March: Speculation on Social and Political Change". In Webster, J.B. 1979 ed., *Chronology, Migration and Drought in Interlacustrine Africa*, Africana Publishing, New York, 203.

77. See Rukudi III, Sir G.K. n.d. , "The Kings of Toro", Typescript. Translated by Joseph R. Muchope, History Department, Makerere University, Kampala. 7.

78. See generally Packard, (1981) chapter 2.

79. See Packard, (1981) 72.

80. Packard, citing Karugire, S.R. 1972. *A History of the Kingdom of Nkore in Western Uganda to 1895*, Clarendon Press, Oxford.

81. Packard, 72-73.

82. See Kamuhangire, E.R. "The Pre-colonial Economic and Social History of East Africa with special Reference to South-Western Uganda Salt Lakes Region", in *Hadith*, 5. edited by Ogot, B.A. East African Publishing House, Nairobi, 1975; and his "The States of South-western Uganda Salt Lakes region during the Nineteenth Century", Seminar Paper, Department of History, Makerere University, Kampala, 11-12; Ingham, K. 1975. *The Kingdom of Toro in Uganda*, Methuen and Co., London, 28-30.

83. Packard, (1981) 74.

84. Kamuhangire (1975), 74-79.

85. Packard, citing Sindani Katsuva and Musienene, Dec. 13, 1974; BHT 128.

86. Packard, (1981) 75.

87. See Packard (1981).

88. Ingham (1975), Chapter 2.

89. Taylor, B.K. 1962. *The Western Lacustrine Bantu*, International African Institute, London, 44.

90. See Doornbos, M. 1970. "Kumanyana and Rwenzururu: Two Responses to Ethnic Inequality", in Rotberg, I. & Mazrui, Ali eds., *Protest and Power in Black Africa*, Oxford University Press, Oxford, and Doornbos, M. 1979. "Protest Movements in Western Uganda: Some Parallels and Contrasts", in Hall, R. L. 1979 ed., *Ethnic Autonomy - Comparative*

Dynamics, Pergamon Press, New York. See also Langlands, B.W. "The Toro Forts and Population Disturbances in the 1890s", in Kahimbaara, J.A. & Langlands, B.W. eds., *The Human Factor in the Changing Ecology of Mwenge*, 24.

91. See Kabwegyere, T. 1995. *The Politics of State Formation and Destruction in Uganda*, Fountain Publishers, Kampala, 50-59.

92. Ford, J. 1971. *The Role of the Trypanosomiases in African Ecology: A Study of the Tsetse Fly Problem*, Clarendon Press, Oxford, 179-180.

93. Howe, G.M. 1976. "Environmental Factors in Disease". In Lenihan, J. & Fletcher, W.W. eds., *Health and Environment*, Academic Press, New York, 1.

94. Howe, (1976) 20.

95. See Kjekshus, H. 1972. *Ecology Control and Economic Development in East Africa*, Heinemann, London; Ford, J. 1971. *The Role of Trypanosomiases in African Ecology*, Clarendon Press, Oxford; Turshen, M. 1984. *The Political Ecology of Disease in Tanzania*, Rutgers University Press, New Brunswick; G. C. K. Gwassa, "The German Intervention and African Resistance in Tanzania", in Kimambo, I. N. and Temu, A. J. eds., *A History of Tanzania*, E.A.P.H., Nairobi, 1969; Mettan, R.W.M. 1937. "A Short History of Rinderpest with Special Reference to Africa", in *Uganda Journal*, 5(1), 22-26; Johnson, D.H. & Anderson, D.M. eds. n.d., *The Ecology of Survival; Case Studies from Northeast African History*, Lester Cook Academy Publishing, London.

96. This insight comes from Janet Ewald's study of state formation and economic transformation in the Greater Nile Valley. See Ewald, J. 1990 *Soldiers, Traders, and Slaves: State Formation and Economic Transformation in the Greater Nile Valley, 1700-1887*, University of Wisconsin Press, Madison.

97. Synge, P.M. 1938. *Mountains of the Moon; an Expedition to the Equatorial Mountains of Africa*, Lindsay Drummond Ltd., Oxford 3rd edition.

98. Synge, (1938) 13

99. See Mamdani, M. 1984 *Imperialism and Fascism in Uganda*, Heinemann, London, 1984; Mamdani, M. 1983. "The Nationality Question in a Neo-colony: An Historical Perspective". In *Mawazo*, Vol. 3 No 3.

100. See Nabudere, D.W. 1980. *Imperialism and Revolution in Uganda*, Onyx, London.

The Rwenzori Ethnic "Puzzle"[1]

Cecilia Pennacini

Ethnic Theories

What do Bakonzo, Banande, Bamba or Batoro, to mention only some of the ethnic groups of the Rwenzori region, mean today when they define themselves using those labels? And for a Mukonzo, does being a Bakonzo mean something similar to what being a Mutoro means to the Batoro, or for a Muganda being a member of the Baganda community? Which historical, cultural, linguistic contents do these ethnic definitions bear for the actors who use them? And what do ethnologists, anthropologists, historians and other African studies scholars mean when employing these same labels? Ethnicity clearly plays a crucial role within the identity construction processes, in and outside Africa, and moreover, in the political arena of the post-colonial state. But despite the wide presence of ethnic discourses in cultural and political life, the concept of ethnicity still presents numerous ambiguities and difficulties.

In the last decades, anthropology and ethnology – two scholarly traditions broadly based on the category of ethnicity – have deeply reconsidered this concept. For too long these disciplines have maintained an essentialist notion of ethnic group, considering it as an unchangeable social reality endowed with a sort of natural substance transmitted down the generations. This conception was connected with the notion of "race" and to that of "tribe", widely used and reified within the colonial administration systems. In the seventies, these notions were progressively replaced by new theories which recognized the historical meaning of concepts of ethnicity, and also denounced the invention of several ethnic groups during colonial period.

An examination of newly invented ethnic labels led Jean Loup Amselle and Elikia M'Bokolo[2] to undertake a radical deconstruction of the concept of ethnicity, conceived by these authors as a "fiction" created only for colonial administrative use. In the last formulation of his theory[3], Amselle suggests that the colonial classification of people into closed and static ethnic entities be abandoned, and that the continuum of cultural and social realities which formed the ethnological landscape in the pre-colonial period, and which still characterizes contemporary Africa, be recognized. According to this scenario, social reality can be described as fluid, where people are constantly engaged in an effort to define themselves in relation to other societies and cultures. As Amselle's critique has shown, the unproblematic, rigid and essentialist conception of ethnic group, as used by colonial administrators, led to a political classification of subjects, with serious consequences, even for the post-independent African states. In line with this perspective, Gérard Prunier[4] has described the evolution of ethnic definitions in Uganda (with all its dramatic consequences). He shows how the pre-colonial ethnic landscape – a sort of patchwork of more than 60 different groups with fluid geographical, linguistic and political boundaries – early became a puzzle for the British administration. The solution found by the British was to extend indirect rule to societies showing a high level of centralization, putting all the other more loosely organized groups under their rule. This often resulted in an entrenched dominance of powerful groupings, leading to long-term resentment and instability.

These critiques of the old notions of ethnicity have opened up important new perspectives in a field that stands at the core of social life. It is thus necessary to rethink ethnicity in new terms, avoiding "throwing the baby out with the bath water". Luc de Heusch denounced this danger in a recent article[5]: "[The fact] that culture could itself be fluctuating and changing does not make it a *poisson soluble*"[6]. Fluid, changing and sometimes indefinable cultural and ethnic realities still exist in the perceptions of members and outsiders, and moreover in the political arena. A theory of ethnicity, which could enable us to understand the complex and often intricate scenario of ethnic and cultural interrelations, is more than ever necessary in the social sciences. In other words, even if the critique of the biological and essentialist notions of ethnicity finds a wide consensus within the scholar community, widespread claims of ethnic identities and diversities all around the world continue to require explanations based on consistent conceptual instruments.

The French paleo-ethnologist André Leroi-Gourhan[7] emphasizes that one of the specific characteristics of our species in the tendency towards cultural differentiation, which takes the shape of ethnicity – in contrast with biological evolution. In Leroi-Gourhan's perspective, ethnicity appears to be a specific human trend, which substitutes biological evolution with acquired functions, historically elaborated and transformed through time and space. Far from taking any biological or natural form, ethnic identities develop through processes of adaptation to the natural environment, as well as to the broad cultural milieu were the group lives, relating to neighbouring groups within wider regional systems. Humanity differs not in its biology, which is fundamentally the same among all groups, but in the diverse cultural responses developed by groups in space and time. These diversities can be observed considering the boundaries which separate groups: the perception and definition of collective identity relies mainly on ethnic diversity expressed in language and culture, which enables the Self to define itself in contrast to some Others.

The shift in conceiving ethnicity not in terms of interior essence, but rather in terms of external factors, mainly in the form of borders and frontiers, was proposed for the first time by Fredrick Barth[8], who suggested that researches on frontier regions and boundaries (that divide but at the same time unite groups) are crucial in the study of ethnic realities. From a study of border zones, we can in fact observe the phenomena involved in ethnic construction (the so-called "ethnogenesis" phenomena), and sometimes even observe the disintegration of groups. Frontiers somehow make groups more than groups make their frontiers. Thus, as many authors have pointed out[9], border areas should be seen and studied as a sort of laboratory, were we can observe the dynamics through which societies and cultures define and redefine themselves in reciprocal comparison.

No longer considered as a biological reality, ethnic groups – defined by borders and frontiers that constantly move and change – still exist today as "imagined communities"[10], and seen from this perspective they "have an history"[11] made up a specific cultural features and by the roles and functions acquired in the broader political arenas. Although not dealing with the subject of ethnic "disintegration", Amselle's description of dynamic and fluid cultures and social formations that connect and disconnect themselves to their neighbours, their rulers and their subjects, gives us a useful theory with which we can observe the Rwenzori region. Here, like probably everywhere else, the study of a specific group is only possible within a wider regional context, were social and cultural dynamics only stand out and become meaningful within the complex framework of inter-ethnic relationships.

It is in this context that Igor Kopytoff developed his theory of the African frontier[12]. He believes that African ethnogenesis originates from the movements of populations and groups engaged on redefining their ethnic identity and their political organization along local frontiers, which alternatively appear and disappear on the basis of such movements.[13] Contrary to the old, now obsolete, image of an unchanging static Africa, made up of small tribal groups that do not communicate with each other, Kopytoff describes a constantly dynamic continent. Modestly sized groups – often distinguished by ancestral ties – break off from the original nucleus for the most varied reasons (political crises, famine, epidemics, lack of land for cultivation or pasture, wars, and so on) and move away to settle in other areas. In the wake of work by Barth, Kopytoff suggests that we consider frontier spaces as fundamental geopolitical dimensions, within which a new social order is literally built on the basis of traditions inherited from the past or transferred from metropolitan centres[14]. We will see how this model can assist us to understand some of the cases in the area under examination, helping us in an attempt to put together the many pieces of the Rwenzori "ethnic puzzle" found in bibliographic sources as well as reflected in the conversations I had with several Bakonzo informants in the Kasese district[15]. In this way I try to find an answer to our initial question: who are today the Bakonzo, the Banande, the Batoro, etc., and which aspects of their past have contributed to their present identity?

The Colonial Frontier

The national frontier separating Uganda from the Democratic Republic of Congo today is the result of complex and intricate ventures of an explorative, political and economic nature. Between the 1870s and the 1890s they led to the colonial divisions of central-east Africa. The division ratified by the Berlin Conference (1884–1885) gave the immense territory of the Congo basin to Leopold II of Belgium. Exploiting Henry Morton Stanley's expeditions and skilfully manipulating European powers, he created the Independent Congo State. Between 1885 and 1908 (the year it was annexed to Belgium) it was a theatre for extreme acts of exploitation of both human and natural resources, conducted with fearful violence and atrocity.[16] Leopold's actions accelerated the processes dividing up the "spheres of influence", which the European powers were consolidating in the African continent. While Germany was negotiating a series of treaties with local authorities for a huge area that would subsequently be called Tanganyika (a German colony until World War I), British commercial and strategic interests in east Africa (whose ports guaranteed navigation towards the Indian colonies) were reinforced by the creation of the British East Africa Protectorate and the Uganda Protectorate, facilitated by the British presence in neighbouring Sudan and Egypt, and Zanzibar.

The border between Uganda and Congo, initially drawn in a virtual and approximate way along the western Rift Valley, was later defined in a series of treaties drawn up between 1907 and 1918, after the duke of the Abruzzi had explored the Rwenzori and compiled the relative maps. The colonial frontier cut the Rwenzori massif and lakes Albert and Edward almost in two and introduced further administrative division into an area already marked by ethnic and linguistic boundaries. The latter were the product of the formation of identities and local political organizations, characterized by the typical fluidity and dynamism of the pre-colonial era.

However fluid and variable, ethnic and political boundaries obviously existed before the colonial frontier was set up. In the period preceding colonization, these boundaries were exposed to redefining processes, resulting also from new external factors that impacted on a large part of Africa during the nineteenth century.[17] Indeed, in this period, external elements (represented in the beginning by Arab and European merchants, missionaries, explorers, and so on) progressively influenced the local inter-ethnic dynamics responsible for the formation of ethnic groups and the frontiers that separated them. They altered the power relationships between groups, creating new political and economic contexts. When the Duke of Abruzzi's expedition got under way, the ethnic situation of the Rwenzori was therefore extremely complex, the result of a succession of migrations, conflicts, violence and the action of external forces, which all contributed to the construction of local identities.

The Pre-colonial Situation

During the nineteenth century, the Rwenzori massif and its immediate neighbouring zones were occupied by various groups that underwent a series of important transformations bound up with local and regional dynamics, in conjunction with a number of wider-ranging phenomena that were impacting on this part of the continent. As pointed out by Calchi Novati and Valsecchi,[18] the nineteenth century witnessed a progressive, growing integration of African economies into the "world system". The slave trade that had catapulted Africa onto the world stage in the worst and most inhuman way possible was beginning to decline under the pressure of nineteenth-century abolitionists. Instead of human trafficking, international trade increasingly began to concentrate on other goods and products required by the world, triggering local transformation processes. During the nineteenth century, the Great Lakes region of Africa was inserted into the commercial network that spread from the east coast as far as Lake Tanganyika and from here towards to the lands of Congo on the one side, and the interlacustrine kingdoms on the other. This commercial network was controlled by Arab merchants, or merchants originating from the Swahili coast converted to Islam ("Arabized"). They followed the old caravan routes and exchanged goods with the populations of the interior (buying mainly ivory in exchange for firearms). Several charismatic figures emerged from among them, capable of exercising military and economic power over vast areas.

The region of the Great Lakes was occupied by a number of different societies, many of which had achieved a remarkable degree of political complexity and cultural sophistication. Despite the differences in language and forms of political organization, many of these cultures showed a marked tendency towards centralization. This was most emphatically pronounced in the southern kingdoms of Burundi and Rwanda as well as in the northern ones of Buganda and Bunyoro, and in that of Nkore. Local differences aside, many of these societies showed a system of social stratification that privileged shepherds (Bahima or Batutsi) over farmers (Bairu or Bahutu). Small pigmoid groups – called Batwa – lived on the margins and in the interstitial spaces of some of the interlacustrine kingdoms, while bands of pygmies (like the Basua now living in the Bundibujo area) lived in a hunter-gatherer economy in the forest zones, on the slopes of the Rwenzori and on the Semliki plain[19].

Despite the variety of political and social organizations, economic models and languages, the interlacustrine area showed, and still shows, a marked cultural uniformity, which De Heusch refers to when speaking of an "interlacustrine civilization",[20] evident in the regional spread of a series of fundamental elements. For example, a similar religious practice, a form of spirit possession called *kubandwa* in the majority of interlacustrine languages[21], is conspicuously a consistent feature of this interlacustrine civilization. However, the wide spread of similar religious practices and rituals does not correspond to an equally marked conformity of spiritual figures (the spirits of the *kubandwa* practiced in Burundi and Rwanda are in fact different from those forming the spiritual pantheon celebrated in the rest of the region). Nevertheless, in the northern and eastern parts of the area, the spirits generally belong to the mythical royal dynasty of the Bacwezi, semi-divine beings who were said to have reigned over the vast empire of Kitara several centuries ago, before a dynasty of foreigners, the Babito, initiated some of the current reigning dynasties. During the possession rituals, the Bacwezi myth confirms and makes topical the common origin of a number of interlacustrine monarchies, and the specific royal ideology they developed.

But when we come to consider the sub-region of the Rwenzori, we find ourselves in a frontier area, where the "interlacustrine civilization" encounters groups and cultures that have also in touch with another major African cultural area: in fact the Mitumba chain and the Semliki Rift Valley mark a very important "cultural divide"[22] between the interlacustrine culture zone and the forest areas of the Congo Basin. The different groups living around the western Rift Valley have usually been considered at the margin of the important Great Lakes kingdoms. But as David Newbury suggests, describing the Havu of the Lake Kivu islands, this area should rather be considered as a "transition zone" more than a peripheral one[23], were cultures and institutions distinctive of the interlacustrine area often mix with groups connected with the Congo basin, producing specific cultural formations. The Rwenzori represents the northern part of this transition area.

The Rwenzori massif and the zones immediately surrounding it are inhabited by numerous communities. From north to south at the feet of the massif, the Bamba are among the numerically most important groups. They are farmers who live on the edges of the equatorial forest on the Ugandan side of the massif, next to the Basua pygmies, once probably connected with the Bambuti of the Ituri forest. Descending towards the plain, the Batoro – who became independent from the kingdom of Bunyoro in the nineteenth century – live in a zone of vast pasture land. The chiefdoms of Basongora, which controlled the prehistoric salt pans of Lakes Katwe and Kaseny, developed on the plain to the south of the massif in pre-colonial times[24]. Lastly, groups of farmers called Bakonzo[25] on the Ugandan side of the massif and Banande on the Congolese side and in the nearby Mitumba, live on the very steep slopes of the mountains. Less numerous groups are also spread throughout this vast territory, which we will not deal with here for reason of space.

Among the above-mentioned groups we find a certain number of sharp diversities at cultural and linguistic level: the Batoro are part of the Nyoro culture, sharing with them a language which belongs to the linguistic family that Makerere scholars have decided to refer to using the neologism "Runyakitara"[26] (which include, among others, Runyoro, Runyankole and Ruhaya, the language spoken by the Haya of north-western Tanzania); the Bakonzo with their Congolese cousins, the Banande, share the same language which is classified in a specific group, called Koonzo/Nande by Schoenbrun[27]; the Bamba show linguistic and cultural similarities with the forest people of the Eastern Congo. The linguistic and cultural landscape, together with the adoption of certain political and social institutions, thus suggest that quite an important "watershed" crosses the Rwenzori massif, where groups belonging to the "interlacustrine civilization" meet other groups that show specific cultural features. While loans and exchanges (of words and of institutions) were and are very common in the area, many traditions continue to keep their specific ethnic identity. The centralized political organization developed by many of the Great Lakes societies clashed with different traditions, being only partially assimilated by them. The fluidity of the borders certainly allowed numerous cultural exchanges, but at the same time the groups living in the Semliki Valley and on the slopes of the surrounding mountains defended their specific ethnic identity against the expansion of the kingdoms.

In this scenario, characterized by boundary fluidity on the one hand and by rapid processes of political and identity formation on the other, I will focus on two cases, considering them crucial for the formation of ethnic identities in the region: the nineteenth century birth, decline and successive rebirth of the kingdom of Toro, and the split and ensuing developments of Bakonzo and Banande societies during the nineteenth and twentieth centuries.

The Kingdom of Toro

The events that gave rise to the kingdom of Toro during the first half of the nineteenth century, are part of the history of the vast ancient kingdom of Bunyoro, which in its turn is rooted in the mythical empire of Kitara. The historical existence of the Kitara empire in the region of the Great Lakes remains a matter of controversy in the literature[28], although its presence is firmly rooted in local traditions. These tell of a dynasty of divine origin, the Tembuzi, from which the Bacwezi descended, semi-divine heroes mentioned above in connection with the cult of *kubandwa* possession, still widely practised today in the larger part of the interlacustrine area. The Bacwezi supposedly gave life to an empire, Kitara, which extended over a huge area including most of the northern interlacustrine kingdoms, over which it ruled for a short time (two generations) before being succeeded by a dynasty of foreign origins, the Babito.[29] Tradition relates the progressive reduction of the Bunyoro kingdom in relation to the supposed size of the Kitara empire, while other important kingdoms rose around it.[30]

The Toro kingdom originated in the 1820s and 1830s from a 'rib' of Bunyoro, when a secessionist splinter group of Nyoro subjects formed an alliance around Prince Kaboyo, described as the favourite son of the *mukama*[31] Kyebambe III Nyakamutukura. They wanted to free themselves of the *mukama*'s power and establish a new distinct monarchy in the southern districts of the kingdom, near the area where the Nyoro princes were traditionally educated.[32] The secession of Toro from Bunyoro reveals some of the features described by Kopytoff as being typical of the paradigm of the African frontier. Steinhart believes that Kaboyo's revolt against his father in fact catalyzed centrifugal tensions present both in the Nyoro court and aristocracy, and at a level of the farmers. In the traditional structure of the kingdom, the latter occupied a position hierarchically subordinate to that of the shepherds.[33] Probably, the Batoro farmers with the Bakonzo, who inhabited the foothills of the Rwenzori and in their turn supported the revolt, saw in the prince's aspirations for independence an opportunity for creating a new society separate from that of Nyoro.[34] However, the kingdom that Kaboyo established was directly inspired by the Nyoro model, and reproduced the same social stratification. This recreated the subordination model typical of the interlacustrine kingdoms, thus dashing the hopes for freedom of the Bakonzo farmers, who had initially supported the venture.

Kaboyo's kingdom covered a fairly large territory, including for a time Basongora chiefdoms with their precious salt works, and the areas occupied by the Bakonzo. It began to decline on Kaboyo's death, which occurred in about 1860. His successors did not manage to maintain order in the kingdom and the inner weakness thus created meant that the field was left open for its reconquest by Bunyoro. In the meantime, Bunyoro was experiencing a period of rebirth thanks to the reforms introduced by the *mukama* Cwa II Kabarega, and to an aggressive "foreign" policy made possible by the formation of military regiments composed of soldiers of many ethnic origins, called Barusura.[35]

In this phase the American explorer Henry Morton Stanley – on his third and last African expedition – traversed the Rwenzori region, after going to Lake Albert to assist Emin Pasha (real name Eduard Schnitzer, a German with Jewish origin with a degree in medicine, who had converted to Islam and was at that time governor of the province of Equatoria), resist a Mahdist revolt. After crossing the Toro, on the way to the kingdom of Nkore, where he would draw up a blood contract with a royal prince, grandson of the *mugabe* Ntare V,[36] Stanley caught sight of the snow-covered peak of the Rwenzori on 24 May 1888:

> My eyes were directed by a boy to a mountain said to be covered with salt, and I saw a peculiar shaped cloud of a most beautiful silver colour, which assumed the proportions and appearance of a vast mountain covered with snow. Following its form downward, I became struck with the deep blue-black colour of its base, and wondered if it portended another tornado; then as the sight descended to the gap between the eastern and western plateaus, I became for the first time conscious that what I gazed upon was not the image or semblance of a vast mountain, but the solid substance of a real one, with its summit covered with snow. I ordered a halt and examined it carefully with a field-glass, then took a compass bearing of the centre of it, and found it to bear 215° magnetic. It now dawned upon me that this must be the Ruwenzori, which was

said to be covered with a white metal or substance believed to be rock, as reported by Kavalli's two slaves.[37]

Stanley's expeditions in Uganda left important traces on local history. During his previous expedition, the explorer spent a period during 1875 at the court of Mutesa I, sovereign of the kingdom of Buganda, which had already been visited by J.H. Speke and J. A. Grant in 1862. In contact with Arab merchants since the middle of the nineteenth century, the kingdom of Buganda had become one of the most important political and military powers in the region in that period. During the latter part of the century however, Buganda experienced a profound crisis, largely caused by the advent of foreign religions and the conflicts these generated. Islam was the first to reach the kingdom through contact with Arab merchants, who arrived along both the southeast routes, from Zanzibar and the east coast, and northern ones, from Sudan and the Upper Nile, in search of ivory and slaves. Later, when the British explorers arrived, they obviously attempted to introduce Christianity. During the period that Stanley spent at Mutesa's court in 1875, he wrote a famous letter that would be published in the *Daily Telegraph*, in which he invited, on behalf of the king, missionaries to come to the country and initiate evangelising work.[38] The letter was received with great interest by both Anglican and Catholic missionaries. In 1877 the first missionaries of the Church Missionary Society arrived in Buganda, followed two years later by the White Fathers of the French Societé des Missionaires d'Afrique.[39] Rivalry soon arose between Anglicans and Catholics, and obviously with Moslems. Interweaved with political affairs at court, the religious conflict was a powerful destructive force that destabilized the country for many years and finally provided the British with an excuse for direct intervention, leading to the institution of a Protectorate in 1894.

The rebirth of the small Toro kingdom, after its decline following the Nyoro invasion, occurred as a direct result of

Britain's official entry into Buganda and neighbouring areas. After the spheres of influence had been set up, Britain had officially taken over the region through the Imperial British East Africa Company, led in Uganda by Captain Frederick Lugard. Aiming to ensure internal order within Buganda, Lugard reinforced the external boundaries of the kingdom, deploying strategies aimed at weakening Kabarega's Bunyoro, Buganda's main enemy. Within this framework, he took action to subtract the lands of Busongora and Toro from Nyoro influence, as they had been reconquered by Kabarega's troops. In the re-established territory of Toro, he reinstated the sovereignty of a descendant of Kaboyo's, who pledged his support,.

Prince Kasagama, who in this way became *mukama* Daudi Kyebambe of Toro, was the son of *mukama* Nyaika, deposed from the throne fifteen or so years earlier, when Kabarega had invaded the kingdom with his troops. Nyaika died shortly afterwards[40] and his wife Kahinju had fled with the young Kasagama and his three brothers, taking refuge first on the slopes of the Rwenzori, where they were welcomed by the Bakonzo. Konzo traditions recount how the Konzo chief Ruhandika, of the Baswaga clan, saved the boy and his mother from Nyoro enemies, hiding them in a cave in the mountains.[41] Subsequently, they were taken into Nkore and from there, after various adventures, reached Buganda. Steinhart, in his book on the kingdoms of east Uganda, describes Lugard's meeting with Kasagama and his commitment to the plans for breaking up Kabarega's fearful Nyoro nation.[42] At the head of a military expedition formed of Sudanese and Zanzibari soldiers, which crossed Nkore[43] and then Busongora, Lugard met up with Kasagama in the Toro territories. Here, on 14 August 1892, Kasagama was reinstated as sovereign, at the same time signing an agreement with the Imperial East Africa Company in which terms of collaboration between the reborn kingdom of Toro and Great Britain were laid down.

Bakonzo and Banande

As already said, the groups located on the eastern flanks of the Rwenzori massif are now called Bakonzo, while the one staying on the western side and on the slopes of the Mitumba recognize themselves using the ethnic label "Banande". Bakonzo and Banande speak the same language, which is well identified among the other languages of the area, but the social and political organization that characterized the two groups during the nineteenth century is quite different. While the Bakonzo remain an a-cephalous society[44], the Banande developed central political structures.

Randall Packard has described the Bashu society[45] – which among the Banande chiefdoms is the closest to the Bakonzo of the Rwenzori and to the area occupied by the Basongora – proposing a hypothesis of the origin of the chiefdom, based mainly on oral and archival sources. According to this hypothesis, a-cephalous communities of farmers that later gave rise to the Banande chiefdoms originally inhabited the lowlands of the Semliki Valley, the region of Isale[46] and the shores of Lake Edward. Demographic pressure, arising partly out of the competition with different groups (especially pastoralist groups coming from Bunyoro), pushed these communities to the flanks of the mountains. In this way the farmers started to colonize the mountains, clearing plantations from the forest. This movement followed various directions: south-east towards the Mitumba and west toward the Rwenzori massif. Packard reports sources which place these waves of mountain colonization at the end of the seventeenth or at the beginning of the eighteenth century[47].

From this moment a slow process of centralization took place inside the farmer groups who had moved west on the Mitumba: ritual specialists started to spread their authority further in the territorial community (referred to with the Nande-Konzo root –*nda*). This process of centralization would have gone on for almost a century until a second group of migrants arrived in the region, at the end of eighteenth or at the beginning of nineteenth century. These new migrants were herders who are considered to be of Babito descent. The emergence of the Bashu chiefship in early nineteenth century can thus be seen as a consequence of the combination of internal and external factors: the alliance between local ritual specialists, who had previously acquired a certain authority, and the Babito, whose expansion in the Semliki had in the same period given rise to the Basongora chiefdoms. Even if the dynasty which gave birth to the Bashu chiefdom can only claim an apparent descent to the Babito, important aspects of the chiefship ideology come from nyoro tradition. In fact, the chief funeral rite of the Banande includes one of the most important symbols of the mystical ideology of nyoro kingship, strictly connected with the Babito dynasty: the practise of removing and conserving the lower jawbone from the chief's skull[48]. Moreover, Basongora and Bashu used to visit an important ritual centre located on the islands of Lake George, where the *kubandwa* cult of the Bacwezi was practised[49].

In Bashu traditions the emergence of a central political organization is described as the result of politics of alliances developed by a clan chief called Kavango, who migrated from the north-eastern Ugandan territories. Below is a version of the myth about the genesis of the Bashu, as reported by Packard[50]:

> Muhiyi lived with his father Kavango in the village of Kavarola, in Uganda. Kavango had many cattle which Muhiyi herded. One day, Kavango noticed that the milk which had been placed in a special hut for him was missing. This continued for several days. Finally, Kavango accused Muhiyi of having stolen the milk. Muhiyi, although innocent, was afraid of his father's anger. He therefore took his spear and hunting dogs and set out across the plains. Muhiyi followed the tracks of a buffalo [...] and when he reached the Kalemba (Semliki) he crossed by means of a fallen tree [...] Muhiyi continued his journey until he reached the foot of the Mitumba Mountains at a place called Kaviro. There he succeeded in killing the animal he had been tracking. Muhiyi butchered the animal and dried its meat. He left some of the meat on a rock and the rest he carried home to his father. On arriving home, he

presented the meat to his father, who welcomed him, for Kavango had discovered that a serpent had drunk his milk. Muhiyi then told his father about the new land he had discovered on the other side of the Kalemba. His father said that he wished to accompany Muhiyi to this new land for there was no more room in their present land. Together they set off across the plains. When they reached the foot of the mountains, they settled at Kaviro. Kavango then gave Muhiyi the land of BuNyuka in the mountains, as a reward for having discovered the new land and for having given him the meat from his kill. Kavango himself settled at Kivika. Together, Kavango and Muhiyi chased away the BaSumba who lived in the mountains and cleared the mountains of forest.

Packard records variations of this myth of the group's origins, which reveal some common elements. The place the first migrant supposedly left from is always located in Uganda: in the version quoted this is the village of "Kavarola" which recalls the toponym of Kabarole, the seat of the Toro court; in other versions the place is generically indicated as being in the kingdom of Kitara. Muhiyi flees from his father after being accused of stealing milk, an episode that could refer to the subordinate relationships of the farmers compared to the herders. He flees across the plain, over the river Semliki, and pauses only on reaching the foothills of the Mitumba mountains. Only after the success of Muhiyi's explorative trip do his father and the rest of the group decide to migrate, urged on by a lack of land. In the new lands they chase out the original inhabitants, the Basumba, and then start clearing the forest, necessary preparations to being able to commence their mountain agriculture.

After having colonized the new territory, the Bashu started to develop a new political system. If previously they were organized according to clan, they now started to build a chiefdom, using some aspects of the Nyoro royal ideology: a religious conception of kingship were the chiefs were sacralized through specific rituals (mainly the enthronement ritual and the royal burial) and through the *kubandwa* cult of the Bacwezi spirit. The Bashu and the other Banande chiefdoms adopted only some aspects of this ideology, integrating it with other institutions which are not known in the "Kitara" tradition. Among these institutions an important role in the chiefship was reserved for a woman, called the Mombo. Donated to the chief during the enthronement ritual, she will later symbolically keep and preserve the chiefship during the chaotic *interregnum* following the chief's death. In this way, the chiefship was doubly endowed, which is quite common in African royal ideologies, often including the queen mother or another female presence who shares and counterbalances the political and symbolic power of the king.

Similar to the Bashu, members of the other Nande chiefdoms – the Bamate, Batangi, Banisanza, Baswaga – are clearly aware of their Ugandan origins. Various migrations from the Semliki Valley[51] avowedly led them westwards towards Congo, leaving the shores of Lake Edward and taking the direction of the Mitumba mountains.[52] In an analysis of the semantic categories of Nande space, Francesco Remotti shows how the Banande represent their history as a process of colonizing and cultivating space freed from the forest. The sense of this journey is clearly indicated in the Nande spatial categories. These describe movements from east to west, from Lake Edward towards the forest, which had to be conquered and destroyed, and then replaced by cultivated fields and banana plantations. This vital move from the lake to the forest is often described as a form of escape (*erihuguta*, a word meaning "to escape" in Kinande).[53] Likewise, as we have seen, the myth reported by Packard about the genesis of the Bashu described the origins of this ethnic group as resulting from flight. Thus, Banande chiefdoms should have arisen around the first half of the nineteenth century, following migrations due to internal and external factors, including the expansion of the Babito political model and the regional repercussions which followed the creation of the Toro kingdom.

Redefining Identities

The new kingdom of Toro created by Kaboyo might well have reinforced the separating and redefining process of the Bakonzo and Banande ethnic groups. While the Bakonzo had pushed their settlements up on the higher slopes of the Rwenzori, escaping Toro rule in this way, the Banande had continued their migration towards the Mitumba, developing more centralized political organizations. Later, when Toro rule was re-established through British support, during the latter years of the nineteenth century and the early twentieth century, this again produced profound repercussions in the Bakonzo environments, triggering a controversial process of centralization within Konzo society, underway from the years of independence.[54]

The analysis of the two ethnonyms Bakonzo and Banande can help to support this hypothesis. As Remotti points out, both were introduced from outside quite recently, probably during the nineteenth century. The term "Ba-nande", or "Wa-nande", refers back to a name used by the Arabized merchants from Zanzibar or from the Swahili coast called Wangwana,[55] who, as we have seen, arrived in the interlacustrine area only after 1850. In the Swahili variant spoken by the Wangwana, the term "Ba-nande" means "those who go", from the Swahili verb *kw-enda*, "to go". Concordant with this etymology, the idea of flight from Uganda again emerges: the Banande would have appeared as an individual group in the moment they decided to leave Uganda and the Bakonzo to *go* westwards and colonize new lands.

Various etymologies have likewise been proposed to explain the origin of the ethnonym Bakonzo. In Pauline Fraas's Nande–English dictionary[56] the term *obu-konzo* indicates "a name of derision for a country or a population that has remained like its ancestors", while the term *aba-konzo* (sing. *omu-konzo*) or *aba-konjo* (sing. *omu-konjo*) indicates "the people or the country of the *Irungu*, the tribe the other side of the borders, closely connected to or part of the Nande". Both definitions are extremely significant: they indicate that the Bakonzo had remained in the same state as their ancestors (a condition considered primitive), whereas the Banande split away from this to develop a more evolved culture and society. Furthermore, the Bakonzo inhabited the *irungu,* an evocative word that recurs in most of the interlacustrine languages. *Irungu* is the bush, the savannah inhabited by wild animals, barren land impossible to cultivate, an uninhabitable space clearly distinct from both the domestic area of fields and banana plantations and from the forest, *omusitu,*[57] which would be destroyed to make room for crops. The latter reference might well indicate Bakonzo settlements at the feet of the Rwenzori and in the Semliki plain, where the type of mountain agriculture based mainly on banana cultivation then adopted by the Banande was not yet established. The reference to the Bakonzo might also be a heteronym, or ethnonym introduced from outside, perhaps by the Banande themselves. As they advanced the frontier of their colonization towards the west, they developed a new identity linked to the emerging of a more centralized social·structure.

Linguistic evidence clearly indicates the common origin of Banande and Bakonzo, which moreover share many of their most important cultural traits. Despite a small number of differences in the lexical repertory of the two variants (Lukonzo and Kinande), produced after the establishment of the colonial frontier, Bakonzo and Banande speak basically the same language and can understand each other very well. On the other hand, Lukonzo-Kinande is quite distinct from other languages spoken on the Ugandan side of the Rwenzori massif, and especially from the languages of the "Runyakitara" group. According to Schoenbrun,[58] the "koonzo" linguistic community (which also includes Kinande) developed in the area of the Rwenzori, differentiating itself from the southern linguistic community of Kivu, to which Rwanda and Buha belonged about 1,500 years ago. Also, when compared to the languages spoken on the Congolese side of the massif, Kinande is a specific linguistic tradition that can be clearly identified from the other languages spoken in the area.

Some scholars have put forward a theory that sees the origins of the Banande and the Bakonzo in a common culture existing before colonization, identified with the term Bayira.[59] Mashauri considers this term to be a variant of the term *bairu*, which means "farmers" in the language of Kitara.[60] The root *-ira*, common in a number of interlacustrine languages, indicates a dark colour, night, being black, black people,[61] while in Kirundi the *abayira* are the "true *hutu* families".[62] Identification of the Bayira or Bairu as peasants would therefore seem to occur thanks to skin colour, darker than those of herders, following a racializing ideology widespread in the interlacustrine cultures.

However, not all the Banande can be identified with the Yira, the darker-skinned peasants. Remotti points out that in the Banande culture the term Bayira was used to indicate the mass of the population as opposed to the chiefs, Bakama (sing. Mukama) and Bami (sing. Mwami).[63] One myth about origins that occurs in several parts of the interlacustrine area, and also known to the Banande, describes the Bayira as descendents of Kayira. In this myth, three forefathers give life to society and its divisions: Kayira (or Kairu), Kahima and Kakama.[64] The Bakama chiefs (sing. Mukama) are supposed to derive from Kakama; the Bahima shepherds from Kahima; and the Bairu or Bayira farmers from Kairu or Kayira. This identification with the Yira would seem to correspond to a definition of occupations, rather than to any ethnic classification: the Bayira are simply peasants. But a claim of a peasant identity in a region where the occupational classification of farmers and shepherds has produced extremely important consequences on a level of social hierarchy obviously takes on political significance.

At this point it is necessary to describe in general terms the features of the "revolution" that led several communities in the region of the Great Lakes to develop and then impose a new cultural–political system, based on the integration of agriculture and pastoral farming into a hierarchic model. Reconstructing some fundamental processes in the *longue dureè* history of the region of the Great Lakes, David Schoenbrun[65] identifies the beginning of this transition around the end of the first Iron Age between AD 800 and 1300. Two great economic innovations brought it about: the spread of specialized herding and that of the cultivation of the banana, from south-east Asia and the Indian subcontinent. The first seems to have developed after two long dry periods that forced the usage of land that was unsuitable for cultivation but that could be used as pasture. It was located in the savannahs that occupy a vast swathe between the Rwenzori massif and the areas bordering Lake Victoria. Occurring several centuries later, the second innovation was connected to the introduction of various types of banana and plantain species. This allowed abundant and constant harvests to be gathered in the wet areas that were unaffected by dry seasons. These two economic factors triggered a complex evolution in social structure, based on the development of client relationships between herders and farmers, which later led to centraliszed political organizations founded on relationships of inequality. This system spread regionally, giving rise to the flourishing of the kingdoms.

For various reasons, Bakonzo and Banande, as many other interlacustrine societies, resisted being assimilated into this system. The Rwenzori and the Mitumba, and the montane land where they had settled, was certainly not suitable for pastoral activities whereas it was good for the cultivation of bananas and plantains as well as other cereals, tubers and vegetables. While they were being inserted into the agro-pastoral system during the reign of the Toro, this obviously meant that the Bakonzo were in a position of subordination. By calling themselves Bayira, the Banande émigrés might have wanted to claim a closely-knit identity with an agricultural economy, opposed to the integrated agro-pastoral system that had characterized the neighbouring kingdoms of Bunyoro and Toro. This reinforces the hypothesis that the Banande and Bakonzo identity was strengthened in opposition to the attempt to assimilate them into the system of occupational classes widespread throughout the region of the Great Lakes. While the Banande took the western route, creating their own *chefferie* that, although relatively centralized within themselves, did not include a system of occupational subordination, the Bakonzo who had remained on the slopes of the Rwenzori developed forms of resistance towards the herders, succeeding in maintaining a well-defined farmer identity.

The Bakonzo under Toro Rule

Now let us see what happened to the groups that decided to remain in Uganda, colonizing and cultivating the slopes of the Rwenzori. The Bakonzo today still keep the memory of their nineteenth-century past alive, together with the period when they were able to live alongside the Batoro. The Bakonzo's initial collaboration in forming the kingdom of Toro and their assistance given to Kasagama's mother on her flight from Kabarega's troops have remained clearly impressed in Konzo traditions. This is confirmed by an old informant, who had been a child porter on the duke of the Abruzzi's expedition. He says that a long time ago:[66]

> ...a Toro woman called Kabirere came here and asked a Konzo chief called Mugharura for permission to cultivate some land. He granted permission, but Kabirere chose not to submit to Bakonzo authority. In the end, a nephew of the woman married the daughter of a Mukonzo, thus establishing family ties between the Batoro and the Bakonzo. Later, when prince Kaboyo rebelled, he used this relationship to get the Bakonzo warriors on his side in defence against the Banyoro. When the young Toro prince was attacked by the Banyoro, he fled to refuge in Bwamba, and was then taken to Kalikura, who could not break the blood pact he had made with the king of Toro. So we defended the young prince against Abalusura attacks.

However, as already mentioned, Kaboyo's undertaking soon turned into disappointment for the Bakonzo who had helped him. Being placed on the lower level of a newly introduced social scale was perceived as a mark of betrayal and ingratitude.[67] Following a scheme which they were to repeat many times, even much later, during the colonial period, the Bakonzo reacted to this attempt by retreating up the steeper slopes of the Rwenzori. The same informant recalls the episode of prince Kasagama's flight of sixty years or so after Kaboyo's rise to the throne. Then, too, the Bakonzo showed themselves initially loyal to the Batoro:

> Later another Konzo chief called Kakule asked for the prince[68] to be taken by him to the area near the Kasinga channel. Kakule helped him cross the channel and then took him to a white man called Kapere[69] [...] When the king returned with Lugard, he brought Christianity with him [...] This prince was not educated,[70] but Lugard had him taught.

Here the informant clearly associates the restoration of prince Kasagama to the position of Toro sovereign – thanks to the intervention of Lugard – and the introduction of Christianity into Konzo territory. Several testimonies confirm that Christianity was introduced to the slopes of the Rwenzori by Toro catechists, during the time when the Bakonzo lands officially came under Kasagama's influence. After Lugard's intervention, the land and functions of the reborn kingdom of Toro were progressively established by means of a series of agreements and treaties. With these the British Protectorate entrusted Kasagama with the government of a multi-ethnic region, covering the entire Ugandan side of the Rwenzori and neighbouring areas. This form of indirect rule, generally the underlying principle for British dominion in its colonies, guaranteed for Britain that this country was administered using its traditional government agencies.[71] In this way, the mother country was assured not only of an extremely economical system (which was self-financing through taxes collected by local chiefs), but also of the loyalty and collaboration of the local authorities directly involved in its organization.

The reinstitution of Toro authority, and its legitimization by the British to govern the whole region through the reapplication of old hierarchies, obviously intensified the Bakonzo's feeling of betrayal and disappointment, with a consequent worsening of relationships between the two groups. The Bakonzo thus came to nurture a profound grudge against the Batoro, who were said to exploit their position of superiority by carrying out raids and forays into the mountains. The old informant quoted earlier narrates how the Bakonzo used high-altitude paths and passes to escape the Batoro:

> That route[72] was used to flee from those used by the Batoro. If you passed along the route close to Batoro territory, they robbed your things. Sometimes the Batoro made raids as far as Nyamutene. I remember a raid led by Kakende.[73] People said: "Tall people have arrived with Kakende". They destroyed the beans and bananas; when you returned from your hiding places in the bush there was no food to be found.

Apart from the incursions remembered by this informant, the Bakonzo were more generally opposed to the imposition of taxes on the part of a system of local chiefs (called *saza*). Their resistance towards the imposed system must be seen in relation to the introduction of a monetary economy – beginning to be spread also in relation to the taxes introduced by the British – which the Bakonzo were reluctant to enter. The Polish anthropologist Jan Czekanowski,[74] who had crossed the region as part of the Duke of Mecklenburg's expedition to equatorial Africa between 1907 and 1908 (a year after the duke of the Abruzzi's expedition to the Rwenzori), noted in his diary – full of ethnographical observations – that the Bakonzo:

> ...seem incapable of adapting to a monetary system, introduced in the form of a tax payable in cash (while payments in the form of

work were reserved for the insolvent). The king of Toro's tax collectors pretended two rupees for themselves and three for the British administration from every hut. Bachelors and those who have no home pay two rupees per head. It is, therefore, analogous to our tax system on revenue or capital. For the polygamous rich it is particularly costly since every woman in possession of a hut is indebted. In this way the tax combats polygamy, the principal obstacle to the Christianization of the country, which is already much advanced.[75]

Taxation and its socio-economic consequences must be counted among the reasons for the Bakonzo's migratory movements in that period. To flee the "obligation of earning money to pay taxes"[76] they preferred to move into neighbouring lands, even at the cost of being submitted to a harsh corvée by the groups holding power in the those areas. This occurred at the end of the century, for example, in the chiefdoms of Busongora where several groups of Bakonzo had moved to. Many continued to emigrate towards Congo, controlled by Leopold's Free State, whose administrative system was undoubtedly harsher and more repressive but at the same time easier to circumvent, especially in the frontier zones:

> The departures of the Bakondjo from the British zone towards Congo surprised me, since everyone everywhere complained of the insatiable *Bergiti*[77] and their incessant need for provisions. Perhaps the Bakondjo did not understand that there the corvées were obligatory while here they only intervened in the case of unpaid taxes. In the case in point, though, the work imposed in Toro for non-payment (and therefore repressive in nature) was so hard that they preferred to flee to the Belgians. The Bakondjo exploited the administrative chaos of the Free State [...] In the Congo and in German Africa (where the inhabitants of Congo met up), the natives extolled the British zone, which became a true paradise in their tales, while here people fled from Toro to Congo...[78]

As well as the harsh tax system introduced by the Batoro under British indirect rule, the Bakonzo also complained of the discrimination which excluded them from the scholastic system when this began to develop, and their consequent inability to join the élite, subsequently charged with administrative and governmental affairs.

Those who did not emigrate soon began to react against the Toro regime. At the end of the 1890s, during the first period of Kasagama's reign, a Konzo medium called Mukeri prophesied that two rebellions would take place later against Toro rule: these revolts would lead to the founding of a Bakonzo kingdom, but only after the "people had suffered heavy loss of life".[79] For the first time, in the form of a prophesy, the Bakonzo expressed their hope to have a kingdom of their own. Realizing that under British indirect rule the a-cephalous groups fall under the control of more centralized and structured societies like the Batoro, the Bakonzo undertook a process of centralization which aspired to transform their scattered political organization based on local chiefs (*bakuru wa bulhambo,* the main political authority present in the organization of Konzo society) into the kingship (*obusinga*).

After the prophesy, two important rebellions against the Batoro occurred, first in the 1920s and then in the 1960s, immediately after independence. The first rebellion became famous with the name of the Abayora revolt.[80] It was led by another medium called Nyamutswe together with the chief of a spur (*mukuru wa bulhambo*), called Tibamwenda. Together they mustered the consensus of a number of Bakonzo who had fought for the Europeans in World War I. As the prophesy had told, the rebellion was violently repressed by the Toro administration, and Nyamutsa, Tibamwenda and a third chief called Kapolya were hanged in 1921.

The second Bakonzo revolt flared up immediately after independence and dragged on for many years, with important political consequences for Konzo society and for the role it played in post-colonial Uganda. It was led by a primary school teacher, Isaya Mukirane, who succeeded in catalyzing Bakonzo retaliatory sentiment and desire for independence within a larger movement that called itself Rwenzururu. Rwenzururu is the local name for the Rwenzori massif, simplified by the first explorers to "Rwenzori" as they were unable to pronounce it correctly. The name of Isaya Mukirane's movement, which rapidly became a strong claim for identity on the part of the Bakonzo, significantly associated the movement with the mountain that the Bakonzo consider the centre of their cosmology.

The etymology of Rwenzururu refers to the word *nzururu* or *nzororo* which in Lukonzo-Kinande literally means "snow".[81] The *rwe-nzururu* is therefore "the place of snow": the presence of perennial snow, possible because of the extraordinary height of the massif, was obviously an exceptional fact at the equator. According to the anthropologist Kirsten Alnaes, snow consequently occupies a central place in Konzo cosmology, believed to be the origin of fertility of the land and of society.[82] For this author, the perennial snow is perceived by the Bakonzo as the frozen sperm of the god Kitasamba – who indeed lives on the highest peaks of the massif. Melting in the rivers and lakes below it fertilizes the ground and Konzo society. In Isaya Mukirane's eyes, calling the independence Konzo movement "Rwenzururu" signified linking up with the central and sacred nucleus of ancient Konzo cosmology.

The Rwenzururu rebellion is remembered to be the first revolt that the new African government of independent Uganda had to deal with. The importance of this movement cannot be underestimated: it has been defined as the most extreme and enduring secessionist movement in all of Africa after independence[83]. Through different phases, the movement has continued to struggle for the recognition of the Bakonzo's identity within the post-independence Uganda: it is emblematic of the numerous difficulties and contradictions inherent in the process of creating a national system on the basis of the geopolitical scenario that emerged from colonial division. Subjected to decades of Toro government in the framework of British indirect rule, the Bakonzo were not willing to recognize that they belonged to the new Uganda nation unless they achieved independence from Toro, so that they could feel as fully legitimate Ugandan citizens, with the same rights and the same duties as the other ethnic subdivisions of the country. Furthermore, they feared independence because they believed, rightly or wrongly, that the British would in some way have defended them from the excessive measures of Toro dominion.[84]

The origins of the second rebellion are to be found in the foundation of the Bakonzo Life and History Research Society, soon transformed from a study centre into a political movement, equipped with its own military organization. On 15 August 1962 the secession of Rwenzururu from Uganda was formally declared and Isaya Mukirane was nominated president of the Association and sovereign (*omusinga*) of the Bakonzo and of the Bamba of the Rwenzori. Ugandan troops, led by British officers, attempted to repress the revolt, but the extremely harsh nature of the mountain terrain and the closeness of the Congolese border made it virtually impossible to defeat the rebels. They established their headquarters – their "kingdom", as they called it – in the high mountains dotted with caves, used as hiding places.

The movement remained active for about twenty years, even after the death of Isaya Mukirane in 1966. In 1972, Isaya's son, Charles Wesley Mumbere Kisembo, who lived in the United States, was declared the Bakonzo's *omusinga* (sovereign) and *irema ngoma* (custodian of the royal drum). From the 1960s onwards, the Ugandan government progressively introduced changes to the administration of the region. Under Idi Amin's regime the district of Kasese was created which incorporated an important part of Bakonzo territory (though many of them lived and continued to live in other districts in the area) and Busongora.[85] On 15 August 1982, twenty years after the secession declared by Isaya Mukirane, his son Charles symbolically assumed power in the presence of the Bakonzo and a minister of the Uganda national government. However, the request for official recognition of the newborn kingdom of the Bakonzo still remains much debated and controversial both within Konzo society and on a national level.

Conclusions

The hypothesis I advanced in these pages postulates a relationship between the nineteenth-century ethnogenesis of the kingdom of Toro and the achievement of two distinct ethnic identities, the Banande and the Bakonzo, concurrent with the introduction of related ethnonyms. They were generated from a common cultural and linguistic background associated with an economy based on farming, and developed in the environment of the Rwenzori massif and the Mitumba chain, both of which present exceptional ecological characteristics for Africa, due to the considerable height.

In the ecology of this environment the forest extends upwards to a remarkable altitude. The climate surrounding the massif and the Mitumba chain is exceptionally wet. The abundant presence of water together with mild temperatures mean that various types of cultivation can be practised even at high altitudes, but the Bakonzo and Banande have to invest much effort in the preparatory work of clearing the forest. This practice, currently forbidden within the Rwenzori National Park, continues to characterize the life of the populations in the valleys surrounding the park and above all created the necessary conditions for colonization of the land along the frontier that advanced westwards in the Congo. This situation was clearly apparent to the first European observers who crossed the region at the end of the nineteenth century. In an article published in the *Journal of the Royal African Society* in 1910, Bernhard Struck attempted to clarify the ethnographic nomenclature of the area that extended along the frontier between Uganda and Congo.[86]

On the basis of sources available at that date, he emphasized the colonizing process of the lands lying to the west carried out by the Bakonzo–Banande, which must have reached its peak during the immediately preceding decades:

> For the sake of completeness, we must here mention also the various *colonies of the Bakonjo,*[87] scattered through the territories of the tribes discussed above. These have advanced considerably to the north since about 1870, in the country west of the Semliki. Thus we have the Baira in several villages north of Mburi, the Baholi in Anderei, and (mixed with the Bambuba) on both the upper and lower course of the Lū river; also the already mentioned Bakonjo in Mboga, and, furthest north of any, the Bahale in the north-eastern Ituri region. "Banande" is a designation for the Bakonjo dwelling at Mbeni's; I should, however, be disposed to doubt that this name is (as Czekanowski was assured by some natives) really of European origin, since Stuhlmann, so long ago as 1891, heard of the "Wanandi–Wakonjo" in the forest behind Mbeni.

As we have seen, Czekanowski had repeatedly encountered both the Bakonzo and the Banande during the long journey made with the express aim of drawing up the first ethnographic map of central Africa. Czekanowski's first contact with the Bakonzo-Banande, recalled in his diary,[88] occurred near Rutchuru, south of Lake Edward. They were "veterans" and "retired workers" from Fort Beni (an important Belgian colonial post to the north of the Rwenzori, beyond the Semliki River), who "call themselves Banande, or Wanande in *kiswahili*".[89] From this moment in his journey, Czekanowski often mentions the Bakonzo, and collects numerous objects of their culture, splendidly reproduced by drawings in his diary.

On several occasions, Czekanowski questioned himself about the Bakonzo and Banande identity issue and about the ethnogenesis underlying the use of the two ethnonyms:

> Monday 16 December at nine I began to study the peasants who provision the column of lieutenant Spiltorie. They come from

Makokoma, to the east of the bay of Vichumbi. The soldiers call them Wanande, but they say that their language uses *lukondjo* or even *rukonjo*. This backs up my supposition that the white functionaries have incorporated the entire Bakondjo tribe under the name Wanande.[90]

After exploring the base of the Rwenzori massif from north to south passing by the Ugandan side, Czekanowski crossed the Semliki plain to get to Fort Beni. Here he could once again reflect on the problem of the relationship between the Bakonzo and the Banande, coming to a conclusion about the origin of these two groups. The inhabitants of the Beni neighbourhood called themselves Banande, but at the same time said that they spoke the language of the Bakonzo, who they thought of as foreigners:

> When I asked why the Bakondjo were *gudi* (foreigners), they replied that the Bakondjo lived on the mountains, and the Banande didn't. So was this the difference? The language issue seemed very important [...] The Bakondjo and the Banande were a single tribe made up of clans with identical names. For the Congolese colonial administration, the Bakondjo did not exist so they called them Wanande, a name made up − as the prefix 'Wa' testifies − by the people who speak *kiswahili*, undoubtedly by the Wangwana who invaded this country for the Zanzibaris. On the other hand, for the people of Toro, whites and blacks, only the Bakondjo or Wakondjo existed, according to whether they had been given this name by natives or by those who spoke *kiswahili*. This explanation given to me by an intelligent guardian of the post, enchanted me, because it put an end to the confusion that reigned in my notes. There was one tribe less.[91]

The sources therefore show the existence of an original cultural nucleus, characterized by a specific culture, an economic system based on agriculture and by the use of a language that appears, as we have said, quite distinct from the other languages spoken around the Rwenzori massif. During the nineteenth and twentieth centuries, this group was subjected to different pressures, mostly due to the situation of conflict and violence connected with the Banyoro's southern expansion and to the birth of Toro kingdom. For this reason, they were forced to progressively colonize the mountains, adapting to a mountain environment that is unique on the African continent. The members of this group struggled to keep their language and their economy, resisting pressures from another powerful political and economic systems, the agro-pastoral hierarchies that reigned on the eastern side of the massif. Maintaining and regenerating their identity as mountain farmers over the years, the community has passed through significant regional changes, giving rise to a migration that separated them into two branches, the Banande and the Bakonzo. From that moment onwards the history of the Bakonzo and the Banande evolved differently and autonomously, though awareness of their common origins has been kept alive.

Notes

1. This contribution is an enlarged version of the paper presented at the conference "Rwenzori. History, Languages and Cultures of an African Mountain". Parts of this article have been previously published in Pennacini, C. 2006 (ed.), *The People of the Moon. Rwenzori 1906-2006*, catalogue of the Exhibition, CahierMontagna, Turin, 215-229.

2. Amselle, J.L. and Mbokolo, E. 1985., *Au couer de l'ethnie. Ethnie, tribalisme et Etat en Afrique*, La Découverte, Paris. Amselle, J.L. 1990. *Logique metisse. Anthropologie de l'identité en Afrique et ailleurs*, Edition Payot et Rivages, Paris.

3. Amselle, J.L. 2001. *Branchements. Anthropologie de l'universalité des cultures*, Flammarion, Paris.

4. Prunier, G. 1989. "Evolution des critères de définition ethnique en Ouganda. Du XVIᵉ à la fin de l'ère coloniale". In Chrétien, J.P., *Les ethnies ont une histoire*, Karthala, Paris, 201-211.

5. De Heusch, L. 2000. "L'ethnie. The vicissitudes of a concept", *Social Anthropology*, 8, 99-115.

6. De Heusch, 2000, 102.

7. Leroi-Gourhan, A. 1964. *Le geste et la parole* Edition Albin Michel, Paris.

8. Barth, F. 1969 (ed.), *Ethnic Groups and Boundaries*, Little Brown & Co., Boston.

9. Anthropological literature on the matter of frontiers is vast. Among the more important are: Kopytoff, I. 1989 (ed.), *The African Frontier. The Reproduction of Traditional African Societies*, Indiana University Press, Bloomington and Indianapolis; Cole, J.W. & Wolf, E. 1974. *The Hidden Frontier*, Academic Press, New York and London. For a review of the anthropological use of the concepts of frontiers and boundaries, see Viazzo, P.P. 2005. "Frontiere e 'confini': prospettive antropologiche", in the conference proceedings *Frontiere, confini: un confronto tra discipline*, 22–23 April 2005, Gragnano, Palazzo Feltrinelli, Milano, Franco Angeli.

10. Anderson, B. 1991. *Imagined Communities*, Verso, London and New York.

11. Chrétien, J.P. & Prunier, G. 1989, *Les ethnies ont une histoire*, Karthala, Paris.

12. Kopytoff, I. (ed.), *The African Frontier. The Reproduction of Traditional African Societies*, Indiana University Press, Bloomington and Indianapolis, 1987.

13. Kopytoff, 1987, p. 7.

14. A reconstruction of cultural dynamics in the region of the Great Lakes, partly based on the application of Kopytoff's model of the African internal frontier, is presented in the book by Schoenbrun, D. L. 1998. *A Green Place, a Good Place. Agrarian Change, Gender, and Social Identity in the Great Lakes Region to the 15th Century*, Oxford, James Currey.

15. The fieldwork was carried out in summer 2004 and 2005 thanks to the support of the Italian Ethnological Mission in Equatorial Africa (Italian Ministry of Foreign Affairs). Researches have been conducted in collaboration with Stanley Baluku, to whom I would like to express my gratitude.

16. See Ndaywel è Nziem, I. 1998. *Histoire général du Congo. De l'héritage ancien à la République Démocratique*, De Boeck & Larcier, Paris–Brussels, 1998, in particular part V; Samarin, W.J. 1989. *The Black Man's*

Burden: African Colonial Labour on the Congo and Ubangi Rivers, 1880–1900, Westview Press, Boulder and London; for an informative synthesis in a journalistic style, see Hochschild, A. 1998. *King Leopold's Ghost,* A Mariner Book, Boston, New York; for Italian participation in the Independent Congo State and collections of Congolese objects, see Pennacini, C. 2000. "Immagini dell'Africa nel collezionismo italiano di oggetti del Congo", in Castelli, E. 2000 (ed.), *Permanenze e metamorfosi dell'immaginario coloniale in Italia,* Edizioni Scientifiche Italiane, Naples, 129–157.

17. For an introduction to some of the issues referred to here, see Calchi Novati, G. & Valsecchi, P. 2005. *Africa: la storia ritrovata,* Rome, Carocci.

18. Calchi Novati, Valsecchi, 2005, Chap. 5.

19. After the institution of national parks the subsistence economy of the pygmies was deeply affected: some groups have consequently migrated towards the Congo while others still live in the area, having been transformed into beggars surviving at the margins of the parks' economy (see the contribution by G. Forno in this volume).

20. De Heusch, L. 1966. *Le Rwanda et la civilisation interlacustre,* Ed. de l'Université Libre de Bruxelles, Brussels.

21. Pennacini, C. 1998. *Kubandwa. La possessione spiritica nell'Africa dei Grandi Laghi* Il Segnalibro, Turin.

22. Newbury, D. 1991. *Kings and Clans. Ijwi Islands and the Lake Kivu Rift, 1780-1840,* The University of Wisconsin Press, Madison, London, 17.

23. Newbury, D. 1991, 17.

24. See Kamuhangire, E.R. 2006. "A Precolonial History. The Hereditary Chiefdoms of Busongora: Kisaka-Makara, Bugaya and Kiyanja (1850-1915)" in C. Pennacini (ed.), *The People of the Moon. Rwenzori 1906-2006,* Catalogue of the exhibion, CahierMontagna, Turin, 2006, 231-236.

25. Often mentioned in the literature with the ethnonym Bakonjo, which is usually used by the Batoro and by the Baganda. Here the term Bakonzo, which they use themselves, has been preferred.

26. See M. Muranga's article in this volume.

27. Schoenbrun, 1998, 54.

28. Chrétien, J.P. 1985. "L'empire des Bacwezi. La construction d'un imaginaire geopolitique", in *Annales ESC*, November–December 1985, No. 6, 1335–1377; Doyle, S. 2006. *Crisis and Decline in Bunyoro*, The British Institute in Eastern Africa, Oxford, Kampala, Athens.

29. Different versions of the Bacwezi myth have been transcribed. Among the more popular, see the one in Fisher, A.B. 1911. *Twilight Tales of Black Baganda*, Marshall, London.

30. Beattie, J. 1960. *Bunyoro. An African Kingdom* Holt, Rinehart and Winston, New York.

31. *Mukama* (pl. *bakama*) is the word used to indicate the sovereigns of Bunyoro and of other kingdoms and chiefdoms in the interlacustrine area.

32. Steinhart, E.I. 1999. *Conflict and Collaboration in the Kingdoms of Western Uganda*, Fountain Publishers, Kampala, 25.

33. Steinhart, 1999, 25. Steinhart holds that the tensions between herders and farmers were at the base of the conflicts and secessions that took place during the nineteenth century on the borders of Bunyoro.

34. Ingham, K., *The Kingdom of Toro in Uganda*, Methuen, London, 1975; Steinhart, 1999.

35. See Kamuhangire, E. R. 2006.

36. Steinhart, 1999, 17.

37. Stanley, H.M. 1890. *In Darkest Africa. Quest, Rescue, and Retreat of Emin, Governor of Equatoria*, London, Searle and Rivington, Vol. I, 405.

38. Karugire, S.R. 1980. *A Political History of Uganda*, Heinemann, Nairobi, London, 51; Chrétien, J.P. 1994. "Les peoples et leurs histoire avant la colonisation", in Prunier, G. and Calas, B. 1994 (eds.), *L'Ouganda contemporain*, Karthala, Paris, 19–53.

39. Chrétien, 1989, 46.

40. Steinhart, 1999, 42 and ff.

41. See also Stacey, T. 2003. *Tribe. The Hidden History of the Mountains of the Moon*, Stacey International, London, 29–30.

42. Steinhart, 1999, 47–50.

43. Often called Ankole in colonial sources.

44. As we will later discuss, on the day of independence a revival movement called Rwenzururu started to claim a kingdom for the Bakonzo, but at present Konzo society remains fundamentally non-centralized.

45. Packard, R. 1981. *Chiefship and Cosmology. An Historical Study of Political Competition*, Indiana University Press, Bloomington.

46. See also S. Baluku in this volume.

47. Packard, 1981, 58.

48. Packard, 1981, 77.

49. Packard, 1981, 77, Kamuhangire, 2006, 97.

50. Packard, 1981, 12–13.

51. See S. Muhindo artiche in this volume.

52. See Remotti, F. 1982. "I Banande dello Zaire", in AAVV, *Uomini e re*, Laterza, Bari, and Remotti, F. 1985. "Concetti spaziali nande. Un tentativo di analisi semantica", in *La Ricerca Folklorica*, No. 11, April 1985, 13–27.

53. Remotti, 1985, 24.

54. For this last phase see Stacey, 2003.

55. Remotti, 1982, 185; Czekanowski, J. 2001, chap. XVIII. *Carnets de route au coeur de l'Afrique. Des sources du Nil au Congo*, Les editions Noir sur Blanc, Paris.

56. Fraas, P. 1961. *A Nande-English and English-Nande Dictionary*, Laubach Literacy Fund, Washington, 51–52.

57. Remotti, 1985, 24.

58. Schoenbrun, 1998, 40.

59. Mashauri, K.T. 1981. "Organisation ètatique des Yira et son origine" in *La civilisation ancienne des peuples de Grands Lacs*, Paris, 1981, pp. 160-172.

60. Davis, M.B. 1952. *A Lunyoro-Lunyankole-English and English-Lunyoro-Lunyankole Dictionary*, MacMillan and Co., London, 275.

61. Fraas, P. *A Nande-English and English-Nande Dictionary*, 40; Davies, *A Lunyoro-Lunyankole-English and English-Lunyoro-Lunyankole*

Dictionary, 51; Rodegem, F.M., 1970. *Dictionnaire Rundi-Français,* Tervuren, 193.

62. Rodegem, 1970, 559.

63. Remotti, 1982, 189.

64. Ibidem.

65. Schoenbrun, 1998.

66. Interview with Bwambale Daudi Isebani, August 2005 in C. Pennacini (ed.), 2006, Appendix.

67. Ingham, 1975, 38.

68. Kasagama.

69. The name used locally to refer to "Captain" Frederick Lugard.

70. Here the informant is referring to Kasagama's conversion to Christianity within the sphere of the Anglican Church Missionary Society (Ingham, 1975, 89 and ff.) and at the same time to the adoption of "modern" customs.

71. Ingham, 1975, 106.

72. The high-altitude route that connects the Mubuku valley with the territory of the Bamba. Interview with Bwambale Daudi Isebani, August 2005, in Pennacini (ed.), 2006, Appendix.

73. This was Namuyonjo Kakende, sovereign of Toro until 1888; also thanks to support from the Ganda court (Médard, H. 2001, *Croissance et crises de la royauté du Buganda au XIXe siècle,* Doctoral Thesis in History, Université Paris I – Pantheon Sorbonne, 219–220).

74. See the essay by Chrétien, J.P. 2006. "An Anthropology Pioneer. Jan Czekanowski in Africa's Great Lakes Region". In C. Pennacini (ed.), 2006, 237-240, and the contribution of Anna Czekanowska in this volume.

75. Czekanowski J. 1958. *Carnet de route au cœur de l'Afrique. Des sources du Nil au Congo,* Edition Noir sur Blancs, Paris, 2001 (orig. ed., *W glab lasow Aruwimi. Dziennik wyprawy do Afryki Srodkowey,* Polskie Towarzystwo Ludoznawcze, Wroclaw, 1958), 153.

76. Czekanowski, 2001, 154.

77. The Belgians were locally called by this mispronounciation.

78. Czekanowski, 2001, 154.

79. Alnaes, K. 1969. "Songs of the Rwenzururu Rebellion. The Konzo Revolt Against the Toro in Western Uganda", in Gulliver, P.H. (ed.), *Tradition and Transition in East Africa*, Routledge & Kegan Paul, London, 243–272.

80. Kabanannukye, K.I.B. 1999. *Bakonzo People: Rwenzururu's Quest for Kingship*, draft, unpublished (by kind concession of the author).

81. Fraas, 1961, 85.

82. Alnaes K. 1996., "The Snow as the Centre of the Konzo Universe", in Omaston, H., Tukahirwa, J., Basalirwa, C., & Nyakaana, J. (eds.), *The Rwenzori Mountains National Park, Uganda,* Department of Geography, Makerere University, Kampala, 288–299.

83. Doornbos, M. 1970. "Kumanyana and Rwenzururu: Two Responses to Ethnic Inequality" in Rotberg, R.I. & Mazrui, A.A. 1970. *Protest and Power in Black Africa*, Oxford University Press, New York, 1009 and 1130.

84. Stacey, 2003; Stacey, T. 1965. *Summons to Rwenzori*, Secker & Warburg, London.

85. Stacey, 2003, 313.

86. Struck, B. 1910. "On the Ethnographic Nomenclature of the Uganda-Congo Border", in *Journal of the Royal African Society*, Vol. 9, No. 35, April 1910, 275–288.

87. My italics.

88. Czekanowski, 2001.

89. Czekanowski, 2001, 93.

90. Czekanowski, 2001, 103.

91. Czekanowski, 2001, 258–259.

Rwenzori, a bridge of cultures

Baluku Stanley Bakahinga Mbalibulha

The Rwenzori Mountains in Western Uganda are to the people who live around it a special feature. The mountains are a mosaic of ethnic groups with variations so deep that in the sub-county of Karusandara, Kasese District, a count of 38 different ethnic groups is an understatement. The 1991 Uganda Population and Housing Census documented 35 different groups, among others in Kasese District. In this cultural variation, aspects of language and social differentiation have defined the way these groups have associated in historical times and continue to define the social political landscape.

This paper aims to highlight the social differentiation among ethnic majorities and minorities, and how they have been brought together by the ambience of the mountain: its rivers, snows, forests, lakes, ridges, plains and vegetation, with the mountain acting as a socio-cultural bridge.

Two old Bakonzo adages stand out: *Twasoka okwa mughongo w'endioka* (we crossed using the back of spirit *Ndioka)* and *itwe twasokera okwa mulihii* (we crossed using the root), which denotes the migration of Bakonzo from Bassu Isale to the Rwenzori Mountains. This is equally true of other ethnic groups found in the region.

The region referred to as Rwenzori flanks the Rwenzori Mountains that occupy a central place in the highland, plain and lake areas in central Africa, lying between the Congo and Nile watersheds. The term Rwenzori has virtually replaced Toro as a reference to this region. It covers Uganda's administrative districts of Bundibugyo, Kabarole and Kasese and also much of DR Congo's North Kivu and southern Ituri. The region presents a complex geography, which mirrors the cultural variety. It has both the highest point in Uganda (Margherita – 5,109 m) and the lowest (Semliki flats 860 m above sea level), and the bottom of the Edward Graben stands at 796 m above sea level. The cataclysmic geographical occurrences in the past configured a landscape of weird terrain: steep slopes and foothills, alpine scenery, flat plains (rift valley) together with associated vegetation (rainforest, alpine, savannah). This environmental diversity also yields rich resources (copper, cobalt, gypsum, fish, salt, rangeland, rivers and besides a fertile soil, beautiful scenery and teeming wildlife). Ruth Fisher, one of the earliest missionaries, remarked "This is undoubtedly one of the world's natural zoological gardens" (1903:45).

A number of writers have advanced the idea that certain locales attract settlement (Schoenbrun, 1998, Pennacini, 2000, Yeoman, 1989), and that in turn leads to the formation of cultures. Schoenbrun's use of glotochronological and lexical calculations has invariably linked the ambience of this region to the ethno-genesis of many of the Great Lakes people. In our case, the consideration is that Rwenzori lies at the centre of an environmentally welcoming region that has attracted a variety of ethno-cultural entities. This has produced, often, identical cultural practices (as the case of the *engoma*, stick dances and circumcision, see Pennacini, 2000:121). The latter fits in well with the argument, especially in the period prior to 1970, when groups of Bakonzo would trek over the spurs of the Rwenzori, asking for the providence of the spirits and partaking in a one-month-long circumcision ritual initiation for which the surgeons were Bamba, a practice also carried on by the Basua pygmies. It has also led to practices particular to an ethnic group (for instance each group takes pride in her identity and customary practices, such as dance (Bakonzo – *Ekikibi, Luma, Endara*; Batoro – *Entogoro, Orunyege;* Bamba – *Luma, Balimu,* etc). This is a consequence of both the environmental and socio-political conditions to which these groups have been exposed.

Table 1 **Ethno-cultural Composition of Kasese District 1991**

Ethnic	Male	Female	Total	%
Bakonzo	131,376	141,404	272,780	80.8
Batoro/Batuku/Basongora	8,871	9,870	18,749	5.6
Banyankole, Bahima	4,711	4,186	8,879	2.6
Bakiga	4,697	4,171	8,868	2.6
Baganda	3,124	2,841	5,965	1.8
Bafumbira	2,807	2,727	5,534	1.7
Banyarwanda	1,400	1,524	2,924	0.9
Iteso	881	538	1,419	0.4
Banyoro/Bagungu	619	607	1,226	0.4
Acholi/Labwor	573	502	1,075	0.3
Basoga	427	285	712	0.2
Alur/Jonam	358	298	656	0.2
Bagisu/Bamasaba	339	271	610	0.2
Langi	332	249	581	0.2
Bamba	241	272	513	0.1
Lugbara, Aringa	315	196	511	0.1
Samia	211	143	354	0.1
Kakwa	130	155	285	0.1
Nubian	116	120	236	0.08
Badama/Jopadhola	126	96	222	0.06
Madi	119	96	215	0.05
Kumam	110	82	192	0.05
Bagwere	81	56	137	0.04
Bahororo	63	42	105	0.03
Banyole	59	41	100	0.03
Karimajong	58	38	96	0.02
Barundi	39	35	74	0.02
Baruli	17	29	46	0.01
Sebei	31	09	40	
Lendu	11	16	27	
Batwa/Basua	09	04	13	
Bachope Bagwe	06	05	11	
Total	**164,383**	**173,074**	**337,457**	**100%**

Source: NEMA (1997), Kasese District Profile, p.18

From Table 1, it can be noticed that the region is a rich mosaic of ethno-cultural entities. The example of Kasese on the table above is illustrative of the region generally. Yet, it is noteworthy that in spite of the numbers, every cultural community lives to express her cultures and customs. However, the table neglects to list a host of other communities integrating within the primary ones, for instance the Basongora, a pastoralist community living in the plains of Busongora, the Banyagwaki, Banyabindi, Baholhu, Bakingwe and non-Ugandan communities like Kikuyu and Luyia have been left out or are merged with other groups. Yet, all these can be found here. The critical cultural issue is that they are able to identify themselves thus and can differentiate themselves from the other groups, having a number of cultural practices that distinguish them (such a totems, dance, occupation, endogamy, dressing, housing and type of livestock kept). In another instance, while the Babwisi are completely different from the Vonoma/Bule Bule (Bamba), they have often been lumped together as Bamba (Winter, 1956) yet they are completely different and very much non inter-intelligible – a consequence of the lack of internal attempts to expose themselves as cultural entities.

Further afield, the Bundibugyo district houses, besides the Bamba and Babwizi, the Bakonzo, Batuku, Batoro and Baswa. The Batuku are a pastoralist community akin to the Basongora in Kasese and the Hema of Eastern D.R.C. Kabarole district is occupied by the Batoro, who occupy the plateau/highland while the Bakonzo live on the mountain flanks in Bunyangabu county. The Bakiga migrants occupy the south of the district.

On the western side of the mountain, i.e. in the D.R.C., the situation is not much different. The Banande coexist with other peoples such as the Mvuba, Bavira, Gegere, Hema, Balegga, Batalinge, Lendu etc. Across our bridge, the Banande and Bakonzo are kinsmen. Similarly, the Batalinge and Bamba, just as the Batwa and Baswa. In each of these cases, the majorities stay on the Congo side of the border. In spite of this, cultural practices remain strikingly similar, tied to the knot of tradition and the commonality of the Rwenzori (Stacey, 1960: 15; 1965: 10).

This ethno-cultural diversity is high compared to the population area statistics as laid out in Table 2 as of 2002:

Table 2   **Area and Population of Rwenzori Region's Districts in Uganda**

DISTRICT	AREA m²	POPULATION
Bundibugyo	2,261.6	212,893
Kabarole	1,818.6	359,180
Kasese	3,389	532,993
Total	**7,468.2**	**1,115,166**

Source: Uganda District Information Handbook, 2005.

Out of this population, only 113,902 (about 10%) are urban. The 90% rural population lives on tilling the soil or claims livestock rearing as a main occupation. The ethno-cultural mix in the urban centres is high, yet urban centres are cultural melting points, with a dwindling trend regarding cultural practices due to exposure to the throes of social change, especially resulting from westernization (Gluckman, 1960:55).

In the cultural bridge of the Rwenzori, cultural variety and distinction remain persistent (Kasfir, 1972:60, Nnoli, 1998:4). Therefore, the Rwenzori region, in spite of a congregation of such cultural variety, is not encouraging ethno-cultural integration, but rather exhibits nucleated ethno-cultural groups, each exhibiting their cultural traits. This is prominent in the nomenclature of places where such groups stay (such as Kitoro, Kikonzo, Kokongo, Kiteso, Acholi quarters, etc.).

Essential to accommodating such a variety of people are the *relations* between the cultural groups themselves. This is expressed either in harmony and peaceful coexistence, or in disharmony (violent conflict, both inter- and intra-ethnic (Stacey 2003:195). The variables may include both internal factors such as dynastic arrangements, trade, religion, supra-cultural rulership over territory, cattle raids, land disputes, local and national ethnic peripherization, resource access, plus the effect of the state. These may work in conjunction with external variables as a common currency, a common foreign language, external religion, colonial policy, ultra national cultural peripherization and competitive ethno-cultural sub-nationalism (Kasfir, 1972:51). All the above phenomena have played a role in the intra- and inter-ethnic relations, which in each case has limited the level of cultural confrontation.

Two developments have added salt to this mix, changing the cultural landscape. Firstly, the introduction of colonial rule, which divided the various cultures into Francophone and Anglophone groupings, often leading to confrontation (as the case of the Bayira, divided into Banande in Congo and Bakonzo in Uganda; Bamba, with the Batalinge and Bavira kinsmen in Congo; Hema with their Batuku and Basongora kinsmen in Uganda etc.). This further caused intra-ethnic divisions (as the case of Batoro versus Banyoro). These people were of the same culture such as the Banyakitara, speaking Runyakitara. Besides, the introduction of external nomenclature as the case of the Italian, German and British names given to various places, replacing local names for Rwenzori (De Filippi, 1909:196-197), imposed a Western culture on this area. Together with colonial rule came Western religion, exploration and tourism. Various accounts from these sources shape the cultural landscape around the Rwenzori (Stanley, 1890:482; Lugard, 1902:182; De Filippi, 1909:196; Fisher, 1904:41; Stacey, 1960:208; Roscoe, 1915:vi), often referring to the people as savages, cannibals, half civilized and natives. A case in point is where Fisher refers to the Bahuku as cannibals who would pay up to six goats for a corpse. These assertions are patently false since we know that the Bahuku (Baswa) do not keep any domestic animals and have until lately been hunter-gatherers in the Semiliki forests.

The second development is urbanization associated with trade, commerce, leisure, mining, etc., which has reinforced the migration pattern in the form of labourers, miners, fishermen, traders and farmers. Their immediate cultural assertion leads to ethnic cleavages of ethno-cultural groups in all urban centres for security, easy communication and propagation of one's group's culture. The urban centres constitute a cultural melting pot in which there is an erosion of tradition and cultural values through the adoption of Western values. Inter-ethnic and inter-clan intermarriages add to the patchwork of ethnic diversity.

Conclusion

Rwenzori presents to us an interesting area. It is one of the exceptional areas where a mosaic of cultures (for both indigenous and immigrant groups) has converged. All the groups, irrespective of their size, are worthy of respect because of their respect of their cultural values, mutual or otherwise. In spite of the pressure on the resources and occasional outbreaks of ethnic conflict, Mount Rwenzori and the adjacent Rwenzori region serve as a symbol to which all these outlined cultural groups look for posterity. The pastoralists will need the rivers, water and pasture while the cultivator needs the soil, and the hunter needs the forest and the wilderness. In this way all Rwenzori's cultures use the environment for cultural enrichment.

Bibliography

De Filippi, F. 1909. *Ruwenzori: An Account of the Expedition of HRH Prince Luigi Amedeo of Savoy, Duke of The Abruzzi.* Rome: Archibald Constable.

Fisher, R. 1904. *On the Borders of Pygmyland.* London: Marshall Brothers.

Gluckman, M. (ed.) "Tribalism in Modern British Central Africa". In *Cahier d'Etudes Africaines.* London: 1:1.

Kasfir, N. 1972. "Cultural Sub-nationalism in Uganda". In Olurunsula, V. A. (ed.) *The Politics of Cultural Sub-nationalism in Africa*. New York: Anchor Books.

Lugard, F. 1902. *The Rise of our East African Empire*. Vol. II. London: Frank Cass.

NEMA. 1997. *Kasese District Environment Profile*. Kampala: National Environment Management Authority.

Nnoli, O. (ed.) 1998. *Ethnic Conflicts in Africa*. Dakar: CODESRIA.

Pennacini, C. 2000. "Religion and Spirit Possession in the Great Lakes". In Remotti, F. (ed.) *Ambienti, Lingue, Culture; contributi della missione Ethnologica Italiana in Africa Equatoriale*. Alessandria: Edizioni dell'Orso.

Roscoe, J. 1989. *The Northern Bantu*. Oxford: Oxford University Press.

Schoenbrun, D.L. 1998. *A Green Place, a Good Place: Agrarian Change, Gender and Social Identity in the Great Lakes Region to the 15th Century*. Kampala: Fountain.

Stacey, T. 1960. *The Brothers M*. London: Pantheon Books.

---. 1965. *Summons to the Rwenzori*. London: Secker and Warburg.

---. 2003. *Tribe: The Hidden History of the Mountains of the Moon*. London: Stacey International.

Stanley, H.M. 1890. *In Darkest Africa*. London: Sampson Low.

Winter, E.H. 1956. *Bwamba, A Structural-functional Analysis of a Patrilineal Society*. Oxford: Oxford University Press.

Yeoman, G. 1989. *Africa's Mountains of the Moon: Journeys to the Snowy Sources of the Nile*. New York: Universe Books.

An Epicentre of Empire: the Rwenzori Mountains in the Western Imagination

Hermann Wittenberg

"These mountains have no fellows on the globe"
John Buchan (1941:124)

Introduction

On this occasion where we are celebrating the centenary of the Duke of Abruzzi's ascent, it also is worthwhile and timely to reflect on the way the Rwenzori Mountains functioned in the Western imagination, particularly in the period associated with colonial domination. Since their so-called discovery by H.M. Stanley in 1888, and even long before that, a rich web of geographic fantasy was woven around the Mountains of the Moon that was not without problematic ideological significance. The snow-capped white Rwenzori Mountains figured large in colonial and racist thinking and were appropriated as a colonial symbol of white mastery over "darkest Africa" by a whole range of explorers, climbers, missionaries, colonial administrators and writers. The Rwenzori had an enormous continental and symbolic significance in the broader context of Western colonialism in Africa, leading Stanley to declare that they were the most significant geographical discovery "in twenty-two years of African travel" (1890:II, 494). When the Duke of Abruzzi reported on his climbing expedition to a meeting of the Royal Geographic Society in London in 1907, the glittering event attracted an elite audience of more than 2,000 politicians, academics, diplomats and military officers, including the king of England. The unprecedented interest and attention given to a remote and little-known range of central African mountains of moderate height raises important questions about the relationship between Africa and Europe, and about the nature of colonialism.

Stanley

To answer this question we need to re-look at history, and examine the context of Stanley's "discovery", on his second trans-African journey from west to east, ostensibly to rescue Emin Pascha, but also to advance the colonial interests of Leopold from the Congo into Uganda and the southern Sudan. Stanley's journeys of exploration and discovery were thus never only purely scientific endeavours, but tied up with colonial expansion. The significance and emotional feeling that Stanley attached to the elevated alpine landscape of the Rwenzori can be partly explained by their impressive *contrast* to the tropical, lowland Congo jungle in which his expeditionaries had suffered months of staggering deprivations and hardships. It was Leopold's insistence that Emin be reached via the treacherous route of the Congo jungle that turned Stanley's expedition into a fiasco, exacting a huge toll in life. The fate of the lost rear column, associated with scandalous allegations of cannibalism, was to dog Stanley for years to come. Stanley describes the Congo jungle as a vast primeval wilderness in which nature assumed the character of a malevolent monster. Stanley's vivid description of a near impenetrable, gloomy and dangerous landscape of entrapment in many ways prefigures Joseph Conrad's more well-known depiction in *Heart of Darkness*, and laid the foundation for the Western myth about the tropical horrors of "darkest Africa".

In stark contrast is Stanley's description of the Ugandan plateau. When the expedition finally emerged out of "the dungeon free and unfettered" they were able to exchange "foulness and damp for sweetness and purity, darkness and gloom for divine light and wholesome air" (1890:295). They stepped on to a

> a rolling plain, green as an English lawn, into broadest and sweetest daylight, and warm and glorious sunshine, to inhale the pure air with an uncontrollable rapture.... A hundred square miles of glorious country opened to our view - apparently deserted - for we had not as yet been able to search out the fine details of it. Leagues and leagues of bright green pasture land undulated in gentle waves, intersected by narrow winding lines of umbrageous trees that filled the hollows, scores of gentle hills studded with dark clumps of thicket, graced here and there by a stately tree, lorded it over level breadths of pasture and softly sloping champaigns; and far in the east rose some frowning ranges of mountains beyond which we were certain slept in its deep gulf the blue Albert. (1890:292-5)

Instead of a claustrophobic confinement in the tangled, dangerous gloom in which the power of the eye is incapacitated and the body constrained, the open rolling grass fields of the plateau and the far horizon give unlimited freedom to the gaze. In this classic instance of a colonial prospect scene, the landscape is rendered as a receptive garden ("gentle", "sweetest", "softly") opening itself to the exploring eye. Mary Louise Pratt uses the expressive term "Monarch-of-all-I-survey" (1992:205) to describe the rhetorical stance of such prospect scenes and links the commanding view over colonial landscapes with surveillance and imperial control. Such strategies appear to be at work in Stanley's passage, where the seeming lack of inhabitants ("apparently deserted") and the detailed description of the homely park-like character ("an English lawn") invite the explorer to take possession.

But the delight in the picturesque rolling grass fields of the central plateau is but a prelude to Stanley's truly sublime landscape of the Rwenzori Mountains. In the two-volume travel narrative, the sighting of the Rwenzori stands out as the climactic moment of the entire two-year enterprise. In sharp contrast to the tropical horrors of the Congo basin, the snow-topped peaks offered a vision of a sublime alpine landscape, set in benign highland pastures and green meadows. The views of the mountains uplifted Stanley

> in speechless wonder towards that upper region of cold brightness and perfect peace, so high above mortal reach, so holily tranquil and restful, of such immaculate and stainless purity, that thought and desire of expression were altogether too deep for utterance. (1890:502)

In a sublime transport away from the dark and violent realities of the African continent he had just traversed, the Rwenzori offers an experience of uplifting spiritual transcendence. Stanley compares this sublime "exultation" to the "peculiar emotion at the sight [of] any ancient work, be it an Egyptian pyramid or Sphinx, be it an Athenian Parthenon, Palmyrene sun-temple, Persepolitan palace" (1890:498), and in this way his language situates the Rwenzori not as an indigenous African landscape, but as part of the historical and cultural heritage of the West.

Stanley's linkage of the Rwenzori and the Mediterranean is based on his claim that these mountains are the true source of the Nile. The idea that any river should have a single, localised source of origin (and that this point of origin is of such over-riding importance) is one of the fictions of colonial geography, that still, today, has wide popular currency. The question of the source of the Nile has a long and complex history tied up as much with the origins of Western civilization as with the geo-politics of late nineteenth century imperialism. It is difficult to underestimate the enormous symbolic significance of this river, and the mystery of its origins, in the culture of the West. The quest for the source of the Nile, as Simon Schama has shown, became invested with metaphysical importance as a riverine metaphor for the West's civilizational origins. While medieval European writers commonly believed that the Nile flowed directly from paradise (1995: 266), early imperial thinkers imagined rivers less in religious than in political terms: "as lines of power and time carrying empires from source to expansive breadth" (1995: 261). Such an imperial model of rivers made the search for a source all the more important, and "it was precisely the denial of this sovereign possession to the Greeks, Romans, French, and British that made the Nile so tantalizing, so treacherous – in a word, so Cleopatran" (1995: 263).

By the middle of the nineteenth century, China, America, and Australia had long become known to Europe, but the mystery of the Nile remained. As Alan Moorehead puts it,

> No unexplored region in our times, neither the heights of the Himalayas, the Antarctic wastes, nor even the hidden side of the moon, has excited quite the same fascination as the mystery of the sources of the Nile. For two thousand years at least the problem was debated and remained unsolved; every expedition that was sent up the river from Egypt returned defeated. (1962: 20)

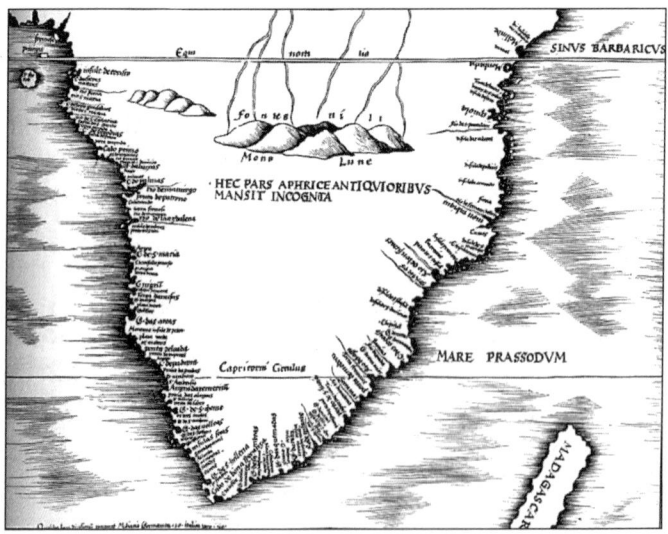

Figure 2   **Martin Waldseemuller's 1513 map of Africa, showing the Mountains of the Moon as the only significant feature in the otherwise blank interior of Africa (Tooley and Bricker, 1976)**

It is in this weighty context that Stanley judged the value of his discovery of the Rwenzori, and accordingly devoted an extraordinary amount of time and effort in securing its status as the ultimate source of the Nile. Making a detailed survey of the geographic features connected with the range, he measured altitudes and calculated gradients, charted the course of rivers, and explored the placement of the catchment areas and watersheds. In establishing a fluvial connection between the Nile and the Rwenzori, Stanley was grandly conscious that he had unlocked the secret that had intrigued civilizations of Egypt, Greece and Rome for centuries; and that this monumental discovery would "win [him] immortal renown" (1890:467). For Stanley, the Rwenzori Mountains are thus altogether the most significant place in the entire continent of Africa: they are "the very mountains before whose shrine Alexander and Caesar would have worshipped" (1890:467).

In order to cement his claim about the historical importance of the Rwenzori, namely that they were identical to Ptolemy's fabled Mountains of the Moon, Stanley devoted an entire chapter of elaborate geographic and historical evidence in *Darkest Africa*, looking at both Western and Arab sources. The Rwenzori is thus not only the point of origin for the famous Nile, but, as Ptolemy's Mountains of the Moon, they are also connected to the origin of Western geography. As the fabled headwaters of the Nile, or Aristoteles's "Silver Mountains", the Rwenzori Mountains are imagined by Stanley and his successors as part of western, not African, history. The people living in the foothills of the Rwenzori are thus not surprisingly seen to be connected to Egypt rather than Africa:

> in their legends and traditions, ... in the form of their musical instruments, in their astronomical symbols carved upon horns, and in certain burial rites, indications have been suggested of relations and contact with ancient Egypt. (De Filippi, 1909: 82)

Stanley's and Luigi Amedeo, Duke of Abruzzi's conception of the Rwenzori is remarkably Hegelian in its denial of history and civilizational agency to Africa. In Hegel's well-known *Philosophy of History* (1834) Africa was seen to be only "on the threshold of the World's History" and "still involved in the conditions of mere nature". Africa was disconnected "with the rest of the World – shut up; it is the Gold-land compressed within itself, – the land of childhood, which, lying beyond the day of self-conscious history, is enveloped in the dark mantle of Night" (1872:130). If the Rwenzori could assume a history for Stanley, it had to be a history that was not properly African, for Africa had supposedly no real history. The Rwenzori is thus connected to the civilization of Egypt, which, according to Hegel, "does not belong to the African Spirit" but can "be considered in reference to the passage of the human mind from its Eastern to its Western phase" (1872:131).

Such mythical historicization continues to exercise a strong influence in the present, if we look at the example of Guy Yeoman, who called for the declaration of the Rwenzori as a World Heritage Site, so that the West would "be keeping faith with the Ancient Greeks" (1989:166). Similarly Rennie Bere, the first president of the Ugandan Mountain Club, rehashed Stanley's antique history in his Rwenzori book, adding that they "may well have been seen by the emissaries of the Queen of Sheba" (1966:76). For a long succession of explorers and mountaineers, the cultural value and significance of the Rwenzori Mountains is less determined by their intrinsic geography and local meaning, but by the way they can be appropriated by a larger narrative of Western history.

White Snows / Dark Africa

Figure 3   Herbert Baker's Cape to Cairo glyph

The symbolic value of the Rwenzori for a continental imperial imaginary can be seen in the iconography associated with Cecil John Rhodes. Rhodes was the greatest imperialist of his time, and dreamt of "painting the whole of Africa red", meaning by that the assertion of British supremacy and control over the continent, from the Cape to Cairo. We can see this imperial trans-continental thinking in an exemplary way in Herbert Baker's suggestive glyph that is reproduced in the frontispiece of his book *Cecil Rhodes by his Architect* (1934); it is also found in a mural in Rhodes House at Oxford University. The glyph represents "Rhodes' Way from Cape to Cairo" in the form of symbols that signify an imaginative imperial control over the whole continent. The four stars in the glyph represent the Southern Cross, the "Pilot stars to the Navigators of the Cape of Storms". They stand for Rhodes's beloved Cape, the southern-most point in the Cape-to-Cairo axis. The two Zimbabwe birds represent the colonies Rhodes founded and gave his name to, namely Southern and Northern Rhodesia. In the centre, surrounded by the other symbols, Baker positioned the snow-tipped Mountains of the Moon from which the waters of the Nile issue. The triangular peaks are also suggestive of the pyramids and in this way complete the northern point of the trans-continental Cape to Cairo axis. The Mountains of the Moon occupy the centre, indicating the mountain's geographical position in the middle of the African continent half-way between the Cape and Cairo points. They are also the largest element in the glyph, indicating the pre-eminent symbolic importance of the Mountains of the Moon as the vital fulcrum in the Cape-to-Cairo axis. Baker's glyph shows that the Rwenzori featured large in the imperial geo-political fantasies of Rhodes and the coterie around him. The irony of course is that while appearing to be symbols of Africa, all four elements of Rhodes's glyph are in fact exogenous to Africa: the Mountains of the Moon and the waters of the Nile are connected to the Mediterranean, the Southern Cross represents the Portuguese voyages of discovery, and the Zimbabwe birds, as "Gleams in Darkest Africa of Northern Lights", are attributed to a mysterious Mediterranean civilization.

For imperialists such as Rhodes, the Rwenzori is a significant ideological location because in a continent which was discursively figured as a place of blackness and darkness, the paradoxical idea of white, virginal snow in the midst of tropical heat assumed a racially loaded symbolic significance. Already Stanley's geographical description of the place thus slips into a racialized discourse of difference:

> What stranger contrast could there be than our own nether world of torrid temperature, eternally green sappy plants, and never-ending luxuriance and verdure, with its savagery and war alarms, and deep stains of blood-red sin, to that lofty mountain king, clad in its pure white raiment of snow, surrounded by myriads of dark mountains, low as bending worshippers before the throne of a monarch on whose cold white face were inscribed 'Infinity and Everlasting' (1890: 502)

In Stanley's sublime vision, the white Rwenzori is an imperious god-like figure which stands out starkly against an almost inorganic background in which tropical climate, local people and vegetation blend into an amorphous, dark mass. The monarch with the "cold white face" is surrounded by lowly bent "dark" worshippers – a scenario which articulates and naturalizes white mastery over black Africa.

The Rwenzori fulfilled a similar ideological function for Ruth Fisher, the missionary wife of the Reverent A.B. Fisher, who went to western Uganda in 1900 "to proclaim the renown, beauty and majesty of Christ among the heathen" (1919:31). Fisher became the first woman to climb up to the Alpine zone of the Rwenzori, reaching the Mobuko glacier – wearing a skirt – in 1903, and again in 1906, a few weeks before the Duke of Abruzzi's more famous climb. In her memoirs, *On the Borders of Pygmy Land*, Fisher recounts her first sighting of the Rwenzori after days of trudging through miles of swamp:

> Huge peaks, sharp and rugged, stretched from north to south in an unbroken range of sixty-nine miles long. Heavy black thunder clouds rolled over some of the summits, while the lightning shot out angry tongues of fire. Torrents of rain were sweeping away to our right, while the sun beat down in full strength upon the valleys. Above all, calm and serene, shone the region of snow. For all ages the sun has directed its equatorial power against that ice fortress. Storms have thundered and crushed against its foundations, but it has stood as the one unsullied and impregnable witness of holiness and purity to God, in a land where darkness has reigned, and the storms of passion, vice and barbarity have laid desolate. (1919: 38)

In Fisher's sublime vision, the impregnable "ice fortress" of the Rwenzori is a transcendent figure for Christianity and Western civilizational superiority withstanding the cataclysmic violent onslaught of the forces of equatorial "darkness". The black storms that ineffectually rage around this unshakable rock of faith are figured as the forces "of passion, vice and barbarity". Similarly, J. Moore, an alpinist who had ascended one of the lower peaks in 1899, held that "the *Mons lunae* were something quite above the monotonous sweltering barbarism of the tropics" (1902: 77).

White Highlands

But part of the appeal of the Rwenzori mountains was also that they could be imagined as uninhabited by Africans. The conquering of peaks in an uninhabited alpine region allowed European climbers to take imaginative possession of African space without the attendant violence of subjugating and dispossessing native people. At the beginning of the nineteenth century, virtually all of Africa had already been carved up by colonial powers, and alpinism remained a way in which inter-European rivalry could be expressed. The expeditions which preceded the Duke of Abruzzi's act of planting the Italian flag on the Rwenzori's highest point, were Italy's imperial rivals in eastern Africa: Germany and Britain. As the duke's own account at a Royal Geographic Society lantern show reveals, the moment of conquest was an overtly political event. Accompanied by triple "Vivas!" he named the two highest summits "Margherita" and "Alexandra", after the queens of Italy and England,

> in order that, under the auspices of these two royal ladies, the memory of the two nations may be handed down to posterity - of Italy, whose name was the first to resound on these snows in a shout of victory, and, of England, which in its marvellous colonial expansion carries civilization to the slopes of these remote mountains (1907:138)

The sense of shared unity and a common idea of sportsmanship among the civilized powers was expressed in John Buchan's comment that "No Englishman will grudge that the honours of the pioneer fell to so brilliant a climber" (1941:121). With the Duke of Abruzzi's ascent and naming, the Rwenzori Mountains do thus not only become a powerful symbolic figure for colonial possession, but also for unity amongst Western powers in their common purpose of rule over "the still unknown and savage wilds of Africa . . . for the advance of civilization" (Abruzzi, 1907:139).

But the Rwenzori Mountains were not just of symbolic importance, but were also, more practically, seen as a natural space for European settlement in Africa, as exemplified by the "White Highlands" in Kenya. This attitude was articulated by Douglas Freshfield, who held the influential position of president of the British Alpine Club. Freshfield, who had climbed in the Rwenzori range in 1905, prior to the Italian expedition, regarded the cool and fertile foothills as ideal "sites for European cultivation and for a sanatorium" (1907: 328). The Rwenzori are thus claimed as an ideal space for European colonization.

The clearest expression of the idea that African mountains and colonial settlement are linked, is found in the literary and political writing of John Buchan. Buchan was not only an eminent British politician and imperial administrator, but also the writer of highly popular works of fiction such as *Prester John, The Thirty-nine Steps* and *Greenmantle*. Altogether, Buchan wrote more than a hundred books, and ended his political career as governor-general of Canada, one of the highest offices in the Commonweath. As a young man, Buchan spent three years in Southern Africa, in the aftermath of the Anglo-Boer War, as a member of Alfred Milner's new imperial administration. Buchan never visited Uganda or the Rwenzori, but his writings repeatedly refer to them. Buchan was fascinated by the landscape of Africa, and in several of his writings he thought deeply about the relationship between topography and colonial settlement.

Buchan believed that colonization was vital for England's renewal and growth, and that a vigorous exposure to Africa would bring out the best in English men. In his autobiography he wrote: "I saw in the Empire a means of giving to the congested masses at home open country instead of a blind alley" (1940:125). In his early political treatise, *African Colony*, he envisioned a vast new Southern African colony that would be "girdled on three sides by ocean, and on the fourth looking north to the inland seas and the eternal snows of the Rwenzori" (1903: 392). In Buchan's imagination, the Rwenzori Mountains help to define the geographic and racial contours of Britain's imperial possessions in Africa and become the birthplace of a newly invigorated English civilization on the dark continent.

The geography of this new imperial Africa is elaborated in an early novel, titled *Lodge in the Wilderness*. Looking out towards the Rwenzori Mountains, one of the characters, Lord Appin, says that permanent British colonial control is only possible on the high ground: "The colonies occupy only the healthy country and leave the lowlands as dependencies under the central executive" (1906:118). High ground, "fortunately", is plentiful in Africa from the Cape right up to Manicaland, the Shire Highlands, and in "East Africa we have this gorgeous plateau as the vantage ground for the coast strip and Uganda" (1906:118). "Tropical administration," declares Appin, must be necessarily spasmodic, "but not too spasmodic." In order to retain the "mental and bodily vigour" of the colonial administrators who have to labour away in "the great hot flats", there need to be close-by

> health resorts where these Englishmen can go when their vitality ebbs and lay in a fresh supply, and where the greater administrative problems can be thought out. They will be what Simla is to India, the workshop of government. They are near enough to be within hail of the lowlands, but they are in another climate, and give a tired man the moral and physical tonic he needs (1906:118).

Like Buchan and Freshfield, Ruth Fisher also believed that exposure to the alpine zone would prove energizing, and she expressed her desire "to inhale this cool life-giving air so that we might be refreshed for a return to work in the hot tiring lowlands" (1919: 175).

The political value of tropical highlands is perhaps most clearly expressed by another Buchan character, Lady Wakefield:

> If only each hot country had been given a habitable mountain, they would be the only places in the world to live in. On the ordinary upland you dominate the flat country because you are higher up, but here we also look down on the plain because we are wholesome and cool and sane and they are fevered. We are a lighthouse to the whole of Equatoria, and if there were fifty other lighthouses in the Empire there would be no tropical problem. (1906: 113)

The contours of an altitudinally and racially mapped empire are extraordinarily clear here: places of elevation are not only the key to efficient colonial administration in the tropics ("you dominate the flat country"), but are also beacons of light, progress and civilization in darkest Africa. This stark altitudinal differentiation also implies a crass racial and civilizational divide between the "cool and sane" colonial elite on the uplands, and the "fevered" African population on plains. In this Darwinian racist conception, the cool highlands are suited for civilizationally more advanced people. The empire needs cool sanctuaries.

Interestingly enough, Buchan's son Johnnie was to find himself in precisely the same situation that *Lodge in the Wilderness* had theorized. As a young district officer in the Ugandan lowlands, he fell ill from amoebic dysentry in 1935 and had to be evacuated to Kenya in order to convalesce (Tweedsmuir, 1953: 210).

Conclusion

In this paper I have looked some of the fantasies and myths of origin that have been that woven around the Rwenzori mountains, and hope that it has become clear how these ideas have also had implications for the views and beliefs of colonial administrators, explorers and climbers. To conclude, I want to briefly present a rather different and more contemporary literary text, namely John Preston's *Touching the Moon* (1990). In this postcolonial travel narrative, Preston satirizes and ironizes the way colonial and imported western myths distort the truth about the Rwenzori.

Preston went to Uganda in 1986 with a copy of Rider Haggard's *She* in his pocket and several packets of Durex condoms in his bag, resulting in an embarrassing search at Entebbe customs. Inspired by the film version of *She* in which Ursula Andress's "white dress still pulled impossibly taut over the jutting splendour of her breasts" (1990:26), Preston hoped to find a fantasy white goddess and the mythical land of Kôr in the Rwenzori:

> Rider Haggard was always the inspiration, the Mountains of the Moon favourite location. Here was the place infused with all the excitement I could imagine. I thought of huge snow-capped mountains linked by a tracery of hanging bridges and tiny paths. There were great fortresses rearing up into the clouds, dark pools where men in armour drank long draughts of inky water, plateaux where armies thundered back and forth in perpetual combat (1990:12).

Instead of this colonial dream fantasy, Preston's Rwenzori experience turned into a gothic nightmare. Wading through thick mud in driving rain, he regards the scene as a "vast secret laboratory for botanic mutations, where hidden hands laboured to produce the most misshapen growths imaginable" (1990:161). The "entire landscape was bristling with aggression" (1990: 145). Appropriately, Preston registers the horror of the landscape as an effect on his body, in particular his genitals. When finally reaching a mountain hut, and feeling very sick, he discovers that his "penis had turned a dark shade of navy blue" (1990:140). Eventually, he realises the extent of colonial romantic fantasies:

I'd miscalculated badly. There were no white-robed immortals here, no eighty-five copper statues from whose mouths the Nile spewed forth. How could there be. This wasn't the Africa I knew – a vast backdrop against which Europeans could act out their romances, covering themselves in self-proclaimed glory. This was a different place entirely. (1990:147).

Preston's narrative is a transgressive, self-reflexive postcolonial text in which the white, heroic explorer figure becomes undone, and European colonial fantasies about the Rwenzori Mountains become unmasked.

The future of the Rwenzori Mountains and the communities that live around them is today closely bound up with the geo-political machinations and wars that have engulfed the Great Lakes region. Ironically, the hopes of local Rwenzori communities are not only linked to the return of peace, but also a continuation of colonial myths about the Mountains of the Moon. In order to draw tourists and attract development, the Rwenzori will in all likelihood continue to be inscribed with a Western history that obscures local cultural knowledge, traditions and histories. The mountains have thus retained, to this day, the names conferred on them by Abruzzi, with only a small change from Ruwenzori to Rwenzori. But otherwise the imperial names remain. In what is now a national park, only one lowly feature is named after a Ugandan: the John Matte hut on the trekking circuit.

Bibliography

Abruzzi, Luigi Amedeo di Savoia. 1907. "The Snows of the Nile". In *Geographic Journal*, February (2): 121-147.

Baker, H. 1934. *Cecil Rhodes. By his Architect Herbert Baker.* London: Oxford University Press.

Bere, R.. 1966. *The Way to the Mountains of the Moon*. London: Arthur Baker.

Bierman, J. 1990. *Dark Safari. The Life behind the Legend of Henry Morton Stanley.* New York: Alfred Knopf.

Buchan, J. 1903. *The African Colony. Studies in Reconstruction.* London & Edinburgh: William Blackwood and Sons.

—. 1906. *A Lodge in the Wilderness.* London: Thomas Nelson.

—. 1908. "Access to Mountains". *Scottish Review,* May 21.

—. 1908. "The Dolomites". In *Scottish Review,* July 23.

—. 1940. *Memory Hold the Door.* London: J.M. Dent.

—. 1941. *The Last Secrets. The Final Mysteries of Exploration.* London: Thomas Nelson.

De Filippi, F. 1909. *Ruwenzori. An Account of an Expedition of H.R.H. Prince Luigi Amedeo of Savoy, Duke of Abruzzi.* London: Archibald Constable.

Fisher, R. 1919. *On the Borders of Pygmy Land.* London: Marshall Brothers.

Freshfield, D. 1907. The Conquest of the Ruwenzori: A Note. *Geographic Journal.* March (3): 326-229.

Hegel, G.W.F. 1872. *Lectures on the Philosophy of History.* Trans. J. Sibree. London: Bell & Deldy.

Moore J. 1902. "First Ascent of One of the Snow Ridges in the Mountains of the Moon". *Alpine Journal,* 156 (May): 77-90.

Moorehead, A. 1971. *The White Nile.* New York: Harper & Row.

Pratt, M.L. 1992. *Imperial Eyes.* London: Routledge.

Preston, J. 1990. *Touching the Moon.* London: Heinemann.

Schama, S. 1995. *Landscape and Memory.* London: Harper Collins.

Stanley, H.M. 1879. *Through the Dark Continent.* Volumes 1 & 2. New York: Harper.

—.1890. *In Darkest Africa.* London: Sampson, Low, Marsden, Searle and Rivington.

Synge, P. 1937. *Mountains of the Moon. An Expedition to the Equatorial Mountains of Africa.* New York: Dutton.

Tooley, R.V. & Bricker, C.(Eds). 1976. *Landmarks of Mapmaking*. Oxford: Phaidon.

Tweedsmuir. 1953. *Always a Countryman*. London: Robert Hale.

Wittenberg, H. 2001. "Ruwenzori: Imperialism and Desire in African Alpinism". In R. Wilson & C. Von Maltzan (eds.) *Spaces and Crossings. Essays on Literature and Culture in Africa and Beyond*. Frankfurt a. M.: Peter Lang.

---. 2002. Imperial Naming and the Sources of the Nile. *Nomina Africana*, 14 (1): 1-18.

Yeoman, G. 1989. *Africa's Mountains of the Moon. Journeys to the Snowy Source of the Nile*. New York: Universe.

Jan Czekanowski's Research in Africa (1907-1909): The Route – Basic Concepts – Documentation

Anna Czekanowska

In 1907 Jan Czekanowski, a young 24-year-old Polish gentleman, had the unprecedented opportunity to participate in the Duke of Mecklenburg's famous Central Africa expedition. He was the youngest participant in this scientific enterprise and grand adventure, and he undertook this challenge with great success. Perfectly prepared by his Swiss and German mentors (Rudolf Martin and Felix von Luschan respectively), he tried to fulfil his obligations as well as possible – taking anthropological measurements, collecting objects for museums (Museum für Völkerkunde in Berlin and the Grassi Museum in Leipzig), learning African languages, photographing, designing maps and drawing small sketches, recording music and interviewing as much as possible. The documentation is fortunately preserved and reveals these efforts accurately.

Czekanowski's route is described shortly, but very precisely, by J.P. Chretien[1], who documents the long trail of almost 7,000 kilometres (covered in 374 days on foot[2]). This study, however, needs additional elaboration, because the bare facts themselves evoke certain questions, if not doubts. Indeed, how was it possible to collect so much material and to observe various cultures so comprehensibly, while at the same time spending so many days marching (374 days in the framework of an expedition lasting 22 months, i.e. 665 days)? If Czekanowski was walking on roughly half the days he spent in Africa, how did he find so much time to do his research?

The explanation of this phenomenon demands knowledge of the scholar's habits and his personal predispositions. The young explorer loved to walk and was in the habit of ordering and systematizing his observations, thoughts and concepts while on the move. According to his daughter, the formula crucial for his statistical concepts was formulated while marching on one his African routes[3]. Perhaps, also important, was the family legend according to which his grand uncle[4], while being deported to Siberia and forced for seventeen months walking on foot to Irkutsk, collected beautiful botanical material and described it precisely. Similarly, the young Czekanowski in Africa covered an extended territory successfully, even though this route was not always easy. A careful reading of his diary and other correspondence reveals many hitherto unknown complications; of which the most dramatic were recurring malaria attacks.

The diary, however, does not dwell on his health problems, even though these were serious and impacted on his work. Instead, one finds only the information that he could not finish his exploration (mostly very exhausting anthropological measurements – encompassing up to 61 different parameters[5]) and that he decided to return later to these places. Czekanowski indeed revisited several locations repeatedly, and therefore the maps of his expedition route, though precisely designed, do not necessarily give an accurate picture of the full extent of his travels, since many of those "returns" were often undertaken by a different route.

A careful study of the diary, especially the problematic last pages where dates are often crossed out and at times wrong, allows one to infer his sickness indirectly, and to presume that on certain days he even lost all awareness of time. The fact that several of the diary's pages got lost also seems to point to his physical weakness. At the same time, however, direct information about his sickness is not to be found in the diary. This is quite different from what one may find in the diary of his compatriot Bronisław Malinowski[6], who had dedicated many pages to this topic.

Indeed, there is only a short notice, "Hoima – 2-7th March"[7], which documents his severe illness and the fact that he was unable to travel, even in a rickshaw drawn by a donkey. He was in fact very close to death. This information one can only reconstruct on the basis of some information found in his correspondence. He never spoke about this crisis.

A Detailed Reading of the Czekanowski's Diary

According to the preserved documentation, the expedition's first long march started on 1 June 1907[8]. The preserved diary-report starts with the expedition setting out and the first field research, which took place already in Kenya in the village Jimba, inhabited by the Wataita. The first proper investigation, however, took place in the place Voi. The results of anthropological measurements and of the excavation of an old cemetery are well confirmed by anthropological documentation. The diary also confirms that some experiences in those days were already very difficult[9], and had a strong influence on the perception of African culture.

The exploration of the "Inter-Lakes" area and of its culture started with their arrival in Bukoba on the western coast of Victoria Lake and lasted until December of 1907, covering the different areas of this region systematically. The stay in the residence of the Sultan in Bukoba (11-16 June 1907) can be seen as the important "initial" point of this investigation. The extended photographic documentation, as well as the quantity of anthropologic measurements, confirms the scientific accomplishments achieved in this period[10].

After the stay in Bukoba, the explorer turned to the west, undertaking some research in Kisiba, and later took a way via Kifumbiro across Mpororo towards Rwanda. The latter was crossed by the explorer in different directions: to the south (Nduga) and to the north (Mulera). The documentation indicates that the material from southern Rwanda is quite different to that from Mulera. The former concentrates on the environment of the residence of Juhi Musinga (the king of Rwanda); the latter documents the culture of farmers evidently of Hutu descent. The record from Mulera includes very rich linguistic material as well as the phonogram recordings of local songs. This song repertory is dominated by topics typical of the Hutu agricultural society, concentrating on family problems, and specifically on warnings for the girls, lullabies and on the most important family event – the wedding. It also includes some war songs, and those expressing particular resentments against the ruler (Musinga). Indeed, the texts of these songs clearly indicate that even in those places quite distant from the Musinga residence, the king was still present in the citizen's mind. The collected material creates a rich vision of a regional culture, its customs, the habits of people, and their beliefs. This repertory, and especially the deeply coded way in which attitudes and feelings towards their king were expressed, also demonstrates that criticism of state power was possible. A proper understanding of these texts, therefore, demands a lot of experience and a good knowledge of the complex structure of particular symbols. The help of missionaries (Father Dufays) was very important to Czekanowski in this case.

At the beginning of the work, cooperation with missionaries was crucial for Czekanowski's study. Later in life he often fondly returned to these remembrances and experiences. Permanent contact with the Nyundo mission was maintained until December of this year.

Very important for the studies undertaken was Czekanowski's stay in Nyansa (10-21 August 1907, and after the return seven more days). Here, in the residence of Musinga (king of Rwanda), he could participate in the court ritual and in an especially rich programme organized for the visit of the Duke of Mecklenburg. Also of importance were the recorded residence songs, which are quite different from those of Mulera. They revolved around the mobilization for war, and were performed polyphonically to pulsating rhythms. Quite interesting are the songs performed by the court choir, which consisted of the highly musical Batwa people.

By studying the results of his own research intensely (as well as materials collected by missionaries), as well as observing, photographing and recording, very thoroughly, Czekanowski could describe the culture of Rwanda in an extended panorama of topics with an evidently deep insight. His diary documents the fact that the contact with his informants was not always easy. Indeed, some interlocutors, and Musinga himself, at first, wanted to manipulate the young enthusiast with false information. After some days the king however recognized the explorer's insights and started to respect him. According to an often-repeated remembrance of Czekanowski, Musinga finally had to admit that "one should not lie, if your partner is clever he will recognize that, if he is not, the discussion with him is wasted time". Musinga stopped pretending that he knew German by changing to the Kiswahili.

The discussions with the king gave the explorer the possibility of not only covering an extended scope of topics, but also of investigating socio-political relations. Czekanowski's material from Rwanda is still of interest today for scholars investigating this country, and especially for those tracing the roots of conflicts between Bahutu and Batutsi[11]. The extensively documented stay in the Musinga residence, as well as the possibility of ascertaining people's opinions in distant provinces, allowed him deep insight into the state structure of Rwanda. This included detailed studies of the tax system and the hierarchy of clerks subordinated to the local power. The detailed descriptions of the citizen's obligations and the principles of tax collection included observations on the principles according to which the material status of the taxpayer could be quantified. This remains excellent material for today's scholars studying the question of state building and bureaucracy in Africa. The expedition concluded its work with research in the area of Lake Kivu and with the long march toward Lake Edward, specifically towards

Kasindi where the expedition members were to meet with the Duke of Mecklenburg for Christmas.

The second part of the expedition was connected with a long campaign undertaken in December 1907, lasting until March the following year[12]. It started with a short journey to the Katwe where the author observed the process of salt melting, which had crucial value as a means of exchange. From the Katwe the explorer turned towards the north, developing his research in the kingdom of Toro.

The residence in Fort Portal (Toro) again became an excellent place for work and relaxation. He received both the cooperation of a local mission and of the Mukama (king) Dawdi Chwa Kasagama. Thanks to the former, the author could obtain material extremely important for linguistic studies (dictionaries of several languages and dialects), as well as very interesting statistics, and many insights into local customs and mythology. In the second case, the most important was the genealogy of the king's family, actually written by the king himself and offered to the explorer personally by the king. This genealogy, with its relations to other family branches as being elaborated by a native person, had unique value. Extremely interesting is the comparison of the two kings. Kasagama was very proud of his family, whereas Musinga, actually being the illegitimate son, had constantly been giving wrong information.

Czekanowski's friendship with the king of Toro, and especially with his brother, was important not only for his work in the local area, but would also help in the next stage of the expedition. Thanks to this friendship and good relations with missionaries, the explorer could be introduced to the local justice procedures. Being accompanied by Brother Van Daille, he could participate in the royal trials conducted by the king.

The main objective of this part of the expedition was oriented towards the exploration of pygmies. These still little-known "small people" fascinated scholars of that time. The explorers wanted to investigate their physique and their little-known culture. The evident difficulties of establishing contact with them enhanced their fascination for the Western explorer. Indeed, the pygmies had an enormous talent for disappearing when they felt the "white" people approaching them. Motivated by this interest, Czekanowski crossed the slopes of the Rwenzori after receiving some information about their whereabouts. Some of this information was completely wrong, but when finally crossing the Semliki River he met a pygmy who travelled in the same boat, and who was quite self-confident – but not interested in being investigated. The proper exploration of pygmies took place in the middle of February 1908, on the western side of the Rwenzori mountains. Later, marching towards the west, the explorer met many pygmies, again in Kulu-Kulu, Mupohe and Djilapanda, and he could explore them quite comprehensively.

The results of Czekanowski's contacts with pygmies not only yield rich photographic records, anthropological measurements and some artefacts, but also interviews, illustrating their extremely interesting way of counting. Czekanowski also documented their art of body painting and other information concerning their beliefs, and sorcery, for which they were famous. The pygmy research also revealed many of their social problems, especially that of hunger and salt deprivation, which has many biological consequences. This part of the expedition was very exhausting for Czekanowski because of long, forced marches and the difficult conditions of staying overnight.

Indeed, the hardships in this area were immense. The explorer usually slept in improvised "camps" located either on the rocks or in the deep forest. In his report he often repeats statements such as: "the conditions are terrible, but the culture I am investigating and the material I am collecting are magnificent"[13]. Quite evidently the conditions in the Congo were much worse than those in Uganda. This pertained both to the badly organized colonial administration and the living conditions of local people (pygmies and others) who were quite hostile to one another. In fact, Czekanowski noted that all the local

Congolese people were terribly exploited by colonizers, pressing them to collect caoutchouc under very harsh conditions. This fact could explain the difficulties in establishing contact with many people, and with pygmies in particular.

At the end of February, the wanderer finally reached the famous "Stanley Route", undertaking a very difficult forced march toward Avakubi. In this area Czekanowski finally reached the Aruwimi River he had been dreaming of since his early youth[14]. The warnings about murders and cannibals, however, dampened his enthusiasm. The last information came from a Mr. Cousement whom he met along the route. This high-ranking person in the colonial administration was knowledgeable of the local situation and his warnings could not be dismissed. He warned Czekanowski of the fact that local people could communicate perfectly over large distances using a drum code. This provoked the scholar to study this drum system.

From Avakubi the explorer turned to the north towards Adjamu. The most interesting people in this area were again the pygmies from the rain forest of the Ituri basin. These pygmies were already known thanks to Stanley, but became more comprehensibly described and studied thanks to Czekanowski. Of particular interest was information concerning their clan organization, family relations, the inferior position of women in society, their religious concepts and the art of sorcery.

The beautiful landscape of this area was described in a seductive way by Stanley, but these charms did not extend to the poor social conditions of the people living there, who were being terribly exploited by the colonizers. The situation was, however, quite different in places where Sudanese influence was more than evident, such as the area of Nepoko where, according to Czekanowski, "the people were looking better"[15]. Their beautiful houses, of evidently Sudanese style, fascinated him.

After reaching Adjamu the expedition turned rapidly to the south-east toward Irumu where they expected to meet the expedition's other members and the Duke, who were leaving in a few days for Europe via the Congo River and the Atlantic. Thus ended the second part of the expedition.

The third part of the expedition, lasting from April to November 1908, is unfortunately not so well documented in the diary. This is the result of dispersed documentation (see below). One finds mostly short notices and one needs to work on the background of correspondence being preserved in the Berlin Museum[16]. The magnificent second volume published in 1924[17], however, shows that the scholar collected a huge volume of material and elaborated it perfectly.

The regions under study presented the conglomeration of different ethnic groups (Azande people, Abarambo, Momvu, Babira). From an administrative point of view it was possible to divide this extended territory located west to the Rwenzori into three districts: Oriental Province, that of the Aruwimi – Ituri River (southern) – and the northern area of the Uele River[18]. The well-preserved maps that accompany the diary, and the basic map, already published in 1912[19], helped to establish Czekanowski's route in this area. For better orientation we have to indicate two basic routes from east to the west: the former from Irumu to Avakubi, and latter from Faradje to Amadi, actually both following the rivers – the Aruwimi-Ituri in the former case and Uele in the second. We have also to indicate the main route from the south (Irumu) to the north via Adjamu, Gumbari to Vanckerchovenville and Yei.

Following the diary in a more detailed way we have to cross the area between Irumu and Adjamu, that is the territory inhabited by the Momvu people, as well as that of the Babira, and Balese. The documentation from this area is replete with rich linguistic material[20]. The social structure of Momvu, based on the clan system, was also of great interest to Czekanowski as it was clearly delineated by the territorial borderlines, an aspect in which these people differed from other groups such as the Babira. The explorer had plenty to do in this area: documenting the rich material culture, experiencing the magnificent musical instruments, learning local languages[21] and elucidating the social structure based on the concept of blood revenge.

The route across the virgin forest (undertaken in April 1908) was very exhausting for the caravan and for the explorer himself. Czekanowski's health was clearly impaired by the climate in the neighbourhood of the big swamp and by the exhausting heat. The caravan also had a difficult time: it had to follow very narrow forest paths. The danger of dysentery and other illnesses overshadowed this march. This explains the brevity of entries from those days, though the collected material is rich and extremely interesting. The friendly relations with the people bore many fruits.

After reaching Adjamu and the area of Gumbari (at the end of May 1908), the explorer went northwards towards Vanckerchovenville, arriving in the area of Azande. In this region he could notice not only a different culture but also a totally different mountainous landscape. The people of this area are generally seen not as the aborigines of this area, but as the descendants of other people formerly living here[22]. The social structure and genealogies of those people are of an uncommon interest. Geographically these people are divided into the western and eastern groups, though there may be also a southern group[23]. The distances between them may number hundreds of kilometres. The explorer had the opportunity of crossing several times into the territories of different Azande people. He was especially surprised by an oriental influence evidently visible in certain artefacts, and specifically in the tradition of dervishes. He also became fascinated with the beautiful Azande tales abounding with animal symbols, which he documented in detail.

Working in the "northern" area close to the Sudanese frontier, the explorer enjoyed the magnificent landscape that he had dreamt of in his early youth. From Dungu he turned westwards as far as Amadi (July 1908). During this long march he collected an impressive volume of linguistic and photographic material documenting this culture. He also had the opportunity to appreciate the artistic nature of the local people (beautiful houses, hair art, dresses). In the last part of this route, Czekanowski turned south-west going from the Poko toward Nala and Rungu, arriving finally at the already well-known Gumbari.

After returning east, the explorer turned to the south-east, via Tagba, Ingeleza, and Kilo, back to Irumi. From there he went once more towards the east, via Djangoba and Dhi, to Mahagi (September 1908), an area inhabited by Nilo-Hamitic people – that is back to the area of cattle breeders well known to him from Rwanda. Very important for our knowledge of these people are the results of a former researcher, Emin Pasha,[24] and the study by Mr. Van den Place, unknown to scholarship at the time.

This part of the expedition could be seen as the end of the big expedition. That is why the last three months, in spite of new discoveries and experiences, are seen as a time of preparation for departure. The comparison of these parts of the diary with earlier entries also reveals the differences between various colonial regimes. The Belgian administration in this part of Congo involved the local political structure in a very limited way only. Indeed, to the duties of the local governors in Congo belonged, above all, the delivery of a clearly defined quantity of crops (e.g. elephant tusks, caoutchouc). These local rulers[25] depended almost directly on the "Chef de District", and had only very limited authority, though quite often they had to make crucial decisions like those concerning the control of the watering system. The documents accompanying the diary (maps, sketches) as well as the preserved correspondence critically describe this coercive administrative policy. One may assume that this exploitative colonial policy depended on the fact that a variety of ethnic groups, some of whom were not well rooted, were living together in a single territory. This fact allowed the colonizers to exploit the inhabitants much more than in the more stable regions. The mass migrations, especially as a consequence of the wars that had been taking place in the last centuries, contributed evidently to this ethnic variety. The populations in the "inter-lake" area in the east, and in West Africa, were evidently more stable than those in the area dominated by the mixed population.

In many regions Czekanowski therefore had to deal with two different structures that evidently clashed, namely the colonial system and the tribal. Although his sympathies may have lain with the latter, he could ultimately not be independent of the colonial system, and in particular of the Belgian military stations such as Faradje, Irumu and Nepoko, which were helping him to deal with the harsh conditions. Thanks to good contacts with the Belgian clerks, he was also able to obtain maps and information.

Traditional vs. New Approaches

It is not only the matter of writing about their own health that distinguishes the diaries of Malinowski and Czekanowski. Most evident is the difference in methodology, very well described in Czekanowski's case by J-P Chretien[26]. Crucial for Czekanowski's methodology was his belief in the power of abstraction, thanks to which he expected to properly interpret the superficial representation of observed facts. Malinowski perceived culture more as a phenomenon of art, focusing on disclosing its deepest structure and concentrating on its transcendental references. One may assume that Malinowski was looking for new impulses in the culture of "others", which could be fruitful for his own reflection. This approach seems to be very close to the ideas of avant-garde artists of that time, among them close friends such as Stanisław Witkiewicz.

Although Malinowski is basically known as a functionalist, explaining the nature of social systems, his fascination with the phenomenon of creative art and his artistic sensitivity cannot to be neglected. The crucial point of methodological discussion is the essence of Malinowski's success. One should ask what was more crucial in his discoveries: was it his approach or the character of the material he had been studying? In the history of the discipline the first assumption is usually accepted.

The totally different conditions, under which these two scholars had to work, obviously left its mark on their interpretation. Indeed, African culture had been invaded for centuries by different influences from Europe and Asia, presenting in certain cases, such as Rwanda, a highly developed multi-strata structure of different dependencies. On the other hand, the culture of the Triobrand Isles explored by Malinowski was much more isolated, though, at the same time, highly developed. The monetary system was already operating in Rwanda at that time and there was no demand for shell currency. The power structure, so well described by Czekanowski and documented in his diary, could not be compared with the one discovered by Malinowski. The principles of taxation and those of personal obligations of particular citizens[27], revealed by Czekanowski, clearly illustrate the "mixture" of European and local systems.

The basic differences concern, however, the different conditions under which they both had to work. Czekanowski, unlike Malinowski, accepted the structure of the framework which he had to investigate, although his criticism, so well described by J-P Chretien[28], is not in question. He befriended colonial and local rulers (e.g. those of Azande), even Kings (Musinga, Kasagama) and local governors of particular provinces, often relaxing in their residences, as well as in missions and military stations. His diary and his correspondence written in seven languages document these friendships in a lively way. Before his departure he also wrote farewell letters to many of them[29].

The friendship and cooperation with missionaries was crucial for Czekanowski's work, especially at the beginning of his research. They actually modified his initial scepticism, whereas Malinowski did not accept missionaries, accusing them of the desire to annihilate authentic ethnic culture. Czekanowski, to the contrary, pointed to their friendly relations with the local people and especially to their defence of women against inhuman rites and an unjust social structure.

The basic question should also concern the relation to the researched. One should ask, who was closer to them, more transparent and who knew them better? The preserved documentation indicates that Czekanowski had identified people according to their personal or clan names, clearly avoiding such terms as the primitive or savage. This choice of terminology may confirm the degree of his affinity with the people he studied. Malinowski, on the other hand, very often used these pejorative terms. Another crucial issue is the hierarchy of values respected by scholars and their evaluation of contrasting local hierarchies. Czekanowski wanted to bring the researched subject closer to himself, to his own criteria and judgement. Should we explain that as the bias with which he was burdened?

When looking at Czekanowski's photographs, the impression is that he was happy to demonstrate how beautiful, skilled, elegant and proud the researched subjects were. By contrast, Malinowski's photos are much more "realistic". The impression is that Malinowski did not like the bearers of the culture he was studying, though their culture itself fascinated him.

Malinowski's relation to his subjects foreshadowed the contemporary "reality shows". This kind of position would have been completely unacceptable for Czekanowski. The latter, as mentioned, admired the strict principles, actually not only in scholarly work, but also in human relations. He admired the concept of balance. Malinowski's fascination with creative art sometimes pushed him to overlook the real facts[30], in the hope of discovering new impulses and explaining better the "unknown" culture. He did not always respect established scientific conventions when documenting anthropological facts. But Czekanowski's diary also contains brutal facts, which in one case of an extremely drastic experience, was commented on in Polish[31]. The ideal and the real overlap in both scholars' relations with the people. Despite some common points, the differences between these two scholars stand out: Czekanowski and Malinowski were two totally different personalities working with different methods and attitudes.

The Documentation

The huge volume of documentation, numbering about 1,200 pages, hundreds of photographs, 84 recordings of music, many maps and short sketches, and, finally, 160 letters written by Czekanowski in Africa, fascinates scholars. It does not mean, however, that this documentation is complete. Many pages are evidently lost, many links in chronology are in question, many questions are not answered. Most painful is the dispersal of some notices written in June and July of 1908, as well as those from the last two months. These gaps are only partly explained by the sickness of the explorer. One may suspect also the difficulties of supply, such as the lack of proper notebooks. Finally, it may be that a part of the proper documentation of that time, i.e. that being organized and rewritten, was lost.

Nevertheless, the diary itself rewards special attention. It is a long chain of observations and impressions complemented by a huge volume of scientific documentation. Czekanowski's personal comments are written mostly in German; the other material, as well as several interviews, is in French.

A careful study of the diary reveals an evident change in Czekanowski's approach. His first entries remind of a diligent report written for his professor who expected him to write three pages every day. This type of report does not neglect any place or fact, and is full of a variety of details. The author's relation with his environment evidently changed with time. His daily reports become progressively shorter, though often complemented by huge annexes of scientific documentation. It is also clear that the author in the later period, concentrated on chosen topics, trying to treat them comprehensively and finding out the basic principles important for the "structure" under study, though he never used this term. It is clear that his long stay in Nyundo (mission) and Nyansa (residence of Musinga), as well as in Kisiba and later in Fort Portal, were very successful in helping him to understand the culture he had come to study.

One may assume that in approximately two months (September 1907) the author changed his attitude, turning from superficial observation towards deep research. Nevertheless, he was still occupied with the taking of measurements, which was strictly demanded by his professor (Von Luschan) and he remained very loyal to his obligations, that is buying objects for museums. But the interviews at the markets and in the houses in which he stayed fascinated him more and more. This change away from the methods he had to implement contributed to conflicts with his colleagues and principals, but, fortunately, he could survive this tension thanks to the Duke's protection. His new attitude finally led him to the decision to be more independent, and to create the concepts of research independently. Progressively, he was constructing the idea of his final report and of his future publications. Fortunately for him this coincided with the ideas of the Duke. The diary confirms these changes on a limited scale only. Much more information may be found in the correspondence and the stories that Czekanowski liked to tell later in life.

The documentation between the period of 8 June and 7 July 1908 is particularly poor. According to the correspondence it is a consequence of the first attack of malaria he suffered. This is also true for the period between the end of December (1908) and February (1909). The last entries, starting with 22 February, actually document the period before departure. Although written almost every day, they are extremely short. They are snapshots rather than narratives, but give a basic picture of the area and events. Indeed, on his way back home, Czekanowski took a steamer from Bukoba to Entebbe, and from there with a small caravan, the gravely ill explorer was conveyed by donkey rickshaw towards the north, via Nimule, Nyonki and Redjaff until

Gondokoro, where on 1 April 1909 he took a boat to Cairo. After almost two years, the grand African expedition was at an end.

Despite his poor physical condition, Czekanowski was still observing and interpreting the countryside, probably considering this journey as his farewell to Africa. His outlook was at that time quite pessimistic. The area he was describing was, according to him, very poor: "the men are totally naked... as even chicken are hardly to be seen, and the houses are in terrible conditions ... the people are rather unfriendly and do not like to be investigated"[32]. To what extent this image is biased by the poor health of the observer remains unanswered. This last narrative presents images like that of a speedily running film, with the observer wanting to record as many impressions as possible in order to preserve them for his memory. His poor health at the time did not however suppress his passion for photography. The final places his expedition passed through (Redjaff) are documented by some pictures[33].

Conclusion

After almost a hundred years many questions posed by Czekanowski still demand answers. This applies mostly to the contemporary political situation and to the roots of conflicts and wars waged in present-day Africa. There are many questions asked by historians and sociologists trying to find the root causes of these political tensions. This discussion also concerns missionaries and their role in these societies. It is well known that opinions about missionaries and their role in society are very controversial. Many methodological concepts also ask for revision. At the same time many former ideas and interpretations do come back with renewed validity. The most promising is the recognition of traditional culture by contemporary African scholars and their vital interest in the history and culture and that which has disappeared. In many cases this interest and knowledge supports people's feelings of identity. It is important to know that their dynastic families have a long history and that their epic tradition complements history in the case where there had been no written sources.

Notes

1. See Chrétien, J.P. 2006. "Jan Czekanowski, Anthropology Pioneer in Africa's Great Lakes Region". In Pennacini, C. (ed.), *The People of the Moon-I Popoli della Luna, Ruwenzori 2006*, Catalogue of Exhibition, CahierMontagna, Torino, 237-240.

2. See Czekanowski, J. 1917. *Forschungen in Nil-Kongo Zwischengebiet.* Vol. 1, Klinkhardt & Biermann, Leipzig, 10-11.

3. In discussion with his daughter (AC) in February 1951.

4. His father's uncle-explorer of Siberia. In the vicinity of Irkutsk one finds a mountain named after him. See Zbigniew Wójcik, Aleksander Czekanowski, Wydawnictwo Lubelskie, 1982.

5. See Czekanowski, J. 1922. *Forschungen.* Vol. 4, 250-255.

6. See Malinowski, B. 1967. *The Diary in a Strict Sense of the Term,* John Hawkins and Assoc., New York.

7. See Czekanowski, J. n.d. *The African Diary (1907-1909),* manuscript in deposit of the University Library in Warsaw, sgn. RPS.D.I, 1, Vol. 8.

8. Unfortunately, the description of the travel between 9 April (departure from Zürich) and 30 May (landing in Mombasa) which concerned the trip by train to Naples and later by boat in the company of other members of expedition, was lost during World War II.

9. It concerns the excavation of the local cemetery, see Czekanowski, J. n.d., *The African Diary 1907-1909,* vol.1.

10. See Czekanowski, J. 1922. *Forschungen,* Vol. 4.

11. See Strizek, H. 2006. *Geschenkte Kolonien. Ruanda und Burundi unter deutscher Herrschaft,* Link's Verlag, Berlin.

12. See Czekanowski, J. 2001. *Carnets de route au coeur de l'Afrique. Des Sources du Nil au Congo,* Les Editions Noir sur Blanc, Montricher.

13. E.g. Czekanowski, J. *The African Diary,* Vol. 5, 2.

14. The reports of Stanley's expedition were published in a Polish newspaper in the late nineteenth century.

15. See Czekanowski, J. n.d. *The African Diary,* Vol. 7.

16. See Ethnologisches Museum, Berlin-Dahlem, Acta I/Mv, 967; *Die Reise Herzogs Adolf Friedrich zu Mecklenburg.*

17. See Czekanowski, J. 1924. *Forschungen.* Vol. 2, 3.

18. See Czekanowski, J. 1924. *Forschungen,* Vol. 2, ibidem.

19. See Czekanowski, J. 1912. *Ethnographische Uebersichtskarte des Nil-Kongo Zwischengebietes,* "Geographische Mitteilungen".

20. See Chrétien, J.P. 2006.

21. See the correspondence with Professor von Luschan, see Acta I Mv, 787, letters from, May, July.

22. They have been documented in this area since the eighteenth century, see Czekanowski, J. *Forschungen,* Vol. 2, 1924, 78-110.

23. See Czekanowski, J. 1912. *Ethnographische Übersichts Karte.*

24. Emin Pasha Mehmed, 1840-1892 (actually Eduard Schnitzer from Silesia), physician, explorer and governor of Equitorial province of Egyptian Sudan.

25. The so-called "Häuptlings" (German term used by Czekanowski)

26. Chrétien, J.P. 2006.

27. See Czekanowski, J. *The African Diary 1907-1909,* Vol. 7.

28. See op.cit.

29. See correspondence, Acta I, Mv, 967.

30. Comp. Czekanowska, A. 2004. "Pour un examen de rechercheur transparent- reflexions sur des journaux des universitaires classiques". In *Regards Croisses : Pologne-Europe-Afrique,* Ecole des Hautes Etudes en Sciences Sociales, Paris.

31. See Czekanowski, J. n.d., *The African Diary,* Vol. 7.

32. Czekanowski, *The African Diary,* Vol. 8, see also Czekanowski, J. 1924. *Forschungen,* Vol. 5, photos No. 131, 132.

33. See *Forschungen,* ibidem.

Language Use and Attitudes in the Rwenzori Region

Oswald K. Ndoleriire

Introduction

In this paper I will discuss questions of language use in the Rwenzori region, specifically the part of that region found in Uganda, the other part being in the Democratic Republic of Congo. This is the region of the fabled Mountains of the Moon that the Europeans first heard about during the time of Ptolemy.

I am a child of this area. I was born 50 kilometres away from the mountains, at the foothills of a 2,000 m high hill called Oruha. We used to collect grasshoppers (one of Uganda's delicacies) from the top of this hill, from which one can admire the full splendor of these mountains. From 1963 to 1968 I did my secondary school studies at Virika in Fort Portal – a place overlooking the mountains, just twenty kilometres away. Virika is the seat of the Roman Catholic Church in this area, and the White Fathers Missionaries gave the name at the end of the nineteenth century. It is said that the missionaries gazed at the snow-capped mountains from this place and asked the locals what snow was called in their native tongue, Rutoro. They were told it was *Ebirika*, and they named the place "Virika". The present cathedral at this place is called Our Lady of the Snow.

The Language Situation

The areas under study in this paper are the districts covering the Rwenzori Mountains and the immediate foothills. I will deal with the districts of Kasese and Bundibugyo, which were formerly part of the Kingdom of Toro and formed the counties of Busongora and Bwamba. To a lesser extent, the study will also cover the

143

district of Kabarole. Other areas comprising the rest of Toro region, Kyenjojo and Kamwenge, as well as the districts of Bunyoro Kingdom, particularly Kibaale and the district of Bushenyi in Ankore, should have been in the study, but could not be included due to time constraints.

The languages spoken in the area can be summarized as follows:

Ethnic Group Speakers[1]	Language/ Dialect	Location	Number
Babwisi	Lubwisi	Bundibugyo	68,499
Bakonzo	Lukonzo	Kasese Bundibugyo Kabarole	608,767
Bamba	Kwamba (Bulebule)	Bundibugyo	35,624
Banyabindi	Runyabindi	Kasese	13,920
Basongora	Rusongra	Kasese	10,599
Batoro	Rutoro	Kabarole Kasese Bundibugyo	606,931
Batuku	Rutuku	Bundibugyo	20,536
Batwa(Basua/ Bambuti/ Pygmies)	Luhuku	Bundibugyo	6,739
Venoma	Kwamba[2]	Bundibugyo	128

Other ethnic groups that have migrated to the area include, among others:

Group	Language
Banyankore	Runyankore
Bakiga	Rukiga
Banyarwanda	Runyarwanda
Baganda	Luganda

Kiswahili and English are also widely used in some areas of this region.

Language Affinity

Among the major languages spoken in this area, practically all are Bantu languages, Rwanba or Kwamba being the most distinct. The mutual intelligibility, based on the percentage of words in common, is the lowest in Kwembe, ranging from 31% between Kwamba and Lubwisi, 32% between Kwamba and Rutoro and 34% between Kwamba and Lukonzo [3].

Generally speaking, one can differentiate between two groups in this area: The Runyakitara group – made of Rutoro, Rusongora, Rutuku and Runyabindi – and the Lubwisi. All the above can be considered as dialects of Runyakitara [4]. Their mutual intelligibility is very high, generally above 80%. Lubwisi, however, shares with Rutoro 73% of words, which is still quite high compared to Lukonzo (57%). The other group is made up of non-Runyakitara languages, the most important being Lukonzo, but also Kwamba (Bulebule or Rwamba), as well as Luhuku. This latter group is made up of languages which are generally not mutually intelligible. For instance, the speakers of Lukonzo and Kwamba are sometimes neighbours, but their languages are far apart (only 34% shared vocabulary). As we shall see later, however, this does not seriously hamper inter-ethnic communication.

Language Use

I am greatly indebted to Syahuka Muhindo and Stanley Baluku for the important information I received from them on this section. I will particularly talk here about which language is spoken where, as well as the status of the language in a given area.

Lukonzo: This is the main language of the Rwenzori region, particularly in the mountain areas. It is the predominant language in Kasese and Bundibugyo Districts. Interestingly, in the latter district, previously called Bwamba, the predominant group is supposed to be the Bamba. In the past, the Bamba were understood to have two languages: the speakers of Kwamba or Rwamba and the speakers of Lubwisi. People knew that those who spoke Lubwisi could be understood while those who spoke Kwamba or Rwamba could not. Today the Bakonzo, the major group in Kasese, are also the major group in Bundibugyo.

Rutoro: This is one of the major dialects in the Runyakitara group. Together with Runyoro, which is very closely linked to it, it is spoken by more than 1.2 million people (i.e. 606,931 for Rutoro and 667,086 for Runyoro). As a matter of fact, these two dialects are often considered as one, and called Runyoro-Rutoro.

The advantage Rutoro has over Lukonzo is that the former was the language of primary education and local administration during the time when this area was part of the Toro Kingdom. For that reason, many Lukonzo speakers also spoke Rutoro. The other advantage that Rutoro has is that it was among the first languages that acquired an orthography in Uganda[5]. As such, the language was able to acquire some written literature. The first grammar of Rutoro was published by Maddox in 1902, entitled *An Elementary Lunyoro Grammar*. The Bible was translated into Rutoro soon after the grammar, but to this day it is yet to be translated into Lukonzo[6].

I was made to understand that most of the Bakonzo today, including the youth, do not understand and speak Rutoro. Since Rutoro is part of the wider Runyakitara language which is spoken in most of Western Uganda, the Bakhonzo can also understand dialects such as Runyankore, Rukiga, Runyaruguru, not to mention Rusongora, Runyabindi, Rutuku and to some extent Lubwisi, all spoken in the inner Rwenzori region[7].

I was also told that the Bakonzo, generally speaking, have the capacity to grasp and use other languages, not only the Runyakitara group. In the same way many of them do understand and communicate in Luganda, which is the most widespread language in Uganda in terms of use. Many Bakonzo are also at ease in Kiswahili, the regional language for Eastern Africa.

Lubwisi: This is a language spoken in Bundibugyo, especially on the lower parts of the mountain and towards the plains. These people have the advantage of speaking a language that could be considered a dialect of Runyakitara, and this facilitates communication with many other groups. Here again, it appears, the Bakonzo are more likely to understand Lubwisi than the Babwisi would be likely to understand Lukonzo.

Kwamba/Rwamba: Although the number of speakers of this language is quite limited, they are among the original inhabitants of this area, as pointed out earlier, at least by the time the colonialists came. It is understood that their language group as well as Lukonzo have more speakers in the Democratic Republic of Congo. In the DRC, the Kwamba speakers are known as Batalinge while the Lukonzo speakers are known as Banande.

As regards Kwamba/Bwamba speakers, they too were under Toro influence and many of them understand and can use Rutoro. Just like Bakonzo, many of their teachers studied in Rutoro-speaking areas, and this has to be reflected in the language medium at school. It is said that a relatively large number of them also understand Lukonzo.

Rusongora, Rutuku, and Runyabindi: These are essentially dialects of Runyakitara quite close to Rutoro. It is argued, however, that Runyabindi also shares much with Lukonzo, although the writer did not verify this. What is clear, however, is that Runyabindi and other Runyakitara dialects are mutually intelligible. In terms of communication, the speakers of the three dialects mentioned above have no problem communicating with Lukonzo speakers, for the reasons given earlier.

Language Acceptability

The term "acceptability" here is not used as we see it in modern grammar manuals (e.g. a sentence should be grammatical, acceptable and should have meaning). Here we are talking about the willingness of a people to make use of a given language, and I will describe the circumstances in which that occurs. We shall examine the different languages and dialects, and endeavour to explain the situations in which they are used.

English: This is the official language of the country, although on paper Kiswahili is also supposed to be an official language. As in other former colonies in Africa, this is the language of education and of upward mobility. The numbers of people in the Rwenzoris with a comfortable command of English are not readily available but the estimated number does not exceed 30% of the population. English is, therefore, not a language used in the family or in other social gatherings. It is a language for administration and education. It is definitely not a language for political rallies, where one would need an interpreter. It remains, however, the most prestigious language.

Kiswahili: This language is well understood especially in Kasese District. It is used for business, particularly along the Congo border. Most earlier traders were either Arabs or Indians and most of them used Kiswahili. This tradition has remained to some extent. It was also pointed out that Kiswahili is connected with Islam. This is understandable, since Arabs, many of whom spoke Kiswahili, introduced Islam.

Luganda: This is a very important language in Uganda and, as pointed out earlier, many people in the region understand it. Like Kiswahili, it is also a business language and is often heard in major towns. There is an enclave in the Lake Katwe area where many inhabitants are fishermen and are said to have migrated from Buganda.

Rutoro: This language is widely used and understood in the Rwenzori region for the reasons given earlier. Despite the stormy history between Rutoro speakers (the rulers) and the Lukonzo and Kwamba speakers (the ruled), it was found out that about 90% of the Bakonzo have no problem using Rutoro. Ethnic rivalries, apparently, do not interfere with language use.

The Bakonzo, particularly, traditionally discontinue conversing in their language and switch to a language that a third party may understand whenever such an occasion arises. This is part of their hospitality, and has undoubtedly helped in their capacity and potential to learn and use other languages.

Because of the Toro Kingdom past, many Bamba can also understand Rutoro and use it willingly. The plains are essentially Rutoro-speaking areas.

Kwamba/Rwamba: This language, whose speakers are quite restricted in number, is generally understood and used by the native speakers themselves. As seen earlier, other languages are available for them to communicate in with the outside world.

Rusongora, Rutuku, Runyabindi and Lubwisi: These Runyakitara dialects have few native speakers. The first three are sometimes confused with Rutoro and it is always difficult to differentiate them from Rutoro. Lubwisi has relatively more speakers and is also more distinct. Generally, these groups have difficulty understanding Kwamba or Lukonzo, but fortunately, the speakers of the latter languages have no problem communicating in Runyakitara.

The use of the above dialects is guaranteed by the fact that they are part of the wider Runyakitara, although it is not sure that they will survive as dialects of Runyakitara or sub-dialects of Rutoro.

Future Prospects

From the above exposition it can be said that there is a great degree of harmony in language use in the Rwenzori region. However, some problems remain and can be defined as follows:

- Some smaller languages, such as Luhuku, spoken by the Baswa (Pygmies) may be facing extinction because of the very restricted number of speakers[8].

- Some smaller Runyakitara dialects such as Rusongora and Rutuku may also face extinction as their speakers are sometimes mixed up with the mainstream Rutoro speakers.

- Problems of agreement about a unified orthography both for Lukonzo and Kwamba, as well as for Lubwisi, exist. This makes it difficult to implement the national language education policy, which stipulates that, as much as possible, children in the first years of primary education should study in their own languages. Lack of an agreed orthography compounds the problem of producing written literature.

However, the Ugandan government has created a relatively enabling environment, which encourages different ethnic groups to promote the use and development of their languages. In such circumstances, one hopes that Lukonzo and Kwamba speakers would mobilize their energies and do more to promote those languages. Furthermore, despite problems posed by the colonial languages, Lukowto and Kwambe speakers could link up with their counterparts in the Democratic Republic of Congo in an effort to promote their languages.

Conclusion

This paper shows how people circumvent linguistic barriers and find ways of communicating with their neighbours. It also highlights the exemplary language use of the Bakonzo, who do not hesitate to put aside past and even some present ethnic rivalries for better communication. All in all, the future of language use in the region looks bright, except in cases where some languages and dialects could become extinct; and should this happen, it would be a great loss of human heritage.

Bibliography

Chrétien, J.P. 2000. *L'Afrique des Grands Lacs: Deux mille ans d'histoire*. Paris: Aubier-Collection Historique.

Ladefoged, P. *et al*. 1971. *Language in Uganda*. Nairobi: Oxford University Press.

Ndoleriire, O. *et al*. (eds). 1996. *Runyakitara Studies* (3 Vols) Manuscript under publication.

Nyakatura, J.W. 1997. *Abakama ba Bunyoro-Kitara – Abatambuzi, Abacwezi, Ababiito*. St.Justin, Canada: W.H.Gagne and Sons.

Rubongoya, L.T. 1991. *A Modern Runyoro-Rutoro Grammar*. Cologne: Rudiger Kopper Verlag.

Rwagweri, Atwooki. 2003. *Toro and Her People: Past, Present and Future*. Kampala: The New Vision Printing and Publishing Corporation.

Uganda Bureau of Statistics (UBOS). 2005. *The 2002 Uganda Population and Housing Census – Main Report*. Kampala: Uganda.

Notes

1. Cf. 2002, Uganda Population and Housing Census, pp.52 and 53.
2. The Venoma are considered as a sub-group of Kwamba speakers.
3. Cf.Ladefoged et al., 1971, pp 70 and 71.
4. From the early 1990s, Makerere University scholars proposed that the mutually intelligible dialects of Western Uganda, Northern Tanzania and Eastern Congo should be known under the umbrella name of Runyakitara.

5. The Runyoro Bible was the second to be translated after the Luganda Bible in the very first years of the 1900s.

6. For the moment, Lukonzo speakers use the Kinande Bible from the Congo.

7. Inner Rwenzori region: i.e. the mountain areas and the areas immediately surrounding the mountains.

8. From some sources, it is claimed that the Baswa (or Batwa) living in the Rwenzori Mountains are only 75 in number, the others living astride the Uganda - Rwanda border.

The Kinande Bilingual Dictionary: A Tool for Learning about the Nande/Konzo Traditional Culture

Philip Mutaka

A danger that lurks for most African languages is their possible extinction as an aftermath of globalization. With UNESCO's recent interest in endangered languages, the need for revitalizing these languages has become urgent (UNESCO Ad Hoc Expert Group on Endangered Languages 2003). The question is how to respond to that need. One possible solution is the publication of dictionaries that are likely to attract the interest of the native speakers of these languages while bearing interest for the scientific community. This paper briefly presents the Kinande dictionary as the type of dictionary that could serve as a tool for learning about the Nande/Konzo culture. This chapter is organized as follows: Section 1 presents the features of the dictionary that are of interest to the linguistic community; Section 2 presents the features that are of interest to the Nande/Konzo speakers who are targeted as its primary users.

1. The Kinande dictionary with the linguistic community in mind

Since Kinande is a language that is fairly well known in the linguistic literature, mostly because of works by Bastin (2003), Mutaka and Hyman (1990), Mutaka (1994), Clements (1991), Gick Pulleyblank, Mutaka and Campbell (2006), among others, and also in the anthropological literature (Remotti 1994, Buffa, Facci, Pennacini and Remotti (1996), it is imperative to present, in the introductory section, background information to the grammar of Kinande. We thus discuss in the introduction such topics as the following: citation forms and root entries, verbal form entries, nominal entries, potential entries not necessarily included in the dictionary, the passive, the causative, other verbal extensions, potential lexical entries using the reflexive –yi-, the auxiliary –ya- "go", various tense and aspectual markers used in the main clause affirmative and main clause negative, some phonological processes such as ATR harmony, nasal + consonant alternations, penultimate lengthening, vowel gliding and deletion, tone realization, etc.

Notice that the choice of the lexical entry is not a trivial phenomenon. One needs knowledge of the use of a form in various contexts to determine its underlying tone representation. Consider the following forms discussed in the introduction for determining the tone of nouns. (The high tone is represented by the acute accent and the low tone is not represented.)

(1) a. okugúlu   leg
        omugóngo   back
        okúbóko   arm
        akáhúka   insect
        omúkali   woman
        omugenda   moon

    b. okugulú kwage   my leg
        omugóngo wage   my back
        okúboko kwage   my arm
        akáhúka kage   my insect
        omúkali wage   my woman
        omugenda wage   my moon

    c. okugulu kulíto   a heavy leg
        omugóngo mulíto   a heavy back
        okúbóko kulíto   a heavy arm
        akáhúka kalíto   a heavy insect

omúkali mulíto   a heavy woman
omugenda mulíto   the heavy moon

    d. Underlying forms in the entries:
       -gulu 15/6 (= singular: okugúlu, plural: amagúlu)
       -gongó 3/4 (=singular: omugóngo, plural: emigóngo)
       -bóko 15/6 (=singular: okúbóko, plural: amábóko)
       -húká (12/13) (=singular: akáhúka, plural: otúhúka)
       -kali % L (1/2) (=singular: omúkali, plural: abákali)
       -genda %L (3/4) (=singular: omugenda, plural: emigenda)

As shown in these forms, although the words for "leg" and "back" have the same surface form in isolation as in (1a), they differ when the possessive adjective or the adjective for "heavy" follows it as in (1b,c). This difference is captured in the underlying representation where –gulu "leg" has no tone whereas gongó "back" has a high tone on the last vowel. Similarly, the word for "insect" and "arm" have the same surface tones in isolation, but they differ when followed by the possessive adjective "my" or "heavy". Only –bóko "arm" has a H tone on the first vowel whereas –húká "insect" has a H on each of the vowels. A more correct tonal representation of this word is a single H linked to two tone bearing units (Mutaka, 1994). As for the words for "woman" and "moon," notice that they end in a low vowel in the various contexts. This has been indicated in the lexical entry by marking them with "%L", meaning that they end in a lexical low tone. A high tone on the penultimate vowel in a word in isolation that does not surface when the word is followed by the adjective, is phrasal and is not represented underlyingly. For more details on tone, see Hyman and Valinande (1985) and Mutaka (1994).

2. The Kinande Dictionary with Nande/Konzo Speakers in Mind

One crucial question that needs an answer and that guided the choice of the material included in the dictionary was: what would motivate a Nande or a Konzo speaker to consult this dictionary? Most probably, it would not be for checking the meaning of the words as he/she already knows. I found the idea of Kavutirwaki (the second author) who initiated this dictionary very compelling; he wanted it to be essentially educational. He recorded notes about the traditional beliefs of the Nande in the lexical entries where such explanations were likely to be appropriate. I have retained those explanations in the French version but did not include them in the English version as I mostly had the linguistic community in mind for this version.

To serve the educational purpose, we thought that Nande speakers would also consult it as a tool to help them learn better French and English. Very often, a native speaker might know the word in his language but he does not know the exact word in the official language. That is when he would need the dictionary. This is the reason why it was decided to write it as a bilingual dictionary, in two separate versions, Kinande-English and Kinande-French.

One other motivation that would motivate Nande/Konzo speakers to consult the dictionary is cultural. Because many Nande speakers grew up outside their native territory and live in cities such as Kinshasa, Kisangani and Bukavu where they cannot experience the daily traditional Nande way of living, the compilers thought they would be interested to use the dictionary to learn more about the Nande culture. That is why the appendices contain sections on Nande names, phrasal expressions, and medicinal plants. Notice that each of these sections is important for a native speaker. With the aid of the dictionary, a native speaker can now choose a more appropriate name for his child, learn new phrasal expressions to express certain realities, or know what medicinal plant is likely to help him to treat certain diseases in case he is not able to obtain more appropriate medication prescribed by a doctor.

For cultural reasons, also included is a section in the appendix on taboos and prohibitions, and on the traditional beliefs, more particularly, the world of spirits as conceived by the Bakonzo. This is a contribution by two Bakonzo speakers and is of special interest for the Banande because they consider Bakonzo and Banande as the same language spoken by people who share the same traditional beliefs. It is true that certain beliefs may be prevalent in the Bakonzo area because the Bakonzo live near Mount Rwenzori. One such belief involves Kitasamba, the spirit of the Rwenzori mountain that the Banande from Butembo will hardly recognize as a member of their spiritual world.

The English version of the dictionary includes an article on traditional medicine by Stanley Baluku. It contains very useful knowledge that the Bakonzo and the Banande will certainly want to read as a way to learn more about their culture.

The remainder of this paper provides samples of these sections to give a feel to the reader of what this dictionary contains.

Samples of lexical entries from the French version of the dictionary (Kavutirwaki and Mutaka, 2006):

ékị́nda *(rad. -ịnda H) n 7/8.* le cadavre, la dépouille mortelle. On a généralement très peur d'un cadavre car l'on croit que l'esprit du mort peut se montrer. Quand un des conjoints meurt, le survivant se couche la première nuit le long du cercueil étendu à terre. Pendant ce temps tous les amis pleurent et les femmes surtout gémissent, se roulent par terre et pleurent en criant très fort. Toutes les personnes amies du défunt gardent cette attitude pendant une semaine "la semaine du deuil". A la fin de cette semaine, le survivant est conduit à la rivière où il se baigne en se tournant vers l'aval. Ensuite on lui coupe tous les cheveux à ras. C'est à partir de ce moment qu'on porte les habits de deuil noirs en général, habits qu'on enlevera le jour de la levée du deuil dans une grande réjouissance populaire.

ekísálị *(rad. -sálị́) n 7/8.* gésier. Lorsqu'on égorge une poule pour un visiteur, on doit toujours lui donner le gésier. C'est de cette façon qu'il sait que la poule a été égorgée pour lui. Et s'il y a plusieurs gens qui partagent la nourriture avec un poulet, on identifie celui à qui appartient le poulet lorsqu'il prend le gésier. **wanáhịrịry' ekísálị́ ky' omo mbóka kwéhi**

*erí*herúka *(rad. -héruk-) v intr.* aller dans la maison nuptiale; se marier. Après l'achèvement de la dot, au soir du jour fixé, un cortège formé des membres des deux familles et de tous les amis des futurs époux se forme, ces derniers en tête, progresse à partir de la maison paternelle de la fiancée vers la résidence du futur mari. L'on chante, l'on danse, l'on proclame dans les chants les qualités de l' un et de l' autre. Pendant ce temps et longtemps encore après la fin du cortège, la tante maternelle de l'homme se tient à côté de la jeune fille, lui transmet conseils et façons d'agir dans sa nouvelle vie de mariée, sans oublier certaines techniques pratiques relatives à l'acte conjugal qu'elle va devoir faire pour la première fois. Car à la fin de la procession, lorsque la jeune fille entre sous le toit du jeune homme, en ce moment précis, le mariage est conclu. Donc, comme ils vont devoir faire leur première union matrimoniale, si réellement la jeune fille est encore vierge, le drap blanc sur lequel ils dorment sera inévitablement taché de rouge. Ainsi au lever, tous les anciens du village attendent à l'extérieur pour être tous témoins de la virginité de la mariée. Si tel est le cas, le jeune homme sera obligé de récompenser les parents de sa jeune femme. Il leur payera une chèvre pour avoir ainsi bien su garder la virginité de leur fille. Cette description concerne uniquement le premier mariage entre un jeune homme et une jeune fille.

*erí*tsúma *(rad. -tsúm-) v.* maudire On maudit soit par simples paroles imprécatoires, soit par un certain cérémonial qui consiste notamment à ôter sa culotte en public (ou esquisser uniquement ce geste) et traîner son séant par terre. Si l'on fait cela pour son enfant, c'est là la plus forte des malédictions. La mère peut aussi maudire en soulevant seulement son sein à l'encontre de son enfant.

omúlímu *(rad. -límu)* *n 3/4.* l'esprit. C'est l'esprit animant l'homme et dont le départ provoque la mort de celui-cị Ces esprits sont parfois nombreux et viennent attaquer un être humain. **Alí kó bálímu** ou **alí kó mílímu** ou encore **alí kó bírímu** pour dire il/elle est possédé(e). Nos ancêtres sont considérés comme existant aujourd'hui sous cette forme. Quand il y a un tremblement de terre, les parents demandent à tous leurs enfants de tenir les mains levées. Ainsi ils saluent les esprits qui passent. Peut-être y en a-t-il de nos ancêtres! Quand la femme prépare de la viande d'une chèvre, elle met sur des bâtonnets autour du foyer quelques morceaux délicieux (foie, coeur, etc.) et dit que c'est le repas que mangeront les ancêtres (les esprits et ancêtres). Même si ces morceaux de viande sont mangés la nuit par les souris, on dira que ce sont les ancêtres qui les ont consommés.

As shown in these entries, cultural information is associated with a word. Since this type of cultural information is not part of the English version, I translate the last entry to indicate to English readers what this information involves.

omúlímu *(root. -límu)* *n 3/4.* a spirit. It is the spirit that gives life to a human being and if it leaves the body, the person dies. There are all sorts of spirits and these may sometimes come to attack a human being. In such a case, people say: **Alí kó bálímu** or **alí kó mílímu** or else **alí kó bírímu** to mean "he is possessed". It is believed that our ancestors continue to exist in the form of spirits. When there is an earthquake, parents ask their children to raise their hands. They thus greet those spirits who happen to pass by. It is possible that one of the spirits may be one of their ancestors. When a woman cooks goat meat, she puts some delicious pieces of meat (liver, heart, etc.) on sticks around the fire and says that it is the meal for the ancestors (the spirits and the ancestors). Even if mice eat these pieces of meat at night, the Nande will say that it is the ancestors that ate it.

The following excerpts in English are from Mutaka and Kavutirwaki (2006). The same information features in the French version of the dictionary, that is, Kavutirwaki and Mutaka (2006).

From Appendix 1: Phrasal expressions:

abíríbinduk' okó lu̧kwi̧: she has got her menses (lit. she has gone round the log)

abíríkíta: she has got her menses (lit. she has gone the other way)

abíriya oko mugeséra: she has got her menses (she has gone to the moon)

bihwére omo nderê: let those things end here (lit. let them finish in the dry banana leaves)

bwámánger' eyi̧hyâ: I had a diarrhea (lit. it became light for me outside)

erihanda omútíma: to not be afraid (lit. to plant the heart)

eri̧heni̧a pe: to refuse categorically (lit. to be white completely)

erilyata ahísi: to refuse categorically (lit. to trample down)

wagenda wáyitwala: do not go (lit. you left you brought yourself)

wáheri̧ré ng' esyónzole: you have disappeared for a long time (lit. you have disappeared like white body marks)

wáholá kera: you do impossible things a normal person should not do (lit. you died long ago)

wámályata omómbátso: you have engaged in a terrible affair (lit. you trample on the wetting instrument of the blacksmith. It is forbidden to step on that instrument)

wámáhi̧sya omulhongo: sit decently (since you are showing your genital parts.) Syn: **wámákunamíra**

wámáyitonger' okw' i̧kála: you are telling a secret in the presence of a person who will betray you (lit. you are telling a secret on the ember)

wakóli̧re omó lw' eBírunga: you arrive just when we finish eating (lit. you stayed in the steep hill of Virunga (a volcano)).

From Appendix 2: The names

1. Chronological order

Mųsókį. Normally, **omųsókį** is someone who leaves his clan and settles with a different clan. He is given a plot of land to cultivate and he pays tribute to the chief of the clan every year. Literally, the term means "the one who crosses" and it derives from erísóka (to cross). As a name given to the first female child, Mųsókį has two different interpretations: (a) by analogy, a girl who is newly married leaves her family and her clan in order to join her husband's family and clan. The union of the couple is a pact between their clans and their families. A girl born from such a union is thus the consecration of such a pact; (b) on the day of her wedding, the young girl crosses one or several rivers in order to reach the village of her husband.

2. Perturbation of order

Kagwálįna (on whom a name falls). This name derives from the verb erigwâ (to fall) and lįna or erįna (name). It is a euphemism for Muhíndo or Mbíndule. It is given to a child who would have had the same name as his father or his grandfather. Since in the Nande tradition it is a taboo for a woman to pronounce the name of her father-in-law or of her husband, the child is given such a name in order to prevent the violation of that taboo. Kagwálįna (or Kawálįna) means that fate caused the child to bear the same name as his father or one of his grandfathers.

3. The given names

A. The place of birth.

e.g. **Kanzíra** (the one of the road). A name given to a child born during a trip, that is, when the mother was on the road.

B. The weather, the time.

1. **Kalúmbį** (small fog). A child born when there was fog.

C. Physical characteristics

1. **Kábúkê** (the one of smallness). A very slender child at birth.
2. **Kalı̧́mbwı̧̂** (the one who has gray hair)

D. State of health

e.g. **Kyámákyâ** (it is daylight). It is daylight at last before the baby is born or a relative dies. This name expresses some kind of relief as the parents were worried that someone would die before daylight.

E. Difficulties of begetting the child

e.g. **Kángitsi** or **Kákitsi** (a subject of worry). The labor was so long that everybody was worried that the mother or the child would die in parturition.

F. The gestation

e.g. **Banémô** (they (i.e. the children) are inside).This name is also given to a male child whose mother was believed to be barren.

G. Death in the family or in the village

1. **Mútsuba** or **Nzúbâ** or **Músubáhô** (the person who replaces, the one who comes back). Somehow the Nande believe in reincarnation; someone who died may resuscitate through the birth of his brother or sister. Nzúbâ means the resuscitated.
2. **Kyábų** (garbage).
3. **Syágúswâ** (he should not be thrown away). This name is given to a female or a male child born after several other dead children.
4. **Kavutirwáki**, more exactly **Kabų̧tı̧́rwákı̧** (why is this child born again? Is it not enough that other children have died before him?)

H. Social events

e.g. **Kándara** (small xylophone). The word designates a musical instrument used for dancing in honor of a dignitary or for putting an end to certain ritual ceremonies such as circumcision, a sacrifice to God or to a Higher Spirit which lasts several days. A child born during such a period is given the name of Kándara.

I. Socio-economic situations

e.g. **Nzáma** (the poor). This name is given to a male child born while his parents were experiencing economic hardship.

J. The daily activities

e.g. 1. **Mųhésį** (the blacksmith)

2. **Kịkųmų** (a big healer)

K. The individual habits

e.g. **Kámabų** (a fan of beer). This name is given to a male child who seems to like beer and whose father is a drunkard. It is also given to a child born while beer was being brewed in the family.

L. The proverbial names

e.g. **Magúlu** (legs), from the proverb **magulu mangú ni mabuy' ịwịtịre** (the quick legs are a good thing if you catch something good; to be present at any event is good as long as one benefits from it). This proverb is meant for a person who goes everywhere where there is an important event. At times he might benefit from the fact of being present at a given event, but there are also some other times when his presence might turn out to be the beginning of his own misfortune. When given to a male child, the name of **Magúlu** may translate the complaint of the mother who considers that she is not respected by the family of her husband; it is a way of telling her in-laws that she regrets having come to their family.

M. Spiritual names

e.g. **Nyábingi** (the mother of abundance). In the world of Nande spirits, Nyabíngi is the goddess of abundance. A special cult is even devoted to her. A female child who shows signs of being connected to her by acting as her medium, is given her name in order to perpetuate her presence within the family. It might also happen that Nyábingi communicates her desire to have a female child dedicated to her through a dream or a medium. In that case, the parents are compelled to give her name to the first female child that is born after that.

From Appendix 3: medicinal plants

A few words to introduce this appendix are in order. Medicinal plants are a cultural phenomenon which is in danger of extinction. This is true for Kinande as well as for other African languages. Notice that the UNESCO fund providers, when they give funds for endangered languages, are not always be aware that, even for widely spoken languages, there are aspects of the language that might be in danger. It is important that such endangered aspects of the language be preserved. Medicinal plants are such an endangered aspect. The authors of the dictionary made it a priority to obtain the names of medicinal plants and record them in the dictionary. Notice that this knowledge is not only precious for the Nande/Konzo people as part of their cultural lore, but it is the kind of information that may be exploited by scientists in search of new medications. If various African cultures were to make available their medicinal plants, this would offer a very rich array of potential sources for developing new medications. Before the arrival of the white people in Africa, people used to treat certain diseases and even today, there are certain diseases which are better treated with traditional medicine. I am not talking of witchcraft, but of the use of medicinal plants with curative properties.

Another feature of the dictionary related to medicinal plants is the treatment of certain diseases. If one thinks about it, why would a Munande use the dictionary? The authors thought that one of the attractions of the dictionary would be the information readers would find for combating certain diseases that are prevalent in the Nande area. Such diseases are poisoning, AIDS, typhus, etc. Here are samples of disease treatment as recorded in the appendix to the dictionary.

Tooth decay

éndugunda (wild aubergine). Fry the fruit on the fire, collect the black ashes. It is preferable to use a fruit that has thorns. One should grind that fruit after having fried it, and then one sifts the ashes that result from the frying; add some table salt (esérwê), mix the whole concoction and keep it in a container. To administer it, take a pinch of that product with the fingers and put it on the tooth for a week.

Poison

omutundúla or **omunundúla**, a type of plant local people use to make brooms (ekifagío). Take the leaves with the yellow seeds of the plant. Dry them inside the house. While drying cover them with a light cloth in order to avoid dirt that flies could eventually deposit on them. Then, one should pound them and sift those dry leaves, and put the resulting powder into a box. Make sure you do not put that powder in a crystal container, to avoid humidity. To administer it, take a pinch of that powder with three fingers, or take a small amount and swallow it with a small quantity of water. It is highly recommended to keep that powder within reach whenever one suspects an eventuality of being poisoned. One could pretend go to the toilets and take that powder, and then, when one gets back from the appointment where one suspects to have been poisoned, one should take some more. The powder is a particularly effective antidote against a type of poison called "akaruho".

Typhus

omurubaíni or **omwarubaíne** (Neem tree). Put 5 leaves in a litre of water, boil them for 30 minutes. Take a glass of this water in the morning, at noon, and in the evening for 6 days. According to Dr. Kamabu (personal communication), this concoction is highly effective for treating typhus. Those leaves also treat malaria. I wish to point out that the genuine name of this plant is unknown. It is a plant that has been imported but which is being grown in several areas of the Nande land. The plant is particularly well known in Kenya (from where I obtained the term). From what an informant of the Luhya ethnic group in Kenya told me, its name means "the plant that treats 40 diseases."

AIDS

éngaka or **ekítenende** (aloe vera). Use aloe vera leaves that are four years old. Cut them into small pieces after washing them carefully. Boil them in water. Take half a cup three times a day. Also, twice a week, use the viscous liquid obtained from the inside of the aloe vera. After mixing it with a little water, use it for an enema. The "cure" will take three months (Mutaka and Bolima, 2004).

To conclude, I wish to reiterate that one of the best strategies to motivate Africans to become interested in their cultures is to publish dictionaries, such as the Kinande dictionary, that feature linguistic know-how of interest to the linguistic community, cultural knowledge associated with certain lexical entries, and cultural knowledge as reflected in certain domains of their daily life: e.g. names, phrasal expressions, terminology of medicinal plants and treatment of certain diseases with medicinal plants.

I would like to end this article by emphasizing the fact that further documents about the cultural heritage of the African people need to be produced, and hopefully translated in languages of wider communication. Such documents could include proverbs, legends, lullabies, traditional games, etc. It is our wish that, in addition to such documents, further documents that emphasize the cultural development of the African people be also produced. Such documents could be written in languages of wider communication and then be translated into African lingua francas such as Swahili and also in local languages such as Kinande for the Nande speakers. It is our wish that our partners in the developed world who have access to funding be our advocates for seeking funds to produce such documents, including the dictionaries. One useful suggestion is, for example, for western universities to have a section in their libraries that contains documentation that is likely to be useful for the group objects of these investigations. As their researchers do fieldwork and as they witness problems faced by the people they work with they can propose solutions published in such works and that might have worked in some other areas. Western universities could thus store such useful literature and seek funds from their governments to enrich this type of useful documentation.

Bibliography

Buffa, C., Facci, S., Pennacini, C. & Remotti, F. 1996. *Etnografia Nande III: musica, danze, rituali.* Torino: Il Segnalibro.

Bastin, Y. 2003. "The Interlacustrine Zone (Zone J)". In D. Nurse & G. Philippson (eds.). *The Bantu Languages.* London: Routledge.

Clements, G. 1991. "Vowel Height Assimilation in Bantu Languages".*Working Papers of the Cornell Phonetics Laboratory,* 5, Ithaca, N.Y.: Cornell University, 37-76.

Gick, B., Pulleyblank, D., Mutaka, N.M. and Campbell, F. 2006. "Low Vowels and Transparency in Kinande Vowel Harmony". In *Phonology,* 23.1. (Forthcoming).

Hyman, L. & Nzama, V. 1985. "Globality in the Kinande Tone System". In Goyvaerts, D. (ed.) *African Linguistics: Essays in Memory of M.W.K. Semikenke.* Amsterdam: John Benjamins, 239-260.

Kavutirwaki, K. & Mutaka, N.M. 2006. *Dictionnaire Kinande-Français Index Français-Kinande*. Musée Royal de l'Afrique Centrale-Tervuren, Belgique, Ms.

Mutaka, N.M. 1994. *The Lexical Tonology of Kinande*. Munich: Lincom Europa.

Mutaka, P. & Bolima, F. 2004. *Wish I had Known*. Yaounde: Editions SHERPA.

Mutaka, N.M. & Kavutirwaki, K. 2006. *A Kinande-English Dictionary with an English-Kinande Index*. Musée Royal de l'Afrique Centrale-Tervuren, Belgique, Ms.

Mutaka, N.M. & Hyman, L. 1990. "Syllable and Morpheme Integrity in Kinande Reduplication. *Phonology,* 7, 73-120.

Remotti, F. 1994. *Etnografia Nande II: Ecologia, cultura, simbolismo*. Torino: Il Segnalibro.

UNESCO Ad Hoc Expert Group on Endangered Languages. 2003. "Language Vitality and Endangerment." Ms. Paris: UNESCO.

Banana Groves and Tree Tombs: "Disappearing" or "Remaining" among the Banande of Northern Kivu (EasternDemocratic Republic of the Congo)[1]

Francesco Remotti

Against the forest

The Banande (to use the name by now established in both ethnographical and bureaucratic fields), or WaNande (to adopt a term closer to local pronunciation), are a large ethnic group of Bantu farmers (currently calculated as numbering about two to three million). Situated in the region of northern Kivu, in the eastern part of the Democratic Republic of the Congo (the former Zaire), they occupy a territory (the Bunande) which lies on the equator, stretching from 28° to 30° longitude east, and from 1° 26' latitude north to 1° 20' latitude south. The Bunande is dominated for the most part by the Mitumba mountain chain that acts as a watershed in a north-south direction between the basin of the Congo (to the west) and the basin of the Nile (to the east). Proceeding towards the west from the peaks of the Mitumba mountains, the slopes descend gradually to flatter plains, entirely dominated by the equatorial forest of the Congo, while towards the east the slopes fall sharply towards Lake Edward (916 metres above sea level). Once, the Bunande was almost completely covered by the great equatorial forest and the Banande distinguished themselves in their history and culture by intense and programmed activities of deforestation. Now settled for various centuries in this region of the Congo, the Banande are nevertheless aware that their origins are 'elsewhere'. In the historical reconstructions that the traditional chiefs in particular are wont to provide, a name constantly referred to is the Kitara, understood by them to be a region of western Uganda which their ancestors had left in search of land to conquer and cultivate. The first migratory movements from the savannas of western Uganda (present-day Toro) to the mountains and forests of the Congo, encircling Lake Edward to north or south, can be placed with a certain amount of accuracy in the seventeenth and eighteenth centuries. The reasons for these movements can in turn be traced to the farmers' hunger for land as they would have had to compete with pastoral populations in their original areas, but demographic pressure, which has always characterized the Banande, can also not be excluded, neither can political pressure from kingdoms that had emerged in the meantime in western Uganda (from Bunyoro to Bunyankole, and most recently Toro).

Despite having had contact with the Ugandan kingdoms, as mentioned above, the Banande have never established a unified kingdom of their own. It is most probable that only under Belgian colonization did the Banande effect a certain centralizing of political power, which led to the formation of *chefferies* (chiefdoms), thanks to which the whole territory was divided up and organized for administrative purposes. From the colonial period to independence and up to today the most important *chefferies*, from north to south, are those of the Bashu, the Baswagha, the Bamate, and the Batangi; certainly, in the pre-colonial period the Banande experienced, above all a spread and fragmentation of power. This is probably a consequence of the type of territorial conquest effected, that is the fight against the forest, which they engaged in as soon as they had entered the eastern regions of the Congo. The fight against the forest was not conducted by any unified political organism, but by a series of groups or clans, who chose a particular point from where to attack the forest and became specialized in forming not just warriors, but "tree fellers" (*abakóndi*) in following in the wake of a "chief" (*ómwami*).

This strategy of penetration and infiltration of the forest required a flexible and even disjointed political organization, which undoubtedly facilitated and made it possible. The pattern of this power structure can be seen as a consequence of this process of segmentation, which comprises a few fundamental elements: in the first place, the figure of the *ómwami*, originally seen as a sort of commander who knows how to guide his men (the *abakóndi*) in their conquest of the territory; in the second place – as the conquest gains ground, establishing genealogically and politically connected villages – figures of secondary leaders, who end by taking titles and positions of a certain stability. This is why, next to the central figure of the *ómwami*, we find that of the *omúkulu* (older brother of the *ómwami*) and that of the *éngabwe*: the first (the *omúkulu*) has religious roles and the second military ones. But – as proposed elsewhere – "it is necessary to think of a proliferation of titles rather than a precise division of roles, duties and powers" (Remotti, 1993b:49). In fact, it is perfectly normal to come across the figures of the *isé-mwami* (sometimes coinciding with that of the *omúkulu*), the *tsongó-mwami*, the *isé-mumbo*, the *omusókolo*, and so on. All these figures are part of the *ómwami*'s "family" in a wider sense – *ekíhanda* – and in fact bear the general title of *abákama*. Along with the stabilization of the conquest of land in this or that place (destruction of the forest and, as a result, construction of permanent villages and fields) a sort of social, political and economic stratification emerged with the *ómwami* at its top, immediately followed by the *abákama* (the above-mentioned secondary figures); then the *abasóki*, described by some authors as "vassals", and finally the *abagúndâ*, the "ordinary people" (Remotti, 1993b: 30):

ómwami
↑↓
abákama
↑↓
abasóki
↑↓
abagúndâ

To understand the proliferation of the figures of the *abákama*, I will not enter into a more detailed analysis of social stratification (for which I refer to the text mentioned above), but only underline two aspects that can be considered as most significant for the issues dealt with in this paper: the first is the existence of a social differentiation, which will also manifest itself in different burial procedures; the second concerns the connection between this stratification and the distribution and use of the land, on one hand, and the taxes for using the land on the other. Until recently the Banande did not buy or sell land. It was, instead, obtained – as we have seen – thanks to the work of the *abakóndi*, literally torn away from the forest; not even the *ómwami* was considered owner of the land. He was, instead, the figure mainly responsible for the conquest and then the distribution of the land, as were the *abákama* in respect of the *abasóki*, and these in respect of the *abagúndâ*. The social entity that mostly held titles of possession to the land was the group or clan (*ekíhanda*) that had effected the deforestation of a certain part of the territory (*ekíhúgo*), winning its battle against the forest. The *ómwami*, therefore, was the chief of this group (*ekíhanda*) in relation to a certain territory (*ekíhúgo*) that was taken, not from other groups, but from the forest (*omúsítu*). The distribution of the land obviously took into consideration the social stratification outlined above, starting from the top (*ómwami*) down to the mass of small farmers or ordinary people (*abagúndâ*). In its turn, the annual tax (*omúháko*), expressed in goats, rose up the social scale, even if most of the livestock collected in this way was then redistributed in the form of donations and sacrifices: as a norm of hospitality the *abákama* who receive goats from the *abasóki* are in fact expected to offer those same *abasóki* part of the goats received in the form of a banquet (Remotti, 1993b:31).

As is only natural, the earth (*omutáka*) occupies a central position in this society of farmers; but the earth (*omutáka*) or, better, the territory (*ekíhúgo*) must not be separated from the violent and destructive process that enabled it to be torn from the forest. In considering the Banande, one cannot forget that the land once belonged to the forest. Elsewhere (Remotti, 1994), it has been shown how the conquest of the territory is expressed in Kinande (the Banande's language) with a term that contains this element of violence and destruction: *erítw'ekíhúgo* (to conquer a territory), where *erítwa* is a verb that means "to cut out"; to conquer a territory is therefore "to cut out a territory", that is, to destroy the forest by felling its trees and burning what remains. The concept of land is central, but it is contained in a process, in a series of phases, that can be described like this:

a)   the land belongs to the forest;
b)   the forest is destroyed;
c)   the land is conquered and occupied by men.

First, the land belonged to the forest, then to men; but this passage is only possible thanks to the destructive force of the *abakóndi*. It is not by chance that the Banande, when pressed to define themselves, do not describe themselves as cultivators or farmers (*avalími*), but in the first place, and proudly, as *abakóndi*, tree fellers, forest destroyers. As demonstrated elsewhere, the Banande do not identify themselves so much in their present culture of farmers, as in the (destructive) process of its formation (Remotti, 1994:141-142). The outcome of the process, the objective that inspired the Nande culture in its historical development, corresponds, without doubt, to the conquest and occupation of the land: men, therefore, took the place of the forest; men with their settlements took the place of trees. This replacement of a mighty and immense natural context with a cultural reality has been the objective of Nande culture, at least since the Banande, a few centuries ago, moved towards and against the great equatorial forest, accomplishing in this way their specific anthropo-poietic aim: they conceived the realization of their humanity by engaging in a battle against the forest, occupying the territory that previously belonged to the forest and its inhabitants.

The Territory and its Categories

What does occupying the territory mean (*erítw'ekíhúgo*)? It means, very concretely, to establish villages and to plant banana trees around each one. It is certainly no chance that the expression "to establish (to found) a village" (*erítw'omuyí*) contains the same verb in Kinande that was encountered in the expression "to conquer a territory" (*erítw'ekíhúgo*): *erítwa*, that is, "to cut out". "To conquer a territory" corresponds to the b) phase of our diagram; "to found a village" gives sense and content to phase c). But even in the definition of phase c), that of the real anthropoization of the territory, the verb *erítwa* is maintained, as if one wanted to preserve the memory of the destructive process that is its premise and unavoidable condition. As we will see further on, the forest, destroyed and lacerated, remains on the physical and mental horizon of Nande culture, and we will even see a sort of return of the forest; but once it has been destroyed and made to withdraw, the Banande establish or build their human world following a precise and consistent ecological scheme. From the point of view of the territory's organization this scheme is basically composed of two elements: the village, where men live, and the banana grove that surrounds it on every side. From an ecological perspective we could summarize this model with the following formula:

$$H = V + B$$

Here humanity (*H*) fulfils itself in an articulate reality that consists of the village (*V*) and of this sort of permanent and inescapable appendage or adjunct, the banana grove (*B*). Even if, today, we are witnessing a few exceptions and seeing this model disintegrate here and there, it is, nevertheless, undeniable that the formula *H = V + B* has been a constant and peculiar characteristic of Nande culture, especially when compared to other cultures (above all the Bambuti pygmies) present in the forest.

To understand the significance of the formula *H = V + B* and to approach the central topic of our analysis one must consider the principal categories by means of which Nande space is organized:

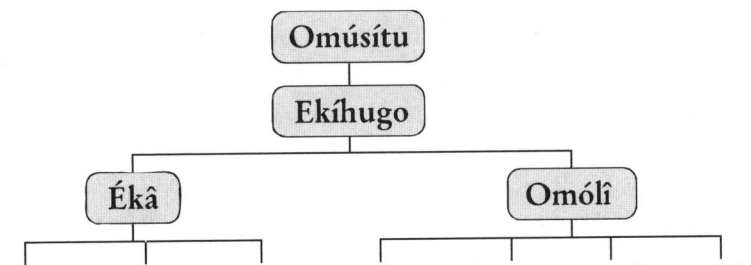

The diagram proposed here is organized on four levels and must be read both in a diachronic and in a synchronic sense. The first level, starting at the top, represents phase a), dominated by the exclusive presence of the forest ("here, once, there was nothing but *omúsítu*"). The second level coincides instead with phase b), the conquest of the forest and the delimitation of the "territory" (*ekíhúgo*). The third and fourth levels include, instead, the categories by means of which the territory has been organized and anthropized. In particular, the third level is formed of two general categories that subdivide the whole Nande territory: *ékâ* and *omólî*. *Ékâ* is the "village". As seen in the previous paragraph, there is however another term for the village: *omuyí*. The difference between *ékâ* and *omuyí* is semantic: while *omuyí* is the village in itself or a village in general, *ékâ* is ones' "own" village. It is important to observe that the two largest territorial categories are not *omuyí* and *omólî*, but *ékâ* and *omólî*; that is, the concept of village conveys a sense of "property" or, better, of "belonging" that structures Nande space. *Omólî*, a concept that indicates everything external to *ékâ*, stands in contrast to *ékâ* (the village "of" an individual or a family, the place where one lives and belongs to).

The fourth level of the diagram contains the subdivisions of the categories of *ékâ* and *omólî*. *ékâ* (ones' own village) is in fact composed above all by the hut where one lives (*ekitétéya*), by an open space (*ekíbúga*) around which the huts are arranged and by the *ékyagándâ*, the men's hut. It must be stated immediately that what we are describing is the traditional village where the huts (both the *ekitétéya* and the *ékyagándâ*) were built of materials of vegetable origin and on a circular plan. Today the *ekitétéya* has almost completely vanished, often being replaced – starting from the period of colonization – by homes on square plans, with walls of dried mud and roofs of metal sheets. The *ékyagándâ*, instead, still maintains its traditional style: strictly circular, with two entrances that face each other without any form of closure, and a roof of straw. The *ekíbúga* is the space of beaten earth in front of the house: it is constantly kept free of weeds and dust so that bananas, manioc and beans can be laid there to dry. The *omólî* starts exactly where the *ékâ* finishes, that is, where the banana grove (*esyómbóko*) starts, which – as already said – surrounds the village on every side. The line that separates the *ékâ* from the *omólî* is very visible, since on one side there is the "aridity" of the *ékâ* and on the other the lush vegetation of the banana grove: it is quite impossible to confuse these two adjacent and opposing categories. *Omólî* is, in fact, the realm of vegetation and it includes – moving increasingly farther away from the *êkâ* – the banana groves, the fields (*amaríma*) that extend beyond the banana groves, the areas of uncultivated territory or the areas on which the scrub has returned (*ekísuki*), and finally the forest (*omúsítu*), which, though destroyed and driven always farther away, remains on the borders of the Nande territory, as well as inside it in some places. Further clarification is necessary at this point. The banana grove is also a "field" (*eriríma*, sing. of *amaríma*); indeed, it is the Banande's prime field, the first field they cultivated. With colonization, the crops beyond the banana grove grew in importance, but – as we will see further on – without doubt the banana grove "field" maintains a cultural and symbolic importance that the other fields certainly do not posses, even though various signs today indicate that this is progressively diminishing.

The marginality of the banana grove

We have seen that Nande space is clearly divided – in a conceptual light – into two categories: *êkâ* and *omólî*. We have also seen, however, that the banana grove (*esyómbóko*) is a subcategory of *omólî* which is closer to *êkâ*: it is in fact adjacent. Where *êkâ* finishes *esyómbóko* starts, and there is no intermediate space between *êkâ* and *esyómbóko*. Even if categorically divided and quite separate, *êkâ* and *esyómbóko* are spatially united, both in the sense that – as said before – there is no intermediate space between the two, and in the sense that there cannot be *êkâ* without *esyómbóko* and vice versa. In its turn, *esyómbóko* is the intermediate space between *êkâ* and any other context of *omólî*: enclosing it on every side, *esyómbóko* isolates *êkâ* like a closed and in some way self-centred world. It is a protective shield that hides even *êkâ* from external eyes and, furthermore, prevents direct access, that is, without crossing the thick strip of vegetation that surrounds it. It is a wide and shady threshold that separates the inside from the outside, so that the pace of whoever approaches may be slowed and his attitude is encouraged to become respectful towards the *êkâ* to which he is going. In turn, for whoever leaves the *êkâ*, crossing the banana grove represents a sort of rite of material passage (to use an expression of Arnold van Gennep (1909)) that gradually introduces him to the outside world.

The banana grove is, however, also a field and so carries out a primary and irreplaceable alimentary function. In the reconstructions that the Banande propose of their faraway past, there is always a reference to the banana tree (*émbóko*) as a plant that they took with them from the regions of Uganda: they came from Uganda, they felled the forest, they built villages and they planted banana trees. Obviously other plants are also grown in the banana groves (above all *taros* and beans); but bananas are the most important and an almost irreplaceable foodstuff. The Banande have lots of different kinds of bananas; here we will point out only the two principal categories: a) bananas that, once dried, milled and made into flour, are the raw material for a kind of "polenta" that accompanies other dishes; b) bananas that are fermented to obtain beer, the well-loved banana beer. Regarding these types of bananas and their different alimentary uses some clarification is necessary. The bananas of type a) are "female" bananas and the product that comes from them (banana polenta) is called *ovúndu*, the same word used to indicate the humanity. The bananas of type b) are instead "male" bananas (they have a sour taste if cooked) and the product that comes from them (banana beer) is called *óbwavu*, "beverage", more precisely *óbwavu bw'esyómbóko*, "the beverage of the banana grove". So, the banana grove produces food that is so important that the Banande call it "humanity" and an equally important beverage, since the Banande do not miss any occasion to drink it with their family, friends, acquaintances or guests. But both the process of production and the process of distribution of *ovúndu* and of *óbwavu* are quite different. (a) For the production of *ovúndu*, we see both the *esyómbóko* and the *ékâ* involved: the "female" bananas, once produced and harvested, undergo a process of desiccation and are then milled and made into flour, which takes place in the *ekíbúga* of the *ékâ*. To become *ovúndu* the flour is then cooked in boiling water and consequently transformed into a dense mass, suitable to accompany any other type of dish, just like polenta. Besides, the distribution of *ovúndu* coincides with family and domestic use. Production and distribution of *ovúndu* is the responsibility of women. (b) For *óbwavu bw'esyómbóko*, the entire process of production takes place in the banana grove: once harvested, the "male" bananas are submerged and squashed in a tree trunk (the *omukímba* tree), which is hollowed out and filled with water, and left there to ferment. To encourage the process the trunk is entirely covered with a mass of rotten leaves and decaying banana peel: this mixture is called *omuhóndo*, from the verb *erihónda*, "to rot". This process of decomposition develops heat that helps the process of fermentation which, after about fifteen days, will result in beer, *óbwavu*. Unlike *ovúndu*, the banana polenta, which is distributed on a merely domestic level, *óbwavu bw'esyómbóko* is circulated much more widely. Beer is an important exchange good and is not produced only for domestic use: it is in fact exchanged, for example, in a systematic way with the goats of other groups, with the groups' relationships based on matrimonial alliance.

As one can see, *ovúndu* emerges from the union of *esyómbóko* and *ékâ*, neighbouring places in which the activities of food production are carried out in subsequent phases to produce a foodstuff – called humanity – that seems to reproduce in its structure and in its name the formula $H = V + B$ (Humanity = Village + Banana grove) proposed in the above paragraph In destroying the forest, humanity fulfils itself, on an ecological level, by constructing a village and a banana grove; on an alimentary level it takes shape by means of a foodstuff that, given from the banana grove, is transformed and brought to the stage of "humanity" by female work in the *êkâ*. The purpose of *óbwavu* is different: its production is exclusively in male hands and occurs entirely in the *esyómbóko*, with the processes of decomposition and fermentation (suitable for *esyómbóko*) rather than of desiccation and cooking (typical of the *êkâ*); besides, its distribution and consumption do not stop at a domestic circle but enjoy wider social networks. This is not about passing from the *esyómbóko* to the corresponding *êkâ* (from the banana grove to the family that runs it); putting a particularly valued good into circulation in a tested network of exchanges, one has the opportunity to pass from one's own banana grove to the entire society.

Coming back to the connection between *êkâ* and *esyómbóko*, our analysis would be seriously incomplete if we limited ourselves to the passage, in the form of food, from the banana grove (where it is produced) to the village (where it is transformed, prepared and consumed). The passage also happens in fact in the opposite direction, the one that leads from the *êkâ* to the *esyómbóko*, now no longer in the form of food, but rather in the form of food waste, personal defecation and other types of disposal. In short, the banana grove feeds the village and the village plies its excretion back into it. The banana grove is the most important food supply for the Nande villages and at the same time it is destined to function as a collector of the *êkâs'* excretion. After its ecologically protective role and its alimentary role, we therefore see a third function emerge which the Banande do not hesitate to recognize with the expression *esyómbóko ni ekyávu*, "the banana grove is a dustbin": the banana grove gives food to the *êkâ* and receives waste and rubbish from it. Even under the profile of this third function the connection between *êkâ* and *esyómbóko* seems to tighten further: an *êkâ* cannot do without its own "dustbin" (*ekyávu*), without its own "dumping ground" and its own "field" (*eriríma*). It is just that, in the banana grove, the field that produces food (*eriríma*) and the dumping ground (*ekyávu*) coincide. The contradiction appears sharper when we realize that the banana grove is also the "place of the dead", where the dead of the *ékâ* are buried. It would be disrespectful to directly and casually compare the corpse of the dead – even in the Nande society – to simple organic waste material: the corpse of a human being is not like that of a dog; indeed, for its burial it requires special treatment. Yet, it is difficult to avoid the idea that corpses – it does not matter in which society (and so even among the Banande) – have an irrepressible meaning of waste. Objectively they are "that something that remains" after the last breath has been exhaled, therefore a "waste" product, abandoned by life to the processes of thanato-morphosis that will soon start to assail it, depriving it of human features and of its apparent integrity, decomposing it in a final and irreparable manner.

Let us go back to the formula $H = V + B$. One could say that this formula becomes increasingly meaningful as the analysis proceeds. From ecology and spatial organization we have in fact passed to the alimentary level, and from this to a consideration of waste and rubbish, up to something that is central to the meaning of humanity, namely the corpse. It seems possible to assert that for the Nande culture everything hinges on the binomial $V + B$, village and banana grove, *ékâ* and *esyómbóko*: once the forest is destroyed (driven back and pushed away), humanity takes form, grows, develops and dies between *ékâ* and *esyómbóko*. *ékâ* is the place where the life of individuals is carried on: obviously not in the sense that they always remain inside the *ékâ* (work, above all for men, happens elsewhere: in the banana grove, in the fields, in the scrub or in the forest, therefore in the *omólî*), but in the sense that they find in the *ékâ* the hearth, the family, food, rest, reunion and conversation with other men. *Esyómbóko* is, on the other hand, the place immediately "nearby": if *ékâ* is – even under a spatial profile – the centre, *esyómbóko* is the place of marginality, a spatial marginality (intermediate space – as we have already seen – between the inside and the outside), but also existential marginality. *Esyómbóko* is in fact the place where one is brought at the end of life; and it is also the place where – once – one was born. Once, indeed, women went to give birth in the *esyómbóko*; and until recently (as births now happen in maternity clinics) the placenta was taken to the banana grove, to be buried under a male banana tree (for beer) if a boy was born and under a female banana tree (for polenta) if it was a girl. The banana grove is (was) the place where one was born and the place where one was buried. One dies, normally, in the *ékâ*, in one's own *ekitétéya*; but it is significant to consider the fact that the Banande immediately arrange to bury the body of the dead in the banana grove: it is as though they want to make the moment of death coincide with one's return to the banana grove. The "margins" of life – birth and death (or at least burial) – are in the banana grove, the "marginal" place compared to *ékâ*, where human beings live, eat, converse and unite: where normal life takes place. *Esyómbóko* is, instead, the place "nearby" – bordering on the *ékâ* – where life (biologically intended) starts and finishes.

Esyómbóko is, indeed, a very biological place; and it is this strongly biological characteristic that allows the contradiction to be resolved (if it is a contradiction) between it being a place that produces food and, at the same time, the place where waste (including corpses) and excretion are deposited. Its biological being and its capacity to resolve the contrast between life and death coincide with what mostly takes place in the banana grove: putrefaction. To putrefy or rot is expressed by the Banande with the verb *erihónda*, which refers to all the processes (not only biological) of decomposition. But the decomposing does not have only a negative meaning or result. In particular – as we have attempted to demonstrate elsewhere (Remotti, 2004) –

putrefaction in the banana grove is not a biological process left to itself; on the contrary, it is subject to the work of men (*omubíri*). The banana grove is a very biological place in the sense that in it life throbs and the transformations that lead from life to death and from death to life take place; but it is also a strongly cultural place, since it is the object of the constant work of humans, and in particular of men, the *aválúme*. This work – which controls the development of the banana trees and intervenes to strip leaves off the banana trees, to clean, in a certain way, the earth between the banana trees, to cut the trunks, when they have produced their only cask of bananas – is essential so that putrefaction does not destroy the banana grove but becomes a factor of new life. In this light, the production of beer – the fermentation of the bananas in the trunk of the *omukímba* tree – is a process with a symbolic value: putrefaction that decomposes, but, at the same time, putrefaction that transforms therefore giving rise to new life.

The banana grove as a place of recycling

What happens in the banana grove is under human control (in particular, the *aválúme*, the men). The *aválúme* are those who, having felled the forest, were able to replace the forest trees with human beings, with their villages and their banana groves. The *aválúme* are also those who, through their industry, direct the processes of putrefaction not towards a destructive and mortal result, but towards new life. The banana grove, therefore, although "very biological", is not abandoned to the spontaneity of biological life, but subject to a real culture (not destructive, like that of the *abakóndi*, but regenerative): the banana grove is the perfect and expert combination of luxuriant vegetable growth and cultural intervention. This combination means that the banana grove is an incessant food and beverage laboratory: a laboratory in the hands of men (*aválúme*) who in this way redeem the destructive role of the *abakóndi*, aiming at a clearly productive and reproductive purpose. The banana grove is, in fact, also a laboratory in which waste and rubbish are collected, to be, however, transformed and regenerated into new forms of life; finally, a laboratory in which even the dead are received, including them in a process of regeneration. In this light, the banana grove emerges as a bio-cultural laboratory that has a central role in the reproductive process of Nande society and culture. Even so, the banana grove always remains in a marginal position compared to the *ekâ* and to life (birth and death of the individual). But it is important to consider above all the binomial nature of this relationship, the union implied between *V* and *B* (between village and banana grove), rather than seeing these two terms as separate elements. Besides, even if the banana grove is a place appointed to marginal moments of human life (birth and death), it must be remembered that the banana grove continuously supplies a) food for the survival of those who live in the *ekâ*, guaranteeing in this way the conservation of their "humanity" (*ovúndu*), and b) the beverage (*óbwavu w'esyómbóko*) that is left to flow without ceasing in the veins of society, in the social relationships in which the *aválúme* are involved. The banana grove, as a bio-cultural laboratory, is always working to the advantage of humanity and the social ties of those who take care of it and work in it. Work in the banana grove is suspended only in the period of mourning – about a month from the burial. This is the period in which the banana grove really becomes "the place of the dead", in which the grave (*eyisínda*) of the buried person remains visible, as do the remains of the disorder that prevails. But one must not forget that two different forces converge in the banana grove: cultural ones, which are briefly interrupted in the mourning period, and natural ones, which, instead, never cease, though always controlled by the work of men. Mourning is a suspension of culture, certainly not of nature; the seeming disorder is a more complex and profound sign of the mere absence of culture (of the work of men), since it is proof of the incessant work of nature. As Lara Giordana affirms, "it is as if the work of men was suspended to allow nature to do its own" (2005-2006: 79): the work of nature is not just disorder; it is instead unceasing transformation and recycling by means of the same processes of putrefaction that in the first place assail the corpse.

Apropos of the dead, a parallel exists between what happens on a biological level and what happens on a social level: while processes of putrefaction take place on the biological level (and we can imagine how much putrefaction is present in a biologically active place like the banana grove), on the social level an inexorable process of oblivion begins. The end of mourning marks (in a decisive and emphatic way) the end of the manifestations of grief; the grave (simply a mound of earth with some flowers) is destined to disappear in the space of a short time; and in the same way – although perhaps over a longer time – the process of the disintegration of memory starts. Whoever is buried in the banana grove is lost to memory: the banana grove – as we have already said (Remotti, 2004: 19) – is a real place of "oblivion": neither memory nor traces of the individual will be conserved, just as the grave will quickly disappear in the environment full of life and vegetation of the banana grove. The dead are, however, "swallowed up in a process not only of oblivion but also of regeneration" (Remotti, 2004: 19). As can be seen, being forgotten is the price the Banande dead have to pay in order to be reintroduced into the vital cycle: "the dead can stay with the living only if they lose their identity, only if they are forgotten. Perhaps because if they kept their identity they could not be truly recycled" (Giordana, 2005-2006: 81). The loss of memory or identity in fact allows the dead to enter the cycle of life, or, more precisely, the "recycling" process that transforms "what remains" (and the corpse is definitely "what remains") into elements of new life. If memory was retained for a long time and in an everlasting way, reintroduction would be difficult into that cycle of life from which food and drink arise; food to nourish humanity (*ovúndu*) and drink to nourish social relations.

The Banande certainly do not eat their dead: funeral cannibalism is not included in their ways of treating the corpse (and one must suppose that they would react to the idea with the same disgust as the Greeks did to the impudent suggestion of Darius, king of the Persians (Herodotus III, 38)). The Banande though, thanks to the incessant work of the banana grove, a place so near and indispensable to the *ékâ*, do not transform the corpses of their dead into "remains of humanity" (Favole, 2003) but reintroduce them into a cycle of life that nourishes humanity and the social relations of the survivors. In this way the dead do not become "remains" of humanity, hard dry objects, preservable relics, having overcome the obstacle or the filter of putrefaction. Ending in oblivion and in the bio-cultural laboratory of the banana grove, they participate again in life, becoming in the end not "remains", but "ingredients" of humanity. On re-examining the case of the Banande (and other societies), Lara Giordana must be owed the merit of directing attention to this prolongation of culture, which does not completely leave its dead but – entrusting them in some way to nature (a nature supervised by the work of men in the banana grove) – arranges to "recycle them" to the advantage of the maintenance of their descendants and of society. In other words, the recovery of the dead to humanity does not only pass through the "bones", the hard parts, preservable, not putrescent, but actually through the soft parts, the putrefaction of the "flesh" – a process that in itself is totally repellent even for the Banande but that nevertheless the banana grove, concealing it in its bowels, succeeds in transforming into an absolutely vital process, capable of regenerating "humanity".

The banana grove is, therefore, a particularly rich and dense place: not only because the vegetation is varied and thick, but also, and above all, because symbols, processes and events of primary importance to the Nande humanity are concentrated here. The banana grove is a concentrate of humanity. In fact, culture and nature, life and death, waste and food, the putrid and the fresh, disappearing and re-emerging all intervene in the banana grove (Remotti, 1993a). Here the Banande find not only the processes that let humanity exist, but also a particularly "thick" representation of human beings. What in fact are banana trees? For the Banande they are not trees; they do not belong to the nominal classes of "trees", those that are countermarked with the following two prefixes: *omu-* (for the singular) and *emi-* (for the plural). "Tree" in Kinande is in fact *omú-ti* (pl. *emí-ti*). The various types of trees are in fact included in the pair of classes *omu-/emi-*. The banana tree is instead *ém-bóko* (pl. *esyóm-bóko*). There is a big difference and indeed opposition between trees (in particular forest trees) and banana trees. Both belong to the vegetable world and are obviously erect, but while the first are hard (and to fell them much force is necessary), the second have a trunk that can be cut with just one blow of a machete. Besides, while forest trees are perennial (they tend to perpetuity or give an idea of perpetuity), banana trees are caducous. A banana tree, after having produced a bunch of bananas, is not able to produce others: it must be felled. And this is what the Banande do in their work in the banana grove: they cut down the banana tree, leaving it on the ground; they also cut it into pieces, so that it will rot and fertilize the soil of the banana grove. But next to the felled banana tree a new banana trunk will sprout, which will be felled in its turn when it has produced its bunch of bananas. It is probably no chance that in a language like Kinande – where the variations of prefixes, suffixes and tones are charged with semantic implications – *eki-hánda* (with a high tone on the vowel *á*) means the root of the banana tree and *ekí-handa* (with the high tone on the vowel *í*) means the family, lineage, the clan. The *ekíhanda* is the social subject that holds possession of the banana grove. The founders and the descendants of the *ekíhanda* are buried there, in the banana grove; many of these are by now forgotten, but all have contributed to anchor the possession of the banana grove – which is also the mark of their settlement – in that territory. The dead are like "roots"; and the banana trees, in turn, are like living men: they rise from the same stump, they produce children (a bunch of bananas), and after that their fate is to be cut down, to fall to the ground and to return to the earth of the banana grove. Likewise, the bodies of human beings are not hard like the forest trees: if you touch them, they are more similar to the trunk of the banana trees; they yield a bit to the pressure of a hand. The Banande affirm for example: *omubirí w'omundú ní kíkuku* "the human body is bark", meaning that it is not solid inside (Kavutirwaki and Mutaka 2006: 150). There are therefore good reasons to assert – as happens among the Banande – that *esyómbóko ni válúme*, "banana trees are men" (Remotti 2004: 21): they protect them, they nourish them, they make them exist and at the same time they represent them.

The *ómwami's* solitude and return to the forest

However, not all men can be rendered similar to banana trees, and not all men, when dead, are buried in the banana grove. One man is different from the others in this respect. The *ómwami*, the chief who – according to tradition – led his men, his *abakóndi*, against the forest, will not be laid to decompose in the *omutáka* (the earth) of the banana grove. The *ómwami* – in truth, the crowned *ómwami* as we shall see shortly – is in fact "buried" in a woven nest of trees, a tree tomb, rather than in the ground. In traditional Nande culture, the *ómwami* has to wait until all the chiefs of his father's generation have died before proceeding with the crowning ceremony (*erísínga*), which consisted of being buried for an entire night in a sort of grave (*evighála*), and on re-emerging the following morning and being crowned with a headdress (*émbita*) made of the skins of various animals. The *erísínga* took place on a specific hill (the place was called *erísingíro*) and signalled a radical change in status in the *ómwami's* life: before the *erísínga*, the *ómwami* was not so very different from other human beings; after the *erísínga* he became a decidedly special being. One of the characteristics that distinguished him was this type of death and burial that took place during the *erísínga* and then, when physical death overcame him, the impossibility of returning to the *omutáka*, of being buried in the ground. The crowned *ómwami* has already known burial in the *omutáka*, and this must not be repeated. The *erísínga* marks an end to his normal life as a human: the crowning ceremony is a simulated, anticipated death that signals a break in the *ómwami*'s life and places him apart, distinct and separate from other mortals. The fact that the *erísínga* is really a type of death is proven by the presence of a character who will reappear on the occasion of the *ómwami*'s second death. In fact, the *omúghúla* (the chief's "official enemy") will be present at the *erísingíro* and will dig the grave in which the *ómwami* must pass the night before becoming a new person. The fact that he is a new person is marked by rules and regulations that will govern his new life: for example, always to sit on a particular stool, never to eat in public, always to keep the fire burning in his hut, never to go about alone, never to meet the *omúghúla* (the man of death, the man who intervenes and has contact with the *ómwami* only on the occasion of his first death – the anticipated death of the *erísínga* – and his second death, the deferred death, as we shall see shortly, which concludes his life). At this point it is important to underline how the moment of the first death (linked to the crowning) gives rise to a situation that is similar to the mourning for the *ómwami*'s second death (that of his physical body). Both when the *ómwami* is crowned and when his physical death is announced, there is a suspension in normal working, social and even sexual life: people do not eat and mothers do not suckle their babies; neither men nor animals may have sexual relations. This suspension, occurring during both the crowning ceremony and the announcement of physical death marks the beginning of a new cycle (*ekirímo*). Therefore the two events are mirrored. More precisely, the *erísínga* is an anticipated death which, by transforming the *ómwami* into a different being with respect to humankind, prevents him returning to the earth on the occasion of his second death (for us, the real death) (Remotti, 1993b: 56-59).

On close analysis, two operations thus take place at the *erísínga*: the first transforms the *ómwami* into a being apart from the rest of humanity; the second relates the *ómwami* to two different spheres of reality. The items used to decorate him for the *erísínga* undoubtedly connect him to the world of the forest: the cloth made of red-coloured bark (from the *omukímba* tree) that he wears, the leopard skin he is dressed in, the necklace of leopard teeth around his neck, the headdress (*émbita*) made of skins of various forest animals. On the one hand, these beings (animal and vegetable) of the forest (first sphere) are made present or symbolized; on the other, he is almost entirely surrounded by the presence of his ancestors (second sphere) – the lower jaw of the last crowned *ómwami* (probably his grandfather), whose name the new *ómwami* takes; the construction of small huts on the crowning hill that can be inhabited by his ancestors; signs of approval on the part of the ancestors in favour of the new *ómwami*; the sacrifices made to the ancestors. There are many of these ancestors; they are not those buried in the ground but those who, having been previously crowned, were given burial in tree tombs. With the crowning ceremony it is as though the *ómwami* is displaced towards these spheres (the forest on one side and the ancestors' world on the other) which certainly represent the "other" compared to ordinary everyday life as it is lived in the *éká* (village) and in the fields connected to it (the banana grove and other cultivated fields). The *ómwami* stands for contact with these worlds, even if it is necessary to distinguish the "polemical" relationship (of struggle) with respect to the forest from the relationship of intimacy and familiarity with the ancestors (the crowned *ómwami* is almost one of them). Connected to these worlds, the *ómwami* is both at the vertex of society while also occupying a decidedly marginal position, due to his separation from the rest of humanity; a position of solitude.

Even the *ómwami*'s real death (his second death) is quite different from that of ordinary people. While the *erisínga* is an anticipated and simulated death, the real death is deferred and also the object of simulation. During the *erisínga* it is "as though" the *ómwami* dies, while at his real death an illness is simulated for a certain period of time: it is not said that he is dead, but that he is ill. In the shadows of this simulation, his body is taken in great secrecy to the crowning hill and here left to decompose on a wooden structure, raised from the ground and completely surrounded by a stockade. The simulation of illness, and therefore of life, continues until the process of decomposition of the body reaches the point where the *omúghúla* can extract the lower jaw of the *ómwami* with the help of a billy-goat. This is the moment of the *ómwami*'s death, the moment at which his end or his death can be officially announced: not the last exhalation of breath, but the removal of the jaw from the body in an advanced state of decomposition. At this point, the contrast between the death of ordinary people and that of the *ómwami* is more than evident. The death of ordinary people is decreed almost in anticipation, in that death is seen (and spoken about) when the individual in the eyes of his dear ones is irredeemably close to dying. Once his last breath is exhaled, his body is taken rapidly – before the sun sets – into the *eyisínda*, where the grave is immediately dug in the banana grove. On the contrary, an advanced state of putrefaction is waited for before officially announcing the death of the *ómwami*, which corresponds to the extraction of his lower jaw. This death, therefore, is not an end or disappearance, on the contrary, the conservation of "remains". The jaw is, in fact, one of the hardest parts of the body, and these "remains" of the body are destined to "remain" and be conserved as a sign of the testimony of the *óbwami*. The power of the *ómwami* is thereby conserved over time, despite the death of the individual. It is a power that crosses generations and is handed from one *ómwami* to the next. The jaw appears to be not just the "remains of humanity", but the "remains of power", that special power (the *óbwami*), that belongs exclusively to the crowned *ómwami* and that is manifested in his capacity to "remain". The *óbwami* truly seems to be a power that "remains", that is conserved, that triumphs over death, that denies and overcomes the biological transformations that other human beings are subject to.

Once the death of the *ómwami* has been made official by the extraction of the jaw, his body will no longer be touched. Trees of the forest have been planted around his body, in particular the *omukímba* tree, having aerial roots. Over time, the corpse continues to decompose while the *omukímba* trees grow, their aerial roots intertwining and thus clasping and imprisoning "all that remains" of the *ómwami* in a luxuriant, verdant embrace. At the end of the process – bodily decomposition on the one hand and tree growth on the other – a very particular type of tomb, the *amáhero*, is attained: it is not dug in the ground but composed of and created by forest trees; it is not underground but raised to the sight of all on the peak of a hill. There is one point in common between the burial of the ordinary people and that of the *ómwami*: in both cases the task of swallowing up the body is entrusted to the vegetable kingdom. But on noting this similarity (this convergence of and preference for vegetation), the differences are also immediately noticeable between burial in the *eyisínda* and in the banana grove on the one hand and in the *amáhero* on the other. 1) The first difference is the ground (the *omutáka*). Ordinary people go into the ground (the bodies, wrapped in material made from bark – the usual *omukímba* tree – were laid in the grave in a foetal position); the *ómwami*'s body instead avoids all contact with the ground. 2) The decomposition of the corpse of the ordinary person is not seen: the body is buried hurriedly, well before decomposition begins; on the contrary, the decomposition of the *ómwami*'s body is a controlled, supervised and even stimulated (fires are lit alongside the corpse). 3) The body of the ordinary person is not manipulated, whereas that of the *ómwami* suffers the violence of the intervention of the *omúghúla*, who extracts its jaw. 4) The body of the ordinary person dissolves completely in the banana grove, whereas the extracted part of the *ómwami*'s body becomes a reliquary to be conserved for future generations. 5) Not only the body, but also, gradually, the memory of the ordinary person is lost (the *esyómbóko*, in which they are buried, is a place of "oblivion") (Remotti, 2004); on the contrary, the chief's tree tomb, in which his body is certainly "lost" or "disappears" (the root *-her-* of *amá-hero* is at the base of the verb *erí-heryá*, which means to "lose something or someone") (Kavutirwaki and Mutaka 2006:65), maintains alive for ever the memory and name of the *ómwami* buried there. 6) In the *esyómbóko*, individuals disappear completely but are incorporated into a collective group, represented by the banana trees themselves (*esyómbóko*, the plural indeed of *émbóko*), which coincides with *ekíhanda*, the family, lineage; the *amáhero* conserves individuality but is totally solitary, lacking any connection with the *ekíhanda*. 7) The graves of ordinary people are closely linked to the village, the *ékâ* inhabited by the living, to such an extent that an inseparable pair is created (*V + B*); the tree tomb of the chiefs, instead, is far from any inhabited centre, in a completely separate and isolated spot. 8) The grave of the ordinary person is immersed in a place of intense production of foodstuffs (food and drink), thus representing for the inhabitants of the *ékâ* continuous nourishment for their humanity and sociality; the *amáhero* instead is sterile from an alimentary point of view: it only nourishes the culture of memory. 9) The grave of the ordinary person "disappears", to the biological advantage of the banana grove; the chief's tree tomb instead "remains" for ever thanks to the biology of the forest. 10) The banana grove is therefore only a temporary "place of the dead", which lasts only for the period of mourning; the tree tomb instead is a perennial monument. 11) Apart from the period of mourning, the banana grove is a place of intense work and constant attention from man, while the *amáhero* is quite removed from all intervention by human beings. 12) The banana grove is a place of constant passage, whereas the *amáhero* is an impenetrable place. 13) The banana grove is a sign of human culture, which has conquered the forest; the *amáhero* instead is the return of the forest.

This last point allows a conclusion to be drawn. As seen, the crowned *ómwami*, "dead" to ordinary life, removed from family and social bonds, isolated in some way with respect to the ordinary community, is placed in a marginal position where he encounters and incorporates the forest on the one side and the world of his ancestors on the other (his ancestors, the *ávami* who preceded him). He represents the convergent point between these two realities: he incarnates the "power" (*óbwami*) of his ancestors, which was not originally so much power over his subjects as power "against" the forest. His power is certainly legitimized by his ancestors (the transmission of the jaw), but the whole line of descent of the *óbwami* is defined by his capacity to overcome the power, strength and exuberant vitality of the forest. To do this, the *ómwami* must appropriate the strength of his ancestors, who are remembered for ever since they succeeded in conquering the land (*omutáka*) of the forest, organizing the territory (*ekíhúgo*) and entrusting it to men under the form of villages (*ékâ*) and banana groves (*esyómbóko*). Among men, the *ómwami* is he who emerges and knows how to affront the forest; for this, he must not die or "disappear" in the banana grove, but must "remain" in everlasting memory in the face of the forest. To do this, his body is transformed, not into food or drink (like the body of the ordinary person), but into a tree of the forest: that particular tree of the forest – the *omukímba* tree – used by the Banande to make clothes (using the bark) and beer (bananas ferment in a hollow *omukímba* trunk). But if the *amáhero* is the representation of the last and definitive transformation of the *ómwami*, who, from the ordinary person that he was before the *erísínga* (crowning), becomes in the end a tree of the forest, it can also be interpreted in a different way: with the death of the *ómwami* – his second and definitive death – the forest reconquers, even if only symbolically, the space and visibility that the *abakóndi* had taken from it. The *amáhero* can therefore be interpreted as a return of the forest; it can be defined as the regeneration of a "small forest" (*akásítu*, diminutive of *omúsítu*), a "re-emerging" of that form of life that the Banande, in their history and for their culture, have been loath to destroy: a "re-emerging" that occurs thanks to the "disappearance" of the body of the *ómwami* and to the "remaining" in collective memory of his name and deeds.

Three Burial Models

A final point before concluding. The *omukímba* tree, a tree of the forest, seems to be especially connected to memory. As outlined in the first section, there are not just the *ávami* (plural of *ómwami*) at the top and the ordinary people (the *ábagúndâ*): there are other chiefs in the middle, generally called *abákama*. Since they are not crowned, they are not buried in the *amáhero*, the tree tombs on top of the hill of the *erísínga*. Like the ordinary people, they are buried in the banana grove, in the grave dug there, thus becoming part of the recycling and transformation process (an underground process that ultimately results in food and drink). But the *abákama* are allowed to avoid the oblivion that will instead be the lot of the *ábagúndâ*. Although buried in the banana grove – the place of oblivion and recycling – they enjoy the privilege of having the exact place of their burial marked by a tree, the *omukímba* tree once again, which is clearly different from all the surrounding vegetation as it is a tree of the forest: in order to remember an *omúkama*, to make sure his memory is conserved and remains over time, the *omukímba* tree is planted precisely on his grave (*eyisínda*). Differently from the crowned *ómwami*, his body is not enveloped in the vital embrace of a tree tomb of a small solitary forest, on the top of a hill far from the bustle of everyday life; instead it is laid in the ground of the banana grove, where his body will take part in the recycling destiny of all ordinary people. However, for his name and memory to "remain", an *omukímba* tree is planted in the banana grove: almost as though saying that if one wants to "remain" one has to have recourse to a tree of the forest. It is also significant that for this type of grave – an intermediary solution sited exactly halfway between the *eyisínda* of ordinary people, destined to "disappear" in the banana grove, and the *amáhero* of the crowned *ómwami* on the summit of a hill – the word *amáhero* is also used. The *omukímba* tree, with its verdant and luxuriant "remaining", distinguishes this category, even if it is not planted on a solitary hilltop, but in the middle of a banana grove, alongside human habitation instead.

The Banande thus dispose of three, not two, traditional burial models for their dead:

a) the *eyisínda*, the individual grave destined to disappear in the banana grove, together with all memory of the defunct, and to be recycled as food and drink to the advantage of the inhabitants of the *ékâ*;

b) the *amáhero* in the banana grove, which consists in a combination of *eyisínda* (grave dug in the ground) and the use of the *omukímba* tree as a perennial mark of memory;

c) the *amáhero* with no *eyisínda*, solitary, on an uninhabited hilltop, conceived as a sort of "small forest" (*akásítu*).

All three models envisage the location of the dead in the *omóli*, outside the *ékâ*, the true centre of habitation. Models a) and b) both use the banana grove though, and are thus clearly distinct from model c). Using the banana grove in fact means laying the dead in a place next to and closely connected with the *ékâ*, while the tree tomb of the crowned chiefs is placed in a solitary and uninhabited place, recreating there a "small forest". Using the banana grove means not only being close to the inhabited area, but also the practice of *eyisínda*, or burial in the ground, and therefore participation in the recycling processes that occur unceasingly in the banana grove. Model c) instead envisages distance from the ground, raising the body above the ground, with the body in contact with the forest trees (the aerial roots of the *omukímba* trees) rather than with the earth. Under another aspect, models a) and b) differ between themselves. Model a) in fact belongs completely to the transforming processes of the banana grove, which provides a constant replacement of bananas and therefore oblivion of their individuality; model b) instead introduces into the banana grove a foreign vegetable element, the *omukímba* tree, which has the explicit function of acting against the banana groves' processes of oblivion, conserving the memory of the chief buried there. In this light (conservation of memory through the *omukímba* tree), model b) is undoubtedly close to model c). But the two models b) and c) also differ from each other in this respect since model b) envisages the use of a single *omukímba* tree, which, although it is a tree of the forest, will never create a "small forest" (surrounded as it is by the banana grove), while model c) pursues the precise objective of recreating in some way an *akásítu*, a "small forest", in an uninhabited place. Indeed, for model c) it is not sufficient to plant an *omukímba* tree as a sign: instead, several *omukímba* trees are planted around the body of the crowned chief, and from that moment men abstain from any further intervention. In model c) it is as though culture is suspended and the whole task of constructing the tree tombs is left entirely to nature (to the trees of the forest, which will close in and progressively interweave their aerial roots). The *amáhero* (model c) are in fact vegetal monuments, built by nature, as opposed to the banana groves, which, instead, represent the signs, testimony and result of the constant work of man and of the persevering interventions of his culture. Tree tombs and banana groves are different: in case of the first these are "natural" places of historic memory, the second are cultural places of biological recycling. Both modes however contribute to dot and mark the territory of the Banande, making up a consistent and in some way inalienable part of their natural and historic heritage.

Bibliography

Herodotus. 1984. *Storie*. Italian trans. A. Izzo d'Accinni. Milan. (K. Hude (ed.). 1927. *Historíai*. Oxford).

Favole, A. 2003. *Resti di umanità. Vita sociale del corpo dopo la morte*. Rome-Bari.

Giordana, L. 2005-2006. *"Carne e ossa. Antropologia del riciclo"*. Master thesis in Cultural Anthropology and Ethnology, Università degli Studi di Torino.

Kavutirwaki, K. & Mutaka, N.M. 2006. *Dictionnaire Kinande-Français*. Tervuren.

Remotti, F. 1993a. *Luoghi e corpi. Antropologia dello spazio, del tempo e del potere*. Turin, Il Segnalibro.

---. 1993b. *Etnografia Nande I*, Turin, Il Segnalibro.

---. 1994. *Etnografia Nande II*. Turin, Il Segnalibro.

---. 2004. "Il secco e il putrido. Luoghi dei vivi e luoghi dei morti tra i Banande del Nord Kivu". In *La ricerca folklorica*, 49, 15-26.

Van Gennep, A. 1981. *I riti di passaggio*. Turin. (orig. ed. 1909. *Les Rites de passage*. Paris).

Note

1. Since Kinande (the language of the Banande) is a tonal language, high tones have been indicated with an acute accent on the interested vowel

(eg. *ómwami*); lack of an accent indicates a low tone. It must also be said that the content of this article was presented at the conference "Sepolti tra i vivi" (University of Rome "La Sapienza" – Department of Historical, Archaeological and Anthropological Sciences of Antiquity – Rome, 26-29 April 2006) and will therefore be published in Italian in the conference proceedings. Lastly, the author would like to point out that the contents and theoretical perspectives contained in this paper have been elaborated within a national research project, of which he was the coordinator, entitled *Luoghi dei vivi e luoghi dei morti. Confini, separazioni, intersezioni* (2000-2002).

From the Forest to the Hospital: Changing Circumcision Practices among the Bakonzo

Cristina Zavaroni

Introduction

In the tradition of the Bakonzo of the Rwenzori, the *Olhusumba* male initiation rite, which traditionally started with group circumcision, represents a way to build the identity of individuals and of society by creating a cohesive group of adult men who are able to become warriors and fathers (Remotti, 1996b). The initiatory aspect of the rite was relinquished some time ago, while the practice of circumcision has been retained by the young Konzo, who, to this day, consider it necessary.

In this article I intend to describe the change that took place in the past four decades, analyze its consequences for individuals and society, and identify those aspects of the practice that have been lost and those that have been preserved in the transition. The data discussed in this article have been gathered in several villages in the Kasese and Bundibugyo districts, and in particular in the areas of Ibanda, Kyondo and Bundibugyo over a total of seven months of fieldwork between December 2004 and January 2006[1].

Traditional *Olhusumba* According to Today's Bakonzo

All elderly informants, both men and women, agree that at the time of their childhood and youth the *Olhusumba* rite was central in the life of Konzo males. It determined and shaped much of the imagery related to the reaching of adulthood and of male sexual adequacy and vigour. The initiation was also a strictly defined male ritual space surrounded by an aura of secrecy that totally excluded women and children. "Going to Bwamba" – as most people refer to the *Olhusumba,* which took place near present-day Bundibugyo – represented the key passage from childhood to adulthood. All informants agree that the focal event of the whole ritual was the act of circumcision, which took place at the very beginning of the segregation period, which was then followed by a long period, up to two months, of isolation in the forest before returning home.

The aim of the rite was to initiate boys to adulthood and to mark the coming of reproductive age, which would allow them to marry, create new families and eventually occupy new farming land. By producing adult males, the *Olhusumba* marked the succession of generations. The young men who were initiated together during the same rite season formed a close group, a forming of a generation marked by internal solidarity, but also separate from the groups that would take part in prior or subsequent rites.

The rite structure that most Konzo informants recall is almost identical to that reported by Bergmans and Remotti for the Banande *Olhusumba,* and it fits perfectly with Van Gennep's classical definition of a rite of passage (Van Gennep, 1909). The *Olhusumba* included a phase of separation, suspending everyday life, a liminal phase during which change took place, and a final incorporation back into society under a new status.

The long and complex initiation rite required the participation of the whole community, and during this period everybody's ordinary life was suspended. This was not only the case for the young candidates and older men who accompanied the initiates into the forest, but also applied to the family members who stayed at home. It was a period marked by several taboos, mainly having to do with food and sex, during which the community, through its behaviour, through propitiatory chants and the cooking of meals to be brought to the forest camps, protected the youth who were going through a dangerously liminal situation.

Information is scanty and conflicting as to who should be circumcised and who should not. Some old informants say that all Konzo males had to undergo initiation; others say that chiefs and their sons had to preserve their integrity; still others maintain that it was actually the healing of the circumcision wound of the son of a chief – performed as a sort of test – that determined that the time was right for a new *Olhusumba* season to start. All of the elders, though, state that they know some adult male, married and with children, who is known for not being circumcised (the wives would be ashamed to reveal that they have sexual intercourse with such a man!). These men supposedly avoided circumcision out of cowardice: they were not initiated when very young and then found ways of escaping a duty that became increasingly more unpleasant and dangerous with time. I had the opportunity to have a long interview with a ridge leader in the Kyondo area who did not undergo circumcision because he was the son of a chief and a future chief. This fact is widely known and ascribed to his noble lineage; nonetheless it is the cause of some embarrassment, as if the younger generations were not fully convinced of the soundness of the reason. And in fact the sons of this chief all say that they are circumcised, in spite of their noble descent. It can be said, in conclusion, that in the past, initiation was certainly prescribed for all non-noble males, but it was equally possible to escape the practice and still have a normal family life.

The rite was performed at rather lengthy intervals. It is difficult to know how often the ritual season recurred and whether it took place at regular intervals. Some informants speak of seven-year cycles[2], others say eleven or twelve years, still others say that there was no fixed interval but that some specific elements in nature indicated that the time was ripe for a new ceremony. Once the time was considered to be right for the beginning of a new cycle, information went around across the whole district and the villagers started to initiate the children's journey.

It is very important to point out that, differently from what it is today, the organizational and moral responsibility for the entire process was shared by the whole community and not limited to the family or the child alone. Informants report that the analysis of omens, indicating whether the times were "ripe" for a new initiation season was done in Bwamba.

Because of the long interval between rites, the age of participants varied greatly. The groups were composed of children of just three or four years of age, up to boys of eighteen or twenty. As it was a hard trial, that actually put the life of the children at risk, only sufficiently strong and healthy individuals would join the departing group. So it could happen that a boy of an appropriate age (eight or nine) might not join the rite if he happened to be of ill health at the time of departure. He would have to wait for the next rite season several years later.

At the start of the journey, small groups of four or five children were entrusted to an initiated man, their *samba* (Magezi, Nyakango and Aganatia, 2004), who would accompany them on their way to the forest, and look after their health, healing and education while they were away. For this service, he would in exchange receive a reward from the children's fathers, such as a goat or some money.

The children were physically separated from the community by walking from their villages to the area of Bwamba, north of the Rwenzori massif. The circumcision that took place here was a second very physical sign and powerful symbol of separation from childhood. The surgical act of circumcision took place near the dwelling of the ridge elder in Bwamba. After that the children were transferred to a camp that they would help to construct in the forest close to a stream. As mentioned, the circumcision started a dangerous period of liminality, the length of which coincided with the time required for the wounds to heal. Every day the initiates were taken to the river where they bathed in the cold water to clean and treat the wounds. The healing process lasted between two weeks and two months, depending on the composition of the group: the higher the age, the longer the time required for healing.

The time at camp was time of pain, of frustration and of training. While waiting for the wounds to heal, the boys learned the secrets that distinguish women from men and the immature from the wise (Remotti, 1996b). The risk of infection was real: one of the participants might get ill or even die during the seclusion in the forest. This explains why, for the duration of the seclusion, all family members were expected to abstain from sexual activity: sexual activity at home would endanger the initiate's healing; perhaps even cause their death.

It is clear from all Konzo testimonies that circumcision and the subsequent training period had the specific aim of separating the child from the world of women they had been part of until then, and to provide a sort of symbolic sexual education and authorization to enter the sphere of reproductive sexuality. To this end a number of training and transition events were organized at the camp. Two of these were recalled by my informants with the greatest frequency: the game of the buffalo, in which each child had to fight hand-to-hand against a character disguised as a wild beast, defeat and tame it, and then ride it. In the other game, the children, now fully healed and ready to return to their villages, were forced to simulate intercourse with a puppet with ugly female features, named Kabiira. This was an unpleasant game, where the children were derided and hit on the back with a bunch of nettles while forced to penetrate Kabiira. Once again the initiates found themselves in an uneasy, painful and shameful situation. Managing to pass through these ordeals would prove their manly qualities.

Besides these activities, the elders remember the long training to learn the rhythms and melodies to be played on the instrument called *Omukumu* (Magezi, Nyakango and Aganatia, 2004:48). Both the instrument and the repertoire of rhythms and melodies are played only by initiated men at the funeral of another initiate. This gives the community a constant reminder that some knowledge is only available to the men who took part in the rite, and that this knowledge would be shared amongst them until death.

According to elderly informants, the rest of the time was spent tending to the painful wounds every morning by the river and waiting for the time of meals. All informants agree that there was a sort of ongoing, implicit indoctrination about the world of men. Only two of them recall that the adults provided explicit moral education through stories and instructions about the behaviour that was expected from them upon their return to the village[3].

Incorporation back into ordinary life started for the newly initiated youth on the way back to their village. Upon their arrival they were welcomed with some ceremonies, generally less elaborate than those we know about with the Banande people. Generally the boys, wearing new clothes, were presented to the village as a group, and recognized individually by their family members. This was followed by a special meal of chicken, the sacrificial food *par excellence* and strictly reserved for men.

Upon returning home, life changed for the children[4]. Some of the main changes that informants reported, are those that concern the initiates' family life: even if quite young, they could no longer be seen naked by their mothers who, up to that point, had looked after their cleanliness and constantly checked their sexual vigour. The young initiate now had to bathe on his own, and had to keep away from females. From the time of their return from Bwamba, males were required to wear clothes covering their genitals at all times. Parents also avoided bodily punishments: the children were supposed to be old enough to be educated through verbal instruction alone. The young initiate was also no longer allowed to cry or show fear; courage being a key trait of adult male personality.

In turn, the new initiate had access to the *kyaghanda*, the hut of the elders. They no longer had to stop at the threshold as children and women should. Furthermore, initiation granted Konzo men the honour of playing in the *omukumu* orchestra at the funerals of initiated men, following the teachings received in the forest.

Discontinuation of the *Olhusumba*

The last traditional *Olhusumba* rite was supposedly performed in 1963, even if some say that rites took place as late as 1978 in the Bundibugyo area. Unfortunately, I was unable to interview anyone who took part in this last rite, nor to gather evidence proving that it actually took place. No single individual or small group can be said to have decided to put an end to the performance of *Olhusumba*, nor is it possible to identify a time when the rite was supposed to be performed but was not. The highly volatile political situation that Uganda experienced for the two decades after gaining independence probably made it very difficult to organize the rite. Since the rite was not supposed to be performed at any specific time, it is quite likely that the Bwamba community – living in a border area sometimes made unsafe by raids of armed soldiers and rebels (Stacey, 2003) – opted to wait for the right, peaceful moment. The right moment never came, and, with time, improvised solutions were found for the circumcision of some young individuals. In the meantime a significant section of the population had converted to various forms of introduced religions.

The spread of monotheism seems to be the most likely reason why the *Olhusumba* rite was not resumed, even when the political situation would have allowed it. The influence of Christianity – and of Islam, if on a smaller scale – on traditional religions is apparent, also from the analysis of female rites relating to fertility, such as *Erikenza*, which was performed for a woman's first pregnancy, and *Eribanira* for the following pregnancies. All these rites were similarly discontinued when families converted to a monotheistic religion. Ministers, priests and imams quite openly oppose all traditional practices as they imply some relation with the world of spirits. The *Olhusumba*, while not focused on communication with the spirits, does require contact with the Konzo pantheon inhabiting the forest and the mountain (Pennacini, 1998).

Among the possible causes of the end of the rite, most informants list health reasons. Parents were apparently unwilling to put the lives of relatively small children at risk. Problems were also cited in reconciling the lengthy *Olhusumba* rite with school attendance, although on this point, one needs to be sceptical: traditionally the Olhusumba was performed between December and January, a time of the year when the children are out of school (In Uganda the school year begins in February and ends in the first days of December).

Although none of the informants made this point, a further contributing factor may well have been the disapproval of traditional rites by various Ugandan governments. It is only recently that President Museveni recognized some traditional kingdoms, and that the government has shown some signs of being open to some aspects of traditional culture and its rites. In this regard, the state is trying to make a rather arbitrary distinction between good tradition and bad tradition. Circumcision in particular is a difficult topic: the government quite strongly opposes all those practices that cause mutilation of children's bodies, but it is also difficult to openly oppose a practice that is fundamental to Islamic religion.

Notes on the Discontinuation of Female Rites

The traditional Konzo society marked women's journey from childhood to adulthood by several different steps. These were situations of passage, which showed that the female individuals had left childhood and that, at the same time, marked their belonging to the Konzo ethnic group. One such sign was belly tattooing (*Esyonzole*). In order to obtain these markings, the little girls ran away in small groups to places where a scarification session was organized. There were also specific rites related to pregnancy and birth. The *Erikenza* marked the definitive entrance of the young bride into the world of women at her first pregnancy. These rites, similar to the male rite, required a suspension of everyday life and the creation of an exclusive female space within which behaviour was allowed that would ordinarily have been unacceptable. This ritual, however, only lasted for a very short time, from a few hours to a few days, and happened after the woman had already left her family group after marriage. *Erikenza* cannot be defined as classical rites of passage: it was mostly a question of acknowledging a change that had already taken place, and of welcoming the mother-to-be into the women's group of the husband's family (see Pennacini, 1996).

Other female rites that were abandoned for the same reasons are the *Omuhulhuko*, which determined and contained the dangerous liminal moment of delivery, and the *Eribanira*, that marked the time when a pregnancy following the first one became public knowledge. Here, too, the rites accompany, contain and direct behaviour; as well as dispel the dangers and contaminations relating to reproduction. But these rites were not actual rites of passage that could make a woman out of a girl child. These rites have not been practiced for many years, mainly due, many say, to the fact that they are not compatible with the monotheistic religion and that there are very few women left who remember the songs, dances and gestures that made up the rites. Despite the cessation of these rites, the aptness of the women to become mothers is not doubted. In the case of men, however, as I will be arguing later, the loss of ritual is more problematic.

Nonetheless, the change of customs has strongly influenced all practices relating to reproduction and has shifted pregnancy and delivery from the public and social sphere to the more restricted family circle. In some cases, a pregnancy is kept secret as long as possible, and sometimes even children are not supposed to know that their mother is about to give birth to a new baby.

This drastic change can be explained, I believe, as a consequence of the fact that the natural quality of reproduction is perceived as a threat and as being closer in kind to animals than humans. This aspect is confirmed by data referring to twin births, around which the Konzo tradition has built a variety of rites and taboos. A woman who gives birth to two babies acts like a goat that produces several kids at a time. It is a disorderly and an unexpected event that puts the community at risk: animal nature taking precedence over human nature. By bringing reproduction within social boundaries, the rites served as a protection against the risk of confusing human persons with animal behaviour. Through the Christianization and westernization of Ugandan society, reproduction has lost its place in the social sphere but, since it is still considered to be dangerous and disorderly, it has been made, as far as possible, invisible.

Circumcision Today

Even if the traditional *Olhusumba* has not been performed for some forty years, all Konzo children are still circumcised. Informants, both men and women, agree that all Konzo boys must be circumcised and that those who are not are under strong pressure from their peers. Uncircumcised boys, the "uncut!", are said to be dirty, smelly, to have two mouths, to dream of sexual intercourse with their mothers, to be unripe for sexual activity and that intercourse with them is not pleasant anyway. The question of cleanliness was brought up by every single informant, whether male or female, adult or child. Another aspect which is deeply felt, is the distinction from other neighbouring populations. The Bakonzo feel the need to assert their embodied difference with the Batoro, in particular, who do not practise circumcision. They believe that their choice is so obviously correct that, when a family belonging to a different ethnic group lives in an area inhabited by Bakonzo, their boys choose to be circumcised because they can clearly perceive the benefit of the practice.

Even in the face of unanimous agreement about circumcision, no one seems to know how and when it should be performed. There is no social prescription telling parents and children how to behave. Still, I could identify three different strategies that are followed by Konzo communities in different areas of the region they inhabit. None of these strategies is exclusive to a certain area, although one will prevail in a certain period and in a certain area.

Escape in Ibanda

In primary schools, both boys and girls make fun of non-circumcised boys, who eventually become annoyed. Wishing to put an end to their hardship, they autonomously escape from the family and go to a circumciser without their parents' knowledge. It is generally a group of friends, brothers or cousins who decide to run away with the help of an older boy who has already been circumcised and can offer guidance. This decision requires some courage because all children have heard terrible stories about the pain they will feel at the time of the operation, about the danger of the wound getting infected, leading to all sorts of complications, even death, and about the chance that the circumciser might not do the job properly. When children escape they seek the help of a man whom they call "the doctor" or "the Muslim". Nowadays many circumcisers who are called Muslims are actually men of all faiths who learned how to perform circumcision and manage the wound. Their reputation is known to the young boys. Until recently, though, Muslim circumcisers who lived in the larger towns in the valleys and plains would visit the ridges, or would be specifically called to circumcise the children, thus taking the place of the Bamba circumcisers with whom the *Olhusumba* used to be organized and from whom the Konzo are said to have learned the practice (Remotti, 1996a).

In some cases, young boys prefer dispensaries or hospitals where they believe they will be operated on in a healthy environment and will be properly treated by doctors or nurses. In hospitals, though, the risk is that a woman may perform the operation. Some boys fear this embarrassing possibility so much that they would rather avoid hospital. When they opt for a "Muslim", the boys generally stay with him for three days to one week, a period during which the man teaches them how to manage the wound. At the first signs of healing, the boys are sent back home. Both the "Muslims" and the dispensary doctors give the children something that will help the healing process, mostly disinfectants, pain killers and, in some cases, antibiotics.

When they go back home, children are usually welcomed rather coldly, although this behaviour disguises the parents' pride in the fact that their children have made a courageous choice and should now be regarded as adults. In most cases children do not go back to their regular life but remain for a while in a secluded room of the house or in a corner of the banana plantation. From there they can reach the river early every morning to manage their wound and be careful to avoid seeing or being seen by any woman. The choice of a secluded place within the house or not far from it, together with other escapes, represents a new twist to a traditional pattern: it is a miniature camp like the ones that used to be organized in Bwamba. It is clear that even if the traditional *Olhusumba* can no longer be carried out, children still feel a need for some sort of initiation. During this short seclusion, children always receive instructions about a particular diet they should follow in order to minimize their pain and help healing, such as avoiding salty foods, or sweet ones or sour ones. Interestingly, the idea of abstinence remains, although shifting from sexual abstinence of the parents (which very few young fathers have mentioned) to food abstinence by the circumcised. This aspect serves the purpose of highlighting the suspension of the child's ordinary life and the liminal state in which he is. The end of liminality is, still, dictated by healing. When the wound has healed, the family prepares a special meal of chicken for the initiate. All the children remember this meal as a very important event: a time when the focus is on the former child for the very first time in his life.

It may happen that the runaways fear the family's reaction. In this case they will try to hide the fact that they were circumcised, readily resuming their ordinary life and treating the wound in secrecy. This case was reported by some informants who escaped to be circumcised when they had already reached the age of ten or more.

Courage is the most relevant residual element of passage to be found in this procedure. By showing courage in dealing with the dangers of circumcision and taking responsibility, the children express their desire to come out of childhood, to be considered able to shoulder responsibility and to join the group of those who can have sexual relations.

The ·age of children who choose to escape varies greatly, from five- or six-year-old children who follow older brothers, to fifteen- or sixteen-year-old boys who can no longer take the mockery they get at home and at school.

Escape is the most frequent choice on the part of the children in the Ibanda valley, but it is not the only one. In fact there is a wide range of alternatives, from a basic respect of tradition, as illustrated by the case of Bundibugyo below, to full medicalization of the operation.

Fathers' Organizations in Bundibugyo

In the area of Bundibugyo I collected several testimonies of small groups of children, friends or relatives, for whom one of the fathers organizes the function, either inviting a circumciser to come to the house or bringing the boys to him. (I learned of examples of this procedure in Ibanda as well, but this choice is much less frequent.) After the operation has been performed, the children are gathered together in a room where they remain for several days. The same restrictions apply as for those who escape. When, as in this case, the ceremony is organized by an adult, parent or uncle, rather than by the children themselves, it is more likely that there is some adult guidance during the period of isolation and healing. Children would be taught the responsibilities of a circumcised man and told stories about tradition, in particular about the *Olhusumba*. Sometimes this training would be accompanied with something reminiscent of the traditional rite. Two children told me about the "riding the buffalo" game; another child reported being taught to play the *Omukumu* instrument.

Also, in this case, the circumcisers give the children disinfectants, painkillers or anti-inflammatory drugs to help healing and check on the situation after a few days or weeks. While secluded, the children follow a special diet excluding some types of food. Again, the end of the isolation is celebrated with a special meal of chicken.

From the information I could gather, the *Kabiira* game, with its strong sexual connotation, is no longer practised. Sexual education is no longer part of the social adult discourse: it has become a scientific task entrusted to educational institutions.

It is rather seldom that Bundibugyo children resort to escaping. Possibly the close links of the Konzo with the Bamba ethnic group who live in the same area and with whom the *Olhusumba* used to be organized, slowed the process of relinquishing tradition. In this area I was able to interview children whose fathers had organized their circumcision in small groups when they were still quite young, starting from age four. Such children believed they should be grateful to their fathers who had organized the event and borne the cost. The aspect of the individual's courage, although present, is less relevant than in the case of the escape. Teaching boys about the duties and privileges of circumcised men is more explicit – and so is seclusion, which emphasizes the liminality of the period and marks a step forward in the status of the circumcised. Boys who are circumcised (following their families' wish) show a stronger awareness of the cultural implications of becoming adult men.

Medicalization of Infant Circumcision in Kyondo

The third strategy, full medicalization, eliminates all remnants of the traditional ritual. In this case parents have the newborn baby boy circumcised at the hospital at the time of birth, or within the first few years of life. The process only takes a few minutes and then the baby is taken home. In this case there is no separation involving space or time, and the family will not prepare the special meal that is supposed to welcome the newly circumcised. Nor is any specific moral or sexual education provided, and there is nothing to mark entrance into the world of sexuality and reproductive life or of taking responsibility for the family. It is clearly rather difficult to presume that the baby understands the symbolic value of the procedure or the possibility for him to exhibit his courage in any way. When you strip the *Olhusumba* of its symbolic value and of the element of separation, circumcision no longer carries any residual aspect of a rite of passage: no separation, no liminality, no incorporation. A new form of responsibility falls onto the fathers, and it is fulfilled within the short time of a visit to the dispensary.

A further effect of the medical circumcision of babies is that there is no separation of the young boys from the female world where they still spend their infancy. Based on traditional standards, these newborns should be considered as adults, but clearly their mothers cannot avoid seeing their babies naked or giving them corporal punishment. Furthermore, having a circumcised baby exempts the mother from the traditional task of checking on his sexual vigour by manipulating his genitals. This practice is now scarcely compatible with the morals of the Christian or Muslim faiths, for which the sexual aspects of life have to do with adult life only. The choice of neonatal circumcision is therefore quite congenial for young mothers who take their faith seriously.

This option is mainly the choice of young fathers who maintain that all Konzo males must be circumcised and that circumcision renders babies cleaner and easier to handle. Such fathers also stress the fact that healing is very quick and virtually risk free in babies. These are young men who have, or aim at having, white-collar jobs, and who see their sons' futures in a national rather than a local dimension. They might end up living in Kampala, or in Kasese, but certainly not along the ridges. Generally these families plan to have fewer children than the average rural family. Neonatal circumcision is mainly chosen by families who can easily reach a medical facility and who live in areas where child delivery is more predominantly medicalized then elsewhere in the district, so that the newborn is repeatedly in contact with health workers during the first days after birth. In the area of Kyondo, surrounding the Kagando hospital, and in the village of Ibanda, this option is much more frequent than in Bundibugyo.

In recent years this solution has become more and more common among Muslim families, since local Imams state that the Quran prescribes that boys must be circumcised on the eighth day after birth. They also advise families against circumcising older boys. Followers of the Adventist church also choose to circumcise very young boys as a sign that they belong to the people of God. It is interesting to point out that the Adventist faith spread very early and widely among the Bakonzo[5], but not among the neighbouring Batoro.

Konzo Opinions about the New Circumcision Practices

The community has lost its involvement in a tradition which saw successive generations of male individuals turn into men by circumcision. In the past, male communal rites ensured that men acquired specific competencies and social responsibilities.

A good indication that the symbolic value of the passage provided by the *Olhusumba* was an integral part of the Konzo culture comes from the markedly negative opinion that some parents hold about the practice of neonatal circumcision. Some fathers and mothers I interviewed in the area of Ibanda profoundly disagree with this practice as, in their opinion, a child must be old enough at the time of circumcision to remember it and understand its importance. Only in this way can he accept the new responsibility that leaving infancy implies. A good age, these informants believe, is six: at this stage the boys will be able to remember the event and at the same time they will not have to endure the mockery at school for too long. The informants who expressed this opinion were of a slightly older generation than the parents who choose to circumcise their children in the hospital. They were also somewhat younger than those parents who had waited for their children to solve the problem of circumcision on their own.

In most cases today it is left to the children to decide on their own to rid themselves of a stigma that confines them to infancy. This act does not imply the acquisition of any sort of knowledge or competence, nor does it enable them to fully acquire the identity of men.

Stages Along the Path of Change

I shall now analyze the cultural path that led from the ritual *Olhusumba* to neonatal surgical circumcision. The various communities in which I gathered information have reached different stages along this path, and within each of them the situation is rather varied.

In the 1970s many fathers in Ibanda were faced with the problem that their children could not take part in a traditional *Olhusumba*. The fact that no specific age was prescribed for the initiation – since the *Olhusumba* had a periodic recurrence – probably enabled many to defer any action. Furthermore, the organization of a rite on the part of a single family is relatively expensive and a father is not likely to decide to spend money for chicken, beer and other food to pay for the circumciser if he is not under social pressure to do so.

Yet some communities, mostly in the area around Bundibugyo, soon opted to adopt this solution and organized small, homely circumcision ceremonies that maintained the features of the group practice: of separation and suspension of ordinary life followed by a short liminal phase of traditional and moral education, during which the children could for the first time exhibit those qualities that are characteristic of adult men. Here too, some fathers did not take any action and waited for their children to decide for themselves.

This option of escape was the most common in Ibanda through the 1980s and 90s, but over the years fathers and families in general become less and less willing to welcome the runaways in a way that was still residually traditional. Lately, these traditional elements and the need for a rite of passage have become irrelevant, especially for young, educated but unemployed men, driven toward a westernized sort of life in which the average age for marrying and leaving the father's house has increased considerably. Nowadays in Ibanda there are quite a few young men in their thirties who are unmarried and do not intend to look after any children they might have had because they are unable to get the clerical job for which they are trained. These same young men are those who, as children, had to escape to be circumcised, their fathers having failed to take responsibility for bringing them into adult life. These individuals have become fathers without having had a chance to become men in the traditional sense, so now they choose to relinquish those rites that would mark the belonging to a community of men.

When they are farmers or diggers, fathers in Ibanda and in Kyondo are more inclined to recognize the importance of preserving some of the traditional elements of the rite of passage; but only a few felt financially able to organize the ordeal themselves. The option of organizing circumcision for a small group of children between four and eight years of age would appear to them as being the best choice, since it allows the children to understand the educational value of the process, to exhibit courage and to avoid mockery from their peers, while at the same time avoiding excessive health risk. This would mean fulfilling, at least partially, both the traditional requirements and the needs of contemporary society. In spite of these advantages, this option is the least frequent choice in the Kasese district and is also becoming less common in the Bundibugyo area.

Manhood and Fatherhood in the Absence of Tradition

As I mentioned above, as far as the traditional *Olhusumba* ceremony was concerned, the whole community shared responsibility for fostering the succession of generations and for inducting young individuals into adulthood. In fact, the fundamental choice of the right time for organizing the rite was made somewhere outside the village. Ever since the rite ceased to be a community affair it has lost its ability to function as a "man-making" device. Such a function cannot be taken up by any single individual.

According to tradition, a Konzo man who had gone through the initiation rite but died without producing any children could not be considered fully a man. Similarly, a young man who became a father before being initiated could not be considered as fully adult and could not assume full responsibility for his child. You are not fully a man if you are not a father and you are not a real father if you are not fully a man. In other words, only an adult and a responsible man can really acquire a father's identity and build his own family. In this view, only society as a whole has the power to make men. If, for some reason, society as a whole relinquishes this role, the succession of adult generations may be hindered.

This is what the elders refer to when they complain that nowadays the youth behave like rabbits, not like human beings: their sexual life is no longer defined by the body of rules that gave reproduction the characteristic of a social event and, as such, fully human.

As an old lady, a well-known midwife from Ibanda, put it: "They run away, they mate, they choose each other and produce children who have no father." The woman's old husband added: "But today children die much more than in the past", meaning that individuals who are not really adults produce a whole generation, which is unhealthy and unstable.

If we consider that pregnancy is also no longer a socially shared event but has rather become a time of life to be kept secret as far as possible, then it can be maintained that reproductive and family life has lost its former social quality. Just as in society and in families, reproduction is no longer ruled by the standards of social production but has become private and scarcely symbolic, so the making of men no longer takes place in the social arena.

The growing inability of parents to actively influence the future of their children goes along with the shrinking of the father's role that many woman informants complain about when they say that their husbands do not devote as much attention to the children as the previous generations did. This, in fact, is a generation of individuals who were circumcised but not made men, so they are not in a position to fully become social fathers. They are fathers only in biological terms.

A large percentage of pupils attending the last year of primary school and the first years of secondary school state that the school they attended was chosen by their mothers with whom they mostly live, and not by their fathers. The reduction of the father's role, or rather the fact that fathers are increasingly unwilling to maintain a normative attitude and to provide a point of reference for their children, could at least partly explain why a large number of children autonomously choose to escape and why, when they return home a few days after circumcision, they receive no specific moral, ritual nor traditional education, neither from their uncles nor from their fathers.

Other Causes that Participated in Ending the Traditional Function of the *Olhusumba*

I will not dwell on the importance of the spread of primary education in the shaping of gender and ethnic identity among Konzo children. It will suffice to note that parents surrender many educational tasks to schools. Parents willingly do so, for the school is thought of as having all those features of power, organization and responsibility over children that society relinquished when it abandoned the *Olhusumba*. The school has been granted the task of making citizens, not yet that of "making men". The introduction of universal primary education is too recent for a shift of the rite of passage from the traditional setting to the educational institution to have taken place.

An analysis of the role of monotheism in shaping a different sense of belonging than that of the traditional social community is beyond the aim of this work. Here I only wish to suggest that the need to define the otherness of society from nature finds a very strong solution in baptism, both from the symbolic and from the social point of view. The affiliation to a monotheistic religion greatly reduces the importance of traditional rites (indeed, all women cease to practice traditional birth-rites the moment they are baptized).

Furthermore, I wish to suggest that a shift from social responsibility to individual responsibility may also be linked to the creation of a new level of power, that of public institutions, which limits the impact of traditional decisions taken by traditional village institutions. It must be noted that state institutions, through school curricula, can only deal with the developmental needs and identity dynamics of children in a limited way.

Conclusions

In comparing new and traditional circumcision practices, what stands out as very relevant is the fact that the responsibility for marking the "making of men" no longer rests with the community as a public concern. A similar trend is apparent in the rituals that revolve around female sexuality.

The implication of this change for Konzo society is that, since the community no longer "makes men", it becomes a society which no longer has fathers in the full, moral, responsible sense of the term. That is to say that it loses its ability to project itself into the future. Women, who still do become mothers, take on the responsibility and the burden of bringing up the new generations. A society that builds its future only through the contribution of half of its members runs the risk of becoming a much weaker society.

Bibliography

Magezi, M.W., Nyakango, T.E. & Aganatia, M.K. 2004. *The People of the Rwenzoris.* Köln: Rüdiger Köppe Verlag.

Pennacini C. 1996. "Danze Nande". In Buffa, C., Facci, S., Pennacini, C. & Remotti, F. *Etnografia Nande, Vol III – Musica, danze, rituali.* Torino: Il Segnalibro, 59-90.

---.1998. *Kubandwa – La possessione spiritica nell'Africa dei Grandi Laghi.* Torino: Il Segnalibro.

Remotti, F. 1996a. *Contro l'identità.* Torino: Laterza.

---.1996b. "'Che il nostro viaggio generi degli uomini': processi rituali di 'atropo-genesi' nande". In Buffa, C., Facci, S., Pennacini, C. & Remotti, F. *Etnografia Nande, Vol III – Musica, danze, rituali.* Torino: Il Segnalibro, 163-244.

Stacey, T. 2003. *Tribe.* London: Stacey International.

Van Gennep, A. 1909. *Les rites de passage*, (Italian edition 2006. *I riti di passaggio*. Torino: Bollati Boringhieri).

Notes

1. The research on which this work is based was partially funded by the Missione Etnologica Italiana in Africa Equatoriale, directed by Dr. Cecilia Pennacini, University of Turin. The field work was carried out with permission of the Uganda National Council for Science and Technology (File No. SS1655) and took place in two different missions over a period totalling seven months, between May 2004 and January 2006.

2. Often, in my interviews, women made mention of the number seven, or said "seven plus seven" to mean a large but indefinite number of children, of years, of goats, etc.

3. As to the reason why informants are so vague about the moral stories and instructions to the youth, two explanations seem possible: either informants did not want to share male initiate knowledge with me, a woman, or the content of the stories was not significantly different from the usual moral education children received in the family, albeit indirectly, and therefore was not worth mentioning.

4. In spite of all these elements of change, it is important to point out that few informants recall that the return from the *Olhusumba* was a dramatic change from their childhood that had ended only a few weeks earlier. True change, state the older informants, takes place with marriage and the birth of children. Once again the Konzo society refuses to acknowledge change when it is too sharp, preferring to metabolize change through lengthier processes.

5. In 1947 the Adventist Church, lead by two pioneering missionaries, reached Mitandi, on the slopes of the Rwenzori. They were the first Christian missionaries to settle among the Bakonzo. Communication by Mr. Stanley Baluku.

Continuity and Change in Bakonzo Music: From 1906 to 2006

Serena Facci and Sylvia Nannyonga-Tamusuza[1]

Music and dance, like any other form of cultural expression, is subject to both continuity and change. While change is inevitable, there is no cultural formation that changes overnight and in a wholesale manner; some aspects are retained while others are lost. Similarly, the aspects of the music of the Bakonzo, people living in Rwenzori Mountain region on the border of western Uganda and eastern Congo (now Democratic Republic of Congo), have experienced continuity and change in the last century (1906-2006). We shall look at continuity and change in terms of performance practices, the types of instruments used, the various contexts of performance, musical structure, and meaning.

However, it is very hard, we could say impossible, to write a comprehensive "history" of the music in the Rwenzori area in the past century. To be historically described, the Konzo music would need regular and intensive fieldwork and comprehensive documentation about musical instruments, as well as pictures, audio and video recordings, musical transcriptions and analysis, descriptions of the context and the occasions when the music and the dances were performed, as well as the musicians' biographies.

In this paper, we will consider oral evidence and written records from the local Bakonzo[2]. Although these studies are very far from being complete, they offer a precious insight into the past, giving an idea of local musical history against which we can predict the future. They are like little windows opened occasionally and for a short time onto the fascinating musical panorama of the Rwenzori. What we offer you is not a real "history", but a more modest *diachronic ethnography*. In fact, there are a lot of gaps, and this paper only aims at stimulating more study of a musical culture that has almost been forgotten.

In this paper, we compare the ethnographic reports, images and sound records of the twentieth and twenty-first centuries in order to trace the historical trend of Bakonzo music. During our research in Kasese and Bwera Districts, we made an overview of the musical characteristics and social-cultural relations (dance movements and motifs, musical instruments, music theory, role of the music in terms of meaning and performance) in the twenty-first century. We presented to the musicians some Bakonzo and Banande music documented in the past in order to discuss with them the historical dimension of this music.

Bakonzo Music Context

When Luigi Amedeo di Savoia, the Duke of Abruzzi, arrived from Italy near the Mountains of the Moon in 1906[3], we can be sure that the musical traditions were very lively. However, the cultural, social and political contexts that have defined the Bakonzo since 1906 account for the continuity and change in their musical traditions. In order to establish the context for this discussion, there is a need to examine in brief the cultural, social, and political atmosphere under which music has existed. However, as John Blacking rightly reminds us, "changes which are characteristic of musical systems are not simply consequences of changes in social, political, economic and other areas"[4].

There is no certainty about the origin and movement of the Bakonzo before they settled in the Rwenzori region. Some historians and oral traditions claim that they broke off from the Batoro, while others claim that they came from Buganda after escaping persecution[5]; others allege that they came from the present eastern Democratic Republic of Congo[6] and yet others say the Bakonzo with the Banande (now living in Congo) were part of a bigger linguistic group: the Bayira[7]. However, whether they came from the eastern Democratic Republic of Congo or were originally one group before they were split by artificial colonial boundaries, the Bakonzo have a lot in common with the Banande of the eastern Democratic Republic of Congo[8]. First, the language Lukonzo and Kinande are very similar, whereas Lukonzo is quite different from the languages of the Batoro and Banyoro in south-east Uganda (Lutoro, Lunyoro). In fact, Margaret Trowell has stressed that, "Whereas in Uganda the name Konjo is in official use, the name by which the same tribe is generally known in Congo [Democratic Republic of Congo] is Banande"[9]. The Banande were separated from the Bakonzo by the artificial borderlines "defined in a series of treaties that were drawn up between 1907 and 1910, after the duke of the Abruzzi had explored the Rwenzori"[10]. As such, there is no way one can talk about the continuity and change of the music of the Bakonzo without referring to that of the Banande. Although we can see many variations when comparing Nande and Konzo music, they look like natural transformations in a main common culture. The hard question would be to ascertain why and when these transformations happened. Moreover, comparisons with the Baganda and Batoro will help us to develop an understanding of the continuity and change that shaped the Bakonzo music.

Despite the strong struggle of the Rwenzururu Movement to liberate the Bakonzo, until the 1980s they were under the political control of the Batoro of the Toro kingdom[11]. As such, to some extent, the Batoro and Bakonzo have had a dialectical influence on each other's music. Tom Stacey reports that, "'Bakonjo [Bakonzo] Life History Research Society' has slowly over the years been turned unto a political movement, the standard-bearer of Bakonjo 'nationalism' with the declared object of overthrowing Batoro domination"[12].

Further, Christianity and Western education, with their ideologies about "traditional" culture, have had an impact on the Bakonzo, like on many other African cultures. Moreover, although a number of the Bakonzo have been converted to Christianity, their belief in ancestral spirits still holds. For instance, Bernard Clechet reports that he "was in Bufuku (14,050 ft) [on Rwenzori Mountain], and tried to get some information about Kitasamba [chief spirit of Rwenzori], a porter, a Christian Mukonjo, with grey hair, asked me to stop talking about Kitasamba because he was evil and it was dangerous to talk about him in such a place"[13]. Actually during our research, Debizi Baluku, a flute player, also told us that we could not talk about Kitasamba while were near the mountains at Nakalengejo village.

Some Aspects of Toro and Konzo Drums in the Early Twentieth Century

Vittorio Sella, the photographer during the Duke of Abruzzi's expedition, took a number of photographs depicting musical activities within the Rwenzori region but, unfortunately, he took none of the Bakonzo, even though the porters during the last part of the expedition were all Konzo. Although these instruments are attributed to the Batoro, later writers, like Klaus Wachsmann (1953), have shown that the Bakonzo too have such instruments, although they may vary in performance contexts, style of playing and design. Two of the Sella's pictures are important for this discussion.

In the first one, we can see a drummer and Sella describes him as "the doorkeeper", greeting him at the entrance of the *Kabaka*'s court at Kabarole (Toro District) (see Figure 4) [14].

Figure 4   **Vittorio Sella, "The watchman at the entrance of the *eriba* of a native chief, who greets visitors with a long and noisy guffaw and a roll of the drums", 1906. Courtesy of the Sella Foundation.**

There is a similar drum in the ethnographic collection of the Museo di Antropologia in Torino. Probably the Duke brought it to Italy after his mission. The drum is the type that Wachsmann defines as the "Uganda drum": "The 'Uganda drum' uses two skins of which only one is beaten. The second skin is stretched across the bottom of the drum body to hold the lacing and is non-sonorous. [...] Bantu Uganda drums frequently have a 'broken' profile as if the top part of the instrument were a cylinder, put on to a conical base [...]"[15].

This type of drum is very common, not only among the Batoro, but also in other Ugandan musical traditions, especially in Bantu cultures. In fact, like the Baganda and Banyoro, among the Batoro the drum is a symbol of power, signifying the existence of a kingdom. The evidence given by Vittorio Sella's photo of the drum at the entrance of Kabarole Court is a sign of the particular role of this instrument, which is typical of courts like that of the Baganda and Banyoro. The drum announces the coming and going of the king and is indeed the doorkeeper. In this case, this drum could not be Konzo, since the Bakonzo did not have an established kingdom.

There is, however, information about Bakonzo drums at the beginning of the century in the ethnographic notes of Jan Czekanowski, who travelled in the area during the time of the Duke of Mecklenburg's expedition in 1908. In his ethnographic reports on Bakonzo and Amba cultures, Czekanowski gives some descriptions and drawings of musical instruments[16]. The drum in Czekanowski's drawing is quite different from the Toro-Nyoro-Ganda type; it is nearer, but not completely similar, to the Konzo-Amba type indicated by Klaus Wachsmann[17], and one that we saw during our research. Moreover, the Czekanowski drum is very similar to the Banande type used in Congo in the 1980s. In general, we can say that the Konzo and Nande drums are both more "slim" than the Ganda-Toro-Nyoro ones. Furthermore, like Czekanowski's drawings, the Nande type has a very short cylindrical part compared to the conical base and yet, it is common to find the recent Konzo drum with a long cylinder on a small base. As such, the contemporary Konzo drum is a variation of Czekanowski's Konzo drum of 1908 and the Nande drum that Facci observed in 1986.

The Konzo drum shares a lot with the Nande drum and a comparison would enhance our understanding of this instrument. Although the design and shape is different from that of the present day, we can find many similarities in terms of the performance practice and roles of the Banande and Bakonzo drums. For example, three drums, in both cultures, are normally played for dances. The biggest has a role of a guide (*enzoboli*). Inside the drums there is a small stone, a symbolic object named "the testicle of a wizard". It is the symbol of the drum's "life"; an aspect also shared in the Toro, Nyoro and Ganda drum traditions.

Facci notes how the drum in some occasions is symbolically linked with the *mwami* (the clan chief). A special orchestra of drums was played during the enthronement of a new chief. *Engwaki* and *erighomba* are the names used by the Banande for the dance in this occasion. As one can note, Nande society, where the most important authorities are the clan chiefs and there is no other central strong power, the *engoma*-political relationship is less strong than in other cultures in Uganda and in general in the Great Lakes region, particularly in the Burundi and Rwanda kingdoms[18].

However, as a result of the Rwenzururu Movement, the Bakonzo founded their own kingdom (although, until now, it is not officially recognized by the Ugandan government). Although the royal symbols are *engoma* and the *endara*, during interviews with the musicians in 2005, we did not receive any information on the role of these instruments in this new monarchy. Similarly, none of them knew the Nande names *erighomba* and *engwaki*, whereas other Nande ritual dances (for example, *amasinduka* for funeral, *omukobo* for war, *omukumu* for male initiation) were known to them. In our impression Bakonzo and Banande both give relevance to another symbolic drum meaning: the relationship with the ancestry. In an interview on 30 December 2005, Davis Walina, a drummer, said that many people have a drum at home because it protects the house and the family from danger, and it is also played to announce death. He also confirmed what a number of Banande said about the role of the drum in relation to the *evirimu*, the spirits of the deceased. As such, the drum, in this way, is a sign of family continuity[19].

Other Musical Instruments

In another photograph, Vittorio Sella recorded important information about the *makondere* orchestra, consisting of side-blown gourd trumpets (see Figure 5)[20].

Figure 5   **Vittorio Sella, "Native musical band at Unioro", 1906, Courtesy of the Sella Foundation.**

While the evidence available in the caption accompanying this photograph indicates that these are trumpets from Toro, Roland Oliver has reported that the Bakonzo too have *amakondere*. However, Oliver attributes their origin to Buganda. He alleges that some clans of the Bakonzo migrated from Buganda and brought *amakondere* with them. He writes that, Rubongo, "brought with him from Buganda the royal trumpets – *amakondere*"[21]. In fact, even today among the Batoro, as well as the Banyoro and Baganda, this orchestra is a royal symbol.

However, in our research we did not find any evidence of this kind of ensemble among the Bakonzo. Nevertheless, another orchestra was very common: *eluma,* a set of twelve to fifteen stopped flutes, each producing a different sound. Just as the *amakondere* trumpets, the *eluma* flutes are played with the ochetus technique, but the functions are different. The *Eluma* orchestra is used to accompany the *amasinduka* funeral dance and it does not seem to be connected to any royal and political symbolism. While Czekanowski did not mention *eluma* in his work, Klaus Wachsmann refers to this orchestra as belonging to the Bamba and the Bambuti in Bundibugjo District. However, he refers to *eruma*, which is most likely the same as *eluma*, and attributes it to the Bakonzo, reporting that it is performed "at the completion of mourning rites"[22].

Further, while all the other instruments documented by Czekanowski are still in use, there is no longer any trace of the pan flute today or in Wachsmann's documentation of the 1950s, even though pan flutes exist in Uganda among the Basoga, for example. Some of the instruments documented by Czekanowski that are still in use include: 1) the leg-bells *esyonzenda* worn by male dancers; 2) the notched four-hole flute *enyamulere*; 3) the gourd rattles (the main instrument for the *kubandwa*, a healing ritual and ancestral worship ceremony); 4) the horn *engubi* used in the past for signalling and during the war dance *omukobo*; and 5) the musical bow *ekibulenge*. The *ekibulenge* is now played with a gourd placed on the mouth. Wachsmann also photographed a man playing the musical bow in this position[23]. However, Czekanowski did not mention any gourd. According to him, the player put the bow between the teeth.

Czekanowski's work and the research done by Wachsmann document a musical panorama similar to the one we observed during our research. Wachsmann's drawings, photos, and objects are conserved in the museum and, most important for us, the musical recordings[24] reveal a bigger number of instruments. In addition to those mentioned by Czekanowski, Wachsmann's list includes: 1) the harp *enanga* (or *ekinanga*); 2) the lamellophone *elikembe* (or *erikembe*); 3) the percussion beam *enzebe;* and 4) the xylophone *endara*.

Another scholar, who went to the Rwenzori area at the same time as Wachsmann, was Hugh Tracey, the founder of the International Library for African Music. He recorded some Konzo music in 1950. We will return to Tracey's and Wachsmann's recordings later.

Vocal Music: A Song Recorded in 1936

Unfortunately, when Czekanowski arrived in Uganda, he did not have the phonograph he had used in Rwanda and so he did not record any music. The first audio recording in the area was made by a Belgian missionary M. Jules Celis, in Beni (Congo), with a phonograph of the Berliner Phonogram Archiv. Celis was also the first to talk about the *endara*, the big xylophone so important for the Nande-Konzo culture. He recorded only two Nande marriage songs before the machine broke. Only one of these songs is very clear. We propose a transcription of the score in Musical Example 1[25].

Musical Example 1

Nande wedding song, perfomed by women, 1936. Extract.

(Solo.Melody A) *Kahumira, kahumira*   [Walking without knowing where (2t)]

(Chorus Refrain) *Eriyakwa ngawetsera*   [Dying while asleep (refers to sex)]

(A) *Kahumira, kahumira*   [Walking without knowing where(2t)]

(B) *Kahumira ly'obakahula mw'eherukare*   [Walking … that's being married]

(A) *Kahumira, kahumira*   [Walking without knowing where(2t)]

(B) *Kahumira ly'obakahula mw'eherukare*   [Walking … that's being married]

(A) *Kahumira, kahumira*   [Walking without knowing where(2t)]

(B) *Kahumira ly'obakahula mw'eherukare*   [Walking ... that's being married]

(A) *Kahumira, kahumira*   [Walking without knowing where(2t)]

(B) *Kahumira ly'obakahula mw'eherukare*   [Walking ... that's being married]

(B) *Kahumira Baghenda w'abene babeghera*   [Walking ... Those who move to other people's houses must adapt]

(A) *Kahumira, kahumira*   [Walking without knowing where(2t)]

(B) *Kahumira ly'obakahula mw'eherukare*   [Walking ... that's being married]

(A) *Kahumira, kahumira*   [Walking without knowing where (2t)]

(Final) *Eriyakwa ngawetsera ly'obakahula mw'eherukare. Eriyakwa*   [Dying while asleep that's being married. Dying]

The song is clearly addressed to the bride. There are explicit references to the new status of the woman (*baghenda w'abene*, those who move to other people's houses), who must become a member of the husband's family[26]. The marriage (*ly'obakahula mw'eherukare*, "that's being married") is a crucial moment; the girl does not know her future life (*kahumira*, "walking without knowing where"). For her this is like a death: her past life in the paternal family is "dying while asleep" (*eriyakwa ngawetsera*). The term *ngawetsera* refers here to the sexual intercourse. When someone enters a new family, they normally "must adapt to" (*babeghera*) the new situation. This is what the song recommends to the bride: to die and to begin a totally new life in the husband's family. In this sense the wedding is like an initiation ritual for the woman[27].

As for the meaning and the style of the lyrics we could regard this song as part of the large repertoire of Nande wedding songs, always performed by women, also used during the 1980s. In this song we also have many of the important musical aspects we noted during our research.

First, the form of call and response is in a very common style of the "Bantu" culture and extensively used by the Banande-Bakonzo. There is a time for the soloist and a time for the chorus. The soloist can freely organize his/her time with changes and improvizations, but the refrain comes in with precision, like a chronometer.

Second, in the soloist's part, we do not have a strophic structure, like often in European music, but a melody divided in two parts, A and B. The soloist can sing these two parts in any order, with all kinds of repetitions and variations. In this case, the form is: A A B A B A B A B B A B A. Moreover, we can hear this form in the instrumental music too, but with more sophisticated segmentations and variations.

Third, the song has a regular beat even if it is not clearly expressed (for instance with hand-clapping). The time of the beat is divided in triplets (--- --- ---), which is also still very common in the twenty-first century Konzo music.

Fourth, the notes used are few (only four), suggesting a tetratonic system. However, in the recording of Hugh Tracey and Wachsmann in the 1950s, Konzo music was often performed in a heptatonic system. It would be an exception among the Bantu (in Uganda, Burundi, and Rwanda), where the predominant system is pentatonic. However, in the 1980s, some Nande songs for marriage, sung by women, had an extensive range of notes, suggestive of a pentatonic system in the background, like the Konzo song recorded in 1936. What does this mean? We can suppose that the pentatonic system was common before the Christianization of the Bakonzo and that the tuning of the instruments became closer to a heptatonic system later. However, some female wedding songs, important for their ritual dimension, resisted in an "older" style. But this is only a supposition: other people in Uganda were subjected to Christianization and to church music during the same period as the Banande and Bakonzo, but the tuning of their traditional instruments is still pentatonic. Neither can we exclude the possibility that, in the past, different kinds of ranges coexisted in Nande-Konzo repertoires.

Omubaliya: a case of continuity

During our fieldwork in 2005, we played a selection of music recorded in the 1950s to some musicians. On the same CD there was also Nande and Toro music. In most cases, the Konzo musicians distinguished the Toro music from the Nande-Konzo. Sometimes they also knew the title of the Konzo music. One of the tracks was *Omubaliya*, a song played on the *enyamulere* flute and recorded in 1950 by Tracey[28]. All the musicians, and also other people, recognized this song and its title, and it is still popular in the twenty-first century. *Omubaliya* means fisherman and the song is about a fisherman who died in the lake, while his wife and his friends waited for him at home. However, the story has various versions. We collected various recordings of this song. All were played on the *enyamulere*. A good *enyamulere* player normally breaks up the melody into short pieces and presents it in many variations and, sometimes, this may include musical motifs completely unrelated to the main melody. If we analyze the *Omubaliya* recorded in the 1950s, we find some melodic patterns, of which some are still in use. In particular, we can easily recognize one of them present in all the different versions of *Omubaliya* we heard.

In Musical Example 2, we present the transcription of an excerpt of the performance recorded by Tracey as played by Bukombe Mukirane. The first melodic pattern is repeated with variations and a second one is named "Pattern A". This model has a particular contour characterized by long high notes between the lower sounds[29].

Musical Example 2

Omubaliya, perfomer Bukombe Mukirane, 1950. Extract.

The melodic contour of Model A in all the performances of *Omubaliya* is easily recognizable as we can see in Musical Example 3[30].

Musical Example 3

A last extract comes from a recording done by Serena Facci with Kambale Kimavi, a Nande musician in North Kivu[31]. The name of the song is *Ekibaliya* (the bad fisherman), and the song tells the story of a man who died in the lake while his friend waited for him. The melody is a little distant from the Konzo group of melodies, and it was impossible to find the Pattern A.

But some similarity could be found with another pattern. If we look at Musical Excerpt 4, there is a melodic cellule characterizing the repeated melody, indicated with "B". It is a simple descending sequence of sounds (with interval of a second and a final third).

Musical Example 4

Ekibaliya, perfomer Kambale Kimavi (munande), 1986. Extract.

This cellule is also repeated in some Konzo versions of *Omubaliya*. See the cellule B in Musical Example 2.

Continuities and Changes in *Endara* Xylophone

Although it is an important instrument among the Bakonzo, Czekanowski did not mention the *endara* xylophone in his 1908 documentation. However, in the 1930s, Humphreys, an explorer climbing the Rwenzori, saw this instrument in the centre of a village[32]. Gerhard Kubik, who came near Bwera in 1962, but only for a very short time, recorded the *endara* and wrote a paper comparing the Konzo and Ganda xylophones. However, details of his findings are outside the scope of the present discussion. The *endara,* played together with the drums, has been an important magico-religious instrument among the Bakonzo; it is not an instrument that is owned by anyone. The *endara* has always been associated with Kitasamba, the head of the Rwenzori spirits, the god of the Bakonzo. In fact, Gerhard Kubik reported that "We soon observed how much the Bakonjo [Bakonzo] music is connected with Bakonjo religion; this holds true for the xylophone music"[33]. Further, narrating his experience during an expedition to the Rwenzori Mountains in 1974, Bernard Clechet (White Father) reported that although they converted to

Christianity, the Bakonzo still built *Kitasamba* "a small shrine in the form of a xylophone"[34]. Similarly, during our research in 2005/2006, we attended the new-year's eve ceremony at Kihaasa village, where the *endara* featured as a prominent instrument during the *kubandwa* thanksgiving ceremony. Florina Mbambu Nyamutooto, about 46 years and formerly a Roman Catholic (she actually had a rosary), was the *mbandwa,* the priest.

While there were definitely some evident changes in the structure of the instrument compared to what Klaus Wachsmann described in 1953[35], there are still some continuities. Similar to what Wachsmann noted, the *endara* which was performed during the *kubandwa* ceremony, had sixteen slabs and was also mounted on banana stem supported by short stumps. However, the slabs where separated from each other by reeds instead of sticks as reported by Wachsmann. Unlike Wachsmann's report, we observed four performers instead of five playing the *endara* in interlocking style. Further, we were given different names for some of the musical parts in comparison to what Wachsmann[36] was given; and these include:

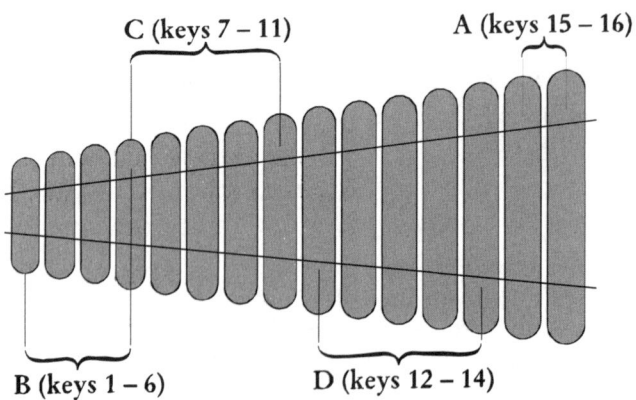

According to Wachsmann, A is *omukirinya* and *muguswe* or *omuhumbiriri*, while we were told that it is *ebikekulu*. Wachmann reported B as *omuhimbiriri*, while we were told that it was *obwana*. We were told that part C was *enzoboli* and this only differed from that of Wachsmann in spelling; it was *"nzhobolye"*. We were informed that part D was *ebidenguli*, while Wachsmann reported them as *omusakulwe*. From this data, it is impossible to establish whether there has been a change in the naming of these parts or whether the differences are accounted for by the difference in informants and their knowledge of the *endara*.

However, comparing research on the *endara* of the Nande, who are closely related to the Bakonzo, might give us a clue to the way in which there has been continuity and change in the Konzo *endara*. In her study of the Nande, Facci reports that the *endara* has fifteen to seventeen keys, which is within the range of what Wachsmann and we observed[37]. While Facci concurs with Wachsmann on the five-player system, she differs in the naming of the parts played on the *endara*. However, Facci's naming is closer to the one we were given during the 2005/2006 research; *obwana* and *"enzovoli"* (but the more correct spelling is *enzoboli*) refer to the same *endara* parts.

In her recent research on Konzo *endara*, Vanna Crupi compares many different instruments and groups of performers[38]. Her study reveals that the number of four players is now common. However, other features such as the number of the logs or the name of the musical parts are various. Crupi's data concurs with Wachsmann's and with other studies in the use of the terms *enzoboli* and *omwana* (or *obwana*). The *enzoboli* is the name of the main musical part and *omwana* is the part played on the smallest high-pitched logs. Omwana is the Konzo word for child (*obwana* means childhood). As we said above, this term is also common among the Banande: they use it for the high-pitched keys of the xylophones and other instruments.

What still holds with Wachsmann's research is that the Bakonzo *endara* is a rare instrument, and besides being performed in churches and during school festivals, outside these contexts, it is performed mainly during the *kubandwa* ceremony.

However, the *endara* takes on new designs to fit in the school and church contexts, and the meaning of the music is also reconstructed. For instance, due to their poor durability, the banana stems are replaced with wood boxes as the frames for the *endara*. Probably the redefinition of the *endara* performance context could help to explain its rarity. Because the *endara* performance we observed was in a ritual context, it had other props around it, and these included a basket in which money and herbs were put. On either sides of the *endara* were a sorghum stalk, a cow's skin, and two flowers of a reed plant. There was constant sprinkling and drinking of local beer made from bananas and sorghum, as well as continuous smoking of tobacco and marijuana by the *mbandwa* and the musicians.

In 1966-67, Peter Cooke recorded Konzo *endara* music in many villages in Bundibudjo, Kasese and Bwera Districts[39]. Cooke arrived during a crucial time during the rebellion against the Batoro by the Bakonzo Rwenzururu Movement. He also recorded many protest songs. Some of them are still sung as accompaniment to dances. However, these songs had multiple meanings and cannot be taken literally. Besides presenting protest, some of these songs emphasized the strong link between the Rwenzori and the people of the mountain: "If a White come from the mountain follow him, if a white comes from the West, don't go with him"[40]. The "White coming from the mountain" is the snow, the symbol of Kitasamba, the white god of the snowy peaks. During the Rwenzururu movement, white became the symbolic colour of the protest. The whites coming from "elsewhere" are the Basungu: the Europeans. They also referred to the Batoro because of their close connection with the British as part of the British divide-and-rule policy. Further, in a joint publication, Cooke and Martin Doornbos[41] reveal that the *enyamulere* was very common at beer parties and the melody always came from a song. The flute was accompanied by the percussion beam *enzebe* or by a drum beating the common pattern of triplets. They also transcribed a new corpus of songs in European style.

Comparing Nande and Konzo Music

The political instability of the late 1960s that culminated in Idi Amin's overthrow of the government in 1971, had as consequence the deportation of all foreigners in 1972. As a result, research on Bakonzo music, like any other music, was curtailed. Facci's study of the Banande later, in 1986-1988, is the only available research that can help us trace the musical development of the Bakonzo in the latter part of the twentieth century, and these findings are useful to compare to our joint study in 2005-2006.

In Table 3, we compare the Banande music in the 1980s and the Bakonzo music we documented in 2005/2006. The important musical ensemble (*engoma, endara, eluma*) is at the top of the list. The solo instruments follow. Some secret ritual instruments (*omukumu*) are at the end.

Table 3 **Nande and Konzo Music**

NANDE INSTRUMENTS (Facci, 1986-88)	KONZO INSTRUMENTS (Nannyonga & Facci, 2005/2006)
• Engoma (drum)	• Engoma
• Endara (xylophone)	• Endara
• Amalenga or Eluma (set of flutes)	• Eluma
• Enyamulere (flute)	• Enyamulere
• Esyonzogha (ankle bells)	• Esyonzende
• Enanga (harp)	• Enanga
• Enzebe (percussion beam accompanying many instruments)	• Enzebe (it accompanies only the harp *enanga*)
• Akasayi, Erikembe (lamellophones)	• Edungu (big harp from Acholi)
	• Erikembe (only mentioned)

• Akaghoboghobo (fiddle) • Endeku (one-hole flute) • Enzenze (zither) • Ekibulenge (musical bow) • Omukumu (set of percussion beams for the male initiation *olusumba*, it was a secret instrument)	• Endingiti (fiddle, only mentioned) • Enzenze • Ekibulenge • Omukumu (now used by cultural groups) • Gourd rattles and bells for *kubandwa*

Comparing the ensemble music, the instruments used (*engoma, endara, eluma, enzende-enzogha*) are the same in both Bakonzo and Nande cultures. The *engoma* and the *endara* are the most important instruments during weddings, funerals, political meetings, traditional rituals and competitions. However, there are some differences: for the Banande the *endara* accompanied dances. This dance, also named *endara* like the instrument, is neither a gendered nor an age-specific dance; any person irrespective of gender or age could dance it. Further, the *endara* has a very important place during the traditional rituals, especially *kubandwa* among the Bakonzo, as we saw before. During the ceremony the spirits are invoked with rattles and bells accompanied by the *engoma* inside a hut, though the *endara* is often played outside[42]. However, in the 1980s the Banande did not practise the *kubandwa* (at least in the open, accessible to Western scholars and missionaries) as much. Was the *endara* a religious instrument for the Banande before Christianization, when they were devoted to the ancestral spirits? If so, is the loss of the *endara* in ritual functions one of the signs of the erasure of the traditional religion? Or, did the traditional priests *embandwa* perform the rituals in secret, without the *endara* (a big instrument producing loud sounds)?

The Banande and Bakonzo musical traditions differ more with regard to solo instruments including harps and flutes. For example, the little one-hole flute *ndeku*, used by the Banande (mostly by children) is completely unknown by the Bakonzo. Moreover, *akasayi*, a Nande plugged instrument with a hemispheric gourd resonator, is not familiar among the Bakonzo[43].

In some cases, the instruments are similar, but their function and relevance is different. In the 1980s, the *enanga* and *erikembe* had an important function for the Banande. Both these instruments (common in many Ugandan cultures) were used during the evening, at home or in the buvettes, and on the local radio. The players sang the old songs used for dancing, as well as some epic songs, but the biggest source for their new repertoire was topical issues or sometimes personal life experiences. Among the Bakonzo of the 21st century, the *erikembe* and the *enanga* is less in use in general ceremonies. The *enanga* is mostly used in the church, accompanying Christian hymns. The strings (eight in the past[44]) are now nine or eleven in number, and the tuning is in the temperate system. This instrument is changing because of influence from other Ugandan cultures. For example, we saw the *enanga* played with the *adungu*, the big harp from the Acholi, in northern Uganda. Are these transformations a sign of "modernity" or was the *enanga* less important to the Bakonzo in the past too? Is that the reason why Czekanowski did not mention the *enanga* in his research on Konzo music? In fact, in Wachsmann's recordings of the 1950s, the songs are short and repeated many times[45]. Similarly, Erisa Muhonja, son of a late *enanga* player in Ibanda, told us in an interview that he could not recall his father's repertoire. It is also interesting to remember that Wachsmann, in his notes on bow-harps in Uganda, talks about the "disappearance [of the harp] from musical life of the Ganda"[46]. After independence in 1962, the harp became one of the instruments used for musical education in school, but rarely exists in the 21st century. Maybe the history of the Konzo harp has to be seen in a larger context of the evolution of this very ancient instrument in Uganda.

The *enyamulere* (flute), documented by all the scholars during the past century among the Bakonzo, is also very popular today. However, it was not the same for the Banande in the 1980s. The flute players were less respected than the *enanga* performers[47].

The Banande and Bakonzo also use the *enzebe*, a percussion beam, in a different way. This object was a sort of obsession for the Banande. The *enzebe*, with rhythmic patterns, accompanied each solo instrument, for instance the harp, flute and zither. In Bwera District, we saw the *enzebe* played only once with *enanga*. However, in 1953, Klaus Wachsmann recorded the percussion beam played with *enanga*. On the other hand, Peter Cooke reported the *enzebe* playing with *enyamulere*, but in a lot of his recordings this flute was accompanied by the drum and not by *enzebe*. In some cases, the *enzebe* of the Banande (maybe also among the Bakonzo) was used as a substitute for the drum. The reason may be because the *enzebe* is a cheap instrument; it can be found everywhere[48], whereas the drums need to be made by a specialist with particular wood coming from the forest and the skin of a cow, or a leopard. However, some aesthetic reasons could be noted: the high-pitched sounds of the *enzebe* are sometimes preferred (in the case of the *enanga*, for example). The Konzo drummers sometimes play on the wooden edge of the instrument to create the effect of the *enzebe*. This kind of beating is named *esyongakatero*.

The musical features including tuning, melodic contours, improvisation and variation, and rhythmic organization are somehow similar. A deeper study must to be done to compare the various repertoires. One key musical concept which must be mentioned is the concept of *e-enzoboli*. It is a sound, corresponding with one specific string on the harp, log in the xylophone, or flute in the *eluma* flute set. It has a particular role in the music, which the Konzo musicians seem to be more explicit in defining than the Nande players[49]. For the Bakonzo, the *enzoboli* "leads". It is the most important pitch or the most important part in an ensemble. In the xylophone one of the four (or five) parts has this name too: it is the part charged with reproducing the main tune in the group.

While we do not deal with any dance in this paper, it would be important at least to include a list of dances as a suggestion for an area that needs future exploration. As such, Table 4 shows, as a comparison, the Nande dances as observed by Facci between 1986-1988 and the Konzo dances as observed in 2005/2006[50]. The dances are in order of relevance:

Table 4 **The Nande and Konzo dances**

NANDE DANCES (Facci, 1986-88)	KONZO DANCES (Nannyonga & Facci, 2005)
• Omunde	
• Endara	• Ekikibi
• Amasinduka	• Amahande
• Amatakio	• Amasinduka
• Omukobo	• Omukobo
• Akasayi	• Akasayi
• Omukumu (secret and only mentioned)	• Omukumu (performed by some cultural groups)
• Erighomba (for *omwami*)	• Other less-performed dances not mentioned in Congo
• Other less-performed dances not mentioned in Uganda	

We can note that some dances are common to both Banande and Bakonzo. For example, some ritual dances: 1) the *amasinduka,* performed during funerals; 2) the *omukobo,* an old war dance in which two dancers do the pantomime of a fight; and 3) the *omukumu,* performed during the male initiation ceremony *olusumba.* However, the most often performed dances, documented during the two researches, are different. The most popular dance for the Banande in the 1980s was the *endara,* the dance around the xylophone. The Bakonzo in 2006 did not use the term *endara* to denote a dance. With the accompaniment of the *endara,* they performed other important dances and mostly the *ekikibi,* a mixed dance (like the Nande *endara*) also documented by Peter Cooke in 1966. The *munde,* another famous performance among the Banande, is an athletic male dance, completely unknown to the Bakonzo. The wedding dance *amatakio* (for young girls) is also specific to the Banande.

Facci's research of the 1980s revealed that the Banande musical customs were very clear about the different performance roles of men and women. Women, for instance, did not play any instruments. Further, many dances were specifically for either men or women. It was only the *endara* dance which was performed by both genders. However, motifs for male dancers were more complex and acrobatic than those of the female. During an interview, some informants told Facci that the Christian missionaries had influenced the style of performing, and the more erotic mixed dances were disappearing. Of course, deeper exploration of the truth of this statement is needed before one can objectively confirm it.

In our research in 2005/2006, we verified on many occasions that Bakonzo women do not play instruments. However, looking at the dance tradition, we always saw men and women dancing together. In the *ekikibi,* the most popular dance, men and women perform different but very explicit erotic movements. This dance is performed during the weddings and has been interpreted as a courtship dance[51]. Maybe the Christian missionaries had less influence on the Konzo dancers than they had over the Banande, or possibly there may be some other reasons that would now be too difficult for us to investigate.

Reinvention of Konzo Music

The establishment of cultural groups and the promotion of indigenous music education in schools and school festivals by the Ugandan Ministry of Education has contributed a lot to the reinvention of not only Konzo music, but also of other music cultures in Uganda[52]. The 1960s were a period when cultural groups were beginning to develop in many parts of Uganda, inspired partly by the troupe "Heartbeat of Africa" (which performed at Uganda's National Theatre and at state functions in Kampala as well as overseas) and partly by the growth in teaching of traditional music in schools and colleges. These "cultural groups" were established with the aim to preserve local traditions through performance. In October 1967 Peter Cooke found an active group from Bwera calling itself the "Rwenzori Drama and Cultural Society" performing in public for the Independence Anniversary celebrations at Kasese. The group had been formed two years previously. Cultural groups are now found in many Bakonzo villages. They perform at public gatherings like political rallies, wedding ceremonies and competitions organized at village, county and district levels. The musicians are often semi-professional and, like in many other parts of the world, prefer the more spectacular repertoires, like the dance with the *endara* xylophone or with the *eluma* set of stopped flutes.

The formation of the cultural groups and promotion of school music and dance festivals has had some influences too. For example, near Ibanda, a local cultural group performed a dance similar to that which Facci and Cecilia Pennacini filmed near Butembo in 1988. This dance was originally performed for the presentation of a newborn to the sun. The woman who led the dance did a pantomime showing how to carry the baby using a monkey skin. Near Butembo the dance was performed by a group of traditional obstetricians. At that time, many birth rituals were disappearing, mostly because many mothers went to hospitals to give birth. These women were however able to perform the old dances and remembered the ritual very well, probably because they had performed it often in the past. All the birth rituals, they said, were strictly for women.

However, when the Konzo Ribuni Cultural Group in Nyakalengija proposed the same dance in 2006, none of the girls present wanted to interpret the protagonist: the women dressing and moving in the monkey skin. It was an informal situation, we arrived without any announcement and the group was not complete. The main dancer and group leader was a boy. He did not mind dancing with the skin, like a woman. Of course the new context (it was not a ritual, but its enactment) permits this change of role. Maybe in the future it would be normal for a Konzo or Nande woman to play the *engoma* or the *endara*.

In conclusion, we can say that while there has been substantial continuity, there have also been a number of changes in the music and dance of the Bakonzo, due to changes in the political, social and cultural environment. We have also demonstrated that due to the close connection of the Bakonzo and Banande, the history of the Bakonzo music can only be accessed through an understanding of the Banande. Finally, the gaps in this paper will hopefully stimulate further extensive research on the Bakonzo, a musically rich, yet largely unresearched culture.

Notes

1. This paper is a collaborative effort based on data collected jointly in December 2005 and January 2006, as well as prior research done by Serena Facci since 1988, on the Banande music.

2. The oral sources are interviews conducted in December 2005 - January 2006. The musicians interviewed included: Manksi Bagheni (Mihunga – Kasese District), Kyiti Erisania, Kule Kosimu, Baluku Bwenge (Nyamurongo – Kyondo Sub-county), Baluku Desesi (Nyakalengija – Kasese); Kule Mbakwa (Mihunga – Kasese), Erisa Muhonja (Ibanda – Kasese), Mbasa Marani, Milton Kule (Kinyabisiki, Kyondo), Nzwenge Gidion (Kabuyiri – Kasese), Thembo Kumasa (Nyamurongo – Kyondo), Isembwa Sele (Nyakalengija – Kasese), Kisamba Cultural Group, Zedekya

Moiyugha (Kisamba - Kasese), Rubuni Cultural Group, Davis Walina (Nyakalengija – Kasese). We appreciate the work by Stanley Baluku and Hilary Baluku Kikumbwa, who were our interpreters. As far as documents are concerned, during the 1950s some ethnomusicologists began to work in the area. Hugh Tracey (1950, 1952) and Klaus Wachsmann (1950, 1953) collected some music for two important African institutions: the International Library for African Music and the Kampala Museum. Tracey also went to Congo and recorded the Banande music. In the 1960s, after the independence and the advent of the national republics of Congo and Uganda, two other scholars arrived in the area, both studying other areas of Ugandan traditional music: Gerhard Kubik and Peter Cooke.

3. On his expedition to reach the highest peaks, see Pennacini, C. (ed.) 2006. *I popoli della luna - The People of the Moon. Rwenzori 1906-2006*, Cahier Museomontagna, Torino.

4. As quoted in Moisala, P. 1991. *Cultural Cognition in Music; Continuity and Change in the Gurung Music of Nepal*, Gummereus, Jyväskylä, 13.

5. Oliver, R. 1954. "The Baganda and Bakonjo [Bakonzo]". In *Uganda Journal*, 18, 1, 31-33.

6. Nzita, R. & Mbaga, N. 1993. *Peoples and Cultures of Uganda*, Fountain Publishers, Kampala, p. 39.

7. Mushauri, K. T. 1981. "Organisation étatique des Yira, et son origine". In AA.VV , *La civilization ancienne des peoples des Grands Lacs*, Karthala, Paris, 160-169.

8. See also Baluku, R. 1999. *Marriage Customs among the Bakonzo in Uganda*, BA (Law) Dissertation, Makerere University, 1.

9. Trowell, M. 1953. "Domestic and Cultural". In M. Trowel & K. Wachsmann, *Tribal Craft of Uganda*, Oxford University Press, London, 8.

10. Pennacini, C. 2006. "On the Slopes of the Rwenzori. Ethnology of an African Frontier". In Pennacini, C. (ed.), 2006, p. 215.

11. On the Konzo rebellion against the Batoro during the twentieth century and on the Rwenzururu movement, see Alnaes, K. 1969. "Songs of the Rwenzururu Rebellion. The Konzo Revolt against the Toro in Western Uganda". In P.H. Gulliver (ed.) *Tradition and Transition in East Africa*, Routledge & Kegan Paul, London, 243-272; Stacey, T. 2003. *Tribe. The Hidden History of the Mountain of the Moon*, Stacey International, London; Pennacini, C. 2006.

12. Stacey, T. 1965. *Summons to Rwenzori*, Secker and Warburg, London, 19.

13. Clechet, B. 1990. "The Rwenzori: The Attempted Ascent by Bishop Guillermain and Fr. Achte". In 1896 - A Commentary, *Uganda Journal*, 39: 37.

14. The photo is published in Pennacini, C. 2006, 57.

15. Wachsmann, K. 1958. "The Sound Instruments". In M. Trowel & K. Wachsmann, 369-70.

16. Czekanowski, J. 1924. *Forschungen im Nil-Kongo-Zwischengebiet*, t.II: *Ethnographie: Uele/Ituri*, Länder Klinkhardt & Biermann, Leipzig, 382-384.

17. Wachsmann, K. 1958, p. 380.

18. Facci, S. 2000. "Les Nande et leur musique". In F. Remotti (ed.), *Ambienti, lingue, culture*, Edizioni dell'Orso, Alessandria, 59-101.

19. See also Waswandi, K.N. 1987. *Anthologie de la philosofhie africaine: les proverbs Yira*. Vol. 3, Grand Seminaire Saint Mbaga-Tuzinde, Bukavu.

20. Fondazione Sella, Biella.

21. Rubango was formerly a Muganda of the Bakunta family who fled after a failed plot to kill Jjunju, the brother of Kabaka Ssemakokiro, king of Buganda, who reigned around 1779-1794. (Oliver, R. 1954, 32).

22. Wachsmann, K. 1958, 342.

23. Ibidem, plate 108. The photo is also in the permanent exhibition of the National Museum in Kampala.

24. The musical recordings of Wachsmann are in the Uganda Museum in Kampala and in the Sound Archive of the British Library in London.

25. The document is still in the Berliner Phonogram-Archiv.

26. On the marriage in Nande culture see Remotti, F. 1993. *Etnografia Nande I*, Il Segnalibro, Torino.

27. Many thanks to Ph. Jean de Dieu Kahangia for the lyric's transcription and translation.

28. The recording is published on the CD entitled *Secular Music from Uganda*, edited by A. Tracey, ILAM, SWP Records SWP 024, 2003, track 17. In the booklet it is mentioned that Bukombe Mukirane, Mukonzo in Toro District, was the performer.

29. A musical transcription is always a compromise; it is even worse when one has to transcribe a Konzo piece using Western conventional systems, which at the moment are the ones available. In this case, we present the

melody in 4/4 for easier comprehension, even if the rhythmic patterns played by the drums are heard in 12/8. Since the drums are not our focus here, we do not transcribe them. We give only the indication of the inner rhythm in 12/8, to show the rhythmic relationship between the flute and the drum parts.

30. List of the recordings: 1) Performer Kule (leader of the group). Kisomoro-Toro District, rec. K. Wachsmann 1954, location British Library C4/36 S1 C3; 2) Performer Manksi Bagheni, Mihunga-Kasese District, rec. S. Facci and S. Nannyonga December 2005; 3) Performer Kyithi Erisania, Nyamurongo-Kasese District, rec. S. Facci and S. Nannyonga, January 2006; 4) Performer Baluku Desesi, Nyakalengija-Kasese District, rec. Serena Facci and S. Nannyonga, January 2006.

31. The recording is published in the CD *Zaire. Entre les lacs et la forêt: la musique des Nande*; ed. S. Facci, AIMP, VDE Gallo CD 652, 1991, track 5c.

32. In Wachsmann, K. 1958, p. 318.

33. Kubik, G. 1962. "The *endara* xylophone of Bukonjo". In *African Music Society Journal*, III, 1: 43.

34. Clechet, B. 1990, 37.

35. Wachsmann, K. 1958, pp. 318-320.

36. Ibidem.

37. Facci, S. 2000, pp. 65-68.

38. Crupi, V. 2005-2006. *Ruoli e funzioni dello xilofono 'endara' nella musica dei Bakonzo (Uganda)*, Tesi di Laurea, Università "La Sapienza", Roma, see also Vanna Crupi's article in this book.

39. The catalogue of Cooke's recordings is available online, on the website of the British Library. Other recordings are in the Uganda Museum of Kampala and in the Sound Archive of the British Library in London.

40. English translation of a song recorded at Kinyabisiki (Bwera District, Kyondo Sub-county), January 2006.

41. Cooke, P. & Doornbos, M. 1982. "Rwenzururu Protest Songs". In *Africa*, 32, 1: 37-53.

42. The Bakonzo used to sacrifice animals to the spirits during the ritual, killing them on the *endara* and sprinkling the logs with the blood. This we witnessed during our research in 2005/2006. See also V. Crupi's article in this book.

43. On the *akasayi* (dance and instrument) see also Facci, S. 2000, 61-65.

44. Wachsmann, K. 1958, 413.

45. See British Library sound Archive C4/35 S2 C6.

46. Wachsmann, K. *The sound ...*, 398.

47. In 1951 Hugh Tracey recorded an extraordinary Nande *enyamulere* player, Mwongolo, published in the CD *On the Edge of the Ituri Forest*, ed. A. Tracey, ILAM, SWP 009/HT 03, 1998, track 12. See also the John Blacking considerations on Mwongolo recordings in Blacking, J. 1955. "Eight Tunes from Butembo, East Belgian Congo". In *African Music*, I, 2: 24-52 and Idem, *How musical is man?* University of Washington Press, Seattle.

48. The Banande also call this instrument *akakete* (a common, but not an important object).

49. See Facci, S. *Les Nande ...*, p. 71.

50. For the Nande dances see also Pennacini, C. 1996. "Danze Nande". In C. Buffa, S. Facci, C. Pennacini & F. Remotti, *Etnografia Nande III*, Il Segnalibro, Torino, 59-89.

51. Mbabazi, P. 2003. *Ekikibi Dance of the Bakonzo*, BA (Music) Dissertation, Makerere University, Kampala.

52. Nannyonga-Tamusuza, S. 2003. "Competitions in School Festivals: A Process of Re-inventing Baakisimba Music and Dance of the Baganda (Uganda)". *World of Music*, 45, 1: 97-118.

The Role and Functions of the *Endara* Xylophone among the Bakonzo People

Vanna Crupi

André Schaeffner, in his well-known book *Origine des Instruments de Musique,* invites the reader to consider musical instruments not only as "significant material traces of musical production" but also as true "signs" that stand at "the multiple crossroads of techniques, arts and rites" (Schaeffner 1936; it. ed. 1986: 334-335).

The *endara* is a log xylophone, which is an important musical instrument among the Bakonzo, a population living on the western border of Uganda, along the slopes of the Rwenzori massif. The *endara*, besides being one of the instruments that most represents Konzo musical culture, is also held in great esteem by virtue of the many functions it fulfils in the social and spiritual life of the community. This "sound object" is, in fact, recognized by the Konzo people as a symbol of their cultural identity and a sign of continuity with their past.

The choice of undertaking ethnographic research, with this particular musical instrument as its focus, stems from the lack of extensive studies on the subject. For many years, in fact, the turbulent socio-political history of the Bakonzo people has prevented in-depth ethnographic research from being carried out. The opportunity of realizing this research project[1] emerged from a productive collaboration with the Italian Ethnological Mission in Equatorial Africa, which has long been involved in important research studies of an ethnographic nature in the area of the Great Lakes.

The xylophones of the interlacustrine area

Central-west Africa can be considered the area where log xylophones, musical instruments which are made up of a series of wooden keys or slats set on a sound box made from banana tree stems, are most widely distributed. The results of extensive research carried out in the 1950s by Klaus Wachsmann (1953) and expanded to include the entire territory of Uganda, offer a detailed report of the types of xylophones existing in the area. During his studies Wachsmann noted the presence of the log xylophone in Uganda among the Ganda, Nyoro, Soga, Konzo, Alur and Gwere peoples (Wachsmann, 1953: 311-414). There are significant differences between the many xylophones existing in the interlacustrine area, both in the specific structural qualities of each specimen (the shape of the keys, for example), and also in the tuning, repertoires, and composition and performance techniques. On the other hand, there are a similar number of affinities between the various instruments, which bear witness to the contacts, exchanges and loans that occurred over time between the many populations of the area. Evident similarities can be noted, for example, between the terms used in different idioms to define the sound object in question. In Lukonzo, the word *endara* is used to indicate the xylophone specific to the Bakonzo people, whereas the term *entaala* was extremely widespread in the past among the Baganda people to indicate the entire orchestra of the *kabaka* (king)[2]; lastly, *ndara*, seems to be the most common appellative attributed by the Alur to their xylophone (*idem*: 318-319).

The Rwenzori *endara*

Limiting the field of observation to the area of the Rwenzori, a mountain range forming the western border of Uganda, we come across the same term *endara* both among the Bakonzo people and the Banande, a population living on the opposite side of the mountain range, in Congolese territory[3]. The analogies, in this case, go beyond mere linguistic boundaries, embracing the instrument in its entirety. In fact, the Nande and Konzo xylophones stem from the same matrix and belong to the same culture.

The first reports of an *endara* orchestra date back to the 1930s, a decade during which L.J. Celis[4] documented the use of the instrument by the Banande in the Congo, and Humphreys (1933) first spotted an *endara* among the Bakonzo. Klaus Wachsmann was to provide the first scientific documentation of the Konzo xylophone and the first audio recordings of the musical repertoire related to it. Subsequently, during the 1960s, Gerhard Kubik (1963) managed to hear and record the Konzo *endara* near Bwera, a town located on the Western border of Uganda. Peter Cooke and Doornbos (1982) recorded the sound of the *endara* in the same area in the years 1966-67.

The first scientific data on the *endara* of the Banande people was collected and processed by Olga Boone in 1936 on the basis of the collection of xylophones kept in the Museum of the Belgian Congo in Tervuuren. From 1986 up to the present, Serena Facci (1988, 1996) dedicated her in-depth research to Nande music, giving wide scope to studies on the *endara*.

Organology of the instrument

The wooden keys, which make up the keyboard of the *endara*, are traditionally placed in graduated order of size on a sound box consisting of two banana tree trunks. The trunks are cut as the need arises and are laid on the ground opposite each other, creating a temporary support for the keys. The length of the trunks is directly proportional to the number of bars on the xylophone. A series of pegs inserted into the trunks separates one key from another. In some cases, twisted dry banana leaves are used to isolate the keys from the trunks. These are made to run between one peg and another for the entire length of the trunks, thus perfectly isolating the wooden keys and intensifying their timbre.

Figure 6   *Endara* of Say Muhando Yokana Visitemi, Lyakirema II village, Bwera.

After performances, the bars are kept in special huts or, in some cases, sheltered from the rain under the roof of dwelling places, where they are tied together with bundles of twigs or ropes. The xylophone is accompanied by three *engoma* (drums)[5], by the sound produced by the *esyonzende* (foot-bells)[6] of the dancers, and by singing, generally in responsorial form between a soloist and a chorus.

When comparing the results of studies on the Bakonzo instrument and the data available on the Banande instrument, the differences observed between the two *endara* appear to be extremely limited. The main difference concerns the number of *endara* players (*munyandara*) who take part in the performances. As Facci notes, the ensemble of a Banande *endara* orchestra consists of five xylophone players and three drummers (Facci 1988:108). Among the Bakonzo, the number of instrumentalists involved is more varied; the most widespread formation sees the presence of four *endara* players and three drummers.

The Bakonzo *endara* consists of four sections that conceptually subdivide the keyboard, with each one entrusted to a *munyandara*. Each of these may have one or more keys in common with the adjacent sections. Observing the instrument from the smallest to the largest key, the series of bars take the name of *obwana* (children), *enzoboli* (he who guides), *ebikekulhu* (older women) and *ebisyakulhu* (older men). This terminology is used in the same way to indicate both the roles of the musicians and, by extension, the sections of keys that they play. Even though some informants report that each section is made up of five bars, from the data collected it would appear that the number of keys in each area is variable.

During performances of the recorded tunes, the order of entry by the musical parts of the xylophone and other instruments involved is, as a rule, the following: *obwana, enzooboli, ebikekulhu, ebisyakulhu*. Only later do the drums, from the smallest to the largest, and the ankle-bells, come into play. Lastly, the singing is superimposed upon this rhythmic-melodic pattern.

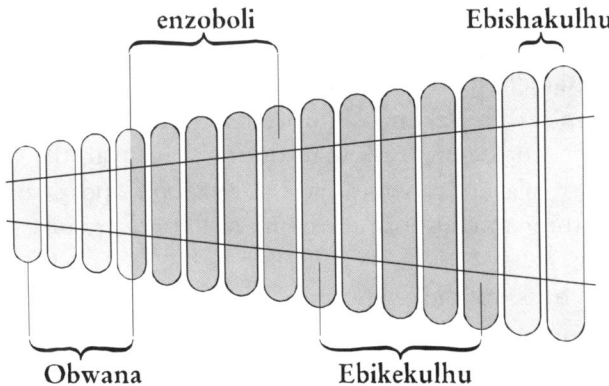

Figure 7 **Endara: an example of the section layout.**

The *obwana*, therefore, starts the tune, and this section almost always has one, two or three keys in common with the *enzoboli*. Although it is said that the first part is the easiest to perform, in reality it very often appears to be one of the most complex. In other cases, however, the *obwana* in effect expresses only a very simple rhythmic pattern on which the tune, built up by the *enzoboli* and the deeper sections, is structured.

The *enzoboli* is recognized as being the most important section of the *endara*, because "the one who plays the *enzoboli* is able to accompany the dancing, even when alone"[7]. Furthermore, the person who plays this part has a role that is more closely linked to improvisation and can create variations, which liven up the tune. The *enzoboli* has from one to three keys in common with the *obwana*, one of which (the key called *enzoboli*, in fact) is often struck at the same time by two players with a regular cadence: this fact – some informants would seem to suggest – constitutes a metric reference for the other musicians. The *enzoboli* key is recognized by the Bakonzo as being the most important. Facci, when investigating the term *enzoboli* used in the musical sphere by the Banande, notes the importance of the key in question, identifying the origin of the word in the verb *erisobolha*, which means "to speak clearly", "to explain" (*Idem*: 135). This same verb is also indicated by Stanley Baluku, a Konzo interpreter who sets a second meaning alongside the one reported among the Banande: "to lead or guide". The two translations are not in contradiction. Without this important bar, explain both the Banande and the Bakonzo musicians, the *endara* cannot be played. Facci further reports that, during a festival, the leader of the group of players can remove the *enzoboli* and take it away, thereby putting an end both to the musical performances and the celebrations.

Going back to the sections of the *endara*, the part of the *ebikekulhu* is often very simple, occurring as a rhythmic *ostinato* constructed on three keys alone. Petero Kivinga, claiming that the sound of this part is encapsulated in the name of the section, sings the rhythm implicit in the word by emphasizing the onomatopoeic role of every single syllable. The *ebisyakulhu,* on the other hand, assumes different roles according to the occasion: at times it seems to be even less present than the *ebikekulhu* in the melodic construction; on other occasions it takes on a structural role, creating a rhythmic-melodic interweaving of a certain depth with the *enzoboli* and the *obwana.*

Wachsmann (1953:318) noted some *endara* consisting of from fourteen to eighteen keys. For Kubik (1963:45-48) the keyboard of a complete *endara* is made up of fourteen keys. The sixteen *endara* instruments that I saw and recorded during my research activities in the Konzo territory have a variable number of keys, of different lengths and tonality: from a minimum of seven to a maximum of 24. The most commonly recurring model would nonetheless seem to consist of fourteen or fifteen keys. Field research has allowed me to understand the reason for this variety in the number of keys that make up an *endara.*

It may often happen, in fact, that when surveys are conducted on the sounds of the single bars, musicians hesitate to include some of the keys set on the logs in the audio recordings. Generally, the largest keys, those positioned at one end of the keyboard, are discarded. The reason for this resistance seems to be linked precisely to the marginal role of those keys that are excluded from the set, which are useful only when a broken or discordant key has to be substituted. The existence of these surplus keys could in part explain the difficulties encountered by scholars, and by the Bakonzo themselves, in defining with precision the number of keys that make up an entire *endara.*

The Functions of the *Endara*

The rediscovery of traditional practices which had seemed destined to vanish, is a tendency, which, for decades, has involved numerous aspects of Konzo society in general. In order to define which functions the music produced by the *endara* fulfils today in the life of the Bakonzo, one needs to take into account the controversial and articulated history of that population, to whom various scholars have long dedicated their research in an attempt to reconstruct their origins and paths (cf. Pennacini, 2006). The mountain farmers of the Rwenzori today find themselves in a complex reality which sees their traditions coexisting with the demands of progress that Western culture has brought with it since its arrival. From the religious point of view, the massive Christianization undergone by the population has compromised the equilibrium in their methods of analyzing, interpreting and responding to a reality, which found its legitimacy in the cosmological philosophy of the Bakonzo, and in traditional religion. If the population today feels the necessity to go back to its own origins, it is also hindered by circumstances: Western progress has inexorably become a model of ideal life for many young Konzo people.

In this multifaceted and complex context, the *endara* still finds a place directly in the middle of these two opposing trends. It is a centripetal force which leads the Bakonzo to return to their own traditions, maintaining the *endara* within the social and ritual space; and it is also a centrifugal force that throws bridges across the traditional cultural boundaries, launching the instrument onto the stages of various districts in Uganda and into the recording studios of the region.

The *Endara* at the Centre of the Village

Although the assemblage of an *endara* today seems to be directly tied to its use, there is information in the writings of Wachsmann about a past collocation of the Konzo xylophone at the centre of the community's space. In the 1930s, writes Wachsmann, the explorer Humphreys, during his reconnoitres, came across an "*endara* firmly fixed in the ground at the centre of the village" (Wachsmann, 1953:316).

In a description of the layout of a traditional Bakonzo village, published in the 1950s, Trowell and Wachsmann (1953) speak of huts set side by side, in such a way as to create two lines of dwelling places that stand opposite one another. In the middle of these, two structural lines were located: the *kyaghanda* (the hut where the adult men used to meet to discuss the running of clan life) and the *kirimba* (where the young people slept and were instructed in the cultural traditions of their clan). The centre of the Bakonzo village therefore represented an essential place in social life, and the *endara*, according to the scant description offered by Humphreys, must have had a stable collocation in this space precisely because of its qualities as a support for social activities.

Even the musical terminology linked to the *endara* reveals the symbolic connection of the instrument to the traditional socio-cultural tradition of the Bakonzo. The names given to the *munyandara* (*endara* players) and, by extension, to the sections of the xylophone entrusted to these players, generally indicate age groups and social roles[8]. The significance of these terms causes one to reflect upon the possibility that the *endara* may mirror an image of society divided into age brackets, given the clear definition that these seem to have among the Bakonzo. With the musical support of the deeper, warmer tones of the "elders" (men and women) and the rhythmic ostinato of the "children", emerges the voice of adult men, "those who guide" the tune, in the same way that they guide the clan. This symbology is not dissimilar to that of various sets of African drums that generally represent age groups or family roles.

One of the principal values borne by music lies in its contribution to integration within a given society or group (Merriam, 1983:226-227). For the Bakonzo, dancing around the *endara* strengthens the sense of belonging to their cultural roots. This function is perfectly portrayed in the drawing, with the title "Dances in Lubero", published in the text by Olga Boone (1936:80), in which some Banande musicians dominate the foreground around the instrument, while dancers holding lances and shields, and positioned in a semicircle, throng the rest of the scene.

The important function of this Konzo instrument also finds confirmation in the oral literature of both the Bakonzo and the

Banande. Facci notes the existence among the Banande of a proverb linked to the xylophone: *endara siki ko mulimba*, which is translated as "There is no *omulimba* for the *endara*" (Facci, 1996:20). The term *omulimba* means "the one who cannot sing/dance" (*ibidem*). The popular saying explains: "There is no-one who cannot sing/dance the *endara*": it therefore follows that everyone is able to "sing and dance the *endara*". In fact, the dances which are linked to this instrument involve the whole community, with no level of specialization or distinction between the sexes, as does occur with the *esyonzole* (female initiation rite) and *olushumba* (circumcision rite). A sentence very similar to this proverb is also found in the text of the song *Kathonda*, recorded among the Bakonzo in Uganda during my research. The fact that this proverb continues to exist even in the present bears witness to the how profoundly rooted this sound object is. It reflects on the extent that the ancient tradition of singing and dancing around the *endara* has remained unchanged.

There are, on the other hand, significant changes in the role of musicians within society. In the past, the *endara* players were required to be highly specialized, undergoing a long period of apprenticeship before they were able to master the instrument. In the 1930s, Olga Boone stated that among the Baswhaga (a Banande clan) "the *endara* is the property of the *watwere*" (Boone, 1936:118), i.e. the artist who, accompanied by his four musicians and apprentices, moved from village to village during the festivities[9]. She continues: "the profession of the *watwere* is not hereditary: once he has become too old, he leaves his place to the player in his circle who shows the most talent" (*Ibidem*). This statement appears to be anomalous when compared with the testimony of many Konzo musicians. They claim that knowledge of the *endara* in the past was an exclusive prerogative of some families belonging to the *Abaswagha* and *Abashukali* clans[10], in particular among the sub-clans of the latter: *Abahimbira* and *Abatwandara* (*omutwandara* from the verb *eritwa*, to cut; *omutwandara* therefore means the one who cuts the *endara*, most probably the one who cuts and builds the *endara*). In some families of these clans the instrument is still handed down from father to son, but nowadays the *endara* can be played by anyone who is interested to do so. The question of who inherits the *endara* and the knowledge connected to it, therefore, appears to be controversial and difficult to define from the outset. Only through further, in-depth studies perhaps could the truth of the matter be verified.

The *Endara* Synthesis of the Bakonzo Space

The *endara* represents a symbolic synthesis of the Bakonzo's double connection with the forest and the banana grove. Its keys come from the *omusitu* (forest) whereas the trunks, which make up the sound box, are cut from *esyomboko* (banana grove).

Francesco Remotti (1994: 52-53) describes the perception and conceptualization of space for the Banande: the *eka*, the settlement or the inhabited village, is surrounded by the *esyomboko*, the banana grove, which is considered to be a threshold area separating the *eka* from the *omoli*. This latter term indicates the external world, which includes, as well as the cultivated and uncultivated fields, the *omusitu*, the forest. As the most extreme part of the *omoli*, the forest, therefore, proves to be the opposite of the dwelling space, the territory of man. In the past, survival of the population required violent actions against the forest, which was cut down and then burnt. Remotti writes: "The Nande proudly present themselves as *abakondi*, tree-fellers" (Remotti, 1994:119). Nowadays, the violent relationship with the *omusitu* appears to be less marked among the Bakonzo, but there is still an evident ambiguity. The scholar further explains that the Banande are dominated by the idea of order and, for them, the *eka* (village) must necessarily be governed by harmony. The *omoli*, on the other hand, represents disorder, a place governed by untamed nature, and inhabited by spirits (*abalimu*). The Bakonzo fear that these spirits may wreak havoc in their lives, and they believe that disregarding the rules irritates these supernatural presences, driving them to inflict punishments, thereby creating "disorder" (*idem*: 53-54). In order to re-establish the lost harmony, it is necessary to placate the spirits by consulting them and satisfying their requests. The *endara*, as well as symbolically representing the continuity between the territory of man and that of spirits, is also considered to be something that contributes to re-establish the "order" between these different worlds.

Figure 8   **Construction of the *endara* inside the Rwenzori National Park.**

The *Endara* and the Forest

The forest, and the Rwenzori Mountains which are covered by it, are under the jurisdiction of *Kitasamba*, the foremost spirit in the Konzo pantheon, who rules his kingdom from the glacier-bound peaks of the highest mountains. Crossing the territory of *Kitasamba* and his spirits requires strict observation of rules and regulations, and the implementation of specific rituals. The act of cutting a tree to build an *endara* also demands a scrupulous ceremony. Every tree is considered to be a perfect being, immortal, a model of perfection. During a lengthy stay in an Ibanda village, I was present at the creation of an *endara*. The instrument in question, built by Walina Davis[11], an artisan in the village of Nyakalenghigya, was obtained from a single tree trunk found inside the Rwenzori Park[12]. The technical procedures and rituals connected to this event highlight the ties existing between the Konzo instrument and the traditional local cult. To cut down the tree, explains Walina Davis, it is necessary to have the agreement of *Kitasamba*. A chicken and an egg must be sacrificed to him: the head of the chicken will be buried and offered to the spirits of the ancestors.

> When you go to build an *endara*, you must sacrifice an egg and a chicken. The chicken must be eaten and the egg left there intact. The chicken must then be completely eaten; nothing must be left in that place (…). This is how you ask permission of the owner of the tree, *Kitasamba* (…). He is the lord of the forest including the tree: when you cut down a tree, *Kitasamba* comes to check what is happening. If he finds an egg under the tree, he might be placated (…). I left the head of the sacrificed chicken there, because when I left home to go and cut the *endara*, the spirits of my family came with me, too, and participated in the ceremony by eating the head.

> When *Kitasamba* arrives to control the situation, he finds blood on the ground and understands that the spirits of my family were present and participated in the meal[13].

Walina carries a special whistle with him into the forest, on the end of which hangs the tail of a small wild animal: blowing this whistle serves to drive away evil spirits and obtain a good sound on the *endara* keys. While Walina's brother, carrying a kind of machete (*omutemi*), climbs onto the first branches of the tree, making his way through the foliage, Walina sets the egg which he has brought with him at the foot of the tree, shakes the whistle in the air as though to drive away someone or something and blows heartily into it, producing long piercing sounds. Leaving the egg as a sign of recognition for *Kitasamba,* and driving away the evil spirits are the first steps to be taken for the construction of the *endara* to be successful. The first part of the ritual is over. At a gesture between the two men, the boy on the branches begins to cut down the tree with blows of his axe.

Only after the first key has been made is the head of the chicken brought from the *eka.* The blood sprinkled on the wood contributes to obtaining the correct sound and timbre from the instrument. Cutting a tree to build an object, even when it is considered sacred, does not diminish the danger that this act implies. The proof of its importance lies in the precise ritual connected to the cutting down of the plant: the offering to *Kitasamba*; the request for protection from the ancestors to defend oneself against evil spirits; the ceremony that must be respected if the action is to be successful. Everything takes on a solemn dimension that is necessary when facing the challenge within the forest.

The Kitasamba *Endara*

In Konzo cosmogony, the spirit *Kitasamba* appears as the firstborn son of *Nyamuhanga,* the divine creator, whose actions in the world are conducted through his children and emissaries. The bond between *Kitasamba* and the *endara* is unequivocally confirmed by various witnesses[14]. Cecilia Pennacini affirms that the social organization of the Bakonzo in Uganda is based on *obulhambo,* territorial units corresponding to the mountain crests. In the past, every *omulhambo* had a chief, the *omukuru,* who performed a purification ritual called *eribhiria obulhambo* when there was trouble in his territory. This ritual foresaw the use of an *endara* through which it was possible to communicate with *Kitasamba* and, carried into the mountains by the chief, accompanied the *ekikuba*[15] dance with music all night long. The aim of this ritual dance was to purify the crest (Pennacini 2006:

138). But the connection between the instrument and this spirit, which is so dear to the Bakonzo, can be noted in many other contexts, which will be analyzed subsequently. Alongside the spirit of the Rwenzori, there is a specific *abalimu* that is linked to the *endara*, called Munyandara, who is recognized by many Bakonzo as being the son of Kitasamba.

Kitasamba, however, does not seem to be recognized by the Banande. This may justify the fact that the xylophone is not used in a ritual sphere among the population living in Congolese territory, who consider the instrument a symbol of aggregation and recreation, used during traditional festivals and various moments of leisure. Further research may, however, shed light on the different function that the *endara* fulfils among the two populations.

From some of the interviews conducted during research among the Bakonzo, it would seem that the missionaries, from the moment they arrived, considered the *endara* to be an object linked with evil. This demonization of the instrument was due to the active role taken by the *endara* in possession rituals, during which it was played to communicate with the spirits. Gerhard Kubik who, in the 1960s, observed an ongoing tendency among the Bakonzo to abandon instrumental playing of the xylophone, attributed the phenomenon to the existence of a close link between the *endara* and their traditional religion, the practice of which appeared in his eyes to be progressively receding.

> We soon observed how much Bakonjo music is connected with Bakonjo religion. This holds true also for their xylophone music. Its religious background may be one reason for its rapid disappearance nowadays. (Kubik, 1963:43)

It is certain that, even today, some traditional healers and various people who are culturally linked to the *endara* play the instrument to communicate with the spirits. The instrument, when used for therapeutic purposes, is considered sacred and subject to specific taboos, as are all the paraphernalia of the healers.

The *Endara* and Albinos

One specific mystic-ritual context in which the *endara* takes on a central role even today, and which appears to sink its roots deep into the past, is linked to the birth of children affected by albinism[16]. The whiteness of skin of albinos is an anomaly for the Bakonzo, which is interpreted as a sign of favour in the eyes of *Kitasamba*. Albinos are considered to be the children of glacier spirits and are welcomed into the community as such. The Bakonzo people do not appear to be entirely free from a sense of disorientation and stupor when faced with "otherness", but the role of albinism in the Konzo culture appears to be unusual when compared with the situation of other African cultures where albinos are often marginalized and ill-treated and their birth considered a misfortune and curse[17]. For the Bakonzo, the albino's bond with *Kitasamba* seems to legitimize their "differentness", which stands midway between a transcendent reality and the world of mankind. The presence of an albino in the family demands scrupulous observation of rules and rituals which the parents generally learn from a diviner. The sound of the *endara* has a primary role in the rite, most probably because of the close bond existing between this instrument and *Kitasamba*. The parents of albinos must keep one of these instruments in the house and play it every month when the new moon rises. Should these rules not be followed, they run the risk that the albinos would be abducted by *Kitasamba*, vanishing into thin air. In that case, the family is obliged to play the *endara* continuously, night and day, to allow the missing child to come home. The Bakonzo believe that an albino who is taken by *Kitasamba* will come home dancing, guided by the sound of the instrument, and remember nothing of what has happened.

The disappearance of albinos brings the social equilibrium into question, undermined as it is, according to the Bakonzo, by lack of respect for the rules dictated by *Kitasamba* regarding the protection of his "children". Yet again social harmony can be disturbed by "disorder": that special disorder which is understood to be "a consequence of breaching the harmony between people and spirits", to which Pennacini (1998:144-145) makes reference in her studies on the *Kubandwa*. The *endara* establishes communication between mankind and *Kitasamba* and, at the same time, its sound serves as a signal for the missing albinos who will follow the music to find their way home. Konzo society's commitment to this rite aims to reorder the equilibrium which has been lost. The return of the albinos confirms, on the one hand, their belonging to the community and, on the other, the return of order to the life of the Bakonzo.

The *Endara* Today

The complex question of the presence of the *endara* xylophone in different contexts, and its use by different social agents, is faced and in part resolved by the Bakonzo who, today, allow the existence of two categories of xylophone: a secular version used by cultural groups and common people, and another, devoted to the *abalimu,* which is played by special families and some traditional healers. In actuality, the two categories of instrument are often not clearly distinct: it is, in fact, more likely that the ritual context cloaks the object with sacredness. On those occasions, playing the instrument becomes a kind of "homage" to the spirits in order to resolve a prior dispute and restore harmony with them.

The response of the population to the social and political changes over the course of time has in some cases led to the abandonment of numerous traditional practices and, in others, their transformation and adaptation to the new conditions. Starting in the 1960s, when the Bakonzo were faced with the risk of the progressive disappearance of their complex and rich traditions, a large number of cultural groups began to emerge[18]. Even today, these associations dedicate their activities to recuperating various traditions, above all the art of dancing and music. They favour the *endara* among the various instruments used in their performances, not only for its recognized "representativeness" within the Konzo musical tradition, but also for its aesthetic and showy characteristics. During this research, among all the *endara* orchestras that were encountered, the vast majority were those composed of traditional groups. The activity of these associations, in effect, fulfils different functions which are adapted to the new social needs: the dances and traditional music are beginning to be structured for the presentation of real shows. So the beneficiaries of the music and dance no longer belong exclusively to the Konzo community, who usually take an active part in the event, but may also be mere spectators. The *endara* of the cultural groups and the members of the group itself are moving from the centre of the village to wherever they are asked to perform, bearing witness to a progressive transformation of music and dance events into the sphere of performance. The figure of the professional or semi-professional modern musician and dancer, whose aim is to live off the earnings from tourism, public events and private parties, is also emerging. The strong influence that these associations have on the process of transformation and adaptation of traditional repertoires should not be overlooked either.

During this research, it was noted on many occasions that various xylophones were kept in public schools. These instruments are generally used by music teachers during their lessons. The school xylophones are normally called *endara*. In reality, they are models that have been purpose-built for didactic use (similar to Orff instruments) and their tuning is clearly pentatonic, whereas the traditional tuning of the *endara* is considered by many scholars to be pseudo-heptatonic[19]. In some cases, the school xylophone comes from the capital Kampala, where one can buy instruments of that design in numerous shops. Music education in Ugandan schools follows didactic programmes which teach the composition and performance techniques of "African music". The term African music is generally associated - and not only in Ugandan institutions - with the use of pentatonic scales, because of their wide diffusion throughout Africa. In the Rwenzori territory, these rules are not in fact violated, even though Bakonzo teachers are asked to teach the children the differences that exist between African music in general and their own traditional local music.

Endara Tuning and Repertoires

In the *New Grove* music dictionary, under the entry for 'Uganda' compiled by Cooke and Doornbos (1980:618-629), which is dedicated to the traditional music of ethnic groups living in the national territory, the Konzo musical system is defined as heptatonic. Nonetheless, the current state of studies reveals the adoption by the Bakonzo, not only of sound sequences composed of seven or more sounds defined as heptatonic or pseudo-heptatonic[20], but also of pentatonic and hexatonic scales, as is noted by Blacking (1955:23-24) and Facci (1988:130). Moreover, the existence, even if remote, of forms of sound organization which are even less defined, and can only with difficulty be ascribed to a specific category, cannot be excluded. The adoption of sound sequences of seven or more sounds, however, is a characteristic feature which differentiates Konzo music from any other neighbouring culture.

Simha Arom (1989:9-26) points to the xylophone as a key element in defining the melodic and modal range of the musical repertoire associated with it. Gilbert Rouget also considers the instrument a preferred means for general study of the scale systems of a people:

> La série de touches de bois dont il se compose rend une suite de sons fixes formant entre eux un ensemble d'intervalles stables (...).

Le xylophone ouvre donc tout naturellement la voie à l'étude des
èchelles musicales, ou si l'on préfère des gammes utilisées en
Afrique. (1986:34)

In point of fact, the tuning of each xylophone can be considered
stable, particularly in those xylophones with fixed keys. In the
instruments with unfixed keys, even though the range of sounds
in use is determined at the moment of construction, the
possibility of varying the arrangement of the bars on the
keyboard makes it difficult to form hypotheses about the
organization of sounds.

Among the Bakonzo people, the *endara* is generally
assembled as it is needed and the keys are removed from the
sound box at the end of each musical event. Reconstruction of
the keyboard is entrusted to the expert ear of the musicians,
generally to the group's leader. The sequence order of the keys
may be conditioned by an infinite number of reasons (a left-
handed musician could, for example, invert the setting of the keys
in his section to make the performance of an otherwise difficult
rhythmic-melodic pattern more accessible). Even without such
variables, and while recognizing that the range of the *endara*'s
sounds fall within one single model, it is not easy to identify
general rules that are able to regulate the internal relationships
between the pitches.

When analyzing two examples of tuning in Konzo *endara*s
recorded by Klaus Wachsmann in the 1950s[21], the pitches of the
keys on one of the two instruments are arranged by a scale
sequence very similar to the heptatonic model. On the other
hand, the tuning of the second xylophone recorded by
Wachsmann does not appear to be so coherent. Gerhard Kubik,
in the 1960s, stated that he had encountered great difficulty in
attempting to associate the tuning of the *endara* with one single,
defined model.

Even if a scale which was very close to the heptatonic model
was in use in the 1950s, it remains to be seen if the origin of this

type of scale used by the Bakonzo is to be sought within the culture itself or whether it stems from outside influences. It could, in fact, be a product which is foreign to the culture, adapted on a pre-existing autochthonous model. A second problem that is raised by the research concerns the limited coherence of the tuning of many modern *endara*s, deemed out of tune by the musicians themselves, but played nonetheless. In these cases, which are not so rare, people dance to the rhythm of the instrument, and the songs are still recognizable, even though they may vary notably from the hypothetical original model. It almost seems as though, for some musicians, the minimum requirement for a specific tune to be recognized as such is the existence of the opposition of high and low sounds within the single sections[22]. In the overall playing of the parts, however, the essential characteristic is to be sought in the existence of different layers of sound, these too in a relationship of opposition to one another.

Tuning Techniques

Tuning of the endara occurs after all the keys have been roughly cut in graduated order of size (on average, from the smallest of about 40 cm to the largest measuring one and a half metres) and set in position on the two strong logs that are used to create a provisional sound box. In this way, it is immediately possible to verify the sound of the keys and carve, file or shorten them until the right tonality is obtained.

During the building of the *endara*, Walina Davis uses a song with the title *Wangenia obwe mirera* to tune the instrument. The choice of this song as a reference pattern would seem to be dictated exclusively by its melodic characteristics[23]. The song, which uses a sequence of seven sounds, has a descending progression and the beginning of every strophe is distinguished by intervals of thirds and fourths. These intervals, however, also distinguish the rhythmic-melodic patterns of the instrumental accompaniment of the song: when playing the tune on the xylophone, Walina is able to check the tuning and, where necessary, modify the pitch of the individual keys and their intervals. Alternate keys will generally be tuned to an interval of a third or fourth. Walina Davis's choice of the interval distance between alternate keys also appears to be conditioned by the motorial rules linked to the playing of the instrument. The right hand will play, for example, keys one and three, and the left, keys two and four. The tuning of the instrument, therefore, appears to rely on the implementation of an interweaving of musical features (the repetition of standard intervals) and the performer's motorial rules (the alternation of the keys). Baily, on the other hand, clearly explains this interaction between sound and movement when he defines the instrument as "a type of transducer, converting pattern of body movement into pattern of sound" (Baily 1990:149).

The importance of the interval of a third in the tuning of a Konzo xylophone is also supported by the assertions of Gerhard Kubik who, in his article on the *endara* written in 1963, notes the repetition of "something similar to minor thirds" among the alternate keys in the low range of one of the two Konzo xylophones analyzed. Kubik further hypothesizes that the standard interval between adjacent keys on the *endara* may be 148 cts, therefore 3/4-tone (Kubik, 1963:44).

The standard intervals between consecutive keys noted during research by the author of this article were somewhere between 140 and 200 cts: therefore, between 3/4-tone and a tone. However, the existence of smaller intervals, about 80 cts, cannot be excluded.

The *Endara* Repertoire

During field research it was difficult to establish which tunes made up the traditional *endara* repertoire. The number of tunes performed seems to be extremely vast and many songs are modern compositions. The Bakonzo themselves, despite claiming that the traditional repertoire consists of no more than four songs, do not agree when identifying the songs in question. On this subject, the following is the testimony by Petero Kivinga, an elderly *endara* player living in the area of Bwera[24]:

> In the past, mainly four songs were played. When people came to realize that the *endara* could be played for entertainment, more songs were composed in addition to those from the past.

This change is closely connected, according to Petero, to the Bakonzo people's understanding of a new practical use of the *endara*. It would not seem out of place to trace this turning point back to the period in which the cultural groups emerged, and to the demands which their appearance created. The family of Say Muhindo Yokana Visitemi[25] also limits the number of songs that they traditionally play:

> We play three songs and their length depends on the time we have available. (One song, *author's note*) can be played for a long time or quickly.

Songs for the *endara* often have the same instrumental accompaniment in common. One could therefore hypothesize that the original repertoire of the Konzo musical tradition consisted of a limited number of instrumental accompaniments on whose melodic-rhythmic patterns the Bakonzo may have composed new songs, thereby broadening their repertoire.

One sole song is generally recognized by the population as being ancient and traditional: its title is *Asawikale Hano Kathondo*. Numerous recordings of this song, made by Wachsmann in the 1950s, are kept in the British Library in London. *Kathondo* is one of the appellatives attributed to the creator and means "Orderer of the world".

Conclusions

According to the results of sound analyzes on the xylophones under examination, the norms which regulate the keyboard tuning of various *endara* do not seem to follow an entirely coherent path. The use of pentatonic scales for tuning traditional xylophones can be excluded, but the question regarding the use of pseudo-heptatonic scales remains open, not only in the intonation of the *endara* keyboard, but also, more generally, in identifying the aspects that are specific to the Konzo musical system. One needs to consider the numerous difficulties which may arise from the use of Western cognitive categories in "other" systems, and underline, moreover, the problematic nature inherent in any attempt to ascribe the musical system regulating *endara* tuning to any one definite category.

The recordings made by Klaus Wachsmann confirm the use of the heptatonic model in the 1950s for tuning some *endara*, but they do not prove that this scale originated within Konzo culture, or that it was implemented before direct contact with the Western world. Analyzes of the tuning show that the sound coherence of individual keyboards is not determined by a stable scale sequence, but by the constant positioning of the pitches in descending order. While recognizing the use of pseudo-heptatonic scales in tuning some modern xylophones, one cannot deny the influence that Western-type church music has had on Konzo musical culture in general. Another important element in this context is the persistent use of intervals of a third, which does not however seem to be sufficient in itself for defining an entire musical system.

Faced with the wide range of ways in tuning – often lacking in internal coherence – one must necessarily attempt to identify the constant factors which permit the Bakonzo to play xylophones even when they are visibly "out of tune"[26]. The existence, in the single sections and in the instrument as a whole, of different sound layers, which are in opposition to one another, often appears to be the minimum requirement demanded of an *endara* to be useable. The characteristic need for a sound opposition of a low-high type is guaranteed by the positioning of the pitches in descending order and does not require any further rules with regard to internal coherence. Only through further more extended field studies of the culture under observation, with the musicians themselves, and with protagonists of the sound world, would it perhaps be possible to identify with greater precision the rules that underlie the Konzo musical system, as well as allowing an assessment of the extent to which external influences have permeated that system.

With regard to the roles of the *endara* in Konzo culture, the instrument is recognized as having a multi-functional nature, which, however, is not matched by a plurality of repertoires, or a diversification of these repertoires on the basis of the contexts in which the instrument is played. The traditional repertoire of the xylophone appears to include a limited number of musical songs. On the other hand the current proliferation of new songs for the *endara*, mainly created by the cultural groups, goes hand in hand with a tendency to simplify and schematise the individual musical parts. The reasons for these choices can be traced to the necessity of rendering use of the instrument accessible even to less expert players. In theory it is clear that there are some differences between traditional and modern *endara*, which correspond to the functions fulfilled by the two models.

In the light of these research studies, it can be assumed that the primary function of the traditional Konzo *endara* aimed, in the past, to re-establish harmony within the community, and also between the community and the pantheon of spirits which give life to the territory. This article has emphasized to what extent the Banande/Bakonzo culture, according to Remotti (1994:53-54), is dominated by the idea of order. The *eka* (village) must, by necessity, be governed by harmony. The *omoli* (forest), on the other hand, represents disorder, a place governed by untamed nature. The *endara* establishes communication between these two worlds and represents a synthesis of them. Its logs come from the banana grove, created and dominated by man, whereas the wood from which its keys are made comes from the forest, governed by the *abalimu* (spirits). These spirits react; creating disorder in response to man's failure to respect rules and taboos. A harmonic relationship must therefore be re-established with them. This reality, despite the fact that many Bakonzo people have embraced the Christian faith, does not appear to have been affected by the passing of time and is a fundamental cultural characteristic. Under these circumstances, the *endara* has become the favoured object for putting men and spirits into contact, and re-establishing a convergence of intent between them. Dancing, singing and the music of the *endara* therefore resolve conflicts with the *abalimu*, as well as strengthening the people's sense of belonging to their own cultural roots.

Another context in which the *endara* appears to be useful in combating "disorder" is that of traditional medicine. Even today, some healers use the sound of the *endara* to communicate with the *abalimu*. There is also a privileged relationship between the *endara* and some families in which there are men, women or children affected by albinism. This condition is considered by the Bakonzo to be a clear sign of the preference shown by *Kitasamba* (the foremost spirit in the Konzo pantheon) towards those who are affected. Albinos, who are thought to be the offspring of this supernatural entity, are obliged to respect the rules and taboos scrupulously throughout the course of their lifetime. Failure to respect the established norms can cause the disappearance of these special people, who would be abducted by *Kitasamba* himself. The disappearance of these children of the mountain spirit would undermine the social equilibrium. Yet again, social harmony is interrupted by "disorder" and the *endara* fulfils its ritual role. It is the sound of the instrument, in fact, which will allow the albinos to return.

Lastly, the new roles assumed by the *endara* have been identified that make it a "modern" instrument and that are superimposed on the traditional roles. The hypothesis that (differently from the mobility which is characteristic of the object today) the *endara* had in the past a stable position in a ditch dug out in the centre of the village, suggests the possibility that some of its structural features and symbolic functions have undergone substantial variations over time. These changes occur as the result of a much wider transformation, which has swept through Konzo culture as a whole.

The Bakonzo probably began to compose new songs for the *endara* when they realized the sound potential of the instrument, and when the image of the *endara* as an object of entertainment came to overlay its function as a symbol of social cohesion. This happened, to a large extent, with the birth of cultural groups, which always favoured the *endara* over the various other instruments used in performances, not only because of it being recognized as representative of the Konzo musical tradition, but also for its aesthetic and showy characteristics. The activity of these cultural associations is also adapting to new social needs: the dances and traditional music are beginning to be structured for the presentation of real shows. So the beneficiaries of their music and dancing no longer belong exclusively to the Konzo community. From the centre of the village, the *endara* of the cultural groups and members of the group itself are moving to wherever they are asked to perform: so we are witnessing a move towards modernization of the music and dance events, with a transferral of the *endara* from the village centre to the centre stage.

From its ancient ritual function to its more recent role as an instrument for promoting traditional culture, the Konzo xylophone sinks its roots deep into a remote past, while nonetheless bearing evident traces of the transformations which the Konzo culture has undergone in the course of time. And it is precisely by virtue of its manifold qualities that the *endara* can thus be considered a multi-functional object and a symbol of identity, which is recognized by the entire community.

Bibliography

Arom, S. 1989. "Un sintetizzatore nella savana Centro-africana. Un metodo di ricognizione interattiva delle scale musicali". In *Culture Musicali*, 15/16. Firenze: La Casa Usher, p.p. 9-26.

Baily, J. 1990. "Music, Performance, Motor Structure and Cognitive Models". In Baumann, S. Wegner (ed.) *European Studies in Ethnomusicology: historical developments and recent trends*, Verlag Wilhelmshaven: Florian, 143-157.

Betto, F. 1996. "L'ultimoapartheid". *Minoranze*. http://www.dweb.repubblica.it/ dweb/dweb/2003/- 07/05/attualita/attualita/066alb35866.html

Blacking, J. 1955. "Eight Flute Tunes from Butembo, East Belgian Congo". In *African Music* 1 (2), 24-52.

---. 1973. *How Musical is Man?* University of Washington Press.

Boone, O. 1936. "Les Xilophone du Congo Belge". In Annales du Musée du Congo Belge, *Ethnographie* (III, 2). Tervuuren, 69-144.

Cooke, P. & Doornbos, M. 1980. "Uganda". In *The New Grove's Dictionary of Music e Musicians*, Vol. XXIV. London: MacMillan, 618-629.

---. 1982. "Ruwenzururu Protest Song". In *Africa*. 52 (1): 37-60.

Facci, S. 1988. "La musica dei Wanande dello Zaire". In *Culture Musicali*. V & VI (10/11), 87-125.

---. 1996. "I Nande e la loro Musica". In Buffa, C., Facci, S., Pennacini, C. Remotti, F. (eds) *Etnografia Nande III*. Torino: Il Segnalibro, 11-55.

Humphreys 1933. "Ruwenzori Flight and Further Explorations". In *Geografical Journal*. Vol. 82.

Kubik, G. 1963. "The *endara* xylophone of Bukonjo". In *African Music*, III, 1: 43-49.

Mazzolini, R.G. 2003. "Sulla storia dell'albinismo dal 1609 al 1812". In *La Natura e il Corpo, Atti del Convegno*. Olschki, Firenze: Mantova, 161-204.

Merriam, A.P. 1983. *Antropologia della Musica*. Palmero: Sellerio. (Original edition 1964. *The Anthropology of Music*. Evanstone: Northwestern University Press).

Pennacini, C. 1998. *Kubandwa: la possessione spiritica nell'Africa dei Grandi Laghi*. Torino: Il Segnalibro.

---. (ed.) 2006. *I Popoli della Luna, Rwenzori 1906-2006*. Torino: Museo Nazionale della Montagna.

Remotti, F. 1993. *Etnografia Nande I*. Torino: Il Segnalibro.

---. 1994, *Etnografia Nande II*, Torino: Il Segnalibro.

---. 1996 *Etnografia Nande III*, Torino: Il Segnalibro.

Rouget, G. 1986. *Musica e trance*. Torino: Einandi (Original edition 1980. *La musique et la transe*. Paris: Gallimard).

---. 2002. "Xylophones africains et Systèmes Musicaux". In *Percussions*, 8: 28-38 (First edition *Almanach* 1986/1987. Paris: Agence de Coopération Culturelle et Tecnique, 293-298).

Schaeffner, A. 1986. *Origine degli strumenti musicali*. Palermo: Sellerio. (Original edition 1936. *Origine des instruments de musique*, Paris-den Haag: Mouton).

Trowell, M. & Wachsmann, K.P. 1953. *Tribal Craft of Uganda*. London: Oxford University Press.

Notes

1. The research area was carried out in the districts of Bundibugyo (the villages of Bunguha, Bumate, Ruhale and Twanzani) and Kasese. In the latter district, the studies concentrated on the zones of Ibanda – a village situated near one of the entrances to the Rwenzori National Park – and Bwera, a town located close to the Congolese border. The research activities, which began on 16 May and continued until 24 June 2005, were carried out in collaboration with Cristina Zavaroni, and involved the contribution of the following informants and interpreters: Stanley Baluku (Ibanda), Hilary Baluku (Ibanda), Kule Cyprian (Ibanda) and Gertrude (Maliba).

2. Wachsmann emphasises that the term *entaala* was used in the past to indicate the orchestra of the *kabaka*, which was made up of xylophones and drums. The xylophone alone, however, was called *amadinda* (Wachsmann 1953: 314).

3. For further investigation into Banande culture see Remotti, F. 1993. *Etnografia Nande I*, Il Segnalibro, Torino; Remotti, F. 1994. *Etnografia Nande II*, Il Segnalibro, Torino; Buffa, C., Facci, S., Pennacini C. & Remotti, F. (eds.), *Etnografia Nande III*, Il Segnalibro, Torino.

4. See Facci, S. in the same volume.

5. The term *engoma* is extremely widespread throughout Central Africa and generically indicates the drum. The *engoma* existing in the *endara* orchestra of the Bakonzo people is of a conical shape and has a double membrane: goat or cattle skins are held together by a stretching system composed of leather laces. The *omugholi* (a smaller drum with a more piercing sound) and the *erithundu* (a medium-sized drum) are played with two thin sticks, whereas the *ebembe* (the largest drum with the deepest sound) is struck with the hands.

6. *Esyonzende* are ankle bracelets made up of a variable number of iron bells of different sizes, are worn by the dancers or musicians to mark time. The ankle-bells have an important role in dancing, but also for the musicians: in fact, there is a rhythmic point of reference in their cadenced and regular sound which is recognized by the entire ensemble. The ankle-bells reveal the metric pulsation, marking time in regular units.

7. Interview with Paulo Maate Kathaligha, artisan, owner of a 15-key *endara*, Buhundo village, 19 June 2005.

8. Name of the sections: *obwana* (children), *enzoboli* (he who leads/guides), *ebikekulhu* (older woman), *ebisyakulhu* (older men).

9. Festivals generally linked to the cycle of the seasons or of the life of the Bakonzo.

10. From the oral testimony of the Bakonzo it is not clear if, by the term *Abashukal*, reference is being made to the *Abashu* clan or to one of its subclans.

11. Walina Davis, artisan, village of Nyakalengigya.

12. To build an *endara,* Bakonzo people use different trees called *Omukoku* (Alangium chinense), *Ekyungu* (Polyscias fulva), *Omulhungulu* (Warbugia ugandensis), *Omusambyia* (Markhamia platycalix).

13. Interview with Walina Davis recorded on 23 June 2005 in the village of Nyakalengigya.

14. See Stacey, T. in the same volume.

15. *Ekikuba* or *ekikebi*: dance style.

16. For a description of albinism, the following is an extract from the text by Mazzolini, R. G. (2003: 161): "Albinism is a human pigmentation disorder characterized by leucoderma, in which there is a normal number of melanocytes, but a vastly reduced content of melanoma in the melanosomes. As well as the milky-white colour of the skin, the main diagnostic signs of true albinism are the pink colouring of the iris and a pupil which instead of appearing black, seems to be pink because of the reflected light from the blood vessels of the choroid and the lack of pigment in the back part of the iris. Another fundamental sign is nystagmus, i.e. the irregular rapid movement of the eyes back and forth".

17. The following is an extract from an article by Betto, F. (1996) dedicated to the situation of albinos in Africa: "When superstition was most ferocious, albinos were even killed at birth, seen as the fruit of divine curses. In South Africa and Zimbabwe today, they are perhaps the last people to be discriminated against (…) Many women spit on the ground when they see an albino. A terrible custom with apotropaic meaning: the women are convinced that if they do not do this, they will in turn give birth to an albino child. But part of the problem stems from another, much worse prejudice: when a woman actually gives birth to a "white" child, she is often treated as an adulteress by her family (…)."

18. Regarding the birth of *Cultural Groups* and their music activities, see Cooke 1982.

19. For an in-depth description of the tuning of an *endara*, see the following paragraph.

20. See Wachsmann 1954, Blacking 1955, Cooke 1980 and 1982, Facci 1988 and 1996.

21. The recordings are stored in the British Library Sound Archive of London.

22. Cf. Simha Arom who, with reference to the oscillations in intonation found in the xylophones of Central-west Africa, defines the margin of tolerance accepted by the population as particularly "wide" (Arom 1989: 9-26).

23. The subject dealt with in the song text does not offer any information about the procedures used in constructing or tuning the instrument.

24. Petero Kivinga, custodian by family tradition of an *endara* in the Abaswagha clan, Kajembe village. Interviewed and recorded on 12 June 2005.

25. Family of Say Muhando Yokana Visitemi, custodians of a 16-key *endara*, Lyakirema II village, sub-county of Nyakyumbu, Bwera. Group interview, recorded on 5th June 2005.

26. Xylophones whose tuning is not accepted by the Bakonzo themselves.

Ambiguous Borders: the Case of Rwenzori

Luca Jourdan

Introduction

This article focuses on the Rwenzori massif that separates Uganda from the Democratic Republic of Congo. This border, established in colonial times, has been at the core of continuous tensions between and within the two states. In the last decades the Rwenzori has been the operative zone of the NALU rebels (National Army for the Liberation of Uganda), and nowadays of the ADF (Alliance of Democratic Forces). Both movements are opposed to the central government in Kampala. At the same time, historically, the Rwenzori has been a strategic area for the organization of numerous rebellions in Congo. The analysis of this particular political space can help us in better understanding the dynamics of state formation and desegregation in post-colonial Africa by showing that frontiers are spaces characterized by political ambiguity and continuous processes of identity negotiations rather than definite and insurmountable barriers.

Borderlands are very delicate spaces where geo-political relations between the different states often take place. Keeping control over these areas is therefore indispensable for the survival and the reproduction of central power. My goal is to furnish an analysis – inevitably partial and incomplete – of the Rwenzori region, focusing on the historical, political and economic variables which shape the dynamics of conflict in this area. Two major features characterize this region: first of all it is a mountainous area, second it is a frontier line. These characteristics make the Rwenzori a privileged territory for guerrilla warfare and smuggling, two activities that are often interrelated.

The case of Rwenzori is not unique. In the history of post-colonial Africa, the peripheral and rural areas constitute a particular political space where the states often show their weakness as well as their coercive attitudes. The leaders who oppose the central governments often organize their armed movements in the borderlands, where they can receive support from other states and easily cross the frontier in case of need, taking advantage in this way of the ambiguity of these spaces. At the same time, these areas allow the development of an economy (formal and informal)[1] based on international trade, smuggling and illegal traffic of a variety of goods: minerals, weapons, drugs, agricultural products, wood, ivory, etc. From this point of view the presence of a border represents an opportunity rather than a limitation.

It is in the rural and peripheral areas, often the less accessible, where the phenomenon of social banditry emerges, taking advantage of the difficulties that central governments have in controlling them. Eric Hobsbawm has argued that "the peasant society creates him [social bandit] and calls upon him, when it feels the need for a champion and protector – but precisely then he is incapable of helping it. For social banditry, though a protest, is a modest and unrevolutionary protest. It protests not against the fact that peasants are poor and oppressed, but against the fact that they are sometimes excessively poor and oppressed"[2]. According to Hobsbawm, bandits are a kind of primitive rebel (actually these two categories seem to coincide) that are usually involved in criminal activities. The historian focuses mostly on European social history (including examples from Calabria, Sicily and Sardinia), but his arguments can be useful in our case too.

The Rwenzori chain, both from the Congolese and the Ugandan sides, is a land of rebellions. Nevertheless, the rebel groups, which have ravaged this area for a long time, cannot be considered to express the political consciousness of the peasant class. These movements partially answer to local grievances, and this explains why some young people join them, but their action has never improved the condition of the rural population. Furthermore, their military and political weakness makes them easy to manipulate from outside. Actually, most of the rebellions in the Rwenzori have spread out because of the will of external political actors, and the local population has always been the major victim of the war. In fact, civilians are often forced to join rebel forces and in many cases they are obliged to support the rebels (with food, money, or by transporting weapons and munitions) and finally they are victims of the counter-insurgency activities carried on by the governmental army.

Before focusing on the specific case of Rwenzori, it would be useful to reflect more widely on the relationship between borders, sovereignty and power in postcolonial Africa. Officially, since the constitution of the African Union in 1963, the relations between African states have always been based formally on two principles: 1) the inviolability of the frontiers inherited by colonization, 2) the non-interference in the internal affairs of the other states[3]. The first principle, the inviolability of frontiers, has been the most respected (from this point of view Africa cannot be compared to the Balkans, where the war has led to a redefinition of internal borders). Until now, the only war in Africa which has led to a change of borders is the one between Ethiopia and Eritrea, while other attempts at secession or annexation have failed (for example in Katanga in 1969, in Biafra in 1967, the Chad and Libya conflict for the Tibesti region, and more recently the conflict in Casamance (Senegal) and in the Anglophone part of Cameroon)[4].

On the contrary, the second principle – the non-interference in the internal affairs of other states – has not been respected. This is particularly evident in the Rwenzori, a region used by Congo and Uganda in continuous attempts to destabilize each other. In the end, this area has been a crucial place for the internal political equilibrium of both Congo and Uganda, and for the equilibrium between the two states. I will focus now on the history of the conflicts in the region.

The Congolese Side

In the turbulent period which followed the independence of Congo (1960), the Rwenzori massif became one of the areas of Simba's operations (*simba* means lion in Kiswahili). Simba was a rebel movement whose aim was the "second independence" of Congo. Three years after the assassination of Patrice Lumumba (1961), who had led the country to independence, some nationalist and Marxist leaders gave rise to a rebellion against the government of Kinshasa, which was considered a puppet, manipulated by western countries. The insurgency aimed to achieve real independence for the country. Pierre Mulele was the first to organize a rebel movement in his native region, the Kwilu (west of Kinshasa). Mulele was an adventurer (from this point of view the contemporary Congolese rebels are no different), and he had made a short trip to China where he had received some rudimentary knowledge of guerrilla warfare. In January 1964 he started his fight, armed with only two revolvers. At the beginning, the rebellion was supported by the local population but the reaction of the government was brutal: villages were burnt and fields were destroyed. When Mulele was about to be defeated, Soumialot, another nationalist leader, started another rebellion in Kivu (the eastern region of Congo) with a movement called Simba. This phase of the conflict, as we will see, involved the Rwenzori massif.

In less than eight months, the Simba conquered the Eastern regions of Congo, and the central town of Kisangani became their headquarters. Most of the rebels were young people between twelve and twenty years old. As Benoît Verhaegen has argued, it was an age class that "l'Indépendance ratée avait particulièrement pénalisée en la privant d'école et d'emploi. Elle n'avait rien à perdre à s'engager dans l'aventure insurrectionelle. C'est elle qui fut le fer de lance des contingents Simba [the failed independence had particularly penalized, depriving them of schools and jobs. It had nothing to lose in the insurgency adventure. This age class constituted the front-line of Simba contingents]"[5]. Despite the initial success, the rebels abandoned themselves to horrendous atrocities and quickly started to disagree amongst themselves. The national army was reorganized and thanks to American and Belgian support (the Belgian parachutists launched in Kisangani), the Simba were defeated. Many rebels were dispersed around the mountains areas of Uviri and Fizi, while some others reached the Rwenzori massif and the nearby areas. It is in these years that the region became militarized since many combatants were never disarmed. Some groups founded villages and became involved in smuggling activities. Many years later, in the 1990s, some Simba veterans joined the rebellions, which until now ravage this region[6].

During the Mobutu dictatorship – Mobutu took power in 1965 and he was overthrown 32 years later in 1997 – trans-border commerce flourished in the region of Beni and Lubero, at the Rwenzori foothills. The crucial point of the trans-border commerce is Kasindi, a town situated at the frontier between Congo and Uganda. After the port of Matadi, on the Atlantic coast south of Kinshasa, Kasindi is the most important place for the transit of goods in Congo.

The Banande (the most numerous ethnic group in this area) had a marginal role in the Mobutist administration and this fact pushed many local entrepreneurs to start activities in the informal economy (most of all, gold and coffee smuggling)[7]. This propensity to invest in the informal sector can be considered as a response to the ineffectiveness of, and neglect by, the state government, as well as a silent reaction against the Mobutu regime. Furthermore, the distance between North Kivu and the capital Kinshasa gave the region a certain degree of autonomy[8]. In the 1980s some Banande businessmen had been able to concentrate the monopoly of trans-frontier commerce in their hands. The Banande business network quickly spread over Dubai, Hong Kong and South East Asia, and the port of Mombassa started to connect these regions with Butembo, the town in North Kivu where most of the Banande businessmen are based[9].

Later on, in the 1990s, as we will see, this fact gave them an economic and political advantage to profit from the new opportunities generated by the war.

The Ugandan Side

During the 1980s the Ugandan side of the Rwenzori was one of the operative territories of the National Resistance Army (NRA), the rebel movement led by Yoweri Museveni, now the president of Uganda. Despite the fact that this region had never been a major area for the activities of the NRA, in April 1985, during the last phase of the rebellion against President Obote, a new front was opened at the Rwenzori foothills, near Fort Portal[10]. A group of NRA rebels, led by commander Fred Rwigyema, settled in this area. Some months later, in January 1986, Museveni conquered the capital Kampala and became the new president of Uganda.

In 1988, only two years after Museveni had taken power, the Rwenzori became the operative area of a new rebel movement, namely the National Army for the Liberation of Uganda (NALU). NALU's objective was to put an end to Museveni's regime and to remove from Uganda the Rwandan refugees, mostly Tutsi, who had supported the NRA. But this program was scarcely evident from their actions: the rebels, in fact, were responsible for many killings and kidnappings of civilians in the Rwenzori villages and they never represented a serious threat to central power. NALU tried to exploit the historical rivalry between the central government and the local Bakonzo[11], who since 1904 have been opposed to their inclusion in the Toro kingdom imposed by the English colonial administration. Despite this attempt to involve the native groups, the rebels never benefited from strong local support while civilians ended up by being the main victims of the conflict.

A Region in the Middle

NALU received support from the Mobutu regime. At the beginning of the 1990s, in fact, the Rwenzori was at the centre of a trial of strength between Kampala and Kinshasa. In these years, some militias began to operate on the Congolese side of Rwenzori. According to Koen Vlassenroot, the first militias to be active in this region were named Kasindien and Bangilima. The first group was based near Kasindi, the village mentioned above, while the second was based in the territory of Beni and Lubero. According to Vlassenroot, Mobutu aimed to support NALU through these militias, in order to destabilize the government of Yoweri Museveni[12]. Mobutu assigned to some local leaders, particularly among the Banande, the task of enrolling young recruits to enforce the rebellion against Museveni[13]. Nevertheless, in a short time, both Kasindien and Bangilima began to act independently and came together in a new movement called Mayi-Mayi, which is still partially active today.

Mayi-Mayi, in Congolese Kiswahili, means "water-water". The term refers to the most important ritual practised by the rebels, namely the sprinkling of special water on young recruits. This water, which has been treated according to secret procedures, is supposed to protect them from bullets. The name Mayi-Mayi does not refer to a united movement; on the contrary it refers to a group of loosely coordinated militias, often riven by internal conflicts. Initially Mayi-Mayi were opposed to the Mobutu regime and in 1996, as we will see below, they joined the Alliance des Forces Démocratiques pour la Libération du Congo/Zaïre (AFDL), led by Laurent Desiré Kabila. Later, in 1998, most of the Mayi-Mayi militias opposed the RCD rebellion, supported by Rwanda, which was considered a Rwandan attempt to conquer Congo.

The Congolese War and the Role of Rwenzori

It is opportune now to focus briefly on the war which has ravaged Congo from 1996 to the present. This conflict is divided into two phases: the first one is characterized by the ascent to power of Laurent Desiré Kabila, an old Congolese rebel who in 1996 became the leader of an armed movement called the Alliance des Forces Démocratiques pour la Libération du Congo/Zaïre (AFDL), which was supported by Uganda and Rwanda. The AFDL campaign started from the eastern regions, from Goma and Bukavu (the chief towns of North Kivu and South Kivu) in August 1996. In a year, the armed movement reached Kinshasa and Mobutu was obliged to flee into exile in Morocco (where he died after some months), while Kabila became the new president of Congo.

As mentioned above, the AFDL was supported by Uganda and overall by Rwanda. The USA was also favourable to the campaign, which represented an opportunity to disengage Congo from French influence and to gain influence over the immense mineral resources of the country. According to some analysts, the US support was not only political but also military. For example, the American journalist Wayne Madsen has argued that the US installed some listening and communication stations on the Ugandan side of the Rwenzori (but, in these cases, it is hard to distinguish rumours from reality)[14].

The official reason for the intervention of Uganda and Rwanda in the Congo was the security of borders. Rwanda claimed to be pursuing the Interahamwe, the militia responsible for the genocide in 1994, who had fled into the Congo. On its side, Uganda claimed that its support of the AFDL was justified by the menace of some rebel groups, especially NALU, which were supported by the Congolese government. But the alliance between Uganda and Rwanda, on one side, and Kabila, on the other side, soon deteriorated. In August 1998 Kabila accused the Rwandans of pillaging Congolese natural resources and he issued a presidential decree to expel them. Some days after, a new rebellion started in Kivu, again supported by Rwanda. The rebel movement organized on this occasion was named the Rassemblement des Congolais pour la Démocratie (RCD, Congolese Rally for Democracy) that quickly conquered North Kivu and South Kivu.

The RCD was soon ravaged by internal divisions and after a year it split up into many factions. On this occasion, Uganda returned to interfere in Congolese affairs by supporting some rebel factions. Referring to our region, the Ugandan government started to support the Rassemblement Congolais pour la Democratie Kisangani, Mouvement de Liberation (RCDK-ML), a rebel movement led by Mbusa Nyamwisi, a Banande warlord. This movement controlled the territory of Beni and Lubero and consequently the borderlands with Uganda.

Once again, Kampala justified its intervention in Congo on the grounds of security. In fact, starting from 1997, a new anti-Ugandan rebel movement had established itself in the Rwenzori: the Alliance of Democratic Forces (ADF). The Ugandan government claimed that this new rebel movement was backed by Sudan and by the government of Congo. According to Gerard Prunier, a major specialist of the Great Lakes Region, the ADF, which is still active, was composed of the following groups: the NALU rebels, some Interahamwe elements and a Muslim rebel movement called Tabliq[15]. The latter had been founded in Pakistan and the Ugandan branch took a violent form: it was composed of combatants from many tribes (Baganda, Banyoro, Batoro and Bakonzo), which, after a failed insurrectional attempt in the Lake Albert region, took refuge in Rwenzori. The ADF is accused of being a terrorist movement (it was on the terrorist list of the US Department of State) and of being connected to Al Qaeda (it is the only movement in Sub-Saharan Africa accused of having such alliances). It is likely that the three main reasons which pushed ADF to establish itself in the Rwenzori are: it is an ideal area for rebellion, the proximity with the border allows the rebels to establish their bases in the Congolese territory where the state does not exercise any control, and finally the presence of some groups, such as the Bakonzo, who historically have some disputes with the central government in Kampala[16].

The ADF committed many atrocities against civilians, resulting in tens of thousands of internally displaced people (IDPs). Furthermore, some terrorist acts have been attributed to this movement: in 1998 two bombs exploded in Kampala, in the Nile Grill restaurant and in the Speke Hotel. In the same year a bus going to Rwanda was blown up, killing 30 people. Since 1998, the ADF actions have become more brutal: for example in February 1998, 30 students were kidnapped at the Adventist College in Kasese. On 8 June of the same year, 80 students of the technical college in Kaborole died after the rebels set fire to their dormitory and in the same month many children were kidnapped from a school in the Hoima district. In December 1999, the rebels' actions became more menacing: the ADF attacked Fort Portal and the districts of Bundibugyo and Kabarole[17]. In recent years, the Ugandan army has reacted strongly and the ADF has been seriously weakened. In the end, the ADF is certainly not a very menacing movement, but the Ugandan government has used it as an excuse for its intervention in Congo[18].

A War Economy around Rwenzori

As we have seen, the Ugandan government has always justified its intervention in Congo by referring to the security of borders (a realistic justification and a pretext at the same time). As mentioned above, a rebel movement supported by Uganda and led by Mbusa Nyamwisi, a Banande warlord, controlled the territory of Beni and Lubero in North Kivu, from 1999 to 2004. During the rebellion, a war economy has become established in this region, based mainly on transfrontier trade. One of the most important sources of revenue for Mbusa Nyamwisi was tax levied on the goods imported to Congo, which transited from Kasindi and reached Butembo[19].

During the Mobutist period, the government of Kinshasa collected these taxes directly, which were quite high since Kasindi is one of the most important places for the transit of goods in the country. On the contrary, during the rebellion since 1998, some important local businessmen (most of them based in Butembo) have made alliances with the warlord Mbusa Nyamwisi. This alliance has been profitable for both sides: on the one hand the traders have obtained a reduction of the import taxes; on the other hand, Mbusa Nyamwesi has collected these taxes, in exchange for security, and in this way has financed his movement.

This alliance was based mainly on an agreement about the price the dealers had to pay in order to clear a container at the border in Kasindi. During the Mobutu regime, to clear a container could cost up to $25,000. Of course, the high level of taxes encouraged corruption and smuggling. Kabila, once he became president, lowered the taxes (at that time the maximum tax for a container was $17,000). Nevertheless he favoured his natal region, the Shaba, where the import taxes on the goods coming from Zambia were nearly halved and this fact provoked the resentment of the Banande businessmen community in Butembo. During the rebellion, from 1998, the import taxes decreased considerably. The dealers started to negotiate the import taxes directly with the RCD-KML. To clear a container could cost only $7,000, depending on the private agreement the businessman was able to reach with the warlord Nyamwesi. At the same time it was possible to pay a fixed sum in advance in order to import freely an undetermined number of containers for a determined period (this last system was defined as a "system of prepayment"). During the rebellion, the economy of Butembo, based on importation, grew enormously: the city was flooded with all kind of goods, sold in a myriad of boutiques, and it became the most important trade centre in East Congo. At the same time, the Banande businessmen started to invest their profits in the construction of new buildings along the main streets and magnificent private houses on the hills that surround the city.

The new system of taxation, including the system of prepayment, was convenient for both sides: the warlord and his military apparatus on one side and the dealers on the other side. Butembo became prosperous, and this is the reason why this area has often been attacked by other rebel movements (the MLC from the west and RCD from the south) that aimed to get their hands on the money coming in from the import taxes or at least to pillage the warehouses of the city. Nevertheless, Mbusa Nyamwesi has always been able to repel his enemies thanks to the prompt help (mostly in the form of cash) he received from the traders close to him[20].

Conclusions

While I was writing this article, in spring 2006, I phoned a Congolese friend who, at that time, was working with an international NGO in the Rwenzori area. I asked him for some updates and he told me that the situation was not clear since some rebels, probably belonging to ADF, had been seen in some villages the days before. I asked him what the people in the villages were saying about that, and he promptly answered "ils ne comprennent plus rien (they don't understand anything anymore)".

I think that this inability to make sense of events is one of the most upsetting effects of the contemporary African crisis. Undoubtedly we are facing a very complex political dynamic. In this article I have tried to simplify the context, without entering into details, by furnishing a reconstruction of the facts in this area that, of course, can be widely criticized. The Rwenzori massif is neither peripheral nor marginal. It is actually a region at the core of many economic interests and political dynamics that overwhelm this mountain chain. From this point of view, the centre-periphery dichotomy, which implies the dependence of the latter on the former, does not have any analytical value: in fact, the central governments seem to be tied to the events which take place in this supposedly peripheral area. The fluidity of the political context in Uganda and overall in the Congo renders any prediction difficult. Until now, the violence in the Rwenzori has constituted an opportunity rather than a problem for many social actors who have fomented social and political disorder in order to affirm themselves. This is certainly a widespread strategy in sub-Saharan Africa[21]. Nevertheless, the recent peace agreement between the Lord's Resistance Army and the Ugandan government on one side and the election in Congo on the other, are perhaps two significant steps towards the pacification of the entire area. This process is very uncertain and success will require time and great effort from the international community. If, in the future, the opportunities generated by peace are going to prevail over the opportunities generated by disorder, the populations in the Rwenzori will have the chance to face a less incomprehensible reality.

Bibliography

Chabal, P. & Daloz, J-P. 1999. *Africa Works. Disorder as Political Instrument*. Oxford: James Currey.

Clark, J.F. 2002. "Museveni's Adventure in the Congo War: Uganda's Vietnam?". In J.F. Clark (ed.) *The African Stakes of the Congo War*. New York: Palgrave MacMillan, 145-165.

Hobsbawn, E.J. 1965. *Primitive Rebels*. New York: Norton and Company.

MacGaffey, J. 1987. *Entrepreneurs and Parasites. The Struggle for Indigenous Capitalism in Zaïre*. Cambridge: Cambridge University Press.

MacGaffey J. (ed.) 1991. *The Real Economy of Zaire*. London: James Currey.

Madsen, W. 1999. "Genocide and Covert Operations in Africa, 1993-1999". In *African Studies,* 50. Lewiston NY: Edwin Mellen Press.

Mararo, S.B. 2002. "Le Nord-Kivu au coeur de la crise congolaise". In Marysse, S. & Reyntjens, F. (eds.) *L'Afrique des Grands Lacs: Annuaire 2001-2002.* Paris: L'Harmattan.

Mbembe, A. 2000. "At the Edge of the World: Boundaries, Territoriality, and Sovereignty in Africa". In *Public Culture,* 12 (1): 259-284.

Ndaywel È Nziem, I. 1998. *Histoire générale du Congo.* Bruxelles/Paris: De Boeck et Larcier.

Ngoga, P. 1998. "Uganda: the National Resistance Army". In C. Clapham (ed.) *African Guerrillas.* Oxford: James Currey.

Prunier, G. 1997. "Sudan's regional war". In *Le Monde Diplomatique*, February.

Raeymaekers, T. 2004. "L'économie politique de Beni-Lubero". In Vlassenroot, K. & Raeymaekers, T. 2004, *Conflit et transformation sociale à l'est de la RDC.* Gent: Academia Press.

Tull, D.M. 2003. "A Reconfiguration of the Political Order? The State of the State in North Kivu (DR Congo)". In *African Affairs*, 102: 429-446.

Verhaegen, B. 1990. *1963-1965: d'oppositions en rebellions.* In *GRIP Congo Zaïre. La colonisation - l'indépendance – le régime Mobutu – et demain?* Bruxelles.

Vlassenroot, K. 2002. "Violence et constitution de milices dans l'est du Congo: le cas des Mayi-Mayi". In S. Marysse & F. Reyntjens (eds.) *L'Afrique des Grands Lacs: Annuaire 2001-2002.* Paris: L'Harmattan.

Notes

1. The distinction between formal and informal economy is more conventional than real. Especially in Africa, it is hard to distinguish these two spheres, which are deeply interrelated.

2. Hobsbawm, E.J. 1965. *Primitive Rebels.* Norton and Company, New York, 24.

3. Mbembe, A. 2000. "At the Edge of the World: Boundaries, Territoriality, and Sovereignty in Africa". In *Public Culture,* 12 (1): 259-284.

4. Ibidem, 271-272.

5. Verhaegen, B. *1963-1965: d'oppositions en rébellions,* in *GRIP, Congo Zaïre. La colonisation - l'indépendance - le régime Mobutu - et demain?* Bruxelles, 1990, p. 94.

6. The reintegration of ex-combatants is a major problem in many African countries. When the disarmament fails, the soldiers often become mercenaries and join different armed groups which menace peace and stability.

7. Cf. I. Ndaywel È Nziem, *Histoire générale du Congo,* De Boeck et Larcier, Bruxelles/Paris, 1998, 751.

8. Cf. MacGaffey, J. *Entrepreneurs and Parasites. The Struggle for Indigenous Capitalism in Zaïre,* Cambridge University Press, Cambridge, 1987, 146.

9. On the political economy of this region cf. T. Raeymaekers, "L'économie politique de Beni-Lubero". In K. Vlassenroot and T. Raeymaekers, *Conflit et transformation sociale à l'est de la RDC,* Academia Press, Gand, 2004.

10. Cf. Ngoga, P. "Uganda: the National Resistance Army". In C. Clapham (ed.), *African Guerrillas,* James Currey, Oxford, 1998, p. 103.

11. The Bakonzo is the major ethnic group in the region and they share the same language, culture and social organization with the Congolese Banande that live on the other side of the massif (the division of these two groups was a result of colonization).

12. Cf. Vlassenroot, K. "Violence et constitution de milices dans l'est du Congo: le cas des Mayi-Mayi". In S. Marysse e F. Reyntjens (eds.), *L'Afrique des Grands Lacs: Annuaire 2001-2002,* L'Harmattan, Paris, 2002, p. 124.

13. The most important leader was Muvingi Nyamwisi, the brother of Mbusa Nyamwisi. Muvingi was assassinated by Mobutu's killers in May 1993. Later, in 1998, his brother Mbusa became the leader of the RCD-ML (cf.

p. 8), a rebel movement that controlled the region of Beni and Lubero. Nowadays Mbusa is minister in the Congolese government.

14. Cf. Madsen, W. "Genocide and covert operations in Africa, 1993-1999". In *African Studies* 50, Edwin Mellen Press, Lewiston NY, 1999.

15. Prunier, G. *Sudan's regional war*, Le Monde Diplomatique, February 1997.

16. Cf. http://en.wikipedia.org/wiki/Allied_Democratic_Forces (consulted on October 2006).

17. Ibid. Because of the atrocities committed on children, ADF has been compared to the Lord's Resistance Army of Joseph Kony.

18. On the motivations that pushed Uganda to intervene in Congo cf. Clark, J. F. *Museveni's Adventure in the Congo War: Uganda's Vietnam?*. In Clark, J. F. (ed.), *The African Stakes of the Congo War*, Palgrave MacMillan, New York, 2002, pp. 145-165.

19. This city, in the last decades, has become a crucial centre for trade in East Congo. Butembo is full of shops that sell all kind of goods: food, clothes, motorcycles, electronics etc. The businessmen of Butembo supply the North and East Congo with their goods, and even partially the Central African Republic. Their influence has increased during the war since the navigation on the Congo river, that connects the capital Kinshasa with the central town of Kisangani, has been blocked.

20. This explanation is an over-simplification of the war-economy in the territory of Beni and Butembo which in reality was much more complex than that. In fact, some members of the Nande businessmen community were much closer to Mbusa Nyamwisi, while others were quite hostile. Nevertheless, every businessman of this area had to look for protection: some of them supported Mbusa Nyamwisi while others supported the Mayi-Mayi militias which were based in the rural zones.

21. Cf. Chabal, P. & Daloz, J.P. 1999. *Africa Works. Disorder as Political Instrument*, James Currey, Oxford.

Marginalization and Uprooting: The Basua Pygmies of the Bundibugyo District[1]

Gianluca Forno

The Basua are part of a multi-ethnic context incorporating numerous other groups such as the Bamba, Bakonzo, Babwisi, Babutoku, and several others. Even though the Basua have always constituted a restricted minority, it is worth considering their ethnic identity at the centre of a socially dynamic complex, and also in the light of political and economic forces. They are thus of considerable anthropological interest.

Identity and Origins

By comparing the information contained in previous research and articles (Schebesta, 1933; Putnam, 1948; Turnbull, 1966; Frankland, 2001) with data taken from fieldwork in 2005, it is possible to trace the presence of pygmy groups in the area of Bundibugyo from approximately the beginning of the 1920s[2]. The name given to identify the pygmies of this zone appears to vary: Bambuti, Batwa, etc. (Frankland, 2001), but it seems appropriate to conserve and adopt the term Basua, which they themselves use. Referring to the study by Colin Turnbull (1961; 1966) carried out on the pygmies from the Congo, it is possible to divide the Bambuti into the Aka, the Efe and the Sua – three distinct groups with significant variations in their spoken language, hunting-gathering techniques and in their various roles in the geographical area where they are found. The information collected during fieldwork confirms the arrival of the Basua, belonging to the Sua group, in the district of Bundibugyo from the Ituri forest. Collected testimonies, in fact, bear witness to a group of around ten individuals who moved from the village of Mahoyo (Ituri) in search of new land. Led by the charismatic family leader Alungama[3], this movement seems to have been caused by a need to find more fertile land to maximize foraging. The band initially settled near the village of Kisiriza, along the banks of the Semliki River, in the depths of the equatorial forest. After some years, the group then divided into at least two subgroups, due to internal disagreements regarding the role of the leader. As a result, a section of the Basua moved to the area where they are currently situated today, along the road that connects Bundibugyo to Fort Portal. As will become clear in the following section, this was a very significant moment regarding the future of the Basua in the district, resulting in profound consequences for their present situation.

Due to the lack of reliable sources, it is not possible to establish a complete reconstruction and localization of consecutive movements. However, it appears certain that the Basua's fragmentation into family bands led to a specific system of economic trade with the agricultural villages (predominately Bamba) of the region. This trade system dominates the network of relations and explains the names of the different clans that are still present today among the Basua: Babukwanga, Bahanda, Bandimundwai, Basendwa, Bandimbela, Bandyegude, Bahombi. These are the names of the Bamba clan to whom the different Sua families were affiliated[4]. The affiliating relations have never been equal; on the contrary, it appears that the pygmies have always been considered inferior to the surrounding groups and a good source of cheap labour. As it will be made clear, this type of prejudice has important consequences for the actual status of the Basua, even though it was previously a result of a compromise which secured their survival.

The clans, or extended family groups formed by a shared ancestry, represent a constituent element of the Sua society, even if the case study presents more than one exception to a "classic" typology. For the Basua, the clan is a strictly exogamic unit[5], guaranteed by the taboo of incest and founded on a patrilineal system; in practice, however, some "anomalies" were registered, partially caused by the peculiar present day circumstances. Firstly, as was mentioned earlier, it remains a rather particular and distinct aspect that the Sua clan changes according to whom they relate with and with whom they share their territory[6]. Secondly, belonging to a clan today has become an arbitrary choice of one or both parents of a newborn, that does not always respect patrilineality and often creates paradoxical situations[7]. Finally, there are some verified cases of adoption and consequent clan changes that, on the one hand, render the whole system flexible and adaptable, and fragile and precarious on the other.

In the attempt to historically reconstruct their appearance in the region, certain characteristics seem to be significant, among which are flexibility and the capacity to adapt to different people and contexts. Regarding their native language, for example, the Basua have conserved their own dialect, Kusua, contemporaneously acquiring competence in the various local languages (Lukonzo, Luamba, Kiswahili, etc.). A system of not only economic but cultural exchange was established among the Basua and Bamba (and subsequently also the Bakonzo) that has partly shaped a new and original ethnical identity[8]. It will subsequently be seen just how the Sua identity today has become prey to socio-economic forces and pressures that are caused by a cultural rarefaction with worrying contours.

Recent History

Before discussing any considerations regarding the present-day situation of the Basua of Bundibugyo, it is still necessary to consider some fundamental episodes in their recent history. One such relevant moment in their history can be placed at the end of the 1970s[9], when, by the will of the elderly Alungama (the head of the dominant clan, the Babukwanga), the Basua reunited into one encampment, in a zone of the forest very close to their present position. From this moment on, the group would always remain united in the vicissitudes that followed, with the exception of some individuals who had decided beforehand to distance themselves from life in the forest, choosing the nearby villages of the Bamba and Bakonzo.

In 1993, the forest area in which they lived was declared the Semliki National Park and thus a protected area and public property. Among the immediate consequences for the Basua was a prohibition of residence, hunting and gathering. From this moment on, two attempts of "resettling" were reported to have been financed by the government, the UWA (Ugandan Wildlife Authority) and by some non-government organizations operating in the region[10]. The first of these attempts, in 1993, saw the construction of new accommodation near the village of Burondo. Two years later, the project failed due to problems created by the distance between the forest and the principal road[11] that connects Bundibugyo to Fort Portal, and due to the difficulties of cohabitation between the Basua and the agricultural groups. In 1995, they were put under government pressure to relocate to the village of Bundimasoli, where, in addition to a new residential solution, they were also offered the opportunity to access state-funded primary education. This also proved to be an ineffective initiative.

A political crisis broke out in 1997 between the Ugandan government and the ADF (Allied Democratic Forces) – guerrilla rebels against the Museveni government – who until 2002 terrorized the entire district with violent incursions, and clashed with the army. During this period a new phenomenon of dispersion emerged: it appears that some individuals returned to the Congo, others returned to the forest (their natural habitat and a secure hiding place), some males were enlisted into the national army, and an exiguous part of the original inhabitants remained in Bundimasoli. The socio-political instability of the area therefore contributed to a worsening scenario for the Basua.

It is not until 2002 that the group would again reunite near the village of Mpulya in a small encampment constructed on the boundary of the forest, in an area granted by the UWA. Here they are considered to be occupants of public land, and therefore without any legitimate claims to land rights. Their new living arrangement is a reduced space, scarcely sufficient to house the nuclear families of the larger group, and directly facing the main road. The area would be completely unfit for subsistence farming, should they happen to decide to compete in a mixed economy including agriculture [12]. From the point of their arrival in the district, it appears that the number of group members has always been between 50 and 100 individuals. Today the total number of the Basua present in this zone is 78, almost all resident in Mpulya.

The present day socioeconomic situation presents many problematic aspects. Social marginalization and uprooting have generated among the Basua a tendency to passively accept their condition, and there is little awareness of their essential human rights.

At the Margins of Society

Numerous anthropological studies have looked at so-called subaltern groups, the marginalized and weakest elements in a given social system. To analyze the *status quo* of the Basua leads in this direction, not so much with the romantic, ethnocentric intention to restore some form of dignity, but with the intention of throwing light on what was observed, offer some explanations and open a debate.

The problem of marginalization clearly emerged during fieldwork, not only in relation to the forest but also with respect to the nearby ethnic groups, inhabitants of the area of Bundibugyo. As mentioned above, the analysis of interviews and participant observation proved just how profound the interconnections are between the different cultural and economic systems of this zone. These interactions are all profoundly marked by the first contact and exchange between the Basua, and the Bamba and Bakonzo.

The ritual of circumcision is a significant example in this regard[13]. Among the ethnic groups that are found in the district of Bundibugyo, all boys "cross" the threshold into manhood through the ritual of circumcision, and it appears that it was the Basua who imported and transmitted this custom to the nearby tribes. This transition rite seems to have been passed down from the pygmies to the Bamba and successively from the Bamba to the Bakonzo and other groups[14].

The fact that the Basua entered into sudden contact with the local population and constructed a long-lasting, economic and cultural relationship does not, unfortunately, signify that their integration into the fabric of society was egalitarian. Different ethnographic research presents the social conditions of the various pygmy groups as subordinate to and at the margins of society (Turnbull, 1966). In some cases (for example the Batwa from Burundi), the dominant groups of pastoralists and farmers identify the groups in question with labels like "pariah" or "untouchables" (De Carolis, 1978), with the intent to express a relationship of subjection, peculation and control.

A great part of the Basua history can be traced back to the dynamics typical of the traditional, affiliating relations between the dominant clans and the small family groups of pygmies (Grinker, 1994). This created a relationship of interdependence that, today, has been remodelled and could be defined as unilateral dependence. This laid the foundation for strong racial prejudice towards the pygmies as inferior human beings: they were without self-determination and deprived of the rights reserved for other ethnic groups. In some cases, they are considered heathens or even animals and not even as human beings. If their relative economic independence in the past incorporated them into a trade system (the reciprocal exchange of meat from the forest traded for agricultural food supplies) that in some way legitimized their presence and above all their group identity. Today their situation has changed, and their role in the internal socio-economic balance appears undefined. Referring to Grinker (1996), marginalization refers to the idea of crossing the frontiers of society without being fully accepted or legitimized: a negative particularism comparable to the conditions of migratory phenomena. The Basua appear as if unrelated to the social balance, to the dynamics of change and innovation and, in particular, to the same cultural roots. A clear example is represented by the type of housing: the passage to a sedentary system has modified the structure, which is no longer an easily movable hut, but a dwelling partly inspired by the Bamba and Konzo models. Poverty, and consequently the inability to obtain material, forces the Basua into residential conditions that seem to underline the social division evident in their society, consolidating initial prejudices and placing them at the bottom of a hypothetical "social hierarchy".

It is said that non-governmental organizations like Uphold, World Vision and ADRA (Adventist Development and Relief Agency) are present in the district of Bundibugyo with the aim of providing "resettlement" for the Basua and to provide socio-economic integration. However, from 1993 until the present day, the initiatives undertaken and the subsequent results obtained seem to be insufficient and rather unfruitful. Fieldwork seems to demonstrate a widening gap regarding the aims of each project that does not take the needs and the future of their ethnic identity into account. Furthermore, the efforts of the various aid entities do not share common goals, nor do they coordinate their strategies.

The present-day Basua pygmies of Bundibugyo are therefore placed in a complex and problematic situation, in that they live on the margins of the forest and the society which accommodates them. There is considerable risk of a progressive cultural "loss" that could lead to their ultimate extinction. The current socio-historic process is leading the Basua to a disheartening and progressive desertion of their peculiar cultural foundations, not only for their identity but also for their physical survival. The uprooting from the forest and the loss of traditional subsistence methods have made them powerless in the face of a multitude of forces and pressures that are continually exerted on them. To be able to safeguard their survival in the region, it is important to comprehend who they are and what they would like to become.

"Forest Ghosts"

It can be confirmed that the traditional Sua identity is best summarized by the expression "forest people", coined by Colin Turnbull in his studies of the Bambuti pygmies of the Congo (Turnbull, 1961); the current circumstances have partly emptied this phrase of its meaning, bringing one to see them today as "forest ghosts"[15], a metaphor of disturbing contours.

The Basua have always had a symbiotic relationship with the forest that has characterized every sphere of their daily living. The forest has been a source of food, a meeting place to make contact with the supernatural, a place to gather herbs, roots and curative plants on which their traditional medicine is based, a natural theatre for celebration, dance, traditional music and rites of passage such as circumcision.

The pygmy groups are usually classified as a society of hunter-gatherers, and in this sense the Basua are no exception; the exceptionality of their current condition lies in the impossibility of living inside the equatorial forest, their natural habitat. They are consequently unable to practise their economic and traditional lifestyle to which they are historically bound. As seen previously, the establishment of the Semliki National Park in 1993 imposed a prohibition of hunting and forest inhabitation. This radical change regarding previous customs and habits has created a precarious socio-economic situation, putting at risk their survival as an ethnic group endowed with its own identity and cultural peculiarity.

The Basua today find themselves deprived of real opportunities, and they are incapable of creating a new type of economy that can ensure an acceptable condition of life. The current situation is only partly new; the error that should not be made is to confuse the Sua identity with a past myth of an uncontaminated origin. The closed relationships studied by Turnbull (1961), those defined as symbiotic by Winter (1956) and the definition of life in the forest by Grinker (1994) could easily lead to an hypostatization of the relations between the different ethnic and cultural groups of the region, and to a rigid, essentialist vision of their culture, which is of course in itself fluid and changeable. The area of Rwenzori and the district of Bundibugyo in particular, which has always been on the limits of the frontier, is a place where a great flow of different people have left their mark on a system of coexistence, including a legacy of colonial exploitation. Therefore, the Basua identity has had to adapt continually to events that could only but generate a new "product", distinct from the ideas that certain authors (Schebesta, 1933, Putnam, 1948) have implied (possibly unintentionally) about the marginalization of the pygmies to Westerners[16].

The impact of tourism that started in the 1940s is a significant example of the changes imposed on the Basua. In fact, in 1938, the road that connects the Semliki forest to the rest of the country was constructed, bringing with it outside contact and the first tourists (Winter, 1956). As was previously mentioned, after having spent their initial period in the depths of the equatorial forest, the Basua divided into family bands and moved closer to the principal road where trade and commerce was easier and a new resource was discovered: tourism. From this moment on, the situation modified profoundly and that which was once considered "living by one's wits"[17] has remained one of the few means of sustenance available today. The Basua are thus considered as a tourist attraction and are forced to live within a precarious economic system that is highly dependant on foreign tourism.

The foreign visitors are accompanied to the village of Mpulya by employees of the UWA, and "escorted" into the Sua reality. An *ad hoc* market immediately springs up offering manufactured goods, handcrafts and the possibility to negotiate prices for posing for photos or films. Naturally, it is difficult to see just how often a casual encounter happens to go beyond commerce. The forest authorities, in effect, have become "landlords" and the Basua try to monetize all that they can, even musical exhibitions and traditional dance, thus creating a theatre where the pygmies appearing in their traditional form become the protagonists, "rewritten" through misleading stereotypical narrations and socio-cultural judgments.

The fluctuating flow of tourism generates chronic economic instability that is incapable of offering security to the group. Furthermore, it creates an alternating "famine" and "an abundant harvest" independent of climate and traditional social relations. Previous research that concentrated on the impact of fluctuating tourism on local cultures is increasingly seeing tourism as an internal element, connected by a circular dialogue of cause and effect (Simonicca, 1998). In this manner, the ritual "performances" of the *Basua* could be interpreted as innovative aspects linking the past and the present, cultural encounters and clashes to the cultural dynamics of change. As previously said, the possibility of remodelling Basua culture is today extremely limited; they are deprived of having access to and exploiting the natural resources of their environment. Once again, what is relevant is the limited freedom to act and react.

Inside/outside, Tradition/modernity

The Basua of Bundibugyo, even if a numerically small group, represent a significant example of what is happening, or could happen, to the culture of the numerous other pygmy groups living in the Great Lakes Region. War, discrimination, environmental conservation policies indifferent to cultural peculiarities, and violation of human rights are all elements that have profoundly permeated their recent past and conditioned their present. Recent studies (Luling, 1998; Lewis, 2000) have shown that the violation of group rights, like those of the Basua, is an extremely current issue in this region.

The principal changes of traditional practices, social customs, rituals, health and economy were channelled by the dichotomy between inside/outside of the forest in relation to tradition/modernity. It is evident that life expectancy is rapidly decreasing: among the 78 individuals, only seventeen have passed into their 30s, while 44 of the individuals are between the age of one and fifteen years. The increasing death rate can be attributed to the conditions of life forced upon the Basua. The substantial changes and the impoverishment of the traditional diet (Ichikawa 1983; 1987) are certainly among the principal causes of the precarious health conditions of group members.

In addition, a social debasement has led the women to prostitution and the men to alcohol abuse. It can be confirmed that the prostitution of the Basua women is an institutional phenomenon today. The sexual intercourse deriving from prostitution (that exclusively involves men belonging to other tribes) is known as "intermarriages"[18], even if in reality they are not genuine inter-ethnical marriages. These relations (with the Bamba, Bakonzo men or others) are limited to conception and never develop into the creation of a nuclear family. The children are not acknowledged or supported by their fathers and end up being raised in the mothers' villages, deprived of a precise family identity. The mother arbitrarily decides which clan her child will belong to, choosing her own[19] or the one which the natural father belongs to. The only certainty for the new group members is to be considered a Basua in every respect; an element that today could even be seen as a "troublesome label".

It is worth underlining that the "intermarriages" are partially forced by a parental network which involves the majority of individuals being tied, in some way, to kinship: they are therefore unauthorized to be united in marriage. This model of procreation constitutes an economic resource for the village. However, it has almost simultaneously replaced the traditional system of marriage among the Basua, placing the continuity of the group in ever-increasing danger and relegating the men to a position of passivity and impotence. Deprived of their right to hunt, today the men find themselves refused by their women and are consequently unable to have their own family. In these conditions, excessive alcohol consumption is becoming an ever-increasing problem.

By studying in depth the themes related to rituals (circumcision, marriage[20], funerals[21], etc.), traditional medicine and economy, it is clear that the process of uprooting from the forest has modified the traditional cultural identity of the Sua. In some cases there is not only a remodelling of the given identity but an actual erasure. In this light, one can see the dialectical relationship between the inside/outside of the forest and tradition/modernity: for the Basua, the modern identity of being outside the forest has meant an estrangement from the practices and customs to which they were once bound. Tradition and cultural roots, by contrast, are found inside the forest.

The spiritual bonds that connect the family to the supernatural, as mediated by the figure of the traditional priest, have almost disappeared. The funeral rite has had to adjust to the current situation[22] and "new" and different denominations attempt to convert the Basua through increasingly insistent proselytism[23] that appears to have increased confusion among these people. Nevertheless, some traditional elements connected to rituals, beliefs and medicine have remained consistent and meaningful, and this should give us hope for the future of Basua society.

In the case examined, the partial elimination of the Basua cultural heritage has been due to an externally imposed process. Today the Basua have very little self-determination, which does not allow them to shape a future on their own terms. Instead they are forced to adapt passively to conditions that do not respect their needs and the right to rebuild and mould their own identity. We live in an era where different cultures take part in a global culture, but in order to participate meaningfully in a globalized modernity, a local culture needs to be independent and grounded: "Today, identity is both global and local, a result of past and present survival linked to origins and state: it is somehow an articulation of all these factors" (Augè, 2006).

The idea that a given society can remain on the margins is no longer sustainable. One needs to look at the entire network of interconnections. The distinction between "us" and "them" has become conceptually more ambiguous: these two categories are often blended, yet distinct (Borofsky, 2000). The Basua can then be considered a subject at the boundary of this movement, and yet placed internally. For a more comprehensive understanding of the Sua culture from an inter-ethnical point of view, it is essential that an up-to-date vision considers the entire web of cultural, economic and political forces that shape humanity.

Bibliography

Augè, M. 2006. *L'anthropologie.* (Italian Ed. 2006, *L'Antropologia del Mondo Contemporaneo.* Milano: Elèuthera).

Beauclerk, J. 1994. *Hunters and Gatherers in central Africa: on the margins of development.* Oxford: Oxfam.

Biesbrouck, K., Elders, S. & Rossel, G. 1999. *Central African Hunter-Gatherers in a Multidisciplinary Perspective: Challenging Elusiveness.* Research School for Asian, African and American Studies. Leiden: University of Leiden.

Bleeker, S. 1971. *The Pygmies.* London: Dobson Books.

Borofsky, R. 1994. *Assessing Cultural Anthropology,* Mac Graw Hill. (Italian Ed. 2000. *L'Antropologia Culturale Oggi.* Roma: Meltemi).

Cavalli-Sforza, L.L. 1986. *African Pygmies*. New York: Academic Press.

De Carolis, A. 1978. *Il Popolo dell'Argilla: pregiudizio etnico ed emarginazione sociale dei twa del Burundi*. Roma: Officina Edizioni.

Frankland, S. 2001. "Pygmic Tours". In *African Study Monographs*, Sup. 26: 237-256.

Grinker, R.R. 1994. *Houses in the Rainforest. Ethnicity and Inequality among Farmers and Foragers in Central Africa*. Berkeley and Los Angeles: University of California Press.

Ichikawa, M. 1979. "The Residential Groups of the Bambuti Pygmies, Tori Region". In *Senri Ethnological Studies*, No 1: 131.

Ichikawa, M. 1983. "An Examination Of the Hunting-Dependent Life of the Bambuti, East Zaire". In *African Studies Monographs*, Vol.4: 55.

---. 1987. "Food Restriction of the Bambuti Pygmies". In *African Studies Monographs*, Sup. 6: 97.

Lewis, J. 2000. *The Batwa Pygmies of the Great Lakes Region*. England: Minority Rights Group International.

Luling, V. 1998. *Forest Foragers of Tropical Africa: a Dossier on the Present Condition of the Pygmy People*. London: Survival for Tribal Peoples.

Magezi, M.W. 2004. *The People of the Rwenzoris*. Koln: Rudiger Koppe Verlag.

Panter-Brick, C., Layton, R.H. & Rowley-Conwy, P. 2001. *Hunter-Gatherers: an Interdisciplinary Perspective*. Cambridge: Cambridge University Press.

Putnam, P.T. 1948. *The Pygmies of the Ituri Forest*. New York: C.S. Holt.

Schebesta, P. 1933. *Among Congo Pygmies*. London: Hutchinson.

Simonicca, A. 1998. *Antropologia del Turismo: strategie di ricerca e contesti etnografici*. Roma: Carocci.

Stacey, T. 1963. *Summons to Ruwenzori*. London: Secker & Warburg.

---. 2003. *Tribe: the Hidden History of the Mountains of the Moon*. London: Biddles.

Syahuka-Muhindo, A. 1989. *The Rwenzururu Question: a struggle for democracy by Baamba and Bakonzo people of western Uganda*. Kampala: Makerere University.

Turnbull, C.M. 1961. *The Forest People*. Ebenezer Baylis and Son. London: The Trinity Press.

---. 1966. *Wayward Servants: The Two Worlds of the African Pygmies*. London: Eyre & Spottiswoode.

---. 1983. *The Mbuti Pygmies: Change and Adaptation*. New York: CBS College Publishing.

---. 1987. *The Lonely African*. New York: Simon & Shuster.

Winter, E.H. 1955. "Bwamba Economy: the developmentof a primitive subsistence economy in Uganda". In *East African Studies*, 5.

---. 1956. *Bwamba: A Structural functional Analysis of a Patrilineal Society*. Cambridge: W. Heffer & Sons.

---. 1959. *Beyond the Mountains of the Moon*. London: Routledge & Kegan.

Notes

1. This article presents research undertaken between July and September 2005, in association with the Missione Etnologica Italiana in Africa Equatoriale. The ethnographic research was undertaken in the district of Bundibugyo, in the Rwenzori region of western Uganda. The research

programme specifically focused on the Basua pygmies, inhabitants of the Bundibugyo area, one of the three main administrative centres in the region.

2. Around four generations have lived in this area up until the present day.

3. Pygmy groups are examples of acephalous and egalitarian societies (Turnbull 1983), but inside the group itself, often a prominent figure is identified who, to some extent, assumes the function of the tribal chief and guide.

4. In the past, the Basua adopted the denomination of the Lese clan (an agricultural ethnic group of the Congo and previous "partners"). This information proves to be salient in attesting the adaptive character of the hunting and gathering bands.

5. It has been reported in the past that there was a diffused practice to return to the frontier in Congo, in search of brides. This was caused by the practical difficulties an exogamous system can bring to a numerically reduced population.

6. In my opinion, this involves the subordination of the families and pygmy groups to a given group who sees them as a form of property.

7. A further explanation of the consequences of the practice of "intermarriages" will be presented further on.

8. A significant explanation, which will be referred to further on, regards the rite of circumcision.

9. Probably tied to the Bamba and Bakonzo independent movement, named Rwenzururu, which emerged after independence in 1962 and who provoked clashes and instability up until 1992 (Stacey 2003; Syahuka-Muhindo 1989).

10. Uphold, World Vision and ADRA (Adventist Development and Relief Agency).

11. A later reference will be made to the importance of establishing the movement towards the principal road, the emergence of tourism and sources for earning a living.

12. The lack of land at their disposition is their principal problem which the group identifies as the main obstacle to changing their customs. They do not refuse this change but it does appear impossible to them.

13. *Liamba* is the Kusua term used to define the overall rite of initiation.

14. This reference can be confirmed by interviews conducted with elderly members of the Bamba and Bakonzo groups.

15. "Forest ghosts" is an expression that is borrowed from the anthropologist Stanley Frankland, with whom I shared some time among the Basua and whom I hold in high esteem.

16. On this subject see: Frankland, S. 1999. "Turnbull's Syndrome, Romantic Fascination in the Rain Forest". In Biesbrouck, K. Elders, S. & Rossel, G., 61-73.

17. Translated as an expression utilized during an interview with Edward Ndige, the eldest (60 years) among the Basua of Bundibugyo.

18. "*Biamangana*" means "inter-marriages" in the Kusua dialect.

19. The situation today, in the majority of cases, sees the newborn associated to the maternal clan; this trend contradicts the patrilineal system and, even if preserving the Basua from further fragmentation, intensifies the matrimonial problem inside the group. The members of the new generation, in most cases, belong to the two dominant clans of Babukwanga and Bahanda.

20. The *Biamana* in Kusua.

21. The *Kukua* in Kusua.

22. Traditionally, the deceased's corpse was not buried, but left inside the deceased's destroyed hut and the encampment was then transferred to a new site; this practice has been abandoned for some time by the Basua, probably from the moment they moved from the depths of the forest towards commercial areas and agricultural villages, becoming sedentary.

23. During the period of time spent on field work, it was suggested that some associations and congregations "court" the Basua often for economical interests: paradoxically, even if marginalized, they represent a potential financial and economic resource.

Being a *Mulokole*:
Physical and Spiritual Salvation
from the East African Revival to the
Contemporary Pentecostalism

Alessandro Gusman

Introduction

In the theology of the Pentecostal movement, the concept of *salvation* takes up a primary value; partially different from the meaning it has in other sectors of Christianity. Strictly linked to the concept of *rebirth* ("to be born again"), the idea of salvation finds a further emphasis in the context of Ugandan Pentecostalism: the term *balokole* (litt. "the saved ones", sing. *mulokole*), which is locally used in several languages of the region to indicate the Pentecostals, actually designates the people who claim to be "saved" (even if the origin of the word is in Luganda, the idiom of the Baganda, the population of the area of Kampala, the capital city). The idea of salvation, more than that of the rebirth, seems therefore to be the crucial notion in the Ugandan version of Pentecostalism.

One has to search for the roots of the term *balokole* in the East African Revival, which started in the 1930s and had its main centre in Uganda in the city of Kabale, and generally in the Kigezi region, at the border with Rwanda. This fact shows how some concepts which are today widespread in the various Christian denominations in Uganda, and especially in the Pentecostal churches, were not been introduced by American Pentecostal missionaries, who reached the country for the first time in the 1960s, but were already present in the earlier history of local Christianity. As several authors have observed, one of the crucial features of Pentecostalism is its capacity to adapt, weaving local elements with the global ones coming from North America. In this way, Pentecostalism has today become the "global religion" par excellence[1]. If one wants to analyze the local peculiarities of the Pentecostal presence, it is not enough to situate the phenomenon in the context of its global diffusion, but it is also necessary to look at the religious and non-religious history of Uganda to be able to understand the *bricolage* of elements which is at the base of the local expression of religion, and to understand the meaning which is locally attributed to some concepts which have taken a global dimension, as elements of identity for the Pentecostal movement. Such is the place, for instance, of the notion of salvation. I will return later, especially in the conclusion, to this aspect.

My paper will focus in particular on two aspects of the Pentecostal presence in Uganda: a) the aspects of continuity which it shows with the East African Revival, which, originating inside the Anglican COU (Church of Uganda), had spread its influence on all the *balokole* denominations (this influence is visible not only in the use of the term *balokole*, but also in some ritual and doctrinal aspects); b) the peculiar meaning taken by the term "salvation" in a country afflicted in the last decades by a long, political instability, with a series of wars, by economic and social problems which derived from this situation, as well by a number of diseases, in particular the HIV/Aids epidemic which has caused hundred of thousands of deaths in the country since the 1980s[2]. It is noteworthy that in such a context, the idea of "spiritual" salvation is linked with a component of "physical" and material salvation, which is even more vital and urgent in this condition.

The Concept of Salvation in the Pentecostal Theology

As I have already asserted, Pentecostalism stresses the idea of *salvation* for the individual (but also, as we will see, for the community) in its effort to revitalize a Christian faith that it considers to be too rigid and nominal. Since the beginning, in fact, the Pentecostal movement took its place against the formalism of the mainstream churches, strongly claiming that salvation can be reached only through a deep and heartfelt repentance, the admission of one's own sinful nature, and the knowledge that it is only by giving oneself to the action of Christ (in particular, the redeeming action of his blood is peculiar to Pentecostal theology) and of the Holy Spirit, that salvation can be achieved. This *gospel of salvation* (which was already present in the East African Revival) becomes in this way one of the main points in the Pentecostal faith, through which it divides the world into two strictly separated groups: the group of the "saved ones", and the other of the "non-saved". It is towards the latter that the evangelical action of the members of the first half is directed[3]. Saving oneself is believed to be the result of an individual decision, which consists of linking one's own life to Jesus Christ, and in accepting him as a "personal saviour". This personal decision is however not sufficient, but also requires the action of the Holy Spirit, and it is for this intercession that collective prayer of the *balokole* community is needed. During Sunday services, usually at the end of the celebration, the pastor asks the assembly to pray for the people who are present in the church but who are not yet saved, so that they give their lives to Christ at that very moment. During the two to three minutes which follow, broken only by the encouragement of the pastor to grasp the opportunity to be saved, in the biggest churches of the town, such as the Full Gospel Church, or the Kampala Pentecostal Church or the Miracle Centre, at least some people often stand up to declare their will to become part of the *Balokole* community. Some members of the staff of the church are ready to approach the new converts and to pray with them or, in some cases, even to bring them to the altar, so that the prayer of the whole community can help them to accomplish the journey which ends with the baptism of immersion some weeks after this event.

The message of salvation is no doubt one of the main tools which facilitated the diffusion of the Pentecostal movement throughout the African continent, as suggested, among others, by Allan Anderson:

> In Africa, Pentecostal-like movements manifested in thousands of indigenous churches have changed so radically the face of Christianity there, simply because they have proclaimed a holistic gospel of salvation that includes deliverance from all types of oppression like sickness, sorcery, evil spirits and poverty. This has met the needs of Africans more fundamentally than the rather spiritualised and intellectualised gospel that was mostly the legacy of European and North American missionaries. The good news in Africa, Pentecostal preachers declare, is that God meets all the needs of people, including their spiritual salvation, physical healing, and other material necessities.[4]

We will see later how this approach reinforced the idea of salvation as a physical and material matter, in addition to the spiritual dimension.

The Origins in the East African Revival

As we have already established, the roots of the word *balokole*, today used in the whole of Uganda to indicate Pentecostals, are to be found in the history of the East African Revival, one of the movements of awakening which marked the history of African Christianity[5]. The origin of the Revival is usually found in the "Christmas Convention" which was held at the missionary station of Gahini, in Rwanda, in 1933, when a group of missionaries and believers started confessing their sins in public, developing an idea of "awakening" of Christianity through the formation of a "regular fellowship" of small groups of people, whose aim was to allow more friendly rituals, and to reach personal salvation through repentance and confession, and with the support of the group to which one belonged[6].

Missionaries came somewhere between 1915-1921, but the group of missionaries who were part of the Revival were a team of medical doctors; they came from England and they came to use their training in medicine to preach the Gospel. There were many complicated diseases in the area, for instance leprosy, and there were no treatments for these ailments. So, when these people came they brought medicine – and the Gospel assisted in the healing of the people. But the churches that they planted not always became viable. People would be baptized and would be, so they said, converted, but there was no change at all, so in the 1930s they started asking themselves: what is wrong with this church? They were not really making disciples: they were baptizing, people were coming to church, but they were not becoming disciples of Jesus[7].

It is interesting to note that Reverend Benoni emphasizes the fact that healing was an important element of acceptance of a foreign religion. If it is undoubtedly true that Pentecostalism's great success is due to capacity to give the answers people need, nevertheless these answers are at the same time spiritual and practical, concerning everyday survival. If the Gospel came together with treatments for diseases or with the means to improve living conditions, it would have a greater chance of success.

The movement grew fast, and spread in the area around Uganda[8], especially in the contiguous region of the Kigezi (with its core in Kabale where, according to many scholars, the Revival started in 1935, after the prelude in Gahini), and from here in the near kingdoms of Ankole and Toro[9], and in Buganda, where it was introduced in particular by some young students of the Bishop Tucker Memorial College[10]. It should be noted that at first, the term *balokole* was not used by members of the Revival, which in its place made use of *Aboluganda*, to indicate that they, by becoming part of the movement, were now all of a distinct family, and belonged to a new clan.

The Anglican Church assumed, since the beginning of its presence in Uganda, a very important political role, being linked to the British Protectorate. Some of the members of the Church Mission Society, influenced by their education in the Keswick Revival in Great Britain, did not appreciate the political connections, and reaffirmed the primacy of the spiritual work of the mission. For this reason, already in 1893, there was a first attempt to instil new life into the Christian faith, the so-called Pilkington Revival.

The East African Revival had much more impact on Christianity in this region of Africa, and on the organization of the Anglican Church. The movement did not, in fact, present itself as schismatic (even if in some moments of particular tension they came very near to a rupture with the official Church), but as an attempt of reformation from inside the Church of Uganda. There were three points in particular on which the *balokole* insisted to "awake" the COU and its pastors and followers: a) the awakening of conscience; b) the renewal of the cult, with the Church being accused of mere ritualism; c) the reaffirmation of the role of theology, with the refusal of the modernist drift (Wild, 1999). On this last point in particular the critics of the revivalists were very strong, and this matter occasioned the hardest clashes with the ecclesiastical leadership. For the *balokole,* modernism, which entered the COU, brought three main problems: the minimization of sins, a reduction of importance attributed to the power of the blood of Jesus Christ, and the lack of preaching about the necessity to live a holy life, setting oneself apart from worldly things. These were the main points of the *Kabale Report,* a document prepared by the group of *balokole* who met in December 1941 to discuss the relationship they had to maintain with the COU (Ward, 1989:209).

Among the other elements of crisis within the Anglican Church, it should be noted that the Catholic missions were penetrating more and more into Ugandan territory, especially in the west of the country (Kingdom of Toro), where the Revival had the greatest impact. Less linked to the colonial administration, the three orders of Catholic missionaries operating in the region (with their centre in the White Fathers' parish built on Virika Hill in Fort Portal) were able to bring off a project of "territorialization" which allowed Catholicism to impose itself on the physical and social space of the region, and attracting a considerable part of the population[11].

During the 1950s the Revival integrated more into the COU, losing part of its reformist energy. In spite of this, the roots of the Revival are today still very visible inside the Anglican Church, where the *balokole* are growing again in number, on the strength of the Pentecostal boom, and inside Pentecostalism itself, which in its Ugandan version caught more than one legacy of the East African Revival, not least the idea of "salvation".

In a sense the Revival has never stopped; just like any Revival it goes up and down. When the Holy Spirit fell on the church, most of the people who first received the power were the Africans – and the African way of expressing themselves is very different from the European one. Somebody is released, or forgiven. Even if it is a person-to-person conflict, and there is then forgiveness, usually two things happen: they sing and dance or they sit down and have a meal together, as reconciliation. So when people accepted Christ and they know their sins are forgiven, they would dance and sing, they would express what is inside on the outside, and this was very difficult for English people to accept. Their tradition eschewed the expression of feelings in public. So the Pentacostalist outpouring of affect was somehow offensive to English people. For this reason, one cannot easily trace this revival to England, although English people were involved. It is much more a local phenomenon that took on the spirit of locality in its expression[12].

In these terms, it seems even more significant that the local term, *balokole*, was utilized, as well as the fact that it is now used to indicate not only members of the COU in the tradition of the

East African Revival, but also the Pentecostals. The central idea is that, from the Revival onwards, in Uganda there is a group of Christians, the *balokole*, who, having accepted redemption through the blood of Jesus Christ and having taken up a certain way of life, called themselves "saved", and this independently from their belonging to the COU or to one of the several Pentecostal denominations which are present in the country. Later on, I will try to illustrate the numerous meanings of the concept of salvation, highlighting how to save oneself often means, in a very pragmatic way, "to survive", or "to reach safety" in a context where diseases and poverty frequently make physical survival itself a problem.

Physical Salvation and Spiritual Salvation

The so-called "neo-Pentecostalism", or the third generation of Pentecostalism[13], has among its assumptions the preaching about prosperity and "divine healing". Chasing away disease, poverty or other misfortunes (interpreted as a chasing away of demons) has become the main mission of the Pentecostal Churches of the "new wave", and to achieve this aim a collective and uninterrupted fight against Evil is fought[14]. It is interesting to note that, by putting the stress on these two factors, the relationship between conversion and salvation is significantly modified. Salvation is no longer understood as an individual "setting apart from the world" to keep away from temptations and corruption (as it was intended by the East African Revival and in the first stages of Pentecostalism), but becomes a "this-worldly" affair (Corten and Marshall-Fratani, 2001:7). From this new point of view, the "rebirth" is both spiritual and material, and "salvation" should also be obtained through the achievement of money, health and success in the life on earth. While the missionary churches often had programs of "holistic healing", in the case of neo-Pentecostalism the miracle becomes the main factor (Simojoki, 2002:272). According to Simojoki this situation depends for a good part on two factors coming from the 1980s: on the one side, the establishment of the media preachers in North America, and the subsequent global diffusion of specialized broadcasts which transmit their sermons; on the other side, the very rapid growth of the "Theology of Success" of the South-Korean Pastor Yonggi Cho, who was able, through a number of "crusades," to bring this theology to various parts of the world, including East Africa[15]. Together with these global factors, an important role is also played by local factors. If it is true that in the Pentecostal theology the traditional idea of the healing of the sick as it is present in the Gospel has been modified to assume the features of "deliverance", this change has been received in a peculiar manner in those countries that live with the dramatic experience of various epidemics (first of all the one of HIV/Aids), whose cures are still very expensive and are therefore only available to a small part of the population. For this reason many people turn to low-priced or alternative forms of healing, like those offered by the traditional healers and several Pentecostal pastors.

The concept of "healing" therefore assumes, in this context, a much wider meaning, which exceeds the strictly physical connotation of taking on social and spiritual features, in the same way the idea of "salvation" goes beyond the limits of the spiritual sense, assuming a physical and social denotation:

> Healing is the practical reaffirmation of a provision of the Kingdom of God. [...] Interestingly enough, the definition of healing goes beyond purely medical problems, and includes a wide variety of personal problems which people have to deal with in this modern global world (Droogers, 2001:55).

In this sense, neo-Pentecostalism exploits the gaps in the wake of liberalism and the emergence of what Ernest Gellner has defined as the "modular man" (Gellner, 1995). For this kind of contemporary man, according to Gellner, the sense of belonging is no longer defined through birth or with a ritual, but it is changeable. Pentecostalism takes advantage of the uncertainties and anxieties which are provoked by the achievement of individualism in African societies, that same individualism which is frequently cited in the sermons of Pentecostal pastors as one of the worst enemies to struggle against in the collective effort to cast away demons.

On reflection, it becomes evident that the use of the term *balokole*, as defined by the various Pentecostal groups in Uganda, revolves around the idea of salvation, and less so around notions of rebirth and being born again. To convert to Pentecostalism, as my interlocutors often told me, means putting one's own life in the hands of Christ, giving oneself to the Holy Spirit, and relying on this revitalizing agency. In this way a new life is given to the individual that is above all redeeming, with protection conferred by the blood of Jesus Christ. As I asserted above, the concept of salvation needs to be analyzed as a double component: it is both a spiritual and a physical process, with the latter component strongly associated with the idea of curing disease. The physical dimension of salvation is thus also connected to the role of religion as an instrument of healing, a topic which finds an important echo in the history of traditional religions of regional diffusion in the Great Lakes Region[16].

As I have already indicated, there are other meanings and situations in which the concept of salvation fluctuates from its spiritual sense to the physical one, and thereby to a social dimension. During my stay in Kampala, one of the themes most frequently recurring in the sermons of pastors was the necessity to forge a new generation of *global leaders*, a generation of young people who are not in debt to the past, but who are always in action, looking to the future and trying to construct it in an active way. What the Pentecostals have been preaching for some years is a "making for changing": first of all, it is a concept indispensable to the actualization of rebirth, which means putting the past behind one, and then preparing Africa and Uganda for a new, successful generation free from Aids and from the other problems afflicting the country (alcohol consumption, corruption, violence, poverty, etc.). This rhetoric of the new generation finds wide acclaim in many of the main churches in Kampala, and more generally in Pentecostal preaching. It is enough to recall the fact that one of the most successful books among the young people attending the Pentecostal churches explains how to bring up children and telling young people to become the future Christian leaders for Uganda. The text refers to the character of Joseph (Asiimwe, 2005) who, in the biblical narrative, resists the unceasing courtship of and attempts to do violence to him of the wife of his Egyptian master, Potiphar. At the end, the woman, in revenge, accused Joseph of having raped her, and Joseph was put in prison[17].

The reference to this biblical figure is particularly significant, not only because, once Joseph left prison he became a leader in Egypt, but also because the beginning of his journey is marked by a moral strength that allows him to refuse sexual temptations. So Joseph has become, for many Ugandan Pentecostals, the symbol of the campaign for abstinence from sex before marriage as the primary method in the struggle against the spread of Aids. This campaign aims to teach the so-called "ABC Strategy" (*Abstain, Be faithful, use Condoms*) supported by the Ugandan government (Office of the First Lady) and stresses, above all, the AB points, considering the condom to be the last frontier of defence against the virus. Several churches and evangelical radio stations spread the message of this campaign; particularly vigorous is the action of the Makerere University Church (MCC), a group that has a good number of university student members. Two years ago the MCC launched a campaign called CAWA (*Campus Alliance to Wipe out Aids*), whose aim was to reduce the impact of the epidemic on campus. These frequent initiatives, led by Pastor Martin Ssempa, are sometimes characterized by mass mobilization (marches inside the campus or in the centre of Kampala, sit-ins, etc.), leading to considerable media coverage. One of the MCC's ideas, namely that "*To abstain is cool*", found itself on the pages of major Ugandan newspapers, and recently even in the Italian magazine *Internazionale*.

These kinds of initiatives are not isolated, but are also organized by several other churches in Kampala; the religious message becomes in this way an incitement to salvation in the wider sense, as I explained above, including both a spiritual and a physical aspect. The problem is often posed in direct terms, reflecting the drama of the "HIV/Aids plague" in the country:

> We cannot build transformational leaders in Africa without dealing effectively with the challenge of the HIV/AIDS scourge. If we didn't, there would be no one to lead or to provide leadership. Africa has lost many emerging and marketplace leaders through AIDS, [...], abstinence is the most effective way of overcoming the scourge of HIV/AIDS (Asiimwe, 2005:69).

Surviving in Times of Aids

The example of Uganda is often cited by international observers and researchers to show how it is possible to deal with the Aids epidemic. In the 1980s, the numeric growth of HIV positive people in Uganda was extraordinary (from the first verified cases in 1982, the epidemic reached the number of about 1 million people infected in 1988, with peaks of more than 20% of the population in certain areas). However, from 1993 there was a steady if slow decrease of the disease, and according to official estimates the rate of infection in the adult population has decreased to about 6%, though not all specialists agree with this data[18].

One of the main reasons for this reduction in the incidence of the virus is probably the insistence of some public campaigns aimed at addressing the problem of Aids "by the light of the sun", recognizing the epidemic nature of the problem and trying to remove the stigma which so often affects people who are HIV positive. As Joyce Namulondo Kadowe of the Uganda Aids Commission (UAC) explains:

... the social diagnosis in the 1980s was often to associate the disease with *witchcraft*, because frequently the first to contract the illness were dealers who had commercial trades with Tanzania. There was fear, ignorance, and stigma. People who felt ill were thrown out of the house and didn't receive the care they needed. At that time only the religious institutions took care of those people, who died in an indecorous manner, deprived of every human dignity. Now, and for the last twelve years now, our strategy is that of opening the problem. People talk about Aids, are well-informed. The stigma little by little went away, even if some prejudices still remain[19].

The action of the UAC changed ideas about Aids so that it could be defined as an *"open secret"* (Williams, Kaleeba, Namulondo Kadowe and Kalinaki, 2000).

But Aids is not the only plague the Ugandan Pentecostals have to face. The stories of the believers (and also of the pastors) are often studded with economic and familiar problems, illnesses, alcohol or drug consumption, violence, etc. It is not uncommon, as during the conversation with a young Pentecostal, to hear a tale of dramatic experiences:

We were in 2000, my father died for Aids some months before, and I felt my sinful nature. At that time, I really was a sinner, too much a sinner, and the Catholic Church, which I frequented, was not strong enough to take me away from my situation. I used to drink, and to do other wrong things, but in that period I was really exaggerating in these dangerous behaviours, I was losing myself, and I felt that I could easily die in every moment, that something could hit me and... Bam! Died. I was really near to this end, before getting saved[20].

The main theme here is fear. In the case of John Bosco, as in several other Pentecostals who I interviewed or heard telling their stories, fear is the mainspring, which pushes many people to approach a church to "get saved". But seen in these terms, what does "salvation" really represent for the people who follow the

Pentecostal message? While one should not deny the idea of a spiritual salvation, which constitutes one of the fundamental points of the Christian soteriology, it is also at the same time clear that the fear that makes people search for a renewal in their lives is a form of worry for their own physical survival. In the stories of their conversion to Pentecostalism, the fact of coming close to the "point of no return" before encountering the new faith is recurrent. So, "to get saved" could mean also "to reach safety" (abstaining from dangerous actions) and to start a new life. For this reason salvation is also represented, with biblical references, as a "going out from the darkness", and as a march towards the light.

With regard to this point, it is significant to quote an extract of a Sunday sermon heard at the Full Gospel Church in Kampala. It referred to an evangelical passage dealing with Jesus's prophecy that Peter would have denied him three times before sunrise, announced by the crowing of a cock[21]:

> That cock brought at the same time reproof and hope: it reminded Peter of his mistake, but also told him that night had gone away, and that a new day was rising. And the new day meant a new beginning, a new birth. That cock told to all the believers that the night had been hard, that they had passed through the darkness, but even that now they had gone through this, and that a new day was rising, and that it brought a new light. That same cock still announces today for all of us that a new day is rising, and gives you a hopeful message, and that Christ is hope. I announce to you that a new day is rising over your lives. Whatever has been passing in your life now is finished; today is a new day.[22]

In the interpretation of Pastor Watante, the crowing of the cock promised good news for the oppressed: that they had survived the night and its darkness, and were moving towards the light. The darkness here is the symbol of the difficulties, of the sufferings, of the mistakes of the past, and of the necessity to repent of these sins, as Peter did, according to the biblical account. Coming out from the night in this way becomes a sort of redeeming initiation, marking the end of a period of suffering: getting through these trials means to rise to a new dimension, that of the salvation (spiritual and physical).

I would like to stress one more point, before concluding: in the speeches of the Ugandan Pentecostals, the theme of salvation repeatedly extends to embrace also a social dimension, instead of being confined to the individual one. Redemption is not only that of the individual, but of the whole country; or rather, the first finds its full realization only if the second is also accomplished, and only if it is used for the aim of the collective well-being.

The core of the theme is again Jesus Christ, and especially his body, which is at the centre of complex representations. It is interesting to note a parallel with what happened in the kingdom of Buganda. Even there, the emphasis was always placed on the body of the *kabaka* (the chief, or the king). In the Buganda kingdom, as in other regions of Africa, the leader of a community had to assure protection for his people, and to guarantee the well-being and security of the collectivity; his own physical wellbeing represented the entireness of the community (Brierley and Spear, 1988). In the periods of great difficulties, people went to the *kabaka* asking for protection and salvation because he had "eaten the kingdom", as they used to say at the moment when the new *kabaka* took the power, and in this way he had become united with the kingdom. But while, for the *kabaka,* the body was that of a human being exposed to illness and corruption, the body of Christ is represented in the Gospel as suffering but indissoluble (resurrection) and incorruptible. On the contrary, it is well known, as in the case of the chronic illness of the *kabaka* Mutesa, this was a period when the Buganda were afflicted by several plagues. The symbolic power of the *kabaka* was deeply weakened by his progressive disease, and from the erosion of his body, he finally proved unable to face the many problems of his kingdom. In the interpretation that Brierley and Spear give of this historical fact, the psychological impact of the lack of protection usually associated with the *kabaka*'s body induced many people to search for other forms of salvation, and this made the work of the missionaries easier; they had been in Buganda for only a few years, and this fact helped them and accelerated the Christianization of the region.

Conclusion

According to Paul Gifford, "Cho and the faith gospel promoters generally cannot be understood in isolation from their American roots" (Gifford, 1998:40), for the reason that a consistent part of the symbols, rituals, songs, music and other elements they use revealed this origin. There is no doubt, as I have shown, that the Pentecostal movement today has a global dimension, and one can easily recognize some of its global features everywhere it flourishes: from Korea to China, from sub-Saharan Africa to the islands of the Pacific seas, from Brazil to some regions of the centre and north of Europe[23]; these traits are present without considerable differences (although often even these small variants can be very significant). In spite of this global uniformity, as Gifford claims, there are always other roots and other elements that are connected to local symbols and beliefs. One can assume that these interlacing elements are a fundamental aspect in the study of Pentecostalism, and it is absurd to reduce it to a mere product of north-American culture (as the mass media often do)[24]. It would also be problematic to try to keep the endogenous elements separated from the exogenous ones in the local manifestation of the movement. These elements are in fact so fundamentally and indissolubly embedded, and in such an irreversibly way, that it is not possible to go back to the origins of each, or to separate them completely for analytic purposes. One can only try to analyze the situation of the phenomenon at a global and at a local level, and to identify the peculiarities of the local manifestation of Pentecostalism, suggesting some socio-cultural-historical reasons that could have led to the actual, distinctive aspect of Pentecostalism in Uganda. One needs to keep in mind that often every church is independent, and has its own history and characteristics, and that this local manifestation is the fruit of a historical process in which elements from different sources mingle.

As Corten and Mary write in their introduction to *Imaginaires politiques et Pentecôtismes* (2000:16), through glossolalia, prophetic visions and other practices frequently performed in the Pentecostal churches, "Pentecostalism recovers some elements and takes possession of schemes which are at the heart of the same popular cultures which they stigmatized (cults of possession in Brazil, *vodu* and witchcraft in Africa)". So it happens paradoxically that the phenomena of pentecostalization and of indigenization of the contemporary African religious manifestations proceed side by side, in spite of the Pentecostals' effort to be "global".

On the other hand, Corten stresses the capacity of Pentecostalism to recover and mingle the available imaginaries, "translating" them according to categories that sometimes distort their meaning. In an evident situation of crisis, where a new, globalized context requires the invention of new symbolic forms, Pentecostalism works to reformulate the preexistent symbolic universe, introducing into the public space ritual devices such as exorcism and miracles, which are able to shift the boundaries of what is possible and imaginable, and in this way opening spaces of complexity which were not acknowledged before, especially by mainstream Christianity.

What I am suggesting, therefore, is that one needs to analyze the Ugandan version of Pentecostalism (as any other version of it) as a cultural product which can be understood only by looking at the connections between local, national, and even global forms. As Coleman affirms, in the moment when they are brought into a new context, "its doctrines and forms of worship take on new symbolic resonances" (Coleman, 1991:7). If there is an external influence and a local adaptation to it, there is also, according to my analysis, "an external adaptation to a local influence", and the two sides of this same process can only be analyzed together, to show how the different elements influence and reinforce one another. It is not wise, I believe, to assume that the local history had no influence on the forms of cult and on the way

Pentecostalism developed and organized itself in a specific country. Looking at the Ugandan case, for instance, the fact that under Idi Amin's dictatorship in the 1970s the Pentecostals were persecuted, obviously had an influence on the way the movement developed in Uganda.

This is only an example of the way in which political, social, economic, and cultural dynamics mingle with the "global" phenomenon of Pentecostalism. In Uganda, as I have shown, Pentecostalism received a richness of symbols, concepts and values from the East African Revival by inheritance, and all these aspects are today strictly embedded with the ones originating from the Pentecostal tradition. This fact, together with the troubled history of the country, led to the peculiar meaning of salvation and of "being a *mulokole*".

Bibliography

Anderson, A. 2000. *Evangelism and the growth of Pentecostalism in Africa.* http//:artsweb.bham.ac.uk/aanderson/Publications/evangelism_and_the_growth_of_pen.htm#_edn3.

Asiimwe, P.R. 2005. *The Joseph Generation. Building a new Generation of Transformational Leaders*. Kampala: GLO Communications.

Brierley, J. & Spear, T. 1988. "Mutesa, the Missionaries and Christian Conversion in Buganda". In *The International Journal of African Historical Studies*, 21 (4): 601-618.

Church, J.E. 1981. *Quest for the Highest*. London: Paternoster Press.

Coleman, S. 1991. "Faith which Conquers the World". In *Ethnos*, 56 (1): 6-18.

Coleman, S. 2000. *The Globalisation of Charismatic Christianity. Spreading the Gospel of Prosperity*. Cambridge: Cambridge University Press.

Corten, A. & Mary, A. (eds.) 2000. *Imaginaires politiques et Pentecôtismes*. Paris: Karthala.

Corten, A. & Marshall-Fratani, R. (eds.) 2001. *Between Babel and Pentecost. Transnational Pentecostalism in Africa and Latin America*. Bloomington and Indianapolis: Indiana University Press.

Cox, H. 1996. *Fire from Heaven. The Rise of Pentecostal Spirituality and the Reshaping of Religion in the Twenty-First Century*. London: Cassell.

Cucchiari, S. 1990. "Between Shame and Sanctification. Patriarchy and Its Transformation in Sicilian Pentecostalism". In *American Ethnologist*, 17 (4): 687-707.

Droogers, A. 2001. "Globalisation and Pentecostal Success". In Corten, A. & Marshall-Fratani, R. (eds.) *Between Babel and Pentecost. Transnational Pentecostalism in Africa and Latin America*. Bloomington and Indianapolis: Indiana University Press, 41-61.

Gellner, E. 1995. "The Importance of Being Modular". In Hall, J.A. (ed.) *Civil Society. Theory, History, Comparison*. Cambridge: Polity Press, 32-35.

Gifford, P. 1998. *African Christianity. Its Public Role*. Kampala: Fountain Publishers.

Hansen, H.B. & Twaddle, M. (eds.) 1989. *Uganda Now. Between Decay and Development*. London/Kampala: James Currey and Fountain.

---. 1991. *Changing Uganda. The Dilemmas of Structural Adjustment and Revolutionary Change*. London/Kampala: James Currey and Fountain.

---. 1994. *From Chaos to Order. The Politics of Constitution-Making in Uganda*. London/Kampala: James Currey and Fountain.

Hollenweger, W. 1972. *The Pentecostals*. London: Student Christian Movement Press.

Martin, D. 2001. *Pentecostals. The World Their Parish*. Oxford: Blackwell.

Mary, A. & Corten, A. (Eds.) 2003. *Imaginaires politiques et Pentecôtismes*. Paris: Karthala.

Meyer, B. 2004. "Christianity in Africa. From African Independent to Pentecostal-Charismatic Churches". In *Annual Review of Anthropology*, 33: 447-474.

Pennacini, C. 1998. *Kubandwa*. Torino: Il Segnalibro.

Poewe, K. (Ed.) 1994. *Charismatic Christianity as a Global Culture*. Columbia: University of South Carolina Press.

Simojoki, A. 2002. "The 'Other Gospel' of Neo-Pentecostalism in East Africa". In *Concordia Theological Quarterly*, 66 (3): 269-287.

Stenning, D. 1965. "Salvation in Ankole". In Fortes, M. and Dieterlen, G. (eds.) *African Systems of Thought*. Oxford University Press, 258-275.

Uganda AIDS Commission, Republic of Uganda Ministry of Health. The MEASURE Project 2003: *AIDS in Africa during the Nineties: Uganda. A Review and Analysis of Surveys and Research Studies*. Carolina Population Center. University of North Carolina at Chapel Hill.

Van Dijk, R. 1997. "From Camp to Encompassment: Discourses of Transsubjectivity in the Ghanaian Pentecostal Diaspora". In *Journal of Religion in Africa*, 27 (2): 135-159.

Ward, K. 1989. "Obedient Rebels: The Relationship between the Early 'Balokole' and the Church of Uganda: The Mukono Crisis, 1941". *Journal of Religion in Africa*, 19 (3): 194-227.

Wild, E.L. 1999. *"Walking in the Light": the Liturgy of Fellowship in the Early Years of the East African Revival*. In Swanson, N.R. (a cura di) *Continuity and Change in Christian Worship*. Woodbridge: Boydell Press.

Williams, G., Kaleeba, N., Namulondo Kadowe, J. & Kalinaki, D. 2000. *Open Secret. People Facing up to HIV and AIDS in Uganda*. London: Actionaid.

Notes

1. The titles of some of the books dealing with the growth of Pentecostalism during the last decades are particularly clear in this sense; one can have a look at, for instance to *Pentecostals. The World Their Parish* (Martin 2001) and to *Charismatic Christianity as a Global Culture* (Poewe 1994).

2. For a better understanding of the events of the history of Uganda during the last decades, one can read the works by Holger Bernt Hansen and Michael Twaddle, who together organized a series of conferences on the phenomenon (Hansen & Twaddle 1988, 1991 and 1994).

3. At the beginning, the Pentecostals insisted on the necessity of living separately from the world to reach individual salvation; but, with the advent of neo-Pentecostalism, a new period started, in which the main mission has become the evangelical action towards the unsaved people.

4. Anderson, A. *Evangelism and the growth of Pentecostalism in Africa*, 6.

5. It should be noted that the term *Balokole*, which derives from *kulokoka* ("salvation"), even if it is used to translate the English "Pentecostals", identifies also the "saved" Anglicans, in continuity with the origin of the word, which was born in an Anglican background. So, *Balokole* indicates today all the saved people, Pentecostals and not, with the exception of the charismatic groups inside the Catholic Church which, even though agreeing with the idea of salvation through the action of Christ and of the Holy Spirit, don't call themselves *Balokole*.

6. In his contribution to *African Systems of Thought*, Derrick Stenning underlines that traditionally in the Ankole kingdom as in other near regions, one of the aspects of the initiation of a cult was the confession: "Having been ritually killed and turned into a dog, the novice was forced, on pain of humiliation, to confess alleged infringements of sexual prohibitions" (Stenning 1965: 263).

7. Interview with Rev. Canon Benoni Mugarura-Mutana, St. Francis Chapel, 10 August 2005.

8. The main figures, charismatic leaders of the movement, were an English missionary and doctor of the Church Mission Society, Joe Church, and a young Ugandan landowner, Simeoni Nsibambi , who met at the hospital in Gahini, in Rwanda, where Church worked as a doctor. Some decades

after the East African Revival, Church wrote an autobiography which remains one of the most vivid accounts of the period in which the movement started and developed (Church 1981). Another central figure of the Revival was Marble Ensor, an Irish nurse. Marble Ensor went to Uganda as a missionary and was working in a hospital, but she was frustrated about what had happened to the church. Marble decided to become an evangelist instead of a nurse, and during the time she was an evangelist she started teaching radical faith in Jesus Christ. She was so frustrated by the leadership of the COU that she started her own church, and called it the Mengo Gospel Church.

9. For the role of the East African Revival in Ankole and in Toro, see respectively Stenning (1965) and Kassimir (1998).

10. See the article of Kevin Ward *"Obedient Rebels" – The Relationship between the Early "Balokole" and the Church of Uganda: the Mukono Crisis of 1941* (Ward 1989).

11. For a better understanding of the dynamics of expansion of the Catholic missions in the Western part of Uganda, see the work of Roland Kassimir, especially Chapter 3.(Kassimir 1998).

12. Interview with Rev. Canon Benoni Mugarura-Mutana, St. Francis Chapel, 10August 2005.

13. For the commonly accepted division of Pentecostalism in three distinct periods, see the review of Birgit Meyer in the *Annual Review of Anthropology* (Meyer 2004).

14. The practices with which the individuals are made free from the evil spirits which possess them are the "deliverance" sessions, which can be individual or collective. In many contexts, the misfortune is attributed to witchcraft, and anyway to the fact of being possessed by demons. In some areas of the African continent, as in Uganda, the traditional spirits are interpreted as demons. The figure of the pastor becomes, in this way, ambiguous: he is able to get into contact with the world of the spirits, as did the traditional healers and sorcerers. This is why accusations are frequently leveled at Pentecostal pastors that they are complicit with sorcery and witchcraft. See for instance the debate which took up the pages of the main Ugandan newspapers (*New Vision* and *Daily Monitor*) in April and May 2006.

15. "Crusades" are huge assemblies which last for some days, attracting thousands of believers. They are usually organized in vast public spaces, such as stadiums, parks, or squares, and their aims is to reach those people who usually do not frequent services at churches, so as to convert them

and to allow them to "save" themselves. These events are organized by famous preachers, often from North America, who in this way are able to spread their message in various parts of the world, helping in the same time to develop Pentecostalism at a local level.

16. With regard to this subject, see for instance the work of Cecilia Pennacini (1998).

17. Genesis 39: 1-20.

18. The estimates reported here are taken from the government document *Aids in Africa During the Nineties: Uganda. A review and analysis of surveys and research studies.* (2003).

19. Interview on 13 September 2005.

20. Interview with Asiimwa Jhon Bosco, 23 August 2005.

21. See Luke 22: 60-68.

22. Ps. Fred Watante, 17 July 2005.

23. Europe is certainly the continent where Pentecostalism finds it more difficult to attract large numbers of followers. In spite of this, there are some interesting cases of success for the movement, especially in central and northern Europe, and in regions like Sicily (see Cucchiari 1990). Simon Coleman's *The Globalisation of Charismatic Christianity. Spreading the Gospel of Prosperity* (2000) provides probably the only in-depth study of one of these cases, the success of the *Word of Life Church* in Sweden. In the last decades then, and recently in Italy, many new churches have been founded in Europe by immigrants coming from countries where Pentecostalism is widespread, and who often in this way kept in contact with the original church and with their home country (for an analysis of this transnational Pentecostalism see, for instance Van Dijk 1997).

24. Speaking of this, it should be kept in mind that Pentecostalism, in the most accepted version, originated in the "black" suburbs of Los Angeles at the beginning of the twentieth century. So even the first steps of the movement are complex, involving a series of elements coming from different social and cultural contexts.

Coping with Babel around the Mountains of the Moon: A Case for Multilingual Patriotism in Uganda and Africa

Manuel J. K. Muranga

Introduction: Multilingualism on and around Mt Rwenzori

On and around Mount Rwenzori, the Mountains of the Moon[1], and in their vicinity, as it were, the following languages and dialects are spoken, among others: Lukonzo/Kinande, Rutoro, Rusongora, Runyabindi, Rutuku, Lubwisi, Kwamba (also called Bulebule and Vonoma), Kuswa (also called Luhuku), Lubwisi, Runyankore/Rukiga, Runyoro, Rufumbira/ Runyarwanda and Luganda on the Uganda side; Bira, Lukobi, Mvuba, Kitalinge, Lega, Tembo, Fulero, Hunde, Gegere and Lingala on the Congo side. English and Kiswahili are also, of course, spoken. With increasing stability in Uganda and the gradual return of Asians to Kasese, Hindi, Gujarati and Urdu are probably also worth mentioning. In fact, Schoenbrun underestimates the figure when he puts the number of languages that are spoken by different people on and around the mountain at 23.[2] In one of the fastest-growing urban centres in Uganda, Kasese (the capital town of the Bakonzo, the majority people of the Rwenzori range on the Uganda side) plays a major role in the growth of this multilingual population. Kasese's position near Kilembe Copper Mines favoured its growth to a multi-ethnic city, particularly in the 1950s and 1960s, for people came from many different parts of Uganda to work in the mines. Also, Kasese has, for decades, remained the most important connecting city between Congo and Uganda in particular and East Africa as a whole, as well as being a transit point for trade from Arabia, India and the rest of Asia. Many goods lorries and trucks loaded with containers destined for Congo enter Africa via the port of Mombasa in Kenya and pause at Kasese. This made it into a significant commercial centre. And, of course, Kasese is also a tourist centre because of its location at the foot of Mount Rwenzori, which people from different parts of the world come to climb. The Queen Elisabeth National Park has also greatly enhanced the tourist industry in this area. The Katwe Salt Lake has for centuries been a source of salt for many peoples from around the Great Lakes Region, who include, apart from the indigenous Bakonzo themselves, the Batoro, Banyoro, Banyankore, Bakiga, Baganda, Banyarwanda, Bahaya, Barundi etc. They would trek long distances to Katwe in order to obtain the salt and sometimes do barter trade with the salt (*okuhonera* in Runyankore-Rukiga). Over the years, these factors led to the growth of Kasese and the area around it (excluding the mountain itself) into a multi-ethnic and multilingual zone, and this development seems likely to be sustained for years to come. As a consequence, however, Kiswahili tends to be used as a *lingua franca* in the Kasese area more than anywhere else in Uganda, except in the area around Masindi and in the army and police barracks.[3]

The languages spoken around Mount Rwenzori can be divided into seven different language groups that are inherently intelligible, so that the speakers of the languages or dialects within each group would not suffer alienation beyond 30% if they were to meet in a situation where there was no common tongue to unite them. These groups are: (a) Lukonzo/Kinande; (b) Lubwisi; (c) Rwamba (or Kwamba); (d) Rutoro-Runyoro-Runyankore-Rukiga-Runyabindi-Rusongora-Ruhema;   (e)   Rufumbira-Runyarwanda; (e) Luganda; (f) Kiswahili; (g) English. The situation around Mt Rwenzori is, in fact, a microcosm of the situation in the entire country of Uganda, where up to 63 languages and dialects have been identified. This, in turn, is reflective of the situation in the entire continent of Africa, which, with its 2,058 languages spoken among some 500 million people is, after Asia, the most multilingual continent of the world.[4] Nigeria alone, with her population of 120 million, speaks over 427 languages.[5] And worldwide there are approximately 6,800 languages. In other words, the question of how to cope with Babel is as valid in the multilingual vicinity of Mount Rwenzori as it is for our multilingual world in general. And the answers to the question will be essentially the same for any multilingual place on earth, though they may differ in the details.

In our answer to the question, we shall focus on the situation around Mount Rwenzori, paying special attention to the mutually intelligible "Runyakitara" group of Bantu languages in the context of the neighbouring other Bantu as well as non-Bantu languages, exposure to which an averagely educated Runyakitara speaker can hardly escape. But before we attempt a solution, we need to make the following general observations:

(a) There is *no common language* around Mount Rwenzori in which *everybody who lives here would feel comfortable enough to be creative in*. We are basing this observation on the hypothesis that creativity in a language is a good indicator of mastery of it.

(b) The language in which human beings are generally and usually most comfortable and most creative, indeed most at home in, is their *mother tongue*, which is the language they first discovered the world with and which was their point of departure into their experience of discovering other, or secondary, languages. The mother tongue or the primary language is the language of their soul: practically, one's identity as human being is inextricably tied up with this first language. A person who tries to deny or exchange this linguistic identity can suffer grave psychological consequences.

(c) Our capacity to learn and master other languages notwithstanding, there remains enough *mother tongue patriotism* in each person, however latent and dormant, for that person to contribute to *language development*. That patriotism, however, needs to be carefully awakened and activated. As long as there is a substantial speech community that cares about its language, that language can form a basis for the development of *an economic sector whose primary raw material is language*: a good number of people can earn their living from products of this sector in industries and markets such as the following: teaching (of the language and the literature and culture around it); the writing and production of teaching materials; the media, both print and electronic (e.g. newspapers, magazines, radio and TV); drama, theatre and film (it can be observed by the critical theatre goer in Uganda that plays and skits in the mother tongue over which the cast is master come out more beautiful and are more effective than when the cast work entirely in English, of which the members of the cast do not have a perfect command[6]); writing and translation; tourist facilitation and education at natural and cultural sights; interpreting.

(d) In the field of education it is well known that *each person learns best in his or her mother tongue*, and so the most important tools of one's education, for example the standard textbooks in the academic disciplines, or any other educationally essential books, should be available in that language for one's normal learning and testing and examination purposes, or at least for consolidation and dissemination of what one may have studied or read in a medium of instruction that is not one's mother tongue, such as English, French or Portuguese in the rural areas of Africa. The books thus coming into existence in various mother tongues should be as beautifully produced as possible, in order to prevent the temptation among speakers of those languages to think that beautiful, well-written, well-illustrated, educationally stimulating books can only be produced in English or French or any other foreign language, but not in an African vernacular. This is a serious, far-reaching fallacy; for any language can of course be developed in such a way as to make its speakers feel proud of it.

(e) An educated person anywhere in the world, whose mother tongue is not international, would naturally love to be able to speak one or two international languages well, though ideally his or her mother tongue should, of course, be duly developed to remain his "strongest" language. In East Africa, this international language will quite naturally be English, followed by Kiswahili and/or French. Since none of our indigenous Ugandan languages are international, an educated person in Uganda will wish, therefore, to benefit from *a three-language education policy that involves the teaching of the local mother tongue, English and Kiswahili or French.* The aim should be to enable students to attain a high level of competence in each one of these; each of these language subjects should provide a basis for professional development for speakers that are good at it.

(f) Any effort at promoting one language at the expense of others in a truly multilingual country or world is inimical to *the fundamental human right to language* and runs counter to the human instinct of linguistic and cultural self-expression, self-determination and self-preservation. This is not only true for individuals struggling to live in a competitive world, but also for entire language communities, peoples and nations affirming and asserting their right to exist and to use their native tongue, even in a globalizing world. To neglect or suffocate the so-called small languages is to kill the potential for further economic growth in a country via viable language-based economies and industries, however small. The thirst for products made out of the raw material of one's mother tongue – whether newspapers, or calendars, or books, both original and translated, or radio programmes, or music, or dance, or theatre, or films, or functional or other educational materials – naturally creates a demand and a market for them, and the satisfaction of this demand and market will be undertaken by cultural groups and other enterprising people who will create employment and produce wealth. The linguistic and cultural diversity of our world that is, in any case, supposed to remind us of our duty to accept and respect others for their differences will, when looked at from this economic point of view, prove to be an asset rather than a liability, for each one of the 6,000 language communities in the world is a potential market for a variety of language products. In this process, however, our many languages in this world, and our natural, individual commitment to and exploitation of them, should keep us grateful, humble and wise, and our actual or potential benefits from this should not go to our heads. We should remember what led to the scattering at the Tower of Babel: the technological over-ambitiousness of the Tower's architects and builders, which had left God out of the reckoning.[7]

Multilingualism around the World: Switzerland, India, South Africa, Namibia and the European Union

Linguistic patriotism is particularly prominent in the multilingual countries of the world. In *Switzerland,* the government policy has for a long time been that all four languages, German, French, Italian and Rhaeto-Romanic, have been allowed to flourish in all fields, including education. Examinations in Switzerland are held in the native language of the people of that particular region. They cope with Babel by (a) teaching the other Swiss national languages in the schools and universities of the area where those languages are not the mother tongue; and (b) training translators and interpreters who can bridge the gap between speakers of different languages.

In *India*, the eighteen major Indian languages, apart from Hindi, which is a *lingua franca*, are Assamese, Bengali, Gujarat, Kannada, Kashmiri, Konkani, Malayalam, Manipuri, Marathi, Nepali, Oriya, Punjabi, Sanskrit, Sindhi, Tamil, Telugu and Urdu.[8] Each of these languages has a flourishing literature, even though Indian literature written in English is said, by Western observers of the scene, to have an elitist position because of its international accessibility.[9] But this "elitism" or "being written in English" must not be automatically equated with "being greater literature than that written in indigenous languages, say Malayalam". Unless we are able to read and judge literature written in two languages truly objectively – which is a rare qualification – we will not be able to compare a good novel written in English with a good novel written in another language. The most reasonable judgement would probably be one arrived at by an international, intercultural panel of some 20 English-reading judges of comparable literary experience who independently read, shall we say, the Malayalam novel in its best translation into English, then the Indian-English novel. A "democratic" decision would then need to be taken through a vote of some sort. We must not remain ignorant of the treasures that are in the literatures, both oral and written, in the many different languages of our world. And since we are living in an age when only English and a few other languages are spoken and taught internationally, we need to emphasize the role of translation, especially literary translation, and to train literary translators. For a truly fair international exchange in the literary field to take place, literary translation should be done between all possible pairs of languages, a "non-international or small" language such as Malayalam in India or Lukonzo/Kinande on Mount Rwenzori, and an "international, intellectual or prestigious" languages such as English or French or Spanish or German. The translating must be done in both directions, even if by two different translators, as is indeed the case normally, in order to give the monolingual readers of the "smaller" languages the opportunity to share some of the best literature of the "greater" languages.

The situation in *South Africa,* with its eleven official languages, is also of some interest in this discussion. The eleven languages are isiZulu, isiXhosa, Afrikaans, Sepedi, English, Setswana, Sesotho, Xitsonga, siSwati, Tshivenda and isiNdebele. The region where each language is spoken is potentially developing an economy, an industry around the language, including a patriotism for that language and culture that will eventually enrich the Republic of South Africa and indeed the entire world through the process of exchange we have outlined above in relation to India, an exchange that should be extended beyond the field of literature to other fields of human endeavour such as music, theatre, film, dance, general knowledge, philosophy, ethics, religion, science, technology and other forms of achievement. For many years in South Africa, Afrikaans enjoyed the privilege of being developed into a language of literary and intellectual and scientific discourse, in the context of a linguistic and cultural patriotism that was exemplary, though racist.[10] It is probably one of the most advanced relatively "small" languages of the world, comparable, I believe, to such patriotically cherished and developed languages of Europe as its near cousins Dutch and Flemish, as well as Danish, Faroese, Icelandic, Finnish, Czech, Slovak, Slovene, Serbo-Croat, Macedonian, etc. The economies and industries based on these languages are sources of livelihood and other forms of self-realization for a great number of people in those different countries. It was wonderful for this author to see huge, beautifully produced, colourfully illustrated general and specialized encyclopaedias, including those of science and – to his joy – even of theology, written in Afrikaans and being sold in bookshops in Bloemfontein, capital of the Orange Free State, in 1997. It is desirable that the Republic of South Africa should now develop all the other languages in such a way that by 2017, there are at least similar encyclopaedias written in Zulu and the other languages also being sold in bookshops in Kwazulu-Natal and other parts of the country. Many people would then be earning a livelihood and deriving other forms of satisfaction and self-realization from their preoccupation with their patriotically cherished mother tongues. By that time, what is happening in Europe on the linguistic and cultural map should also be happening in South Africa with language and culture well understood to be a beautiful, non-material raw material that can be processed into material products. A book is, indeed, a material product of a non-material basic element called language; a book is a materialization of language.

What is happening in South Africa is also happening in *Namibia*, though on a smaller scale because of a smaller population. Government policy has nationalistically and patriotically come in to ensure that each of the thirteen major languages of Namibia (Oshindonga, Rucgiriku, Rumanyo, Otchiherero, Rukwangali, Mbukushu, Oshikwanyama, Tswana, San, Khoekhoegowab, English, Afrikaans and German) comes into its own, each having a committed officer – always a writer or otherwise engaged language developer in that language – employed by the Namibian Institute of Educational Development (NIED), the equivalent of the National Curriculum Development Centre (NCDC) in Uganda, on a full-time basis to reproduce himself or herself, as it were, across the length and breadth of the region of his or her language community. With this wise approach, many writers have been developed through writing workshops and a substantial literature has come into being, besides textbooks for the learning of the languages from Grade 1 to Grade 12. These books are well-produced and attractive to use. Namibians follow a maxim that is well expressed in the Luganda proverb *Ensiba mbi edibya mutere* (Poor wrapping can cause the dried bananas to be rejected by buyers). A badly produced book will devalue itself by creating the impression that its contents are not worth the effort to "wrap them up in a nice, skilful, professional manner that ensures long life". The contents of the textbooks follow the "integrated" language textbook writing approach, whose point of departure is the realization that it is language that "integrates" all knowledge. Thus all registers of language are introduced in these textbooks, so that the student will find stimulating texts, not only from oral literature or modern poetry or fiction or drama, but also from history, geography, geology, biology, chemistry, physics, even philosophy and religion, complete with comprehension, lexical and stylistic questions on each text. Teachers of these languages are trained at teacher training institutions of the country and a Namibian child grows up at least bilingually respecting and developing his native Namibian-African heritage in the context of cosmopolitanism and globalization. He/she has something to offer to the rest of the world in the global village, even as he/she takes in something from other parts of the world. Translation into and out of the Namibian languages is in fact part and parcel of the language education curriculum. Under the GTZ-sponsored project Upgrading of African Languages (AfriLa), moreover, the NIED has been able or is still undertaking to produce paedagogically appealing books in all school subjects in all the Namibian languages, so that they are not only available in English but also in each other language. They are practically the translation-based indigenizations of the English-language textbooks, and these will help with mass education. The Namibian's bilingualism is not limited to ordinary day-to-day conversation; it also stretches into more academic and intellectual discussions. It is intended that via his knowledge of his/her home language and his/her other knowledge, and via knowledge dissemination, *inter alia* through writing, the educated Namibian will be able to contribute to the economy around his/her home language; it will be part of his/her patriotic vocation.[11]

In the *European Union,* they have accepted that multilingualism is part and parcel of the European heritage and so they are prepared to pay what it takes to maintain it. Each member country is proud of its own heritage and enters the Union with its linguistic heritage. The Union spends dearly on translation and interpretating. At home in each country, the national budget also consciously supports the teaching of the mother tongue(s), as well as at least two foreign languages, usually taken from one of these five: English, German, French, Spanish and Italian. The classical languages of Europe, Ancient Greek and Ancient Latin can also be studied in some schools. But at home again, there is a dynamic mother-tongue-based economy which employs a good number of people in direct or anciliary industries.

Literature as the highest medium for the celebration of the gift of language is written and studied in the different mother tongues; an active literary translation industry contributes to the necessary intra-European intercultural exchange. True democracy demands that every person is free to express himself in the language he/she feels most comfortable in, but the state has a duty to train competent translators and interpreters who will facilitate the exercise of this linguistic freedom. In Africa too, we cannot talk of true democracy until we are consciously promoting the full exercise of the right to self-expression without linguistic barriers, coupled of course with a strong sense of responsibility.

The way to "cope with Babel", then, is for each linguistic community to organize itself patriotically, whatever their number, and to make use of the "raw material" that is their mother tongue. The European Community countries have a long history of linguistic patriotism that we in Africa can learn from. We should aim to produce good, learner-friendly and learner-centred books in our mother tongues for both school and general use. We should grow writers that can enrich and ennoble their mother tongues and add literature to them. This, in turn, should unleash a reading culture that will again encourage experienced writers and stimulate new ones. If the language community itself can institute a prize for good writing, the writers would be further strengthened. Indeed the multilingual state should itself institute its own prize for good original writing in each language, plus a prize for translation into and out of each language. The state needs to promote both cultural and intercultural activities.

However, we should also make use of our socio-linguistic history: in Uganda and indeed elsewhere in Africa where English is used, we need to maintain the teaching of English up to a high level of competence (and confidence!) in both spoken and written forms, yet without striving unnaturally to speak it with an accent like that of the people of Britain or America or Australia, or to write it with idioms and imagery that are totally foreign to our countries. The Africanization of English in written form may at times indeed involve what Dambudzo Marechera puts in the following terms: "The writer should be mastering the [English] language. The language should be the slave, we must brutalize it into our own shape"[12] (Williams 1998:1).

Kiswahili is already so well developed as a school subject and is an increasingly useful medium of communication and education; the smaller but robust languages can learn from it. Particularly, its language studies curriculum and textbooks, from primary school to university, contain good examples of the approaches that can be used by the writers of the mother tongue textbooks. Similarly, the growth of literature from poetry and academic and scientific knowledge to newspapers and magazines and functional applications such as usage manuals and labels indicates what could happen on a smaller but viable scale if we had enough linguistic patriotism.

Trilingualism within Multilingualism: A Viable Language Policy for Uganda and other Multilingual Countries

I believe that the way forward for Uganda in matters of language policy and education is that each educated Ugandan should know, as well as possible, at least three languages, namely: his/her first language, which is normally the mother tongue, then Kiswahili, then English. This will cater for the local, regional and global needs respectively of the individual and the nation very well.

However, at the local Ugandan level, we need to understand one another across the potentially 63 languages in the country. We cannot afford isolation because that would cost us the chance to grow into an internally dynamic nation that derives wealth and pride from each of its many languages and the cultures around the languages. Therefore I propose the following approaches:

(i) The government should consciously *promote linguistic and cultural patriotism* within each linguistic community, yet this must be well understood as different from, indeed the opposite of, promoting linguistic and cultural chauvinism. In a country of 63 languages, a continent of 2,058 and a world of 6,800 languages, we cannot afford to be chauvinistic, indeed we need to be humble. As a matter of fact – and I have already hinted at this – a Christian interpretation of the theology of the growth of multilingualism in our world practically states that this phenomenon was meant to keep us human beings humble due to our difficulties in understanding one another. If we are all united due to ease of communication, we shall develop the kind of megalomania that led to the building of the Tower of Babel, with the intent of challenging the Creator. This means that the effort to promote each language in this multilingual world contributes to the growth of humility and the reduction of megalomania, power hunger, pride, even a tendency to cultural and other imperialisms among nations. We may have a world language, or even just an international language, yes; but it would be a healthy development in the countries where such a language is on the whole not the people's first language if this language was deliberately kept at the level of a second or third language, acquired alongside a very profound commitment to and appreciation of one's first language or mother tongue. To work with or in this first language must be promoted to become a very rewarding activity intellectually, socially and financially. This is partly the way Afrikaans was promoted over the decades: a reading and writing culture was deliberately nurtured, leading to the emergence of a great literature in all major academic and artistic disciplines; English was not emphasized over Afrikaans, though it was taught as an important language in Afrikaans-speaking schools.

Our situation in Uganda (and probably in some other multilingual countries of Africa and elsewhere) will necessarily be a little different, for we have to accommodate English and Swahili more generously in our school curriculum. Indeed, while the implementors of the multilingual policy are working out a method for the distribution of classroom hours and space at the grassroots, it appears prudent to give the local mother tongue class at least a single double period per week, while the rest of the learning is done through a mother tongue resource centre or laboratory in which co-curricular activities can be carried out between teacher and students. Also, students should be required to undertake a personal project, especially in writing. With some imagination and enthusiasm the mother tongue subject can be made into a fascinating discipline, examinable with good results. If Kiswahili is given similar weight and attention, but English, being the medium of instruction, is done more intensively, it will not put the mother tongue at a serious disadvantage. The purpose of introducing the mother tongue subject is primarily to accord our linguistic heritage its due respect in this and the coming generations, including the redeeming of it from the stigma of inferiority to English and other so-called "greater" languages, plus challenging the assumption that the many mother tongues are virtually valueless to the economy of a multilingual nation. Learning and teaching of each mother tongue subject at school is tantamount to developing a potentially important and viable sub-sector of the economy, out of which a substantial number of people can earn a living, dependent on their knowledge of their mother tongues.

(ii) The government should *encourage interethnic and intercultural exchange through requiring people who work in regions of the country that are not their places of birth to undergo a linguistic and cultural orientation exercise,* based on an appropriate manual. This way, a Mukiga doctor working in Soroti, for example, will get to know the Iteso better, apart from learning some Ateso. An Ateso linguistic and cultural orientation manual will prove handy in this effort, as a supplement to some formal classes conducted, say, at district level. Similarly, a Lango engineer or teacher or bank official assigned to work in the Fort Portal-Kyenjojo area would integrate better into the host society if he had this orientation. If the American Peace Corps and the German International Development Agency staff, and indeed any other groups, demand this kind of orientation from their people, it is important that we understand why and learn from them.

(iii) The government should *encourage translation of good writing* from language to language, if need be via English. It is important, for example, that the folk tales, proverbs and riddles of the Alur or Acooli or Lugbara are read in translation in any other language of Uganda and that they are identified clearly as folk tales of the Alur etc. This exchange is extremely healthy for nation-building in a multilingual and multicultural setting. Translations of good literature from the languages of other nations and cultures of the world into the Ugandan languages is also important for shaping of a cosmopolitan attitude in individuals, which in turn is important for world peace. Of course, our own original writing – and writing in the mother tongue can be more successful and more prolific than writing produced with kicks and cramps in a foreign language[13] – should also be translated into the "greater" languages of the world, such as English, French, German, Spanish, Chinese, Korean etc., not to mention the more regional African languages such as Kiswahili, Hausa, Bambara, Amharic, etc., in addition to translations into fellow "local" languages. Ideally, this exchange of literature both from oral sources and from modern creative writing achievements in the many mother tongues of Africa, plus the exchange of factual or scientific knowledge written in different languages, should not remain limited to the relatively few speakers of that language. Africa should learn from Africa even as she learns from elsewhere; and other countries of the world should also learn from Africa. The best way to achieve this is through translation. Translation is a skill and an art that needs to be learnt, mastered and perfected. Therefore governments should encourage the teaching of translation and the development of the relevant tools, such as dictionaries, thesauruses, encyclopaedias, etc. Universities should have translation courses at both graduate and postgraduate levels. It has been observed too that translation is one important way of learning how to write in the target language. Indeed, many a translator is or has also been a writer[14]. And through translation, the target language and its literature grow both quantitatively and qualitatively.[15]

(iv) As pointed out earlier, governments should *introduce a system of rewards and awards* for commendable work in at least three areas, namely: original writing, editorial work and translation. Each language needs to have its own awards. People who excel in preserving their mother tongues by producing literature in them need to be celebrated as heroes. These awards are an integral part, therefore, of value addition to our languages and cultures.

(v) Ideally, at our present stage of development, *each language should have a reasonable presence in the media world*, e.g. at least one good weekly newspaper, an attractive, well produced, well-edited magazine with good quality pictures in colour; a radio station; and some programmes on the national television channel.

(vi) To encourage the growth of interethnic and intercultural exchange and understanding, cultural groups with music, dance and drama presentations should *undertake intercultural visits* to the capitals of the country's different districts or regions. With carefully composed repertoires that take into account the local languages along the itinerary, they can promote a healthy intercultural and international awareness and education in the districts.[16] This approach could spread to the rest of East Africa as part of the effort to arrest or rescue the creative potential of the mother tongue. It is, indeed, not an accident that many of the most successful popular music pieces are sung in the mother tongues of Africa. Certainly in Uganda, such popular compositions as *Obangaina* (Lusoga), *Wipolo* (basically Luo) and *Yesu, Beera Nange* (Luganda) owe their success not only to the power of the music itself but also to that of the poetry.

(vi) For closely related languages, such as those in the Runyakitara cluster, which are virtually dialects of one another, it will be prudent to *nurture and promote two important qualities: mutual intelligibility and "mutual legibility"* in order to bring *their speakers closer to one another and reduce dialect-based psychological barriers.* Mutual intelligibility can be encouraged *inter alia* through, for instance, academic and intellectual discussions; but also in the context of church, where this could be done through intentionaly organized multi-dialect fellowship meetings and Bible studies concluded by communal, conversational prayers[17]. In both situations each participant would endeavour to use their mother tongue as intelligibly as possible, so that the appreciation of one another's languages can gradually lead to the philological enjoyment of aesthetic qualities that may exist in the participants' use of language. Multi-dialect discussion and interaction could in fact grow into a culture with its own art. Mutual legibility, on the other hand, can come from a deliberate effort to produce readers with texts in all the dialects or languages of the inherently intelligible group. The ability to enjoy "Runyakitara", i.e. multi-dialect, textbooks and readers for schools, universities and the general public could, for example, not only produce a high sense of satisfaction, achievement and fulfilment for the individual student or adult; it would also sharpen the sense of essential closeness, even oneness, among the Banyoro, Batoro, Basongora, Batuku, Bahema, Banyankore, Bakiga, Banyambo and Bahaya.[18] It would be a matter of broadening the experience of mutual understanding from listening to reading. What would be needed would be a glossary of potentially confusing or unshared words and *faux amis,* plus some basic grammatical notes on the major differences.[19] When it comes to the productive language skills of speaking and writing, each person would have to speak and write in their own "mother tongue" or even "mother dialect" without fear or embarrassment.

Conclusion: Multilingualism as an Opportunity for Personal and Social Expansion

We wish as intimate participants in the total – i.e. linguistic, cultural, social, economic, political etc. – experience and adventure of life in the shadows of these Mountains of the Moon[20] to conclude this discussion on a rather personal note.

Where there is no common language comfortably uniting the speakers of the different, closely-related dialects/languages, we propose multi-dialect and even multilingual prayer meetings as a method of trying to achieve inter-dialect appreciation and enjoyment, eventually leading to co-existence such as that found in Kabale/Kigezi: the Rusigi–Ruhororo co-existence. In my own family this is manifest: my mother stayed with her *Ruhororo-ized* Rukiga dialect even when surrounded by the *Runyarwanda-ized* Rukiga dialect, called Rusigi, which was spoken in our part of Kigezi. Why can't we achieve this at the Runyoro-Rutoro/Runyankore-Rukiga level? Both in spoken and in written form! We propose that there be as many opportunities as possible for formal (in addition to the informal) inter-dialect or inter-language encounters. Among these we recommend prayer in our freest, most intimate language – which is usually the mother tongue – as one good, effective, peace-enhancing way to internalize the diversity of our linguistic heritages. Before God, all our languages and dialects are equal; English is not greater than Rukiga. God hears all languages. We can re-enact the Pentecost marvel among Jesus' disciples,[21] with the experience of tongues, in a human way. God is not limited, and we humans have fewer limitations than we think. God understands all our languages. Christians are busy translating the Bible, God's Word, into many languages in order to make known His indiscriminate love for all humankind. In this same spirit we need to "expand" in our own mentality and experience, from our nucleus that is our native dialect through the languages that are related to our own and those that we are easily exposed to, on to the outer reaches that are the international languages within our range. Expansion is addition and gain; it entails no loss. Here is a diagram to show my own linguistic "expansion" in a lifespan of some fifty years:

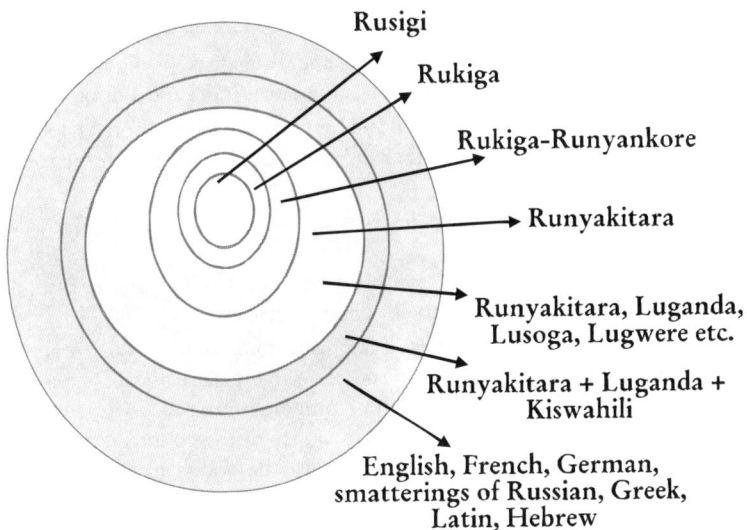

Rusigi

Rukiga

Rukiga-Runyankore

Runyakitara

Runyakitara, Luganda, Lusoga, Lugwere etc.

Runyakitara + Luganda + Kiswahili

English, French, German, smatterings of Russian, Greek, Latin, Hebrew

Notes

1. Stacey, T. 2003. *Tribe. The Hidden History of the Mountains of the Moon.* London: Stacey International, 34. Stacey traces the name Mountains of the Moon to Herodotus, of Greek antiquity, who "vouchsafes the name *(te ourea tes selenes)* - the Mountains of the Moon – which, with the lakes, were the ultimate watershed", for he held the belief of classical antiquity that the seasonally flooding Nile had its source in a range of snowy mountains in the heart of Africa. The name Rwenzori or Ruwenzori is believed by folk etymology to be an ellipsis of *Olusozi rw'Enjura* (meaning "Mountain of Rain" in Rutoro), which was corrupted to *Ruwenzori.*

2. I owe this information to historian Stanley Baluku's gleanings from his reading of Schoenbrun, D. 1998.

3. The area around Masindi has been a meeting and merging zone for the Bantu-speaking people of western and central Uganda and the Nilotic- and Sudanic-speaking peoples of northern Uganda, for a long time, which has favoured the growth of Kiswahili here; which in turn has favoured the coming and settling in of groups from Congo and Kenya. In the Uganda police and army, similarly, Kiswahili has traditionally been the *lingua franca*, the language of training and command. This development was initiated during World War II, when the British recruited many East

Africans from all over Uganda, Kenya and Tanganyika to fight against the Italians and the Germans in Somalia, Abyssinia, India and Burma.

4. Cf http://www.nvtc.gov/lotw/flashDemo.html, accessed on 31 October 2006. According to this website, 2197 languages are spoken in the various regions of Asia.

5. Cf ETHNOLOGUE Languages of the World, 1992, p. 354. However, according   to http://www.nvtc.gov/lotw/months/november/worldlanguages.htm, accessed on 31.10.2006, Nigeria has 515 languages.

6. In Uganda there are three types of linguistic communities: (i) communities of which practically everbody speaks the same local language, i.e. one of the 63 mentioned above, and such communities are most naturally found in rural areas, and they make up the majority of the country's population; a few closed urban communities may also be added to this group; (ii) communities where the majority of the people basically speak the same Ugandan language but due to education and/or urbanization code-switch much and quite naturally between the Ugandan language and English; most of the skits, plays and films produced in Uganda are characterized by code-switching and they are consequently popular; (iii) communities, also usually in the urban centres or the boarding educational institutions, where people come from different linguistic backgrounds, are relatively well educated, and mostly use (Ugandan) English in their communication; there is an upward trend both numerically and socially among this part of the population, and children of educated, ethnically intermarried couples who live in the cities grow up speaking this English, which is also the medium of instruction in the urban centres from nursery school to university.

7. Cf. comment in the *New International Version Study Bible* (2002) on Genesis 11:4: "At Babel, the rebellious human race undertook a united and godless effort to establish for themselves, by a titanic enterprise, a world renown by which they would dominate God's creation".

8. There are many other languages in India apart from these eighteen. *Ethnologue* 1992 lists 416 languages for India, 11 of which are extinct. The Indian Constitution, however, protects the interests of linguistic minorities in Article 29 (Protection of interests of minorities), Sections 1 and 2, thus: "1. Any section of the citizens residing in the territory of India or any part thereof having a distinct language, script or culture of its own shall have the right to conserve the same. 2. No citizen shall be denied admission into any educational institution maintained by the State or receiving aid out of State funds on grounds only of religion, race, caste,

language or any of them." (See . Thirumalai, M.S. 2002. Language in India, Vol. 2, 2 April 2002).

9. See, for example, an article in the literary supplement *(Literatur-Beiheft),* page 2, of the German weekly *Die Zeit,* Number 34, Volume 61, of 17-8-2006, which was dedicated to India, in line with this year's main theme "Indian Literature" at the Frankfurt Book Fair in October.

10. The post-Apartheid constitution of the Republic of South Africa provides for a redress of the injustice done to the other language communities of South Africa. It stipulates in Article 6 (2) under Chapter 1, as follows: "Recognising the historically diminished use and status of the indigenous languages of our people, the state must take practical and positive measures to elevate the status and advance the use of these languages." In Article 29 (2) under Chapter 2, it furthermore states that "[e]veryone has the right to receive education in the official language or languages of their choice [...] In order to ensure the effective access to, and implementation of, this right, the state must consider all reasonable educational alternatives, including single medium institutions, taking into account (a) equity; (b) practicability; and (c) *the need to redress the results of past racially discriminatory laws and practices."* (our emphasis!)

11. Cf NIED's statement on the theoretical basis for the importance of using the mother tongue in learning: "Learning and developing in one's mother tongue is crucial to establishing a positive self image, an affirmation of one's own culture without being chauvinistic and to the primary understanding of the world. Learning a second or foreign language widens one's way of experiencing and interpreting the world, and enables wider communication. However, if learning the mother tongue stops at an early stage of schooling, it makes it more difficult for concept formation, and to relate what is learnt through another language to one's personal experience and culture as one grows up. *It also has a strong signal effect that the mother tongue is inferior to the second or foreign language.* Therefore, both in terms of improving learning, strengthening identity and for language ecology, the mother tongue should be taught all the way through school". (Our emphasis) Cf. http://www.edsnet.na/Resources/LearnerCentredEd/lce.pdf. Accessed on 1-11-2006.

12. Marechera, however, indicates that this process is by no means easy and it involves patience and endurance; no mastery over the foreign language comes without hard work: "This is the best way to fight back our own former slavery. But every time we try, language escapes. And so we have to beat it again and again and to capture and to punish it again and again."

13. Cf. J.G. Herder's statement and essay with the title "A True Poet Must Write in His Own Language," in *Classical Readings From German Literature. From The Middle Ages To The Present Day,* compiled by Wolfgang Langenbucher, Werner Rehfeld and Frank Auerbach. East African Publishing House, Nairobi, Kenya and Horst Erdmann Verlag, Tübingen and Basle, 1969, 54-56.

14. E.g. Johann Wolfgang von Goethe, August von Schlegel, Ludwig Tieck, Walter Benjamin; Ngugi wa Thiong'o.

15. See Muranga, 1990. "Translation as a Means of Developing and Enriching the Target Language". In Mukama, R. (ed.), *Makerere Papers in Language and Linguistics,* Kampala: Makerere University.

16. The Makerere Travelling Theatre of the 1960s is a good example of how effective such visits can be. Though they concentrated mainly on schools, they visited all three countries of East Africa and their presentations always left a strong impact.

17. While this may already be happening in some churches in the Rwenzori Diocese of the Church of Uganda, the planned Centre for Intercultural Learning and Prayer (CILP), Kasaali Village Branch in the foothills of Mount Rwenzori, intends to promote this activity in a more deliberate way. (See "Proposal for the Establishment of a Centre for Intercultural Learning and Prayer", available from the author at <mmuranga@arts.mak.ac.ug>).

18. When the Subject of "Runyakitara" was introduced at Makerere University in 1990, it was falsely assumed that a new language had been or was being artificially created out of Runyoro, Rutoro, Runyankore, Rukiga and potentially also Ruhaya, Rusongora, Runyambo and Ruhema. In fact, however, what was being fostered was a greater linguistic and pragmatic appreciation, understanding and even enjoyment among the students of one another's inherently highly intelligible dialects and mother tongues. Indeed, to enhance the mutual legibility, the principles used in the production of the Runyoro-Rutoro and Runyankore-Rukiga standard orthographies could be harmonized and applied to all the other members of this group.

19. Until the Runyankore-Rukiga Bible was finally published in 1964, the Christians of Ankole and Kigezi used to use the Runyoro-Rutoro Bible and prayer and hymn book for their devotions and worship. Whereas this was linguistically not entirely satisfying for them, it would go a long way in satisfying their spiritual needs.

20. The author's parents, who were Bakiga, migrated from Nyakagyera Village of Ndorwa County, Kabale (formerly Kigezi District), to Nyamba and

Kasaali Villages in the immediate foothills of Mount Rwenzori, Bunyangabu County, Kabarole District of Toro Kingdom, in January 1980, due to the well-known economic hardships of cultivator families thriving on pieces of land scattered all around the village, in its valleys and on the mountain slopes and crests that define it geographically from the next village. Such cultivator hardships are bearable in the earlier years of life; beyond the age of 50 or so, the body gets worn out. The villagers in Toro on the other hand, usually Batoro, had larger, more consolidated pieces of land to sell to immigrants from Kigezi. Bakonjo live in close proximity, on the Rwenzori slopes next to Nyamba Village. The Rwenzururu conflicts between Bakonzo and Batoro have affected the immigrants, in addition to the occasional, but so far non-violent, manifestations of Batoro-Bakiga tribalism.

21. Cf. Acts of the Apostles 2:1-13.

Index